Securing the West

RECONFIGURING AMERICAN POLITICAL HISTORY
Ronald P. Formisano, Paul Bourke, Donald DeBats, and Paula M. Baker, Series Founders

Other Books in the Series

Michael Goldberg, *An Army of Women: Gender and Politics in Gilded Age Kansas*

Mark Voss-Hubbard, *Beyond Party:*
Cultures of Antipartisanship in Northern Politics before the Civil War

Douglas B. Craig, *Fireside Politics:*
Radio and Political Culture in the United States, 1920–1940

Kate Weigand, *Red Feminism:*
American Communism and the Making of Women's Liberation

R. Rudy Higgens-Evenson, *The Price of Progress:*
Public Services, Taxation, and the American Corporate State, 1877 to 1929

Donald DeBats and Paul Bourke, *Washington County:*
Politics and Community in Antebellum America

Leigh Ann Wheeler, *Against Obscenity:*
Reform and the Politics of Womanhood in America, 1873–1935

Liette Gidlow, *The Big Vote:*
Gender, Consumer Culture, and the Politics of Exclusion, 1890s–1920s

Jeffrey O. G. Ogbar, *Black Power: Radical Politics and African American Identity*

Robert E. Shalhope, *Bennington and the Green Mountain Boys:*
The Emergence of Liberal Democracy in Vermont, 1760–1850

Dennis Deslippe, *Protesting Affirmative Action:*
The Struggle over Equality after the Civil Rights Revolution

Williamjames Hull Hoffer, *To Enlarge the Machinery of Government:*
Congressional Debates and the Growth of the American State, 1858–1891

Securing the West

Politics, Public Lands,
and the Fate of the Old Republic, 1785–1850

JOHN R. VAN ATTA

Johns Hopkins University Press
Baltimore

Johns Hopkins University Press
2715 North Charles Street
Baltimore, Maryland 21218-4363
www.press.jhu.edu

Library of Congress Cataloging-in-Publication Data

Van Atta, John Robert.
Securing the West : politics, public lands, and the fate of
the old republic, 1785–1850 / John R. Van Atta.
pages cm. — (Reconfiguring American political history)
Includes bibliographical references and index.
ISBN 978-1-4214-1275-7 (hardcover : alk. paper) — ISBN 978-1-4214-1276-4
(electronic) — ISBN 1-4214-1275-6 (hardcover : alk. paper) — ISBN 1-4214-1276-4
(electronic) 1. United States—Territorial expansion—History—19th century.
2. United States—Territorial expansion—Government policy. 3. Federal
government—United States—History—19th century. 4. Public lands—United
States—History—19th century. 5. Slavery—United States—Extension to the
territories. 6. Indians of North America—Government relations—History—19th
century. 7. Manifest Destiny. 8. West (U.S.)—History—To 1848. I. Title.
E179.5.V33 2014
978'.02—dc23   2013025017

A catalog record for this book is available from the British Library.

*Special discounts are available for bulk purchases of this book. For more information,
please contact Special Sales at 410-516-6936 or specialsales@press.jhu.edu.*

Johns Hopkins University Press uses environmentally friendly book
materials, including recycled text paper that is composed of at least
30 percent post-consumer waste, whenever possible.

For the two Lucys, as always

CONTENTS

List of Maps   *ix*
Acknowledgments   *xi*

Introduction   1

Prologue: "A Great Country, Populous and Mighty"   8

1 "Republican Notions—and Utopian Schemes"   17

2 An Embryo of Empire   45

3 Rise of the Radical West   85

4 "A World within Itself"   113

5 Foot's Resolution and the "Great Debate"   139

6 Whose West?—Alternative Visions   170

7 "A Lawless Rabble"   205

Epilogue: The West Secured?   232

Notes   *245*
Essay on Sources   *279*
Index   *285*

Land Ordinance of 1785   38
Distribution of U.S. Population East of the Mississippi River, 1790   48
Distribution of U.S. Population East of the Mississippi River, 1810   82
Distribution of U.S. Population East of the Mississippi River, 1830   148
Distribution of U.S. Population East of the Mississippi River, 1850   234

Over the many years it took to finish this book, I have run up a daunting tab of debts, most of which can never be paid. There is room here to acknowledge only a few. Both the motivation to complete the manuscript and the inspiration for its central themes of nation building and social development came from a National Endowment for the Humanities seminar, The Early American Republic and the Problem of Governance, at the Library Company of Philadelphia in summer 2011, sponsored by the Society for Historians of the Early American Republic (SHEAR). For that remarkable experience, I especially thank the seminar's codirectors, John L. Larson and Michael A. Morrison, along with fellow scholar-participants Patrick Bottiger, Melissa Bullard, Christopher Childers, Thomas Cox, Andrew Fagel, Scott King-Owen, Helen Knowles, Albrecht Koschnik, Gabriel Loiacono, Daniel Mandell, Patrick Peel, Andrew Schocket, Nora Pat Small, and Sarah Swedberg. My gratitude extends also to John Van Horne and his Library Company staff for their exceptional skill and warm welcome to researchers.

In addition, I wish to thank the library staffs of the University of Virginia, Ball State University, Indiana University, the University of Michigan, Smith College, Amherst College, Hiram College, the National Archives, and the Library of Congress. I am also grateful to the staffs of the Library of Virginia, New York Public Library, Salem (Ohio) Public Library, Greenwich (Connecticut) Public Library, the South Caroliniana Library, Virginia Historical Society, New-York Historical Society, South Carolina Historical Society, Ohio Historical Society, Indiana Historical Society, Pennsylvania Historical Society, and the Western Reserve Historical Society.

Parts of the manuscript appeared in earlier versions as articles in the *Journal of the Early Republic* ("Western Lands and the Political Economy of Henry Clay's American System, 1819–1832," vol. 21 [Winter 2001], 633–665; and "'A Lawless Rabble': Henry Clay and the Cultural Politics of Squatters' Rights, 1832–1841," vol. 27 [Fall 2008], 337–378). I thank the *JER*'s anonymous readers for their insightful comments, past *Journal* editors John Larson, Michael Morrison, and Roderick Mc-

Donald—along with their staff members—for expert guidance, and the University of Pennsylvania Press for allowing further publication of this material.

For many years, the annual SHEAR meetings have rejuvenated my interest in the early republic in all kinds of ways. I wish in particular to recognize my cohorts in the SHEAR poker group: Jim Broussard, Richard John, Gene Smith, Dan Preston, Sam Watson, John Belohlavek, John Ifkovic, Mark Cheathem, and others who have joined from time to time, especially Jim Bradford, for helping to make those meetings all the more enriching and a whole lot of fun.

This project began long ago as a Ph.D. dissertation at the University of Virginia. I am not sure what possessed Merrill D. Peterson to accept me as one of his students, but it proved my great fortune that he did. William W. Abbot and Charles W. McCurdy also kept watch over my progress; their advice never failed. Along with Peterson and Abbot, my parents, Robert E. Van Atta and Mary E. Van Atta, passed on before we could see what might finally become of this work. I shall keep trying to learn from their examples.

Many thanks go to all those at the Johns Hopkins University Press who have had a hand in the production of this volume, especially my editor, Robert J. Brugger. His patience, wise counsel, and scholarly know-how have made a huge difference for me and many others. Anne Whitmore's knowledgeable and meticulous copyediting also proved of enormous value. As a great favor both to me and the press, Andrew R. L. Cayton kindly read the entire manuscript and sent his excellent suggestions. I owe a large debt to the anonymous reader for Johns Hopkins, who recommended my work for publication while proposing several other valuable improvements. Beyond all that, my youngest brother, Matthew Van Atta, contributed the benefit of his constant encouragement, sharp eye for detail, and years of professional editorial experience.

Among many friends at The Brunswick School and our sister-institution, Greenwich Academy, I wish to thank Brunswick headmaster Thomas W. Philip and former headmasters Norman Pedersen and Duncan Edwards, along with my history department colleagues on both campuses, for supporting my scholarly efforts. In particular, John Booth and Kristine Brennan went over and commented on parts of the manuscript. Robert Taylor clarified a number of elusive points in the field of economics. Steve Mandes's curiosity and enthusiasm buoyed my spirit. The reliable, ever-resourceful Margot Beattie took from her own free time to draw all the maps. John Pendergast, chairman of our philosophy and religion department, has guarded my sanity over many years and generously provisioned our weekly "business meetings." Brian Freeman of our English department not only models everything a true academician should be but is also the finest dinner host and chef I shall ever meet. Thanks to Sunil Gupta and the school's excellent technology staff for keeping my laptop well-serviced and operating. Paul Withstandley may despair over my poor ability in the Spanish language he so ably teaches, but our lengthy friendship matters more. Valerie Fenton, her predecessor Gene La Faille, and the staff of the Brunswick School library came to my aid innumerable times. Certainly not least, I thank the many great students I have taught over the years in regular and advanced placement United States history and in constitutional law for always refueling my commitment to those subjects and the teaching profession.

My longtime spiritual mentor and constant ally Fr. Robert E. Kennedy, S.J., has rescued me on many occasions and in many ways. But my greatest personal debt is, of course, to the two Lucys, wife and daughter, to whom I dedicate this book— and everything else.

Securing the West

Introduction

Edmund P. Dana was a good man to know. As of 1819, he had found employment for several years as a land agent for more than 1,300 settlers headed for the northwestern frontier of the republic in hope of a new and better life. By his own account, Dana had lived for six years among the natives in the Great Lakes Region. He could tell you the way through the new states of Ohio, Indiana, and Illinois, and the wilds of the Michigan Territory. He had trekked over the prairies and the salt licks, explored the rivers, and seen firsthand areas where some of the best farming soil in all of North America still awaited the plow.

An easterner by birth, from Cambridge, Massachusetts, Dana stood apart from other agents, who seemed in the job mainly for personal gain. He held a certain awe for how congressional policy makers of the 1780s had designed a land system around republican principles and with some thought to how a stable society might be established in what largely remained a vast wilderness. "So great an influence has civil government in shaping the mental features of a community," he gushed, with prideful exaggeration, "it is not strange that the wisdom of illustrious statesmen and lawgivers should have caused them to have been classed among the gods." In spite of the American Revolution, he thought, the people of the eastern states had never really succeeded in forming a "uniform national character." Their progenitors had been settlers from different parts of Europe—"English, Scotch, French, High and Low Dutch." In them, "the manners and customs of the mother country" had been "but partially obliterated in their descendants."[1]

But in the "western country," as Dana saw it, a different story unfolded. There, "the settlers[,] being more promiscuously located," a new identity of opinions, manners, and customs slowly formed—"a new character . . . from the various materials constituting the compound, which may with propriety be denominated national." May we not anticipate, he asked confidently, "that the arts which abridge manual labor will be improved—that the stock of useful knowledge will be increased—and that the condition of man will generally be ameliorated?" Dana answered *yes*, of course, but only conditionally; he also believed that a government which "lacked strength to enforce obedience to its will, and to resist the violence offered to public authority, by punishing the licentiousness of faction," would be doomed, like the republics of ancient times, to ultimate dissolution.

At the time he wrote these words, in 1819, a terrible financial panic, the worst Americans had yet seen, was ravaging the country. People all over had reason to wonder whether the political and economic framework the founding fathers had constructed could withstand the crisis. Many had lost everything, including confidence in the future. Dana, however, counseled hope in the face of despair. Salvation lay in an ever-optimistic, westward-expanding citizenry: "Virtuous propensities, correct principles, intelligent understandings, and skillful industry, are the substantial pillars on which free republics rest. Such institutions, without them, are mere hay and stubble."

Alas, Dana, like many others, would prove a better salesman and promoter than prophet of the American future. No one knows whether his views shifted markedly between 1819 and his death in 1840. We can say with certainty, however, that western development occurred in radically different ways from the plans and expectations of the Revolutionary generation. A number of critical, and sometimes questionable, decisions of policy makers between 1815 and 1850 largely accounted for that difference, along with the inertia of expansion and the realities of a distant, hard-to-govern frontier.

The chronicle offered in these pages says as much about how early dreams died or took unexpected turns as it does about why certain land policies emerged after 1783 and why Congress later modified (or killed) them. The realization that a new hemisphere existed across the Atlantic had once transformed the European imagination, offering some of the oldest utopian dreams an actual chance of fruition in America. And yet, the frontier realities of this new West would confound successive generations of dreamers, settlers, and policy makers with the unplanned and the unexpected. Vaunted "solutions" to Old World problems never seemed to apply as intended in the New. The hope of transcending time and place and even human nature, by building societies meant to work in fairer, better ways, would prove to be what it always had been—elusive.

But apart from environment and the vicissitudes of chance, history turns on the dynamic of conscious *choices* and the frameworks of belief influencing them. For one thing, the building of a new society from scratch involved concepts of political economy. Whatever terms are used to describe it, "political economy" refers to the ways people choose to organize the economic and social structures of the environment they inhabit. In any culture, the distribution, use, and political significance of the most basic economic resource—land—must be a central part of the design. In the aspirations of the earliest New World settlers and for long thereafter, America represented above all the opportunity for people to own land. Institutions, sanctions, rituals, regulations, social structures—in short, the foundational elements of a civil society—all related to who controlled land, the manner in which they controlled it, and for what purposes. From the start, while the land in the New World may have been vacant, to some eyes, it was never empty. The very survival of Indian tribes lay in question after white settlements started to appear, and whether or not those original Americans failed to grasp the European concept of property, they could not have foreseen the long-term implications of white occupation. In contrast with Native groups, Euro-American settlers thought of land more as a commodity, something to be owned, divided, bought, and sold. The development of land markets would eventually undercut the "middle ground" of intercultural relations that once existed between whites and Native Americans in western regions. Whether white settlers intended to generate moral or social perfection, or just the unbridled pursuit of material wealth (either way, at the expense of Native Americans), the settlement of land had to be the basis for it. From the origins of New England Puritan towns to the filling of the Ohio Valley and beyond, the same fundamental questions remained: *Whose* West was it and whose *should* it be? How should it be "secured" and by whom? The answers proved to be conflicting, complex, and subject to radical changes over time.[2]

Public policies of the early republic not only reflected elements of society and culture but aimed also to influence societal and cultural change. The structure and purposes of that change usually replicated the environmental contexts, worldviews, and personal backgrounds of the various policy makers themselves and of spokesmen and agitators who sought influence from outside the policy-making sector. Federally owned lands in the West became a divisive subject, especially after 1815, when settlers of all descriptions started to fill those lands more rapidly than ever. Quarrels over the proper character and means of western development raged throughout the first half of the nineteenth century. These land issues—and public-policy battles in general—exposed intense ideological conflict and momentous class and cultural tensions that carried into the political arena. We see these tensions operating powerfully *within* sectional and party struggles of the period, but we must view that political arena in a broad sense, not so much as a matter of election competition and the winning of public office, but as the shaping of opinion within an extended and hotly active public sphere.[3] To down-play the importance of philosophical rivalries by seeing them as part of an overall entrepreneurial consensus, wherein rival sides essentially shared the same goals and only disagreed over the means to reach them, tends to obscure crucial realities. The risk is that we may understate the more radical implications of political, social, and economic change and miss key perceptions that people living at the time expressed.[4]

In all, the story told herein tries to explore dimensions of federal land policy that other historians have minimized or left out. Most of the older studies, such as those of Paul Wallace Gates and many others, have told us more about how the system worked and less about what motivated the system makers. Political historians, not only in the long-ago days of Frederick Jackson Turner but also the best in recent decades, have stressed the sectional rather than the social and cultural implications of land policies. As a result, we need to learn more about the broad contexts of public lands–related issues. In addition, some scholars, being rightly skeptical, have dismissed too much of the actual content of political discourse in this period, at times regarding those voices as little more than artful cover for personal ambition, party advantage, or economic interests.[5]

By 1830, a host of other economic issues had become critically tangled with land disposition, including policy-making hallmarks of the economic transformation that historians have identified as the post-1815 "Market Revolution." Protective tariffs, federal use of public land revenue to encourage internal improvements, reduction or graduation of land prices to promote western settlement, distribution of land proceeds among the states, preemption rights and donations of land for the poor—all of these animated the ideological tension among rival sections, parties, and interests in the early years of the republic, particularly in Jacksonian America. At the grassroots level, agriculture in the West and the policies governing its expansion underpinned much of the commercial development essential to the progress of capitalism in America, which included security for mortgages and loans, capital accumulation, and market integration. To examine this network of subjects, I draw upon a range of sources known to influence public discourse, from congressional debates and committee reports to editorial writings and news coverage in small town newspapers. Much of the attention, of course, focuses on Congress, the principal elected leaders who took positions and advocated choices about western lands. In Congress, more than any other place, public leaders articulated basic concerns about the character, structure, direction, and destiny of society in the early United States. Its members, like those outside of government, operated within a political vocabulary that may seem strange to nonhistorians, an ideological vernacular reflecting a political culture, pressing issues, and common worries often different from today's.[6]

Attention to the cultural roots of political conflict—the underlying beliefs, values, assumptions, forms of expression, rituals, and other common practices that influenced thought and behavior—is nothing new, and yet recent scholarship along these lines has stimulated fresh interpretation of the early republic. Over the past generation, many researchers have developed and refined the rich interpretive potential of "republicanism" as an early American ideology that incorporated social and economic concerns as well as political ones. But this paradigm of republicanism, applying best to the Revolutionary period, does not by itself unravel the complexities of American politics and belief for the decades after 1815, when the influence of the new West became more and more a dominating force in national politics. It might be that different manifestations of republican governance, interworking with newer political notions, important events, and conditions on the ground, helped to frame major questions of public policy and shape the enlightened—or sometimes not so enlightened—responses of policy makers.[7]

In some of the most compelling recent studies of early American politics, including a few on policies for governing the West, state building and the role of the nation-state have received much more extensive attention than just ten or so years ago. Far from the old, romantic image of scrappy pioneers cutting their way westward while policy makers left them, laissez-faire style, mostly to their own devices, the picture that now emerges is one of a federal government busy "cultivating partnerships with state governments and local businesses, thereby fostering a commercial economy" in frontier zones, carrying forward the early intention of a "well-regulated society," while individual settlers and entrepreneurs pursued their private, self-defined (and often self-serving) interests. One writer identifies a European-style military-fiscal-state tradition emanating from the Federalist side of the ratification debates in the late 1780s and in subtle ways guiding central government decision making through the 1790s, only to be challenged and undermined by an older, oft-resurging anti-statist impulse in American political culture. Another author describes the federal government throughout the early republic as having been "more powerful, capacious, tenacious, interventionist, and redistributive" than historians had realized before. Still another argues that "the positive use of government power for popular constructive purposes . . . never was proscribed by American republicanism but lay well within the presumed legitimate authority of revolutionary governments"—just as Edmund Dana believed. Among the latest works, one goes so far as to find centralizing tendencies operating consistently through the nineteenth century but "out of sight" of most Americans.[8]

In what ways and how well does this state-building profile apply when looking at the varying directions of western land distribution and its social consequences during the period up to 1850? This study extends the nation-state literature by carrying the inquiry beyond the earliest decades of the republic and asking how major changes in federal land policy may further illuminate the ongoing narrative—and, indeed, depart from it at critical junctures.

More specifically, examining the history of western settlement in the first half of the nineteenth century raises some interrelated questions: How did competing economic beliefs and divergent cultural mandates influence outcomes of the broad debate over the means, timing, and purposes of settling the trans-Appalachian West? What alternative visions of western society lay behind the battles among policy makers within the government and the interested parties who would sway them from outside? Why did settlement of the West take such a different turn in the end from that which the earliest leaders of the republic intended?

Discussions of the early United States incur the inherent problems of using the word "nation." The republic then was a plural entity, sovereign states within a sovereign union, and not a unitary "nation-state" until after (probably *long* after) the Civil War. In this study, the terms "nationalist" and "statist" refer to people who favored centralized federal power, and "anti-national" and "anti-statist" are at times employed to describe those who opposed that vision. The expression "political economy" is used here as Americans of the early republic understood it—not simply as a body of literature representing important classical sources but a wider understanding that intertwined social, economic, and governmental concerns. The term "frontier" refers somewhat loosely to what scholars have described as a "zone of cultural competition," where various groups and interests on the fringes of settlement, some indigenous and many not, some defying and others following the rule of law, asserted conflicting values and beliefs and vied, at times violently, for agency. Except where specific tribal designations are more appropriate, the terms "Indian" and "Native American" appear interchangeably. "The Northwest" refers to the region above the Ohio River, stretching to the Great Lakes and westward from Pittsburgh to the Mississippi River. Missouri relates to, but also—significantly—fits outside, this framework. "The Southwest" constitutes the area south of the Ohio, from western Georgia to the Mississippi borderlands.[9]

In structure, this book addresses a selection of major themes within a chronological format, beginning before the Revolution. Many of the fundamental social and cultural questions that would later influence federal land policy found urgent expression right after the Revolutionary War—especially in deliberations of the Confederation Congress of the 1780s—and tied closely to the republican aspirations of that time. Those questions included how and to what extent to use land sales for revenue—as well as how, if possible, to regulate settlement so as to encourage "desirable" persons (those who shared the basic republican values of federal decision makers) and discourage the "less desired." The land system that emerged in the 1780s reflected nation building by *design*, but within that general agreement appeared conflicts that would persist for decades. Successive Federalist and Jeffersonian Republican regimes attempted to refine the land system and adjust policy in the 1790s and early 1800s, each side informed by considerations of belief but also frustrated by the problems of distance, by settlers operating without regard for law, and by divisions within the leadership itself.

Major economic downswings jarred perceptions and altered the political landscape of the early republic much as they still do. The Panic of 1819, the first such moment in the nineteenth century, produced calls for important—and in some cases, radical—changes in federal land policy. The responses included a judicious land reform law in 1820, Thomas Hart Benton's more drastic plan for the graduation of land prices, the evolving case for preemption (legalization of squatters' claims), and Ninian Edwards's idea in Illinois that federal lands lying within state boundaries ought to be ceded to those states. The latter three points proved "radical" in the sense that they challenged the fundamental principle of federal control and undercut the 1780s intentions. The Panic also affected the way Henry Clay and his intellectual supporters calibrated the early "American System" in the 1820s; it compelled clarification of the West's place in their overall scheme. Some historians, siding more with the Jacksonian view of the argument, have exaggerated the conflict between settlement and revenue objectives in the land policy of economic nationalists like Clay. Viewed more fairly, those nationalists, like the republican framers and the moderates who supported the Land Act of 1820, primarily favored maintaining a well-ordered, governmentally controlled land system and promoting a commercially oriented, middle-class society in the West.

By the end of the 1820s, two fundamentally different perspectives—one antigovernment, the other not; one stressing individual freedom, the other seeking order and community—would be on a collision course. One of the most dramatic political expressions of that conflict would come in December 1829 on the floor of the United States Senate—an extended controversy over Samuel A. Foot's little-understood resolution that became known, somewhat misleadingly, as the Webster-Hayne Debate. Within several more years, a new economic crisis, that of 1837, would send both policy makers and ordinary Americans on another psychic loop, with political implications to follow. The climax of the story featured here would arrive in the form of another debate—in the late 1830s, on preemption—conducted both in Congress and around the country and culminating in the passage in 1841 of a long-term federal commitment to "squatters' rights." No decision could have been more pivotal, in light of the dominant considerations of earlier decades; it threw into relief just how radically public land policy had shifted over the first half-century of the republic. The forces that drove these changes produced— indeed, by the late 1830s had *already* produced—an American West vastly different from the one the original republican framers had expected, with far-reaching consequences for the years beyond.

"A Great Country, Populous and Mighty"

When Benjamin Franklin, aged 42, retired from his publishing business in 1748, he expected to devote more time to scientific and philosophical studies. Having achieved both fortune and status in Philadelphia, he now considered himself a "gentleman," a "Man of Leisure" and disinterested reflection. In his case, this included studying the differences between American society and that of Europe, particularly England, then in the early stages of industrialization. His major work on the subject, an essay entitled *Observations Concerning the Increase of Mankind* published in late 1754, circulated widely in both Europe and America for more than a decade and likely influenced the writings of Adam Smith, Thomas Malthus, and David Ricardo. Franklin intended the *Observations* as a blueprint for the long-range expansion of a self-sufficient British Empire, but it also expressed widely shared American beliefs that would help inspire coherent visions of a westward-expanding New World civilization for generations to come.[1]

While writing the *Observations*, Franklin did not anticipate, or desire, the independence of the colonies. Like most colonial Americans, he regarded the British Empire as the freest and most enlightened since the fall of Rome. Some of Franklin's views on settling the western regions resembled later economic belief on that subject, but in the early 1750s he prescribed only a course for British empire building and saw America's western lands as key to that enterprise.

Looking at empires more as processes than structures, that is, the creation of people involved directly on the ground as well as decision makers in faraway metropolitan centers, the British approach had been distinct from the start. Theirs was an empire based on conquest and settlement of the land and the building of permanent, self-sustaining colonies as opposed to the commercial style of their principal rival, the French, whose New World expansion pursued more the trading of goods that their trappers and adventurers extracted from unsettled regions with the cooperation of native inhabitants. By the mid-eighteenth century, however, British imperial officials had come to see their increasingly prosperous American

colonies not just as a source of agricultural materials but as a market for English manufactured goods. While colonial Americans remained intractably committed to land development—no more than one in twenty made a living apart from
farming—their growing propensity to consume drew some into occupations like
rudimentary textile production and shoemaking. The gradual emergence of small-
scale manufacturing in the colonies, despite the ongoing shortage of investment
capital and the high cost of labor in America, registered in London as a threat to
homeland mercantilism, a competitive danger to English investors. Parliament
responded in 1750 with legislation that outlawed colonial manufacture and export
of specified textiles, and it issued the Iron Act, which banned American construction of slitting and rolling mills, plating forges, and iron furnaces—a drastic limitation on production of finished iron products in the colonies. Believing these
moves to be based on misinformation, overreaction, and a logic of mercantilism
that Franklin found faulty, he argued that England had little reason to fear competitive development in America, especially when the coming of war between Britain
and France for ultimate control of the North American continent seemed only a
matter of time.[2]

Influenced by European physiocratic thought, which argued the primacy of
agriculture for the health and progress of civilization, the main point of the *Observations* was that America's vast territorial reserve would enable population to
increase dramatically without heavy reliance on domestic industry. Such industry
at that time offered the only means of employing surplus labor in geographically
small European nations. "In countries full settled," Franklin wrote, "all hands
being occupied and improved to the Heighth: those who cannot get Land, must
labor for others that have it."[3] But no such difficulty threatened expansion-minded
Americans—only the French presence west of the Appalachians and the Native
Americans. With the eventual removal of both, the colonies easily could withstand
a doubling of inhabitants every twenty years. So vast was the territory of North
America, Franklin explained, "that it will require many Ages to settle it fully; and
till it is fully settled, Labour will never be cheap here."[4]

With a lot of available land to lure away would-be industrial workers, little need
for New World manufacturing could exist, he thought. "The danger therefore of
these Colonies interfering with their Mother Country in Trades that depend on
Labour, Manufactures, &c. is too remote to require the Attention of Great Britain,"
said Franklin. By long delaying the arrival of industrial modernity, American colonial societies could maintain their agricultural simplicity and virtue, forestalling
the rise of inequalities, the increase of "luxury," and a corresponding degeneration
of public morals.[5]

Even so, westward agricultural expansion ideally required migration of the "right" kinds of people—a culturally homogenous, law-abiding mixture—and not just anybody who wanted land. Here the British ran into major obstacles that policy makers for the American West, too, would encounter, in the decades following the Revolution of 1776. Land development and trading systems in the Ohio Valley, for example, proved notoriously difficult for imperial administrators to control. No comprehensive plan of empire, at such great distance from its center in London, could succeed very well in restraining excessive expansion, arranging efficient surveying and fair purchasing of land, achieving enforceable agreements with Indians, and fostering well-ordered communities. Squatter invasions of Indian lands made a mockery of practically every peace accord on the frontier and provoked justifiable countermeasures by tribal leaders. Franklin, for one, believed that the development of any culture depended on the formation of virtuous character. He had, after all, deplored Britain's earlier policy of exporting its convicted felons to America, suggesting that Americans should reciprocate by sending cargos of rattlesnakes back to the mother country. "It grieves me to hear," Franklin would lament, "that our Frontier People are yet greater Barbarians than the Indians, and continue to murder them in time of peace."[6]

Similarly dismayed by the tens of thousands of non-English immigrants then arriving in Philadelphia—mostly Germans recruited by Quaker merchants to supply labor and fill up the Pennsylvania backcountry—Franklin wondered what kind of place his colony was becoming and what the impact on the "Englishness" of the British Empire might be: "[W]hy should the Palantine Boors [German peasants] be suffered to swarm into our Settlements, and by herding together establish their Language and Manners to the Exclusion of ours?" German pacifists had refused to cooperate with Franklin's 1747 militia "association" in Pennsylvania, and rumors circulated that the clever French were plotting to establish a colony of Germans in the Ohio country as a buffer against English expansion there. "Why," Franklin asked, "should Pennsylvania, founded by the English, become a Colony of *Aliens*, who will shortly be so numerous as to Germanize us instead of our Anglifying them, and will never adopt our Language and Customs, any more than they can acquire our Complexion[?]"[7]

The idea of populating western settlements with people of demonstrated virtue, productive potential, loyalty, respect for law, and willingness to defend the country would echo for years to come in other voices. Franklin's friend Richard Jackson, after reading the *Observations* in 1755, thought Franklin should have addressed even further the inculcating of morals among settlers in new territories: "Inhabitants may be encouraged to settle, and even supported for a while; a good government and laws may be framed, and even arts may be established, . . . but many necessary moral habits are hardly ever found among those who voluntarily offer themselves . . . to people new colonies." Franklin, in 1756, mused to evangelist George Whitefield that the two of them should go west, found a colony on the Ohio, attract "a large Strong Body of Religious and Industrious People" to increase the "Territory, Strength and Commerce" of the British Empire, and introduce the Indians to "a better Sample of Christians than they commonly see in our Indian Traders."[8]

A rapid peopling of the West had been one of the themes of Franklin's Albany Plan of Union in 1754, which prescribed joint action of the colonies on matters affecting their common interests, notably Indian relations and frontier defense. With French attack looming, Franklin argued that such collaboration could have offered Great Britain a major advantage, not only for colonial dealings with the Indian tribes, but also, more importantly, in facing imperial rivals in the future. Any one colony had scarcely enough strength "to extend itself by new settlements, at so great a distance from the old," but the strength of a union of colonies could do so "greatly to the security of our present frontiers" and break off "French communication" between Canada and Louisiana, while stimulating intercolonial trade and population growth.[9] Two years before, in a report on behalf of the Pennsylvania Assembly's committee on the state of currency, Franklin had characterized speedy colonial expansion as part of what amounted to a home market within the British Empire: "[B]y rendering the Means of purchasing Land easy to the Poor, the Dominions of the Crown are strengthen'd and extended; the Proprietaries dispose of their Wilderness Territory; and the British Nation secures the Benefit of its Manufactures, and increases the Demand for them." Offering the deserving poor opportunities in the West, an idea he had first advocated in the *Observations*, would keep wages for labor in America high, "and while Labor continues dear," he continued, "we can never rival the Artificers, or interfere with the Trade of our Mother Country."[10]

At about the same time, Franklin toyed with his own design for the settling of two colonies west of Pennsylvania. Private schemes to cash in speculatively on colonial frontier lands proliferated on both sides of the Atlantic. In 1747, Parliament had chartered the Ohio Company with a mandate to settle an area of 200,000 acres and build a fort. The extensive land claims of colonial governments, Virginia's especially, constantly whetted the appetites of American land grabbers. Like the rest, Franklin marveled at what he heard of the Ohio country: "the extreme richness and fertility of the land; the healthy temperature of the air, and mildness of the climate; the plenty of hunting, fishing, and fowling; the facility of trade with the Indians; and the vast convenience of inland navigation or watercarriage by the lakes and great rivers, many hundred[s] of leagues around." Pursuing a land grant from the Crown, as many others did, he dreamed of speculative profits on

western lands while filling the trans-Appalachian frontier with exemplary Englishmen. This had to be done before the French, who now made "open encroachments" there, became too strong to be dislodged. Were Britain to be defeated in
the approaching confrontation—a great war for empire—its colonies would be
left clinging to a narrow coastal strip and would face not just higher military vul-
nerability but a hastened social decay: "Our people, being confined to the country
between the sea and the mountains, cannot much more increase in number," for
a virtuous population increased only "in proportion to their room and means of
subsistence."[11]

To ignore frontier possibilities, or let speculators retard settlement by holding
rather than developing their western grants, invited an imperial disaster no less
devastating than to lose a war with the French—for several reasons. As in a military
defeat, the English colonies would be confined to the East, increasing in population without room to expand and leaving to the French "room and plenty of subsistence and become a great people" instead of the English. Moreover, those who
benefited least under British rule—debtors, "loose English people," "our German
servants," African slaves—would desert to the French, increasing their numbers
and strength while further weakening that of the British. In addition, enhanced
French control would cut the British off "from all commerce and alliance with the
western Indians," further inhibiting sale and consumption of manufactured goods
from the mother country. And finally, as bitter colonial experience had shown,
the empowered French, in both peacetime and war, would induce the Indians
"to harass our frontiers, kill and scalp our people, and drive in [back eastward]
the advanced settlers," without whom the essential growth of population through
expansion would never occur.[12]

Franklin's *Plan for Settling Two Western Colonies* therefore made a case for the
filling of trans-Appalachian lands quickly, fortifying the wilderness with Englishmen willing to stay, implant their culture, and provide military strength—all key
to Britain's survival as a power in North America. This scheme required a granting
of two royal charters, "*each* for some considerable part of the lands west of Pennsylvania and the Virginia mountains, to a number of the nobility and gentry of
Britain." Franklin assumed that these gentlemen aristocrats and other "leisured"
people, as he now styled himself, would be accompanied by migrants of common
means who would constitute the majority of new colonists—"such Americans as
shall join them in contributing to the settlement of those lands, either by paying
a proportion of the expense . . . or by actually going thither in person, and settling
themselves and families." A variation on the old colonial headright systems, these
charters would entitle each settler to a small tract of land for himself and one "for
every poll [person] in the family he carries with him." Franklin, the quintessential

self-made American, believed justice and necessity demanded incentives for individual advancement: "extraordinary privileges and liberties, with lands on easy
terms, are strong inducements to people to hazard their persons and fortunes in
settling new countries."[13]

Given the need for the "right" sorts of people to guide western colonization, it
bothered Franklin when the "wrong" sorts often took interest. As Richard Jackson
reminded him in June 1755, many "fruitless attempts" to found colonies resulted
from a lack of "necessary moral habits." Samuel Hazard, according to Franklin,
exemplified the "wrong" type. Hazard, a Philadelphia merchant, had gotten caught
up in the Great Awakening via Gilbert Tennent's Second Presbyterian Church.
"He aims at great Matters for himself, hoping to become a Proprietor like Mr.
Penn," Franklin complained to Peter Collinson. Hazard reportedly had assembled
"a great Number of Settlers" to accompany him westward. All he lacked was a land
grant from the Crown, but his ambition exceeded his organizational abilities. "I
wish to see it done," Franklin declared, "yet I think this man not the fittest in the
World to conduct such an Affair." And worse than people like Hazard, an abundance of would-be western land monopolists, intent on keeping lands uncultivated
and waiting for a speculative windfall, also vied for royal favor during this period.
Franklin called them "land jobbers" and thought that their obsession with personal
gain held little hope for benefit to society.[14]

⁃⸱⁃

British victory in the Seven Years War, ending with the 1763 Treaty of Paris, brought
extensive territorial gains. The French gave up all territory west of the Appalachians
to the Mississippi and all of Canada. Now, Franklin's mental picture of a vast New
World empire became more grandiose than ever. With the major military and economic threat to the thirteen colonies eliminated, American agriculturists might
proceed westward almost at will, averting the social evils of industrialization for
many generations to come. He wrote in his *Canada Pamphlet*, circulated through
Britain in the early 1760s, "A people spread thro' the whole tract of country on this
side of the Mississippi, and secured by Canada in our hands, would probably for
some centuries find employment in agriculture, and thereby free us at home effectually from our fears of American manufacturers." Maintain the colonies in their
mostly preindustrial condition, he argued, and America would remain a lucrative
market for British manufactures. He gushed to Jackson on March 8, 1763, "Since
all the Country is now ceded to us on this Side of the Mississippi, is not this a good
time to think of new Colonies on that River, to secure our Territory and extend our
Commerce; and to separate the Indians on this side from those on the other[?]"[15]

But British policy headed elsewhere. The new secretary of state for the Southern
Department, George Montagu-Dunk, second earl of Halifax, wanted to central-

ize and streamline western policy for the colonies. The changes would follow no expansive vision of empire but only reinforce the colonies as a market for English manufactures and make them a focus for George Grenville's (ill-conceived) revenue-raising plans to pay for the eighty regiments of British regulars expected to remain in the colonies. In fact, Halifax showed scarcely any interest at all in using the trans-Appalachian West for economic purposes. In reaction to Pontiac's Rebellion in the Northwest, which had erupted in May 1763, British policy emphasized keeping future peace by getting settlers out of the western regions and preventing further agitation of Indian hostility. The presence of redcoats stationed at forts beyond the Appalachian ridge would, he felt, help to deter frontiersmen from defying imperial power.

On Halifax's instruction, King George III issued the Proclamation of 1763, a first step toward governance of the newly enlarged empire. The Crown designated all British claims west of rivers that flowed into the Atlantic—from the Great Lakes to Florida—as a gigantic reserve for native tribes. It banned further colonial land grants in that area, suspended surveying, restricted frontier trade, and forbade British subjects "from making any purchases or settlements whatever" in that region without first obtaining "special leave and license for that purpose." It ordered all whites living within the new Indian reserve "forthwith to remove themselves from such settlements." The prohibition of private purchases within the Indian domain attempted to curb reckless speculation and land fraud, while leaving Indian land titles to be negotiated only by official agents of the Crown. Migration could occur within the established colonies, directed northward and southward, but not westward—with the aim of a more compactly settled colonial population under tighter imperial control. It was a sensible policy for Great Britain, perhaps, but hardly for colonial land speculators, ordinary farmers who hungered for frontier lands, or advocates of rapid expansion like Benjamin Franklin.[16]

The proclamation, of course, did not work. Drawn hastily because of the Indian unrest, the settlement line along the crest of the Appalachians placed some colonial settlements within the confines of the Indian reserve. Frontier Americans ignored regulations on whites who attempted to trade with the Indians. Lobbyists on behalf of speculative interests, including the Grand Ohio Company, which coveted millions of acres in the Ohio Valley, pressured for the settlement line to be shifted westward. The proclamation left hanging the fate of legitimate grants and claims already established. Were all trans-Appalachian settlers to just walk away from their homes, no questions asked? Were the colonies to repudiate patents that in some cases extended all the way to the Pacific? What of the western land bounties promised to British soldiers who had served in the French and Indian War?

Meanwhile, land speculators with powerful connections in Parliament could, and often did, receive exemptions.[17]

Britain's territorial gain in 1763 had made North America a potential world within itself. Franklin saw that better than anyone, and he predicted the outcome as well. Unless British political economy changed in ways more conducive to a "union" between the mother country and the expanding colonies, nature instead of design would dictate policy: "[A]n immense Territory, favour'd by Nature with all Advantages of Climate, Soil, great navigable Rivers and Lakes, &c. must become a great Country, populous and mighty." It would "in a less time than is generally conceiv'd be able to shake off any Shackles that may be impos'd on her, and perhaps place them on the Imposers."[18] Franklin's *Observations* had offered a vision better suited to a westward-expanding agricultural nation than to Britain's post-1763 governance. At that time, the influence of European physiocratic writers—Quesnay and Turgot in France and Lord Kames in Scotland—had spread within the English philosophical community. Not long afterward, Adam Smith in the *Wealth of Nations* (1776) would delineate the merits of free market economics. Agricultural husbandry constituted the only real source of riches, the physiocrats maintained. Franklin agreed. As he put it in 1768, for example, "Agriculture is truly *productive* of *new wealth*; Manufactures only change Forms; and whatever value they give to the Material they work upon, they in the mean time consume an equal value in Provisions." Moral advantages accompanied the economic ones. "Agriculture," kept free from governmental interference, Franklin wrote, "is the only honest Way; wherein Man receives a real Increase of the Seed thrown into the Ground, . . . as a Reward for his innocent Life, and virtuous Industry."[19]

Serving as America's key foreign minister during the Revolutionary struggle, Franklin would point to America's vacant lands when assuring potential allies and creditors that the former colonies could maintain their independence and discharge their debts. In doing so, he obviously hoped that the trans-Appalachian West would be among the fruits of American success in the Revolution. As he saw it, the war pitted a geographically limited, morally decaying nation against a spacious country of agriculturists. That could give the Revolutionary states a long-term financial advantage their enemy would no longer enjoy. Britain, he wrote, "will have fewer People to assist in paying her Debts, and that diminished number will be poorer." America, by contrast, could rely upon "her Lands already cultivated," along with "a vast territory yet to improve." And the value of those lands would rise as they filled with a population to be augmented not only by "*natural Propagation*," but from abroad a steady "[a]ccession of *Strangers*," no longer so distrusted in Franklin's scheme of things, "as long as Lands are to be had for new

Families; so that every 20 years there will be a double Number of Inhabitants oblig'd to discharge publick Debts; and those Inhabitants, being more opulent, may pay their Shares with greater Ease."[20]

This argument, like much of Franklin's writing after 1750, anticipated some of the views that frontier westerners and congressional pro-settlement advocates would take during the early decades of the nineteenth century. He disregarded the objections of those who feared that westward expansion necessarily would bring a depopulation of older-settled areas. To any man with a disposition for honest labor, he thought, the new land promised that "every one" would "enjoy securely the Profits of his Industry." Yet, as he quickly added in his September 1782 "Information to Those Who Would Remove to America," the emigrant who did not bring his fortune with him from the start "must work and be industrious to live." Little but moral virtue could guard against "luxury" and social corruption in republican America, but the land itself, he thought, could sustain the character as well as the prosperity of the people. Franklin would write in 1784, six years before his death, "The vast Quantity of Forest Lands we have yet to clear, and put in order for Cultivation, will for a long time keep the Body of our Nation laborious and frugal." On that lasting agricultural base, he believed, individual Americans, like the nation they inhabited, could remain free and independent.[21]

CHAPTER ONE

"Republican Notions—and Utopian Schemes"

On November 15, 1782, as he pondered the prospects of westward expansion in post-Revolutionary America, James Madison had good reason to be worried. It was not just that American independence had yet to be finally confirmed in negotiations with Great Britain. A few weeks earlier, the Confederation Congress, where Madison sat as one of the delegates from Virginia, had received a disturbing communication from General William Irvine at Fort Pitt, near what would become the town of Pittsburgh. It reported an impending crisis on the frontier.

With no governmental force to restrain them, recounted Irvine, "the people are in great numbers flocking over the Ohio into what has hitherto been called the Indian Country & are busy in taking up & improving lands as well on what is supposed to be within the bounds of Penna." and "beyond the Western line thereof." More specifically, a body of some four hundred men from the western-most reaches of Virginia had decided to establish a settlement on the Muskingum River, gladly committing "many wanton & unprovoked acts of cruelty" against tribal neighbors. The most likely result, he cautioned, would be Indian retaliation, the first of "many evil consequences that must result from such lawless measures." If Congress failed to act, or if the states claiming these unsettled lands did nothing, neither the United States nor any of its member republics would ever "reap much advantage" from the vast trans-Appalachian frontier. In a letter to Virginia governor Benjamin Harrison, Madison conveyed Irvine's news and added a further, equally troubling conclusion of his own: "[T]he inhabitants of this State West of the Alleghany Mountains are openly proceeding towards a separation of Govt. It is certain that they have for some time had such a scheme in contemplation."[1]

Three gigantic issues of public policy loomed here—not just for Madison and other officials in Revolutionary Virginia, but for all who recognized the need to secure western America within some basic framework of republican values and well-connected to the independent nation beginning to emerge. One matter, of course, was financial. The states with western land resources hoped that the sale of their lands would help them retire the massive Revolutionary war debts they had incurred, thus relieving legislators of the need to overburden their taxpayers. Historians have long emphasized that Congress and the landed states needed to use western lands for revenue to pay their mounting bills, which included recompense to the soldiers who had been promised land bounties for their service. A second reason for government to be involved in settlement of the West was political. As Parliament had foreseen with its Proclamation of 1763, any sudden release of land-hungry whites into the areas beyond the Appalachians would likely provoke the hostility of Native American groups and risk the costly distraction of frontier warfare between white intruders and the indigenous inhabitants. In addition, only governmental authority could guarantee the legality of land acquisitions in unsettled areas, so that initial and future purchasers could count on safe title to tracts they believed to be theirs. The third issue, even more critical to the American future but less often addressed by historians, was social. The fear had started to spread that frontier regions were filling all-too-rapidly with a crowd that recognized no real authority other than themselves—settlers who, if left to their own will or the intentions of scoundrels, could in no time degenerate into "white savages." If so, then western America might be overrun by people of no character, no ethics, no regard for native inhabitants, and no respect for law. The result, put simply, could have been the loss of the West, ending any hope of building a great republic to extend not just to the Appalachians, but far beyond.[2]

If chaos is the law of nature, order is the goal of policy makers. The American West at the time of the Revolution featured chaos in abundance and precious little order. The vast expanse of territory from the Appalachians to the Mississippi belonged to the several states that held claims dating from early colonial times, Virginia being the foremost. Little would change until Virginia ceded its claims to the United States in 1784, a precedent that other states eventually followed. Colonial governance of the frontier, apart from British efforts at control, had been a hodgepodge of rules and regulations, traditions and innovations, styles and practices that varied from region to region. The historical roots of this medley lay in origins as diverse as township grants in Puritan-dominated New England to the great Hudson River estates bestowed upon favorites of the Crown and farmed by lowly tenants. Policies had varied; Pennsylvania, for example, sold tracts of every size, while the headright systems in Virginia and throughout the colonial South resulted in large accumulations of plantation lands. Colonial governments had been mostly interested in moving lands into private ownership as quickly as possible. Their haphazard ways of doing that—the absence of limitations on the acreage one could own, the non-enforcement of "seating" or settlement requirements, and the poor handling of Indian relations, to mention just a few lapses of governance —

had left large areas in the western parts of colonies underdeveloped, caused widely dispersed patterns of population, and fostered the arrival of too many settlers who felt no more regard for colonial authority back east than for that of the British an ocean away.[3]

—◌

All pursuits of a more ideal society in America had begun, to some extent, as refracted images of the perceived "good" and "bad" being left behind. One of several dominant views in political economy that historians have linked with the English settlement of North America, and with the origins of the United States, appeared in England during the late seventeenth and early eighteenth centuries. In that era, reform-minded writers were shaping a critique of Britain's growing commercial, military, and imperial power. The questions that occupied English political thought of that time included the extent to which government should direct and regulate economic growth, how to promote opportunity without sacrificing the community benefits of restraint, and how to achieve expansion while maintaining vital elements of social control. Informed Englishmen understood these questions not merely as relating to the means of prosperity—land, trade, and credit—but also as they affected political stability and public virtue. The relatively sudden appearance of wild financial speculation, excessive "luxury," and a public debt—features of an increasingly urban society—alarmed old-fashioned agrarians who thought that only the wide distribution and cultivation of land could provide a national community of moral and autonomous citizens.[4]

James Harrington's *Oceana*, published in 1656, expressed these sentiments better than any other such treatise. The goal of this work was visionary: a prescription for a republican commonwealth, protected from political instability and secured against internal corruption. Such a commonwealth, he assumed, could be possible only with the material circumstances necessary to support it, widely distributed landownership in particular. Like some writers before him and many to follow (including Benjamin Franklin), Harrington believed that humans acted rationally, pursuing recognizable economic interests. If landholding were widespread on a popular basis, an agrarian commonwealth like the one Harrington envisioned, where law guarded against too much land in too few hands, would become feasible. As landownership widened, he argued, so too could the privileges and obligations of citizenship: the right to vote, the holding of office, the bearing of arms to defend one's interests, the paying of taxes, and so on.[5]

Some early designs for new colonies in British America, especially the scheme for Pennsylvania in 1683, had borrowed structural ideas from *Oceana* and other classic texts to avoid replicating the Old World social order. Later, Thomas Jefferson seemed to echo Harrington as well as John Locke when he wrote in 1785: "Whenever there are in any country uncultivated lands and unemployed poor, it is clear that the laws of property have been so far extended as to violate natural right. The earth is given as a common stock for man to labor and live on. . . . [And] it is not too soon to provide by every possible means that as few as possible shall be without a little portion of land."[6]

Whether the principal influence came from Classical republicans, Lockean liberals, Scottish Enlightenment thinkers, the various permutations of Calvinism, or anything else, historians have regarded the American Revolution as an effort to shield American "virtue" against the spread of English corruption and decay. The Revolution also promised to defend the traditional "rights" of property holding against the presumed British threat to this and other fundamental liberties. Such beliefs took deep root in eighteenth- and nineteenth-century America, not just because they represented a rich ideological inheritance, but also because they accorded with daily experience in colonial and postcolonial societies. Widely distributed property made individual economic autonomy a normal way of life for millions. Yet, in the two or three decades after 1776, political leaders disagreed sharply as to what sort of republic best suited America. Being in some fashion men of the Enlightenment, almost all agreed that human behavior could be altered by the willful shaping of environment. The American West provided an open place for political leaders, and those who influenced them, to project a new social vision with design as the key, as opposed to unleashing energies at random. But *whose* design? And to benefit *which* sorts of people? Publicists and policy makers in the Revolutionary states and the Confederation Congress argued over a variety of problems, each seeming to bear on the fundamental character of American society and institutions. Western land policy ranked high on the list of concerns. The existence of so much open territory in America called for much transforming of traditional ideals, if not always a rejection of them.

—◦—

Most men and women who originally settled in English colonies reflected a post-Elizabethan world of set traditions, strict practices, and established hierarchy. However much some of them may have expected the New World to offer circumstances different from the Old, they still generally assumed that society should be a tightly knit fabric of relationships among people and organized according to "status," that is, distinct levels of superiority and inferiority—not simply according to occupation or financial situation. Those deemed naturally "superior," the highborn, expected to achieve the highest education, enjoy greatest wealth, exert political influence, do the leading, and become the most respectable and dignified members of their communities. People who lived in the colonial offshoots of English society often tried to reproduce the best values that had governed the collective order and overall character of society back home.[7]

That applied, too, in Puritan New England, where the primary goal had been to build a new commonwealth that served the Godly purposes of escaping worldly corruption, materialism, and greed. One way to achieve such lofty aims was to establish public authority over economic relations, which included a "well-regulated" allocation, exchange, and use of land. In America, as in the Old World, land was to be the principal means of advancing one's fortune, but in early New England the motive behind one's accumulation had been all-important. The urge to acquire had to be tempered by respect for the common good, as articulated by governmental authority and fostered in churches, schools, and families. With landholding and the opportunity to build one's personal fortune came the responsibility to uphold the community need. Moreover, since Puritans believed that God rewarded the industrious, why should settlers be entitled to more of nature's bounty than they could use? Clearing land and building farms, constructing shops, shipyards, and forts, erecting bridges and ironworks—all of these, and much more, fell under the Puritan notion of communal capitalism (as opposed to more predatory forms already working in the Chesapeake and West Indies). As Puritan leader John Winthrop cautioned in 1639, "a man can have no right to more than he can subdue," and all proper acts of economic development were to come "by the sweate of our browes." In 1634, the Massachusetts General Court declared "improvement" to be the "price of possession." Anyone who had received a land grant of any sizeable quantity and did not build or otherwise improve it within three years would forfeit ownership. In Massachusetts, the General Court controlled land grants and used its power for targeted economic development. Shipbuilding, fishing, and metalworking enjoyed governmental favor. New England towns valued shopkeepers, millers, smiths, tanners, and other occupations that enhanced the welfare of the community as a whole. Traditional Puritan social hierarchies emerged in land grants to recipients who merited favor because their behavior and judgment seemed most likely to advance the religious principles and various needs of the commonwealth.[8]

The vastness of land, however, quickly forced Puritan magistrates to realize that they could not easily control the character of settlement and the movement of population. This realization would come to governmental authorities again and again in the extended story of westward expansion. With land abundant and labor scarce in colonial New England, tying "artificers and workemen" to their parishes, regulating their economic activities, or making them stay put geographically proved difficult. As a result, the landholding system that developed allowed land to be alienable, divisible, and inheritable, as opposed to its being restricted by an assortment of archaic rights and obligations like those of the Old World.[9]

By the mid-1700s, traditional concepts of social order had deteriorated not just in New England but throughout colonial America. One reason, as Benjamin Franklin had said, was that colonial population exploded at a rate unknown anywhere else, doubling to two million between 1750 and 1770, and four million by 1790. Along with natural increase, hundreds of thousands of immigrants, mostly from the British Isles and central Europe, added to this growth in the decades preceding the Revolution. Historians have estimated that some 300,000 more whites arrived between 1783 and 1819, a large number of whom filled backcountry regions, where fertile land beckoned and the prospect of competition with slave labor lessened considerably in comparison to much of the East. By the 1760s, exorbitant rents in Ireland and Scotland had driven tens of thousands to North America. Imperial administrators, including Lord Hillsborough, the American Secretary from 1768 to 1772, even began to worry that the fringes of the British Isles might become depopulated. In America, lands along the Atlantic coast settled thickly, making them harder to obtain either by purchase or inheritance. More and more young men and women, undeterred by distance, hardship, or restrictive edicts like the Proclamation of 1763, pinned their hopes for agricultural happiness on developing western regions of the colonies or across the mountains. In his letter to Madison, General Irvine would refer to conditions north of the Ohio, but a similar story had been unfolding south of the river. Kentucky, as part of Virginia's claim, had scarcely any white residents before the mid-1770s. By the early 1780s, more than 20,000 settlers lived there, many of them psychologically empowered by the antigovernment ethos of the American Revolution. That number would multiply more than tenfold by 1800. Almost before governing officials could grasp what was happening, westward expansion outran the political ability to control it. The farther migration spread, the more traditional authority, social connection, and the rule of law seemed to disintegrate. In all, it seemed not only the Celtic parts of Britain but also much of "old" America really was breaking up and moving westward.[10]

For many of these migrants, the pressure of necessity accompanied the lure of new land. Though appearances often misled traveling visitors to the contrary, inequality characterized post-Revolutionary American society. All through the former colonies, more and more families experienced significant economic hardship. During this period, about 15 percent of Philadelphians lived in poverty, as did roughly a fifth of New York City's inhabitants. Although landownership remained far more widespread than in Europe, landlessness increased in longer-settled rural areas, where 90 percent of the overall eastern populace lived, most depending in some way on the soil for their livelihoods. In Chester County, Pennsylvania, the number of landless laborers, including dependent farm workers, would nearly double between the mid-eighteenth century and 1820. Patterns of growth and inheritance caused average farm sizes in the older parts of New England to shrink from about 120 acres in the early 1700s to less than 40 by the time of the Revolution.[11]

The same sort of story unfolded in many parts of the upper South, which, along with southern New England, produced an overwhelming number of westward-bound families in the decades after the Revolution. In Albemarle County, Virginia, in Thomas Jefferson's day, despite soil exhaustion, disruptions in the tobacco trade, and a shift of many farmers to grain production, only about 10 percent of the names on the census of 1800 owned the vast majority of farm tracts. Farther east, in Caroline County, the number of household heads without land increased from 154 to 572 between 1787 and 1830, a percentage change from 16.8 to 34.1, while the number holding fewer than 50 acres jumped from 42 to 197, 4.6 percent to 11.8. In the Shenandoah Valley county of Augusta, just west of Albemarle, the number of landless grew from 182 to 1,348 in the same period, a percentage rise of 13.5 to 47.2. Meanwhile, the percentage of yeomen holding 100–500 acres also fell dramatically, from 50.2 to 32.3 in Caroline County and from 61.5 to 33.0 in Augusta. In Jefferson's Virginia, many small farmers became landless whites; the dream of small-scale independent freeholding was evaporating.[12]

An unprecedented population boom in the 1780s—proportionally, one of the greatest in American history—resulted by 1800 in an unusual increase in the number of white Americans of younger age—more than 68 percent of them no older than 25 years. This change, viewed together with the diminishing agricultural opportunities in the East, goes far to explain the pressure for westward expansion in the early decades of the nineteenth century. In all, about a fifth of all Americans had removed to frontier regions by 1800, expecting—and sometimes demanding—that their respective governments, dominated by an eastern establishment, address their most pressing needs.[13]

These changing social conditions, especially the swelling of settlement in western regions, inspired consternation but little sympathy among the ruling classes. The explanation involves more than wealthier men seeking to gain economically from the distresses of their social lessers. *Control* was the main issue. For elite merchants, planters, and speculators, the period after 1763 brought not only deteriorating relations with British authorities but also escalating social pressures from below. The frontier upheaval that would vex officials like Madison in the early 1780s occurred in a broader context of social cleavages involving a variety of disputes that had shaken one backcountry region after another since the 1760s. The Paxton Riots in Pennsylvania, the Baptist challenge in Virginia, the Regulator movements in the Carolinas, the land riots in New Jersey and New York—all of these denoted popular resistance to propertied authority and political control *within* the colonies. Even during the War for Independence, the clamoring of angry western farmers, disgruntled tenants, defiant squatters, and various others continued to distract patriot leaders like James Bowdoin in Massachusetts, the Livingstons in New York, James Wilson and Robert Morris in Pennsylvania, Charles Carroll in Maryland, and Richard Henry Lee and George Washington in Virginia—to name a few. British- and loyalist-inspired slave unrest, especially in the plantation states, along with reactivated Indian hostility in the West, complicated the picture still further. Revolutionary ideology carried powerful, if unintended, implications for all kinds of men and women tired of deferring to their social "betters." In the eyes of the propertied classes, these restless sorts often appeared to be "licentious" elements that would have to be suppressed.[14]

Of course, as Benjamin Franklin noted, plenty of merchant-speculator types pushed forward with one community design or another to bring order and "civilization" to the western areas, along with greater riches and notoriety for themselves. One example is William Judd, a lawyer from Farmington, Connecticut, who in 1774 led an expedition to set up a Connecticut settlement on the west branch of the Susquehanna River, in the Wyoming Valley, the site of a jurisdictional tug-o-war between Connecticut and Pennsylvania. Judd's project seemed to hold promise, because he and some of his fellow settlers had been men of respectable standing back home. Eliphalet Dyer, one of Connecticut's delegates to Congress, wrote Judd on July 23, 1775: "I am Very glad that a Gentn. of the Capacity & Abilities I esteem you . . . to be possessed of is about to move into that Country as Gentn of knowledge & prudence may be of great service there especially at this Critical time when a jar between two Colonies may be of almost fatal Consequence to the Whole." Another, James Hogg of North Carolina, was an investor in the Transylvania Land Company, which aimed to found a colony west of the Alleghenies between the Cumberland and Kentucky Rivers. He showed up in Philadelphia on October 22, 1775, with a plan for the Continental Congress to add this colony of "Transylvania" to the united colonies and recognize himself as its delegate to Congress. The Virginia delegation, perceiving among other things an encroachment on their interests, managed to dissuade Hogg and send him packing. John Adams, representing Massachusetts, suspected all such fortune seekers, to say the least. He remarked in his diary on October 25, 1775, "These Proprietors have no Grant from the Crown nor from any Colony, are within the Limits of Virginia and North Carolina, by their Charters which bound those Colonies on the South Sea." And yet, like so many others, including members of Congress, these entrepreneurs came "charged with Republican Notions—and Utopian Schemes."[15]

Yet another illustration is Silas Deane of Wethersfield, Connecticut, who, like Judd and Dyer, cited the importance of carrying westward some of the more refined ways of New England. Born in 1737, the ambitious, Yale-educated Deane made money as a Connecticut River merchant, but his questionable reputation in business (and later in politics) would cover the spectrum from mere opportunism to outright rascality. Entering colonial politics in 1768, he advanced quickly with the help of the wealthy Saltonstall family, into which he had married. By the mid-1770s, he had established himself as the most fervent westward expansionist in Connecticut. This enthusiasm derived in no small part from his own commercial connection with the Susquehanna Company, a body of fellow merchants who hoped to exploit the "sea-to-sea" clause in the colony's royal charter to justify a major land speculating endeavor in the Wyoming Valley of Pennsylvania. By 1774, Deane ranked easily among the richest men in Wethersfield.[16]

Chosen in 1774 as one of Connecticut's delegates to the First Continental Congress, Deane presented his "notion"—or, rather, his "scheme"—in November 1774, promising to undercut Parliament's Quebec Act by establishing a colony of New Englanders in the Great Lakes region. After presumably being granted money by Congress to purchase from Indian tribes a tract of land sufficient for a large settlement, he told Samuel Adams, "a Number of Settlers, at least one Thousand strong should instantly move on the Land, with every Necessary for carrying on, and supporting their plantation"—a body sizeable enough to "awe the natives" and remote enough to be free from British authority, including that in Quebec. According to the plan, these colonists would quickly organize their own government along the lines of the earliest commonwealths of New England. While Deane thought "no extraordinary pains" would be needed to recruit migrants, he considered it still to "be the very best policy to open Our Doors wide, and use every means, in Our power, to invite the poor, industrious Inhabitants of Scotland, Ireland &c to come in and join Us, and with but little incouragement they will flock over in Numbers, and soon render [the colony] important." Of course, most of these inhabitants had to be Protestant in religion, so as to carry westward the "New England Inheritance." Via successive tiers of colonies to follow, he predicted, "Our People, & their descendants, will give Law, not to North & South America alone, but to the World if they please."[17]

A few months later, now touting a venture to fill the Ohio River region, Deane tried his luck with Patrick Henry, one of Virginia's delegates. Again, his idea offered to reproduce west of the Appalachians the pattern of New England towns: "The lands given should be divided into lots of about two or three hundred acres to each family and not more, for a Connecticut farmer with two hundred and fifty or three hundred acres of good land, is a rich man, that is, as rich as he wishes to be, for this Colony is now so full of inhabitants that there is not more than twelve acres to a person." That estimate was about right; the percentage of independent whites in Wethersfield who owned land had shrunk considerably since 1756. By the time of the Revolution, a third of this population was landless (nearly twice as many as fifteen years before), and of the landholders, over half owned fewer than 100 acres and 40 percent fewer than 50 acres. Deane boasted that he could raise enough settlers for one town right away, following as much as possible "the New England Plan," by which he meant a self-governing community of at least 70 families, enough to support a minister (preferably Congregationalist) and provision a schoolmaster. Whatever their merits, these expansionist overtures went nowhere. Apparently, Deane's reputation had more than sufficiently preceded him, and besides, the Continental Congress had quite a few other things to think about in 1774–1775. Several years later, he conspired unsuccessfully with Robert Morris and several other leading Pennsylvanians involved with the Illinois and Wabash land companies; and finally, in 1785, he would try for a deal to connect Lake Champlain to the St. Lawrence River by way of a canal.[18]

No one contrasted with Deane more than 33-year-old Thomas Jefferson, who had little interest in land speculation and no connection to land companies. As he saw it, the solution for disorder on the frontiers lay in populating the western regions with virtuous yeomen and providing them powers of self-government as quickly as possible. Few at the time actually shared this agricultural idealism. Jefferson's sole claim to fame before arriving in the Second Continental Congress in June 1775 was his widely circulated pamphlet *A Summary View of the Rights of British America*, published the year before. There, he had argued that Americans possessed "a right, which nature has given to all men of departing from the country in which chance, not choice, has placed them, of going in quest of new habitations, and of there establishing new societies, under such laws and regulations as to them shall seem most likely to promote public happiness." Like David Hume, whose *History of England* had appeared over a decade before, he regarded the feudal land tenures in England as a foreign contrivance, part of the system introduced by William the Conqueror and alien to the "Allodial" system presumably originating in "the earlier ages of the Saxon settlement." As Jefferson saw it, British colonists' "saxon ancestors held their lands, as they did their personal property, in absolute dominion, disencumbered with any superior." Referring to the 1763 Proclamation Line and other efforts to retard western settlement, Jefferson accused the Crown of impairing further the proper acquisition and settlement of colonial lands by setting the terms of purchase at double their current worth.[19]

Far more radically agrarian than he would be after 1800, Jefferson in these early years of the Revolution might have struck John Adams as *both* "republican" and "utopian." As in private life, so in public affairs: Jefferson deplored debt but had little frugality or sense of finance. He wanted to imagine ordinary rural Americans as the eighteenth-century avatars of their "antient" eighth-century Anglo-Saxon "ancestors"—holding their small parcels of land in full and free possession, without obligation of service or rent, the opposite of feudalism. Although most in Congress later would expect western land sales to answer the mounting public debt, Jefferson opposed selling the lands at all. Doing so would throw them into the hands of propertied men to the exclusion of the poor, who could not successfully bid against wealthier competitors. Further, he told Edmund Pendleton in August 1776, those who migrated west would already be subject to their proportion of the states' collective debt, and they would be the sorts "little able to pay taxes." There would be "no equity in fixing upon them the whole burthen of this war, or any other proportion than we bear ourselves." By selling the lands, he continued, "you will disgust them, and cause an avulsion of them from the common union." Besides, they would still go ahead and "settle the lands in spite of everybody."[20]

This advice implied that governmental power might be insufficient to enforce a sales program, particularly if many of the migrants from eastern regions would be people with no intention—or economic wherewithal—to pay for the land. Nor would they crumble under threats of coercive rulers or the intimidation of their wealthier "betters." So why not win western allegiance by making the burden of migration and resettlement as light as possible? The benefits of rapid settlement might outweigh the need for government revenue. Jefferson would eventually have second thoughts about that, too.

Returning to the Virginia assembly from late 1776 until 1779, young Jefferson tried to reshape his own state's land policy. In his draft of the state constitution of 1776, submitted unsuccessfully to the legislature in June of that year, he proposed: "Every person of full age neither owning nor having owned (50) acres of land, shall be entitled to an appropriation of (50) acres or to so much as shall make up what he owns or has owned (50) acres in full and absolute dominion, and no other person shall be capable to taking an appropriation." He also proposed that all lands previously held by the Crown be converted to fee simple. These suggestions, however, contemplated no sudden releasing of settlement to occur wherever nature might dictate. Jefferson specified that government somehow exert authority over frontier administration *prior* to settlement: "No lands shall be appropriated until purchased of the Indian native proprietors; nor shall any purchases be made of them but on behalf of the public, by authority of acts of the General assembly to be passed for every purchase specially."[21]

In all of this, Jefferson faced the formidable weight of the past. Historically, as Virginia expanded westward, the tobacco barons who ran the politics of the colony assumed that they could shape the expansion of culture and social organization as well, thus extending and preserving the distinctive character of the Old Dominion. No process so pivotal to Virginia's future, and its dominant families, could be left to chance. Leading planters like Robert Beverly and William Byrd II had expected their own descendants to take part in the filling of the Virginia frontier, tying it to the Tidewater and the authority of its elite. Western regions could not be risked to ordinary settlers, especially those of lawless disposition and questionable loyalty. If Bacon's Rebellion of 1676 had taught them anything, it was that such types would, unless controlled, flock to the standard of a demagogue.[22]

In "An Act for the better strengthening of the frontiers," the Virginia assembly in 1701 had tried, without success, to lure whole societies of "warlike Christian" settlers, offering them ten thousand–acre to thirty thousand–acre grants in return for their willingness to defend the western reaches of the colony. There, lawmakers hoped, they would recreate the traditional power structure that so much favored order and the prerogatives of the rich. In 1711, Governor Alexander Spotswood had spoken of Virginia's own frontier inhabitants as mostly degenerated former indentured servants—crude, lazy, and profligate. "It is pretty well known what Morals such people bring with them hither," Spotswood lamented. In his *History of the Dividing Line,* Byrd in 1728 had dismissed backcountry folk as people who "detested work more than famine." Virginia's western residents, he thought, scarcely rose above the white savages of frontier North Carolina. The future danger to—and importance of maintaining—Virginia's precious social hierarchy showed plainly to him.[23]

On October 14, 1776, Jefferson introduced in the state assembly the first of his famous bills intended, as he explained later, to "annul . . . an aristocracy of wealth" and "make an opening for the aristocracy of virtue and talent." Here, too, appeared elements of the social reform program he envisioned for the West. Passing in the House of Delegates on October 23 and in the Senate nine days later, the legislation granted landholders in fee tail throughout Virginia the privilege to convey their lands in fee simple. This meant that holdings previously restricted, or "entailed," to a specified class of heirs could now be divided or sold however the owner might wish. The measure also dispensed with the principle of primogeniture, whereby entailed lands were to pass intact, through inheritance, only to the eldest son— making "one member of every family rich, and all the rest poor." These changes could gain acceptance with relative ease; for some time Virginians already had circumvented such vestiges of feudalism by specifying the disposition of property holdings in their wills. In years to come, most states would adopt a system of partible inheritance, whereby children of the deceased would receive equal shares of the estate in the absence of a will. But Jefferson wanted not just to repudiate outdated practice but also uproot Virginia's privileged and influential class of great landholders—a patrician order immersed in luxury. Perpetuating property in "certain families," the bill stated, "tends to deceive . . . fair traders who give a credit on the visible possession of such estates, discourages the holder thereof from taking care of and improving the same, and sometimes does injury to the morals of youth by rendering them independent of, and disobedient to, their parents."[24]

Obliterating "unnatural distinctions" remained central to Jefferson's view of ideal social reform and good land policy, even though Virginia lawmakers more often moved in the opposite direction. The first of the two bills, mainly Jefferson's work, included a pair of egalitarian provisions that the legislature quickly pruned. The other, entitled a "Bill for Establishing a Land Office," joined the progress of settlement with deriving public revenue from the sale of some lands. The two ill-fated sections of the first bill shocked Virginia's gentry, who found them far too radical. Similar to Jefferson's constitutional proposal of 1776, these sections originally promised 50 acres of vacant western land for free to "every person removing from any foreign Country or at his charge importing any Inhabitants not being Slaves"—in effect a democratized headright system. The assembly also excised from the initial draft a proposal "for the more equal Distribution of Lands, and to encourage Marriage and Population by making Provision for the Natives of the Country." In this, Jefferson and James Madison had collaborated in advocating a grant of 75 acres in the West to each freeborn Commonwealth citizen upon marriage and residence in Virginia for the following year. The opposition to these ideas reflected not only the influence of land syndicates and powerful individual speculators but also the fear that such encouragement to settlers would too rapidly drain population from eastern Virginia and invite Indian conflicts in the West. Frustrated in this attempt to reform Virginia's land system and prescribe the course of western policy, Jefferson and his Virginia allies dropped the issue until after the Revolutionary War.[25]

—◦—

Whatever the merits of this or that speculative concoction, and however insightful Virginia's reformers might later have seemed, Congress in the years before the Treaty of Paris in 1783 cared more about coaxing the several states with western land claims to cede the lands to the United States, thus creating a single public domain under central control. Success in this endeavor would make the national government, too, a speculator in western lands but would also make Congress the prime shaper of western land policy. At the time of the Revolution, Massachusetts, Connecticut, New York, Virginia, North and South Carolina, and Georgia held extensive grants stretching from the Atlantic coast to the Mississippi River. The largest of these claimed regions was Virginia's nearly 177 million acres, the smallest New York's "Erie Triangle" of slightly more than 200 thousand. Parliament had tried to reduce these holdings in the Quebec Act of 1774, transferring the area north of the Ohio River to the province of Quebec. Far from resolving boundary questions between colonies, that measure succeeded only in provoking certain Americans, like Deane, who already resented faraway lawmakers whose decisions they could not influence. After 1776, the smaller states and those without western lands—New Hampshire, Rhode Island, Maryland, New Jersey, and Delaware—could prevent the growing political influence of their larger partners (under the Articles of Confederation each state had a single vote) but faced a major disadvantage against those with room to expand and frontier revenue to amass.

Among the smaller states, Maryland insisted most forcibly that the larger states, particularly Virginia, had no "exclusive" right to the West and that any territory won in a war for independence against a common enemy ought to be regarded as "common property." But when the proposition of giving Congress exclusive control of the states' western holdings came to a vote on October 15, 1777, opponents defeated it. So important to Maryland was the issue of western land cession that its legislators had refused to ratify the Articles of Confederation until definitive movement in that direction occurred. Raising soldiers to fight the British, Maryland had promised bounties for land it did not have and could not afford to purchase. Virginia's resistance to cession voiced the interests of speculative land-company investors in the Old Dominion, along with others in Pennsylvania and Maryland.[26]

Pressure on the landed states to give in would increase steadily over the coming years—and for substantial reasons. For one, there was the problem of credit abroad, which became increasingly critical as the months passed. The Revolution was doomed without allied help from Europe, both military and financial. As the Congressional Committee for Foreign Affairs stated in late 1777 to the American commissioners in Paris (shortly before the October 15 vote), the question stood undetermined whether such land would be "common stock or the exclusive property of the state within whose charter bounds it may be found." Until Congress settled that business, and the states approved, the commissioners would "readily discover the difficulty of doing any thing in the way of raising money by appropriation of vacant land." Two years later, "A Citizen of Philadelphia" lamented in the *Pennsylvania Packet* that Congress at that very moment could borrow "more than forty million of livres on the credit of the unlocated land," if only the states would transfer it to congressional authority. "What . . . have twelve of the United States done," asked Assistant Superintendent of Finance Gouverneur Morris, "that they should be excluded an equal participation of the lands in that immense Western country?" Moreover, what had Virginia done "that she should at once grasp and rapaciously seize on one hundred and twelve millions of acres to the annihilation of her national debt, and the creating of an enormous fund for purposes yet unknown?"[27]

Congress had its own land bounties to fill for soldiers risking their lives in the Continental Army, along with revenue obligations that exceeded any of the states'—not to mention speculative groups that stood to gain more through national than state control of the lands. Also of persuasive force was a statement from Congress, adopted in October 1780, that any lands ceded to it would be "settled and formed into distinct republican States," destined to become "members of the Federal Union," with the same "rights of sovereignty, freedom and independence" as the original states—music to the ears of would-be speculators and settlers alike.[28]

The language of early nationalism rang all the more convincingly in light of the mounting difficulties the landed states had with managing their sprawling claims. The expense of clearing Indian title and administering legitimate sales and settlement was one thing. In addition to that came the states' inability to control the tide of migrating population, the proliferation of squatter strongholds, and the threats of separatist movements on their frontiers. And then, in late fall 1782, Congress received the foreboding advisory from General Irvine—the one that distressed Madison—on the large numbers white intruders crossing the Ohio into "Indian Country" west of Fort Pitt. From another quarter came news that inhabitants west of the Alleghenies had "by Beat of Drum declared Themselves an independent State, by the Name of Transilvania . . . 5000 Men, good Marksmen, who have associated Themselves to defend their Independence." At about the same time, North Carolina delegate Hugh Williamson fretted, "[The] spirit of migration prevails to a high" in the middle states, "and the Spirit of making new States is become epidemic." He also suspected that troublemaking "People of Vermont & their abettors in the minor States are endeavouring to persuade the People in General on the Western Waters to revolt." Revolutionary ideology seemed to have unleashed forces of near anarchy on the frontiers, and state lawmakers, facing other problems closer at hand, stood at a loss as to how to respond. But to some, the solution seemed obvious. As Jonathan Arnold of Rhode Island noted to Daniel Cahoon on November 4, 1782, for states to cede these lands to the nation would be to "disencumber them of their unwieldy bulk, which now is productive merely of Pride & poverty, but which in the hands of Congress, might become the sources of Wealth & power to the United States, and relieve them from the burthens under which they now groan."[29]

After further negotiating, and incessant lobbying from the Wabash, Illinois, Vandalia, and Indiana land companies—all basing their claims on dubious purchases made from Indian tribes or grants from Great Britain—Virginia passed an

act of cession in 1783. The measure conveyed to the United States title to all western lands north of the Ohio River and east of the Mississippi, with no provision
for private company interests but on several other conditions. Those conditions
included a clause that lands therein not promised as bounties to Virginia's Revolutionary War soldiers be regarded as "a common fund for the use and benefit" of
all the states—disposed "for that purpose and for no other use or purpose whatsoever." In early 1784, Congress agreed to accept Virginia's cession of the massive
territorial claims northwest of the Ohio to the United States.[30]

Two fundamental and ultimately incompatible concepts accompanied this
pivotal deed of cession. Virginia had insisted that the lands of its former claim
be disposed "for the common benefit." Yet, any new territories to emerge from
within the cession were to be guaranteed eventual admission to the Confederation
as "distinct republican States, . . . having the same rights of sovereignty, freedom,
and independence as the other States." Still, these provisions rejected the prevalent European theories of colonial empire. Politically, the newly settled territories
of America now existed not for the use and benefit of the original states only,
but it remained for Congress to prescribe a new mode of land development and
administration to ensure the evolution of western wilderness into tightly settled,
self-governing republics.[31]

Following suit, Massachusetts ceded its claims in 1785; Connecticut in 1786,
except for its 120 mile–long Western Reserve in what would become northeastern
Ohio; South Carolina in 1787; North Carolina, after various complications, in 1789–
90; and, at last, Georgia in 1802. In all, prior to the Louisiana Purchase in 1803,
the United States would come to rule roughly 220 million acres of "vacant" land
west of the Appalachians. But many serious questions loomed and would continue
to press: the rights of indigenous Indian tribes; the organization, administration,
and distribution of lands to white settlers; and above all, whether the social and
cultural underpinnings of republicanism, whatever form those might take, could
be established, encouraged, or expected to develop naturally in frontier America.

—◊—

In some ways, the actual fact of independence changed the whole picture of land
policy. A goal ardently pursued was one thing; a great prize finally won, at considerable sacrifice, quite another. Still, the West held the prospect of providing
desperately needed income for the government. Important as this was, however,
money raising never sufficed as the "great design" of land-policy makers in the
years after the Revolutionary War; it never trumped the higher aim of creating the
foundation for a westward-expanding republican society. Virginia's Arthur Lee,
while ever-mindful of land proceeds, held a more comprehensive benefit in view
than just paying current bills when in January 1784 he wrote, "The finest & most

fertile Country in the world if properly managed will be a source of wealth to the U. S. superior to that of any Power upon Earth." The scholarly David Howell of Rhode Island, renowned in Congress for expertise on land questions, said it better on February 21, 1784. "The Western World opens an amazing prospect," he declared to Jonathan Arnold. "As a national fund, . . . it is equal to our debt. As a Source of future population & strength it is a guaranty of our Independence. As its Inhabitants will be mostly cultivators of the Soil, republicanism looks to them as its Guardians." What Howell then added *seemed* prophetic at the time: "When the States on the eastern Shore . . . shall have become populous, rich & luxurious & ready to yield their Liberties into the hands of a Tyrant—*the Gods of the mountains will save us—for they will be stronger than the Gods of the Vallies.*"[32]

The peace treaty with Great Britain signed in Paris on September 3, 1783, and ratified by Congress on January 14, 1784, gave the United States all the lands east of the Mississippi, south from Canada, and north from Florida. From the standpoint of finance, most members of Congress from the beginning of the Revolutionary War had assumed that revenues from this extensive region would at some point retire the public debt. On this, immediate necessity compelled action. By 1785, with the war won, independence secured, and a public domain in creation, the Confederation *did* face a financial emergency. Expenses soared. Credit plunged. In the West, speculative buying and selling by "land jobbers" abounded, as did colonizing by schemers. War veterans expected the bounty lands promised to them. Squatters, nothing deterring them, swarmed onto vacant lands. Congress had to forge an agreement on the disposition of the western regions it now controlled and might acquire in years to come—but hardly for the sake of revenue alone.

To address these issues at all invited conflicts, mainly sectional, but within the sectional came cultural and philosophical contests as well. Rhode Islander William Ellery alluded to one troubling divergence when he observed, "Eastern politics are still republican, the Southern it is said verge towards Aristocracy." More accurately, southerners for the most part favored the old Virginia policy of issuing warrants from a land office allowing settlers to locate wherever they wanted, with the surveying of the lands to follow. Here was the most direct way to promote individual initiative, rapid settlement, and the expansion of plantation-style agriculture, including slavery—all with minimal administrative costs. The approach accommodated the natural flow of migration rather than restraining it to fit a plan. "In this way the good land is looked out & seized on first," as Howell understood it, "and land of little value & in all shapes left in the hands of the public." But this refuse land, he added, "soon rises in value & is bought by the holders of the adjacent good lands in their own defence." Major drawbacks of this system included scattered distribution of settlements, minimal restraint of squatters, the absence of population centers, slow development of cultural institutions, and the likelihood of extensive private litigation to resolve conflicting claims, as would happen in western Virginia and Kentucky.[33]

Others in Congress, especially northeastern delegates, favored the meticulous order of traditional New England—township grants to proprietors, surveying and recording of tracts before occupation, built-in provisions for religion and schooling. The development of villages, towns, and nearby small farms—all tightly settled—held the prospect of quicker, more diverse, and fluid access of goods to and from distant markets. In Howell's words, "the custom has been to sell a township by bounds, or certain lots, taken flush, good & bad together, & to push out settlement in compact columns." This scenario in time would also encourage merchants, bankers, lawyers, and other middle-class types—a capital-gathering, class-structured society, propelled by free labor. Yet there were drawbacks here, too: higher costs to ordinary settlers, delays of settlement until surveys could be completed or until township owners decided to sell in subdivided pieces, and, as always, the aggravation that some migrants would not wait for legal proprieties to be answered. Moreover, a systematic surveying of lands in New England–style rectilinear grids would treat all subdivisions as the same, making little or no adjustment for variations in topography and soil quality.[34]

Amid the maelstrom of debate, one southerner, Jefferson, who returned briefly to Congress in 1783–1784, championed the New England option. As chairman of a committee on territorial administration and land management, he advanced in April 1784 a comprehensive proposal for the disposition of the Virginia Cession. For the region north of the Ohio, he favored a methodical survey in rectilinear units of 10 miles square, after the clearing of Indian title to these lands. These units, reflecting Jefferson's obsession with the decimal system, were then to be divided into "hundreds"—100 lots, each a mile square (he preferred using the geographical mile of 6,086 feet, which would have made each section 850 acres as opposed to the 640 acres in the standard square mile). Contrasting with the southern practice of indiscriminate settlement and subsequent survey by metes and bounds, the plan opted for the New England style of scrupulous planning and careful organization of lands prior to sale.[35]

Although Jefferson accepted the necessity of sales for some length of time, the idea of vending the land still bothered him; with Madison, he naturally recoiled from any land-distribution system that gave an advantage to men of means while excluding those too poor to purchase at any price. As in 1776, he would rather have seen government function as an agency for distributing tracts on an egalitarian basis, letting further transactions proceed from that point. To guarantee every settler a freehold, he still thought, was to encourage the best in human nature, promoting a virtuous community of citizens. On February 20, 1784, Jefferson and his fellow Virginia delegates Arthur Lee and James Monroe brought before Congress a petition from Kentucky inhabitants who expressed exactly this view: "It is a well known truth that the riches and strength of a free Country does not consist in property being vested in a few Individuals, but the more general it is distributed, the more it promotes industry, population, and frugality, and even morality."[36]

When Jefferson left Congress to succeed Benjamin Franklin as minister to France, his fellow Virginian William Grayson, a lawyer and major property owner in the town of Dumfries, assumed the role Jefferson had been performing. Sitting on the "grand committee" in Congress that between March and May of 1785 would put together the great Land Ordinance, Grayson now helped lay the organizational foundation for all subsequent land policy of the early republic. The committee consisted of one member from each state, but Virginia, because of its prestige and the size of its cession, carried considerable weight. Grayson, as it turned out, more or less agreed with Jefferson on the merits of the "Eastern" model, but he did not share his predecessor's radical agrarianism. During the war, Grayson had risen to the rank of lieutenant colonel and served as aide-de-camp to George Washington, with whom he still kept in close touch. In a letter to Washington on April 15, 1785, he revealed his preference for the idea of townships, with "support for religion & education" as contributing to "neighborhoods" and "the purpose of purchasing and settling together." This he opposed to the "Southern mode." That style "would defeat this end by introducing the idea of indiscriminate locations & settlements, which would have a tendency to destroy all those inducemts. to emigration which are derived from friendships, religion and relative connections." But Grayson (like others) had also considered the potentially disruptive implications of the West's being settled "out of the bowels of the Atlantic States." The plan had to be one that would build a strong frontier society without debilitating the East by draining its population, undercutting its land values, or competing with property sales there.[37]

After months of wrangling, the essential part of the compromise between proponents of "Eastern" and "Southern" modes emerged with the rectangular system of survey, historically perhaps the best known and the most lasting part of the Land Ordinance of 1785. Beginning at the intersection of the Ohio River and the Pennsylvania border, the public domain was to be surveyed in parallel lines of longitude and latitude, resulting in an initial seven ranges of townships. Each of these townships was to be 6 miles square (23,040 acres), divided into 36 sections of 1 square mile (640 acres). Alternate townships were to be sold whole to accommodate communities of settlers, as New Englanders wanted; the others would be opened for sale by sections, favoring individual buyers as southerners generally favored. Another concession to New England was the reservation of section number sixteen in each township for revenue to finance public schools. Absent from the final agreement, however, was the New England practice of reserving a section for religious purposes, which had received support from only five of the states. Madison, when he heard the religion clause had been voted down, expressed relief that a provision "smelling so strongly of an antiquated Bigotry" had been kept from becoming a part of the nation's land policy.[38]

Rufus King, then of Massachusetts, had wanted to include a prohibition against slaveholding in the Land Ordinance (like the one that would appear in the Northwest Ordinance two years later), but he thought "great benefits" still had been achieved in the 1785 law. "[Y]ou will find it bears strong features of an eastern System," he wrote to Elbridge Gerry. Grayson, though satisfied, thought the outcome ironic: "The Eastern people who before the revolution never had an idea of any quantity of Earth above a hundred acres, were for selling in large tracts of 30,000 acres while the Southern people who formerly could scarce bring their imaginations down so low as to comprehend the meaning of a hundred Acres of ground were for selling the whole territory in lots of a mile square."[39]

The grand committee also recommended an auction system for selling public lands. This recognized three things, all indicative of a capitalistic transformation in America, expressed in a new political economy that based land policy on changes then occurring in the perception of land. First, western tracts would be of unequal value—some better for farming than others—and therefore should be determined in worth according to the law of demand. Second, the purchase of land at market value, though favoring those with money, would have the effect of drawing westward families of economic substance, willing to invest not just time, effort, and good intentions but also the capital resources needed to build a new society on principles of republicanism. Third, more and more landowners in the older parts of America had come to see their holdings not just as a possession, a mark of status with intrinsic value, but also as a commodity to be traded (bought for speculative purposes and resold at a higher price) or to be divided up for sale to settlers. The buying and selling of land thus would become, both in the older and the newer areas of the country, a capital-building enterprise. It could potentially attract anyone with the means and the opportunity to acquire a piece of earth. Some members wanted to vary the minimum price according to the value of the land—why should refuse tracts command the same monetary sacrifice as precious soil?—but this idea would attract little interest until the 1820s.[40]

In the end, for all the animated talk about revenue, the framers of the Land Ordinance *seemed* willing to ask very little for trans-Appalachian lands. Part of the reason is that they were operating under certain preexisting constraints. The United States Military Tract of one million acres, Virginia's Military District, and the Connecticut Western Reserve—all in Ohio—were off limits to national government sale in the first place. By 1785, some of the states offered remainder lands within their boundaries for no more than a few cents per acre in specie, forcing Congress to limit expectations of what it might receive for its far more distant lands in the Ohio country. With the minimum purchase set at one section, or 640 acres, the minimum price of one dollar an acre stated in the Ordinance became payable in depreciated Continental securities, which converted to just pennies per acre—an amount expected to make Confederation lands competitive with state lands being offered at the time. Adding to this picture the costs of prior surveying, which was expensive as well as time consuming, and the government's chances of making much money from land sales in the near future looked remote at best.

In setting the terms of their sales strategy, however, the land-policy makers in Congress showed their elitist colors more than anywhere else. While rightly concerned about the expansion of lawlessness, they offered nothing in their program to entice squatters, impoverished as most were, to come back within the law. Many poor whites had poured westward from Virginia in the late-eighteenth century, choosing wilderness over a world where slavery undercut the value of their labor. Of those involved in congressional decisions, only Jefferson and a few others had shown the audacity to think that the lands might be given away in small parcels rather than sold; few took that option seriously. Who among the lower classes, including those now settling unlawfully, had 640 dollars in hard money to meet even the minimum price and acreage requirements at auction? Who among them held Continental securities at all, no matter how depreciated in value? They could not hope to purchase from private speculators, who expected to sell the lands they held for no less than they themselves had paid. Besides, the minimum purchase of 640 acres was far more than an average non-slaveholding small farmer could manage by himself. Plainly, in no way did the designers of the original land system intend the public domain to be—or become—a refuge for the poor. Except for those who had earned military bounties, this land-policy design of 1785 would not encourage members of the "humbler classes" to go west, at least not as owners of the land.[41]

The provisions that the ordinance did *not* include reveal even more. For one, the omission of limits on the amount of land anyone might purchase surprised nobody. The ethic that John Winthrop had long ago articulated—to no one man more than he can "subdue"—had been, even in Puritan New England, a restraint more often stated than practiced. The investment potential of the extensive West loomed irresistible. Pennsylvania delegate Joseph Gardener commented in March 1785: "[T]he land Speculators already Smell a rat and expect fine picking. . . . There will be a scram[ble to] the land offices in this new Country, Many hav[e al]ready applied." Of all the energies the Revolution had unleashed, the forces of avarice

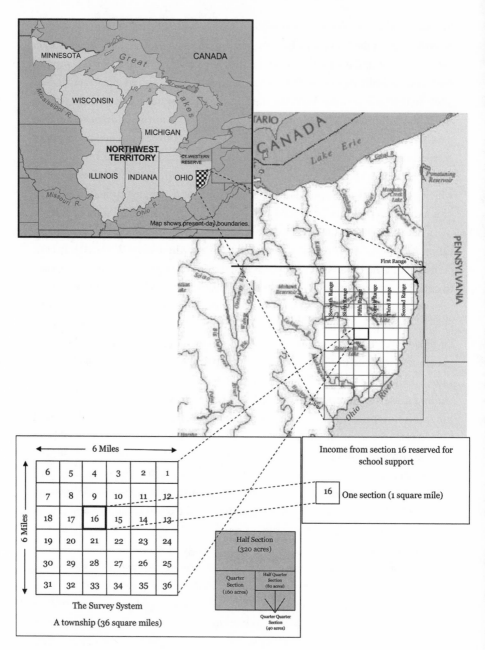

Land Ordinance of 1785. Map drawn by Margot Gibson-Beattie.

would have been most difficult, if not impossible, to hold back. On the other hand, Grayson contended that if the land were to be sold in whole townships, the "poorer class" would come out better than expected, as "speculators & ingrossers," forced to purchase such an amount at the outset, would feel compelled to start selling soon afterward to recoup their large investment, or else face "the consequent loss of interest" while the lands remained "in their hands uncultivated." Howell, as well, stressed "the duty of Congress to open their land-office on terms which will at once secure the greatest possible revenue therefrom & give no undue advantage to any class of citizens, or to any district of the Foederal Union."[42]

Still less surprising was the absence of a right of preemption to protect squatters' claims. The ordinance did not specifically address the squatter issue, but concern about it had become widespread. Many premature settlers knew perfectly well that squatting had received favor in colonial times, especially in Virginia, and that preemption (the post facto legalization of claims) often had been granted, so they supposed that the same would be remain true. But with regard to distant western lands, squatters had plummeted from grace during the Revolutionary period. The choice of Congress not to endorse such earlier practices followed similar efforts in the states before 1785. Pennsylvania in July 1783 had ordered all judges, sheriffs, and other officers to crack down on the "divers disorderly persons" who had lately, "in contempt of the laws of this state," moved onto "vacant and unappropriated lands" in its western regions, and even tried to sell "pretended rights to such lands." Later that year, Connecticut governor Jonathan Trumbull threatened persons who were freely "entering upon or settling" upon its western reserve with "pains, penalties and forfeitures." The reasons for such anti-squatter pronouncements, which to those targeted must have looked all too much like Britain's Proclamation of 1763, had to do not only with problems of debt and revenue-raising via land sales, but also principles of citizenship in a republic—the acceptance of responsibilities along with freedoms. If some could get away with skirting the law, why should others bother to obey? A society rooted to any extent in the rule of law and "the common good" could not be established on a foundation of lawlessness and disrespect for governmental authority.[43]

Meanwhile, the idea of settling the frontiers with former officers and soldiers of the army, men well-acquainted with discipline, good order, and the constraints of law—many of them entitled to land bounties in any case—had gained considerable appeal. "It hath ... the immediate effect of procuring a number of good industrious subjects," thought Gouverneur Morris of such a possibility. "Perhaps I should not go too far in saying that every man so acquired would be worth two." Unlike Great Britain, colonial America had never developed anything like a national governing class, intermarried across provincial boundaries, interconnected by military comradeship or associations like the post-Revolution Society of the Cincinnati. The concept of settling frontiers with former soldiers who might eventually constitute such a class was anything but original. By the time of Caesar Augustus, Roman soldiers upon retirement often received land in far-away provinces where imperial authorities wanted citizens of proven virtue as leaders of society. Virginia, though lax in its colonial land policies, had been the first to lay out western districts to be reserved for and defended by its war veterans. In early 1779, General Benedict Arnold, not yet the famous traitor, had proposed in New York to lead a similar effort for the officers and men who had served under him. The idea appealed to the New York delegation in Congress. Recognizing "the Necessity of strengthening our Frontiers," they pointed to the policies of other states: "Virginia we learn has taken the Lead and already passed Laws for laying out a District of Country for Settlement, & assigning Farms for their own Soldiers, as well as those of Maryland, Delaware, and New Jersey." George Washington, too, declared in 1783 that the frontiers could not "be so advantageously settled by any other Class of men, as by the disbanded Officers and Soldiers of the Army." In no better way could the West receive "a brave, a hardy and respectable Race of People."[44]

Revolutionary ideology, loaded with "commonwealth" principles passed down through English reform tradition, had mandated certain rules for landholding. All remnants of feudal tenure, redolent of monarchy, had to go. In an American republic, landownership would be opened to a wider representation of citizenry than in the Old World or in colonial experience, but "the landed" would not include all. The ones who deserved to be freeholders, trusted most to defend their western homes and those of their neighbors, would be the individuals and families who had worked, earned, sacrificed, and perhaps bled for the privilege—those living within the law, demonstrating moral virtue and regard for others.

Major landowners and speculators, Washington for one, had long resented the increasing presence of intruders on their own frontier holdings, but Congress by the early 1780s had framed the issue more critically than that. Such trespassing upon the public domain threatened to diminish the value of land Congress hoped use for revenue purposes, dampened the interest of law-abiding people willing to bid for the land and pay accordingly, and posed an enormous problem of governmental control. American success against Britain in the Revolution had ended whatever imperial restraint there had been against illegal settlement in the trans-Appalachian region and weakened the power of native tribes to resist incursion on their lands. The Confederation already, in September 1783, had issued a proclamation reminiscent of the British Proclamation of 1763, prohibiting settlement without official sanction on western lands north of the Ohio River. The regular posting of a powerful military force might have given real teeth to such a proclamation, but that possibility remained untenable financially and unthinkable ideologically. Ellery reflected in December 1783, "It may be necessary to maintain some temporary posts to secure the lands . . . from intruders and to check the Indians, but from a standing army in time of peace Good Lord deliver us." More than a year later, Richard Henry Lee would complain that it had been "impossible to get a vote for more than seven hundred men to garrison all the posts to be fixed in the trans-Alleghanian country" and called this "a number very inadequate . . . to the purpose of even suppressing illegal trespasses upon the western lands."[45]

Nevertheless, in spring 1785, while the grand committee busily hammered out the Land Ordinance, Congress sent Lieutenant Colonel Josiah Harmer, a Pennsylvanian, with a small military force to clear squatters—at least 2,000 of them— from the region of southern Ohio near the mouths of the Miami, Scioto, and Muskingum Rivers. Apart from their taking lands illegally, squatters looking for the slightest excuse to expel the native inhabitants had literally gotten away with murder for decades, especially in the Old Northwest. Their actions had prompted Indian retaliation, turning the frontier into a venue of mayhem, and worsening the problems of centralized governance. Marching an arduous 370 miles westward from Fort McIntosh (on the Ohio River below Fort Pitt), Harmer's soldiers torched buildings and crops, sending the interlopers scurrying back to Pennsylvania, Kentucky, and western Virginia, from whence they had come. Pennsylvania congressman David Jackson conceded, "[I]t seems rather a species of cruelty, yet something must be done to prevent more confusion & bad consequence hereafter." But as soon as the soldiers left, the squatters returned, this time a safe distance from the forts. "These men upon the frontiers," Harmer complained, "have hitherto been accustomed to seat themselves on the best of lands, making a tomahawk right or Improvement, as they term it, supposing that to be sufficient Title." Indian commissioner Samuel Holden Parsons spoke for many in the government when he declared unauthorized settlers in Ohio to be "our own white Indians of no character who have their own Private Views without regard to public benefits to Serve." To be Indian-like meant standing outside the accepted boundaries of civil society—a potential threat to legitimate authority.[46]

The difficulty of keeping such people off lands reserved for bounties, sales, and other purposes would bedevil policy makers for decades to come. Meanwhile, further masses of illegal settlers would pour into the Ohio country and elsewhere, claiming a natural right and waiting for lawmakers to grant them title to soil they occupied. At the very least, they would expect compensation for the value of improvements made on property they did not own.

—◦—

By November 1786, Madison's mail had become even more interesting but not less troubling. A different general this time and more bad tidings from the West: George Washington deplored the news coming from the Berkshire Hills of Massachusetts—Shays' Rebellion. Defying unfair taxation, indebted, and fearful of losing their land, the Shaysites may have been more justified than General Irvine's scofflaws north of the Ohio River; but to the ruling authorities, disorder was disorder, and Massachusetts would send an army to crush the rebels just as Congress had sent one to clear out squatters west of the Appalachians. For the "monied" men who wanted their own economic interests kept safe and the gains of the Revolution protected from agrarian radicalism, nothing seemed more important. "We are fast verging to anarchy & confusion!" Washington exclaimed. The Massachusetts rebels, from what he heard, wanted unbacked paper money and repudiation of all debts, public and private. Like western squatters, they believed that property won from Britain "by the joint exertions of *all*" now became "the *common property* of all." According to Washington's intelligence sources, such radical doctrines now extended far beyond just the western counties of the Bay State and had permeated New England, gathering support from an estimated "twelve or fifteen thousand desperate, and unprincipled men." These were "chiefly of the young & active part of the Community," exactly the sorts most likely to move farther westward if eastern lawmakers would not, or could not, accommodate their demands.[47]

Washington's impressions could only have heightened Madison's simultaneous concern about the excesses of democracy being practiced in state legislatures, like Virginia's, where he now sat. Rash new men to power, their parochialism, their service of particular private interests, the stay laws they passed, the reckless issuances of paper money some states had authorized, and debtor-relief measures that targeted creditors and threatened individual property rights—in short, the radical side of the American Revolution—all of it seemed to Madison evidence of populist forces "so frequent and so flagrant as to alarm the most stedfast friends of Republicanism." Others shared this perception. Benjamin Rush, a prominent Philadelphia physician, expressed in 1788 the belief that social order had unraveled to the point that many Americans were "degenerating into savages or devouring each other like beasts of prey." Madison, Washington, Gouverneur Morris, Richard Henry Lee, and others among the eastern elite employed the same language, similar in vocabulary and comparable in the expression of alarm, to describe the absence of governmental control in the far western reaches of the country.[48]

Poor relations with foreign powers and the failures of Confederation diplomacy did nothing to comfort the growing number of nationalists who found in strong central government the only remedy for turmoil in the states and disorder on the frontiers. The United States had yet to establish its "treaty-worthiness"—and *could* not do so until the newly ratified federal Constitution in 1789 provided the format needed to achieve credibility among other nations. At that time, the British in Canada and the Northwest, along with the Spanish in Florida and the trans-Mississippi region, would have been happy to weaken the new United States by luring away the disgruntled part of its population. Many in Great Britain already predicted that the American republics would quickly dissolve for lack of internal unity. Spain held the strongest hand in the West as long as it exerted commercial control of the Mississippi River and its outlet at New Orleans. To frontier settlers who felt no great affinity for the United States, little stood in the way of their conspiring with, or even joining, the Spanish in return for the market access they needed. The 1785–1786 negotiations between American foreign affairs secretary John Jay and Spanish minister Don Diego de Gardoqui, in which Jay had been willing to surrender the Mississippi in favor of New England's Atlantic trade, hardly inspired western loyalty.[49]

Despite questions from right and left and answers being in short supply, the inventors of land policy for the new United States still agreed on a few key things. One was the need to bring order on their western frontiers, even though they knew not how to maintain it. Better to open more western lands to speculators than entrust the region to the rabble said to be threatening it now. A second was the desire for westward migration in systematic fashion—compact and community-oriented, with surveys preceding settlement. And yet squatters continued to scatter wherever they pleased, locating and relocating at will, spurning community life and violating Indians' rights at every turn. Neither Congress nor the states had explored ways to entice such people back to mainstream values and behavior, much less make them a legitimate part of the body politic. Third, the policy designers wanted a land system for America that, like its government, differed in fundamentals from those in the history of England and the rest of Europe. In America, landownership *was* liberty, and, as Hugh Williamson put it, "the value of land increases in proportion as the Government is more free."[50] Property would be held and conveyed in fee simple—no primogeniture and entail, no quitrents, personal obligations, or other strings attached. For ordinary Americans, too, that definition of liberty easily hit home. While many people remained slaves, others slaveholders, and still others landlords, no man or woman aspired to live under another's thumb. Fourth, these leaders agreed that, in a modern republic, the extension of landownership should be as wide as possible or practicable. And yet, landholding remained more a privilege than a right, a status earned through sacrifice of treasure or service to others. Finally, they shared an anxiety about the actions of those whom the elite regarded as lawless and irresponsible, and not just in frontier areas. Rumblings from below increasingly illustrated the extremes to which American revolutionary principles might be carried—a challenge that governing authorities thus far knew not how to address.

CHAPTER TWO

An Embryo of Empire

In December 1804, the Public Lands Committee of the House of Representatives received a petition, in two sections, from "inhabitants" of Randolph and St. Clair Counties, Indiana Territory—284 signatures in all. Danel Stuky and Larence Shuk featured among the names, along with two men from the Jarvis family and three of the Prewits. Thomas and James Crokker signed, as did three Killbreaths and three Carrs, four of the Fultons and four Kirkpatricks. Every signer was male. All admitted being illegal residents on "unlocated lands."

These petitioners claimed they had "been placed" on the frontier "by various turns of fortune"—some purportedly "on account of their wives and children being carried away" into captivity by hostile Indians living north of the Ohio River. In the hope that Congress "would put it in the limits of their Power to become owners of the soil," they had (so far) refused "all offers held out to them" by the Spanish government and resisted the temptation, unlike certain "fellow citizens," to migrate into the newly acquired Louisiana Territory. Alas, "the very great scarcity of cash" and "an indifferent Market" for their produce had left them unable to purchase their farms under the strict terms of federal land law, and, unless they were granted a preemption on more favorable terms than the government price minimum, their "hard labour" would be sacrificed to others coming later to buy the very soil from under their feet. The petition went on to characterize these lands as "far from being the best in the country on account of the present settlers wishing for safety to be near to towns stations and settlers to whom titles of land have been given already." Such areas would be of little interest to "Monied men while there is such a vast tract of country for them to make choise of." Finally, these squatters described themselves as "patriotic sons of freedom, some of whom have fought and bled in defence of their country, and the support of Liberty and of equal Laws." The writers and others like them had already started to abandon the deferential colonial rhetoric of "faithful subjects" pandering for favor. They saw themselves more as "citizens" and former soldiers with "rights" due to them from their own sacrifices and in keeping with principles of the American Revolution.[1]

Family, constant toil, devotion to country, the evils of speculation, the promise of equality—many western settlers did, of course, hold such values close to their hearts. Some of the petition's arguments made sense: the dearth of money, the "indifferent" economy, the opportunism of speculators. Indeed, a number of women and children *had* over the years been taken captive by hostile tribes. But the appeal asked suspicious lawmakers to amend not only their policy but also their basic perception of squatters as self-serving trespassers—a leap of faith that few, at that point, could bring themselves to make.

In its Land Act of 1800, Congress had lowered the minimum purchase required from 640 to 320 acres at a minimum auction price of $2.00 per acre, while offering four years' credit to pay. The idea was to encourage settlement along with revenue. In March 1804, a Jeffersonian Republican majority had further slashed these amounts to 160 acres and $1.64, keeping the credit provision. These modifications helped, but did they go far enough for ordinary settlers? Did squatters deserve something more? Were they, as they claimed, intrepid men and women who faced the terrors of trans-Appalachian wilderness, survived it, and prevailed—all despite daunting odds and an unfair government? Or were they just land grabbers, uninterested in legalities, differing in means but not in motivation from the "monied men" they so resented? Whatever the truth here, these petitioners and others employed a variety of tactics, including exaggeration, prevarication, and even threats, to persuade distant federal authorities. Sometimes it worked. Usually it did not.

⁓

To accompany the Land Ordinance of 1785, the Confederation Congress in its Northwest Ordinance of 1787 had aimed for tight control over the West, mandating the expansion of republicanism, freedom of worship, trial by jury, and public support for education, while at least nominally prohibiting slavery north of the Ohio River. To prevent the disordered outcomes expected of frontier democracy, the policy required dictatorial government in the early stages of territorial development—an appointed governor with the advice of an executive council—to be joined by an elected legislature (based on strictly limited suffrage) only when the population reached 5,000 within a designated territory. Statehood had to wait until that number ballooned to 60,000, but when new states did enter, it would be "on an equal footing with the original states"—a distinctly un-British strategy of empire. In the new United States, frontier provinces would evolve toward full membership rather than stay as mere colonies. Other than that, the provisions of the 1787 Ordinance reflected the urge to guard propertied men against ignorant and lawless elements of western society. Richard Henry Lee explained: "It seemed necessary, for the security of property among uninformed, and perhaps licentious people, as the greater part of those who go there are, that a strong toned government should exist, and the rights of property be clearly defined."[2]

Confronted with the difficulty of launching a new federal government after 1789 and at the same time quelling Indian unrest on the frontier, Congress delayed until 1796 any refining of its public land policy. But neither then nor soon after did it give much ground to westerners who simply *took* their land rather than purchasing it. Americans acting outside the law were not to be excused—much less rewarded—for what they had done. Most lawmakers believed that bowing to lawlessness only increased contempt for law and cost government the support of more "respectable" people who obeyed the laws, paid their way, and worked hard to raise the value of what they had.

The Federalist policy makers who ran the country in the 1790s hesitated to bring new western states into an already unstable union. In the first place, many frontier inhabitants loathed the Federalists. In the three states that did enter the Union during this period—Vermont, Kentucky, and Tennessee—political opposition to the Federalists quickly became dominant. Steadiest Federalist support would come from old-stock English voters living in traditional northeastern communities where the rate of growth lagged way behind the newer regions. In addition, some people on both sides of the political divide regarded the "foreign fashion" of empire building across space as likely to undercut the public and private virtues needed to sustain a republican form of government. This view would persist despite the newly ratified Constitution's retooling of central governmental powers in ways more appropriate for an expanding nation. Montesquieu's caution in *De l'Esprit des Lois* (1748), that overextension of Roman influence had produced the erosion of values responsible for bringing down the greatest empire of ancient times, still carried considerable weight. "In an extensive republic," the widely read French theorist had said, "the public good is sacrificed to a thousand private views." In *Federalist No. 10*, Madison had argued to the contrary, setting out his "theory of factions," which contended that proliferation of competing interests in a large republic would lead such groups to check and balance one another, leaving "disinterested" men, an aristocracy of the honorable and talented, to administer enlightened governance at the national level. He added in *Federalist No. 51* that "the larger the society, provided it lie within a practicable sphere, the more duly capable it will be of self government." No one really knew which view to trust. There was only Madison's theoretical assurance that "for the *republican cause*, the practicable sphere may be carried to a very great extent, by a judicious modification and mixture of the *federal principle*." And yet, untested formulations would not quickly outweigh the lessons of historical experience.[3]

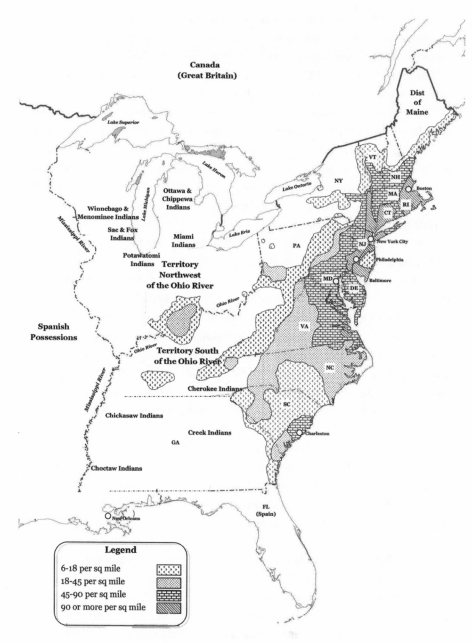

Distribution of U.S. Population East of the Mississippi River, 1790. Map drawn by Margot Gibson-Beattie.

Besides, on an agenda dominated by the immediate problem of restoring American financial credibility, opening the West ranked comparatively low. The strength of Native American forces on the frontier—the sometimes-combined powers of the Miamis, Shawnees, Delawares, and Potawatomis—made early expansion problematic in any case. The Shawnees in particular, like the Senecas, Mohawks, Onondagas, and Cayugas in western New York, had fought fiercely against the Americans during the Revolution. After the war, the United States, assuming they had won both sovereignty (right to govern) and property rights (ownership) as part of their victory against the British, tried to confiscate native peoples' land, as opposed to following the traditional American practice of buying it. That enraged the Indians of the Old Northwest, who hardly regarded themselves as "conquered" and still had access in the region to supplies, weapons, and encouragement from the British. Startling Indian victories against Generals Harmer and Arthur St. Clair in the Ohio Territory, in 1790 and 1791, respectively, not only highlighted the risks of premature migration but also deterred new settlers. St. Clair's defeat took the lives of 623 of his soldiers and, in addition, several dozen of their wives and children who had been allowed on the trip. It was one of the worst disasters in warfare with Native Americans in U.S. Army history. As a result, the United States government would return to its old approach of purchasing Indian lands (and trying to prevent private parties from doing the same). Meanwhile, cautious settlers and speculators turned instead to available, cheaper, and safer tracts in New York, Pennsylvania, Maine, Kentucky, Tennessee, Georgia, and also eastern Canada. Government sales before 1796 remained disappointing, with individual purchasers taking a mere 108,431 acres and eventually forfeiting almost a third of that total. Sales by 1795, counting auction proceeds, a 202,187-acre deal with Pennsylvania, and payments by the Ohio and Scioto companies for large grants they had received, barely provided enough revenue to cover 1 percent of federal obligations.[4]

Another reason for the slowness of Congress in advancing western development was the fear of many easterners, including a number soon to champion Alexander Hamilton's financial program, that rapid western settlement would mean a corresponding social and economic decline of the Atlantic states. That consideration loomed large in the Treasury Department, which, under Hamilton, looked to advance northeastern commercial and proto-manufacturing interests. By the 1790s, similar reservations had found expression also in the South, where attitudes toward developing the remote frontier remained ambivalent at best. Federalist paranoia inspired by the rapid proliferation of "Democratic Societies" in the mid-1790s compounded all of this. Those inflammatory groups, often modeled on the Jacobin clubs in France, supposedly aimed to carry forward in America some of the radically egalitarian implications of the French Revolution. Partly as a result,

Congress in 1796 stopped short of extending federal land sales to resident aliens. The notion persisted that a republican society had to be a homogenous one, politically as well as culturally.[5]

Hamilton envisioned one kind of American empire, one of power—economic and otherwise—where the West mattered only peripherally. With the ascension of Thomas Jefferson and his followers to federal leadership, the so-called "Revolution of 1800," came a limited refocusing of both theory and policy, regarding the West in particular and the political economy of the nation in general. Here, another conception of empire prevailed, one Jefferson would characterize in terms of liberty—individual and otherwise—in which the West figured critically. This reorientation, however, would not quickly follow along lines of Jefferson's earlier agrarian vision. And again it would be the Treasury Department, then under Albert Gallatin, that would prescribe some basic parameters of land policy for young America.[6]

—◌◌

Dissatisfied with the slowness of land sales, the Confederation Congress in 1787 had taken up some of the grandiose proposals of well-connected individuals and companies. That year, for a million dollars in return, it transferred 1,500,000 acres of the seven ranges running north of the Ohio River into the hands of Manasseh Cutler's Ohio Company. Arguing the increasingly persuasive view that former soldiers would make the most trustworthy settlers, Cutler's joint-stock company of former Continental Army officers made sense. The deal included a provision that the Ohio Company might apply for another 4,500,000 acres under the auspices of the Scioto Company, being organized along similar logic by William Duer, the Confederation's Board of Treasury secretary, who would serve a few years later in Hamilton's Treasury Department. Another speculator, John Cleves Symmes, purchased 1,000,000 acres in southwestern Ohio, the region that would later encompass the city of Cincinnati. Meanwhile, the Connecticut Land Company obtained 3,000,000 acres of that state's Western Reserve, near modern-day Cleveland.[7]

Cutler, Duer, Symmes, and most other land company magnates had no intention of personally living on these giant tracts, but one did, William Cooper, the most successful of all. Some elements of his own land policy would appear later, at least for a time, in federal land law. In the mid-1780s, Cooper, the father of novelist James Fenimore Cooper, bought up an enormous chunk of the Otsego Lake area of upstate New York. American success in the Revolutionary War had driven the Iroquois, allied with the British, out of the region and into Canada. In New York City, Alexander Hamilton managed legal technicalities of Cooper's purchase. Like Hamilton, Cooper had grown up without privilege—in an impoverished Quaker family outside Philadelphia—but he aspired to the status of a "gentleman," a member of the wealthy elite. As a large landholder and the founder of Cooperstown, he imagined himself as a paternalistic benefactor for those less fortunate. Cooper resold the land in freeholds at prices attainable to ordinary buyers and, as Congress would do in 1800, on the offer of long-term credit. Refusing not only to be a landlord but also an absentee speculator, Cooper went to live among his settlers and help develop market access for their goods.[8]

Dovetailing with the stated intentions of this private monied gentry, Federalist leadership after 1789 assumed that the new federal Constitution provided at least the broad outlines of a modern, empowered nation-state. They hoped to pursue a coordinated western policy aimed at regulating the pace and character of westward settlement and making sure of the political loyalty of frontier settlers. George Washington in 1784 had articulated the fear that, without the guiding force of central government, frontier inhabitants could easily "become a different people from us, have different views, different interests," including possible sympathy with the Spanish and British in western North America and, "instead of adding strength to the Union, may in case of a rupture with either of those powers, be a formidable and dangerous neighbour." With the "seeds of population" now dispersing far into the wilderness, he also worried that without adequate transportation improvements, roads and canals linking frontier areas to eastern markets, the people of the West might find "no excitements to industry," live too easily on the "luxuriency of the soil," and let themselves degenerate into habits of indolence and immorality. To address such dangers, governmentally paternalistic Federalists envisioned a frontier dominated by a patriotic elite of officials and speculators, committed to the building of orderly, prosperous, well-educated, religiously grounded communities, and willing to invest private capital in projects of internal improvement. The result, they expected, would be a new western world rooted in the strictures of the 1785 Land Ordinance and the 1787 Northwest Ordinance, where lawlessness could be thwarted, by military force if necessary, and solid republican values and practices nurtured. The decision in 1787 to sell hundreds of thousands of acres, at just $1.00 per acre, to Cutler's Ohio Company (former army officers of presumed virtue and proven devotion) exemplified the socially elitist concept that Federalists meant to follow. The Washington administration's crushing of the Whiskey Rebellion in 1794, which to them seemed reminiscent of Shays' uprising in Massachusetts, indicated the extent to which the military could enforce law and maintain order in frontier areas. That forceful response also helped to show foreign powers that the federal government held—and would use—coercive power to rule its own house.[9]

Meanwhile, the Federalist-dominated Congress reinforced the army, enabling General Anthony Wayne to lead a 5,000-man force into northwest Ohio and, on August 20, 1794, rout a massed contingent of Potawatomi warriors and others on the Maumee River—the Battle of Fallen Timbers. In the resulting Treaty of

Greenville, signed August 3, 1795, twelve tribes, including the Shawnee, ceded title to a large area that included the southern two-thirds of Ohio and southeastern Indiana. At that time, one army officer stationed in Greenville wrote of seeing long-lost white captives being returned to their families. "I have been a witness," he reported, "to parents receiving their children, who have been absent fifteen or sixteen years, and had grown to an adult state, but could not speak one word of English." Shortly thereafter, as part of the Jay Treaty of 1795, the British, who had done their part in provoking Indian hostilities, agreed finally to evacuate the western forts they had first promised to leave in 1783. That further weakened the Indians' position and prompted so strong an upsurge of legitimate settlement that Ohio would qualify for statehood in 1803. Perhaps most important, the October 1795 Treaty of San Lorenzo with Spain—Pinckney's Treaty—succeeded where the Jay-Gardoqui negotiations had failed nearly a decade before. It quieted western commercial discontent and separatist agitation for a time, by providing American frontiersmen free navigation of the Mississippi River and the right to deposit their goods at New Orleans, and carried a minimum duration of three years. With these developments, the Federalists asserted national supremacy over the West, defining boundaries with Indian groups, claiming exclusive right to purchase Indian lands, and regulating settlement on the frontier. The Greenville treaty gave the United States the right to build forts anywhere it chose within the Indian country that remained, but it also declared squatters who crossed the boundary and settled on Indian lands to be "out of the protection of the United States."[10]

In the 1790s, Federalist policy for the West also had to fit within the framework of Alexander Hamilton's economic program. When Hamilton looked upon the United States, he saw the early stages of an emerging colossus, "the embryo of a great empire," he said in July 1795. But the place of westward expansion in his vision remained limited and somewhat ambiguous. When late-eighteenth-century Americans used the word "empire," usually they referred not to the conquest and subjugation of other peoples, notwithstanding the Indians' fate, but rather sovereignty over an area of territory. One Connecticut columnist, for example, borrowed his definition from the eighteenth-century Swiss philosopher Emer de Vattel: "when a nation takes possession of a country that never belonged to another, it is considered as possessing there, the empire or sovereignty at the same time with the rights of domain. The whole space over which a nation extends its government is the seat of its jurisdiction." Still, Hamilton did not much imagine the building of an empire across space. Westward expansion, he thought, should occur quite slowly, in measured steps, and never at the expense of commercial and budding manufacturing interests. His "great empire" would be financial, not spatial, capital being the prized factor of production, not land. His unsettled West mattered less for agricultural purposes than as massive collateral to establish the credit of the nation. He valued most the artisans and manufacturers on whose shoulders American investors might, in a not-too-distant future, construct an industrial giant.[11]

Well aware of Montesquieu's caution (and the Romans' experience) that a republic could not sustain itself across extensive space, Hamilton considered the size of the United States—particularly the area of its unsettled western territory—as a potential danger to political unity. In this, he echoed Washington's concerns. Hamilton had written in *The Federalist, No. 23* that "the extent of the country, is the strongest argument in favor of an energetic government; for any other can certainly never preserve the Union of so large an empire." It would take strong central power—a military-fiscal state—to prevent squatters from overrunning the frontier.[12]

But by 1790, Hamilton would doubt the ability of any government, no matter how powerful or energetic, to control a nation so vast. As treasury secretary he worked to delay the development of the West. He designed the plan for the federal assumption of state debts in part to prevent a depopulation of the old states. Without assumption, heavy state tax burdens would drive inhabitants out of the East. The alternatives, he explained, would not only weaken eastern states but "retard the progress in general improvement and . . . impair for a greater length of time the vigor of the Nation by scattering too widely and too sparsely the elements of resource and strength." Hamilton later viewed the Louisiana Purchase in the same light. Should "our own citizens, more enterprising than wise, become desirous of settling this country, and emigrate thither," he wrote in 1803, "it must not only be attended with all the injuries of a too widely dispersed population, but by adding to the great weight of the western part of our territory, must hasten the dismemberment of a large portion of our country, or a dissolution of the Government."[13]

Because land proceeds composed a part of federal revenue, much of the initial responsibility for prescribing land policy rested with Washington's treasury secretary. From the start, Hamilton viewed settlement of the West as secondary, though related, to the more immediate problems in the nation's political economy: securing public credit and encouraging domestic manufactures. As an early economic nationalist, he advocated a balancing of agricultural and commercial interests, and he believed farming and trade to be "inseparably interwoven." As he had put it in *The Continentalist* of July 4, 1782, "[o]ne cannot be injured, without injury nor benefitted, without benefit to the other. Oppress trade, lands sink in value, make it flourish, their value rises, incumber husbandry, trade declines, encourage agriculture, commerce revives."[14]

In the same piece, the New Yorker referred to the "unlocated lands" of the West as "a valuable source of revenue, and an immediate one of credit." The latter phrase indicates his belief that the trans-Appalachian region should be managed indefinitely under federal, not state, supervision and then conveyed into private hands, but not too much or too quickly. Always conscious of long-range sources of national wealth, as well as being determined to harness various means of public revenue, Hamilton advised governmental reservation of the mineral deposits and precious metals, regarding these as "rather a future than a present resource."[15]

Five years later, with the Constitution being prepared and ratified, Hamilton reflected further on the value of the frontier and its place in a more consolidated Union. To him, the main purpose of a republic, or any other form of government, was to curb man's passions and harness his interests. At the Constitutional Convention on June 22, 1787, he declared: "Take mankind as they are, and what are they governed by? Their passions. There may be in every government a few choice spirits, who may act from more worthy motives. One great error is that we suppose mankind more honest than they are." He identified the prevailing passions as ambition and interest, and so "it will ever be the duty of a wise government to avail itself of those passions, in order to make them subservient to the public good." More specific to land policy, Hamilton told the Convention, "You have to adopt necessary plans for the settlement of your frontiers, and to institute the mode in which settlements and good government are to be made." Several months later, his *No. 7* of *The Federalist* reflected on the political dangers and security considerations of a poorly supervised frontier—and also on the likely use of the military to enforce law, keep order, and settle disputes: "In the wide field of Western territory, . . . we perceive an ample theatre for hostile pretentions, without any umpire or common judge to interpose between the contending parties. To reason from the past to the future we shall have good ground to apprehend, that the sword would sometimes be appealed to as the arbiter of their differences."[16]

The new Constitution protected contracts, guarded property rights, and gave Congress authority over the western territories, including power "to make all needful rules and regulations" for areas en route to statehood. Hamilton saw these provisions, along with the financial powers of Congress, broadly interpreted, as sufficient to address the problem of land devaluation under the Confederation government. While the falling of land values during the politically tumultuous decade of the 1780s did not strictly reflect supply and demand, many easterners, including Hamilton, agreed that to glut the market with cheap western lands during the early years of the new national government could only depress further the worth of property in the older states. For sure, eastern landowners featured prominently among the people Hamilton hoped to rally to the cause of the federal Constitution and the Washington administration. He believed that the funding of the public debt would help restore confidence in property generally and benefit all sections at once, especially the South, where, according to the January 9, 1790, "Report on Public Credit," more than half the value of cultivated lands had been lost (a trend well-noticed by southerners themselves). Prompt federal action might also prevent a sudden renewal of western migration, encouraging proprietors to retain their eastern holdings instead of abandoning them at reduced values and finding better investments and new homes farther west.[17]

During its first session, in 1789, the House of Representatives had ordered the new treasury secretary to advise "on a uniform system for the disposition of lands and property of the United States." At about this time, scattered voices in Congress advocated generous pro-western measures intended to benefit common settlers and limit the advantages of large speculators. In an impressive speech on May 29, 1789, Representative Thomas Scott of Pennsylvania called for a land office to be located in Ohio for the convenience of several thousand prospective buyers there. Without this legal alternative, Scott observed, settlers would either lodge themselves as squatters, demanding preemption measures to validate their claims, or leave United States territory altogether and seek homes in Spanish Louisiana. Only a few members stood behind this argument at the time, but one happened to be James Madison. The Virginia representative feared the potential repercussions of an illiberal attitude of policy makers toward land disposal. "A further reason for keeping the lands at market," he warned the administration in November of 1789, "is that if the appetite for them be not regularly fed, it may produce licentious settlements, by which the value of the property will not only be lost, but the authority of the laws impaired."[18]

Hamilton, by contrast, had no intention of promoting a westward diffusion of population. He never saw the potential of trans-Appalachian America as clearly as later treasury secretaries would. "There is a Western Country. It *will* be settled," he conceded. But the larger picture, as he saw it, required a concentration of labor to help jumpstart manufacturing enterprise in the middle-Atlantic states, including his own New York. Wise policy therefore dictated that groups of new immigrants (as opposed to eastern workers) fill the West gradually, under the mandates of the Northwest Ordinance. In May 1790 Hamilton wrote to Arthur St. Clair, governor of the Northwest Territory: "It is in every view best that it [the territory] should be in great measure settled from abroad rather than at the entire expence of the Atlantic population. And it is certainly wise by kind treatment to lay hold of the affections of the settlers and attach them from the beginning to the Government of the Nation."[19]

In the document he finally submitted to the House on July 22, 1790, the "Report on Vacant Lands,"—without doubt the least studied of Hamilton's treasury reports—the secretary offered specific ideas on public land disposition. Unsurprisingly, the report focused on the "operation of finance"; yet this consideration, of premier importance to Hamilton and eastern Federalists, could not entirely preclude "the accommodation of individuals now inhabiting the Western Country, or who may hereafter emigrate thither"—people whose main interest, he knew, was to obtain the tracts they wanted with as little trouble and for as little cost as possible.[20]

Reconciling these two aims might prove difficult, but Hamilton proposed offering something to each of "three classes" of land buyers: "moneyed individuals and companies" who would buy and then resell, associations of persons "who intend to make settlements themselves," and "single persons, or families" already residing in the "Western Country" or soon to be. The first two groups obviously would require "considerable tracts," the third preferring generally "small quantities." On the assumption that the greatest aggregate amount of land would go to the largest buyers, he figured that the system would be calibrated mostly to their advantage, as it had been earlier for men like Cutler, Duer, and Symmes. Smaller buyers, in turn, could eventually purchase from them, as they did from Cooper in New York. As a particular convenience for men of capital, the report suggested locating a general land office at the national seat of government: "'Tis there, that the principal purchasers, whether citizens or foreigners, can most easily find proper agents, and that contracts for large purchases can be best adjusted." For the sake of westerners, however, the report recommended two additional offices (*only* two) closer to the lands in question, one in the Northwest Territory, another in the Southwest.[21]

In suggesting rules and limitations for the land system, the secretary refrained from mentioning the Land Ordinance of 1785; in some respects, the "Report on Vacant Lands" philosophically rejected the ordinance's important features. Most striking of all is that Hamilton made no direct allusion to the rectilinear survey system. Only in vague references to "townships" of 10 square miles, the size prescribed in Jefferson's 1784 plan, did the report indicate much interest in the earlier provisions for structuring the West. The greatest difference between the two approaches was that in 1785 Congress had advanced a design for speedy retirement of the public debt, being concerned with freeing subsequent generations from the burdens of governmental finance and guarding against the corruption they understood as likely when government became indebted to the creditor classes. Hamilton held no such fears of perpetuating the debt. Better to ally domestic creditors—the economic power in society—with the new federal regime that would now promise to pay them. Unsold lands free of prior settlement represented a form of collateral to the government's creditors. After extinguishing Indian titles, Hamilton urged, Congress should set aside sufficient space for "satisfying the subscribers to the proposed loan in the public debt" and should offer for this purpose no tracts smaller than 500 acres. In addition, however, "convenient tracts" from time to time might be set apart for "actual settlers" in quantities not exceeding 100 acres to each household. To encourage group settlements and to attract European settlers as opposed to migrants from the eastern United States, the report proposed reserving "townships of ten miles square, except where they shall adjoin upon a boundary of some prior grant." Finally, the secretary suggested that additional sales might occur "by special contract, comprehended either within natural boundaries or lines, or both."[22]

Hamilton's views on land pricing and conditions for payment also diverged from the 1785 Ordinance. The "Report on Vacant Lands" proposed that Congress set the price at just 30 cents per acre, "to be paid, either in gold or silver, or in public securities, computing those which shall bear an immediate interest of six per cent, as at par with gold and silver, and those which shall bear a future or less interest . . . at a proportional value." This offered greatest advantage to private land companies, corporate associations of settlers, individual speculators, and, especially, holders of shares in the public debt. Here again, the idea was a land policy consistent with a funded public debt, Hamilton's primary concern.[23]

Another key issue remained: that of allowing credit sales to individual settlers. The Hamilton report suggested no credit for quantities "less than a township of ten miles square" and no more than "two years credit for any greater quantity." Thus, the privilege of partial payment should go only to purchasers of extremely large tracts, which the secretary, like Congress in 1785, apparently expected in time to become homogenous, tightly filled communities, with the original purchasers enjoying maximum speculative benefits in the process. Following long-established colonial practice, he added that such townships should be located by the "subscribers to the proposed loan" or their clients within two years, or else be resold "on the same terms as any other land." A quick occupation of these tracts would foster prompt increases in land values, another lure to speculative investors.[24]

Concerned with political unity, promoting capital growth above agricultural settlement, and favoring East over West, Hamilton's view of policy for America's vacant lands reflected his overall political economy. The government's sanctioning overly rapid filling of western lands would hamper other sectors of a national economy, particularly domestic manufactures. A fast diffusion of population westward might break up concentrated capital resources in the East. Building up the West at a potential sacrifice of eastern growth and prosperity could therefore undermine the balance of economic pursuits—agricultural, commercial, and manufacturing—that Hamilton and other early nationalists prescribed. In his "Report on a National Bank" of December 13, 1790, the secretary argued that the "progressive settlement" of western lands, "while it promises ample retribution, in the generation of future resources, diminishes and obstructs, in the meantime, the *active* wealth of the country." Expansion threatened to draw off a substantial portion of the "circulating money" important for the vitality of production and consumption in eastern states. Capital in the hands of westward migrants reverted, Hamilton thought, to "a more passive state." "In the early periods of new settlements," he wrote, "the settlers not only furnish no surplus for exportation, but they consume a part of that which is produced by the labor of others." As a result, he cautioned, "manufactures do not advance or advance slowly."[25]

While touching on the theme in several other treatises, Hamilton addressed excessive population dispersion most directly in the "Report on Manufactures" of December 5, 1791. He drew on a vast array of contemporary pro-manufacturing tracts, including Tench Coxe's draft of a similar report, along with numerous pieces that had appeared only a few years before in Mathew Carey's periodical *American Museum*. Here, Hamilton targeted European physiocrats, who argued that agriculture alone provided the most beneficial and productive direction for human enterprise. In addition, the manufactures report challenged the contention in Adam Smith's *Wealth of Nations* (and also Benjamin Franklin's vision) that North America should remain predominantly agricultural for as long as its vacant lands remained plentiful and accessible.[26]

Smith's arguments furnished formidable weaponry for American agricultural theorists and free traders, including Jeffersonian intellectuals who would say that a westward expanding, agricultural "empire of liberty" promised the most for America, especially if European markets opened to American produce. Not for many decades to come would the United States face an industrial revolution on the scale of the one then under way in England. The "workshops of Europe" could go on providing manufactured goods for Americans, but Hamilton saw this as too much reliance on foreign economies and said so in the "Report on Manufactures." He doubted that Europe could be counted on to absorb the anticipated surfeit of western agricultural goods: "Considering how fast and how much the progress of new settlements in the United States must increase the surplus produce of the soil, . . . there appear strong reasons to regard the foreign demand for that surplus as too uncertain a reliance, and to desire a substitute for it, in an extensive domestic market."[27]

"To secure such a market," Hamilton contended there was "no other expedient, than to promote manufacturing establishments." A domestic laboring class attached to manufacturing industry could then become the "principal consumers" of surpluses from the land. Governmental encouragement of manufactures, whether in bounties, premiums, or protective duties, would not necessarily injure the interests of agriculture. The same idea had appeared in Carey's *American Mu-*

seum of October 1787: "a constant demand for the productions of our lands, cannot be secured without manufacturing towns to consume them." Hamilton did not seize upon this town concept, however. He perhaps did not imagine economically integrated regions, with agriculture and manufacturing side by side, but rather a sectional balance of economic spheres, with western settlements and the plantation South supplying agricultural raw materials for a manufacturing-oriented East. Hamilton believed that the rise of manufacturing would increase, not undermine, the rewards of farm life. By the influence of domestic industrialization, he wrote, "the condition of each individual farmer would be meliorated, the total mass of Agricultural production would probably be increased."[28] He then added, "[I]t does, by no means, follow that the progress of new settlements would be retarded by the extension of Manufactures." Still, for the time, it was better to deter any westward diffusion of either labor or capital and instead concentrate these precious resources in the East.[29]

—◌—

If Hamilton balked at westward expansion in the empire he envisaged, some other Federalists, especially in the Northeast, vented everything from distrust to outright hostility toward the West. At the time of the Jay-Gardoqui negotiations, Confederation congressman Rufus King had counseled against an agreement providing frontier use of the Mississippi River, for fear that such commerce would undermine any connection of westerners with the East. He also objected to a rapid dispatch of the national debt by selling western lands. Once the sales were made, King figured, both the lands and their owners would be "forever lost to the Confederacy." Ten years later, Congressman Fisher Ames, a High Federalist from Dedham, Massachusetts, and one of the harsher voices against frontier development, would declare it "infinitely more probable" that the West would "sink into barbarism than rise to the dignity of national sentiments and character." The whole region, as far as he could see, was little more than a "capacious wilderness" filled with ignorant men "who think it their right to be exempted from all tax, restraint, or control."[30]

To these eastern eyes, the West had already become associated with radical democratic notions and antigovernment attitudes, making it all the more susceptible to destabilizing influences from Europe, particularly France. Everything from constant settler conflicts with western Indian tribes to the Whiskey Rebellion of 1794 further strengthened the view that frontier settlers raged out of control. While it was annoying enough that the whiskey protest had risen over Hamilton's excise tax on alcoholic spirits, federal officials learned that "Democratic Societies" had stirred the rebels' passions to fever pitch. Told that the insurgents numbered as many as 7,000, Hamilton urged President Washington to respond with a force of some 9,000 infantry and 3,000 cavalry—an army significantly larger than the

Harmer expedition that Congress had sent to eradicate illegal settlers from Ohio in 1785. Washington's September 25, 1794, proclamation on the rebellion closely paralleled his earlier alarm over the disorderly Shaysites in Massachusetts, but it obviously was intended to address the "democratic" agitators as well. The "combinations" operating in Pennsylvania in defiance of the laws of the United States, he commanded, were to desist in "propagating principles of anarchy, endeavoring through emissaries to alienate the friends of order from its support, and inviting enemies to perpetrate similar acts of insurrections." The actions of the Whiskey Rebels, Washington that same day wrote to Burges Ball (a fellow Continental Army officer, cousin, and sometime aide), were "the first *ripe fruit* of the Democratic Societies," provided by the French minister "Mr. [Edmond Charles] Genet for the express purpose of dissention, and to draw a line between the people and the government."[31]

Some western inhabitants, too, abhorred the uncivil behavior they saw around them, likewise attributing it to sharpening ideological conflict back east and events abroad. In December 1795, an anonymous letter purportedly from a resident of the Northwest Territory to Federalist John Fenno's *Gazette of the United States* characterized the "good people" of the "western country" as welcoming desirable migrants but not "Democrats" settling on lands north of the Ohio. Better to dispatch beyond the United States—to Spanish territory west of the Mississippi—all such members of the radical, French-inspired "Democratic Societies," whose "principles and politics" seemed no more civilized than those of the "savages." At last on the verge of delivery from "the *tomahawk* and *scalping knife*," the writer went on, "we beg, for Heaven's sake, not to be visited by the *Guillotine*."[32]

Some of the more strident antiwestern voices issued from the South. In April 1795, Charleston's *City Gazette*, offering advice to immigrants who might settle in South Carolina, revealed a subtext of unease over competition with frontier regions. The newspaper emphasized how safe the state was from Indian attack, how likely the land to rise in value and be cultivated easily by "white men," how accessible to navigation and soon-to-be-built canals, how inviting to capital investment (especially wheat flour milling) and advantageous to mechanics and tradesmen, and how enlightened in the "cause of republicanism" and reformed in its land laws. Six months later, another Charlestonian, writing in the *Columbian Herald*, bemoaned the pro-western features of Pinckney's Treaty of 1795, which opened trade access to the Mississippi River. Had South Carolina's interests been considered as much as Kentucky's, the writer reflected, the result might have differed: "all those who are acquainted with the nature of our staple productions, and those of the western territory, much anticipate with a fearful anxiety the opening of a navigation which will enable that country, peopled with inhabitants, whose views are hostile to the Atlantic states, to be our *rivals* at foreign markets."[33]

In Virginia, St. George Tucker, for one, shared with Hamilton and other northeasterners the apprehension that precipitate sales and extensive migration would debilitate the economy and governmental influence of the old states. A judge of the General Court, Tucker had been against ratification of the federal constitution in 1788, perhaps anticipating a net loss in Virginia's prestige and political sway. He would live to see one of his own sons, Beverley Tucker, abandon the Old Dominion in 1816 for the fresher lands and open opportunities of the Missouri Territory. Another son, Henry St. George Tucker, moved from the Tidewater region to western Virginia—beyond the Blue Ridge into the northern Shenandoah Valley, where vibrant trade among market towns like Winchester, where he finally settled, had begun to appear.[34]

In an anonymously written 1795 pamphlet that circulated in Philadelphia, at that time the nation's capital, the elder Tucker cautioned against a vigorous prosettlement policy. Instead of *"promoting* and *encreasing* population," he contended, rapid expansion would only produce "a still more *dispersed location*, than already prevails among us." With regard to political consequences vital to Virginia and its slaveholders, he predicted, "[A]s representation and population are inseparably connected by the constitution of the United States, the representation of the *present States* in Congress will *decline*, in proportion as that of the *new States encreases*."[35]

Tucker also warned against letting territories fill with European immigrants, "strangers to the language, government, laws, and policy of this country, and the habits of the people, and of each other." The result would be not community but a frontier "Babel," he thought. Better, again, to put the older states (and the "land in abundance" remaining there) to more comprehensive use. The "fugitives from Europe" could then "acquire an earlier acquaintance with the principles of our government, Laws, manners, and language than could possibly be affected in a distinct settlement." Tucker disagreed with Hamilton on the pricing of lands— and certainly on the principle of a funded federal debt. To him and many other prominent Virginians, including Richard Henry Lee, John Taylor of Caroline, and, of course, Madison and Jefferson, a double danger loomed. First, it would be "a most improvident sacrifice" if Congress, "instead of applying the annual revenue of the United States to the redemption of the national debt, should sell the lands at a low value." He might have added that the impact on Virginia land values, already in decline from too many generations of tobacco-growing, could have been disastrous. Second, for western lands to be offered at too low a value would too much encourage "a few rich, and ambitious men, disposed to aggrandize themselves and their posterity"; there would be no preventing "the seeds of an aristocracy" from being sown. This was not just another way of saying a landed aristocracy of slaveholding planters would be preferable to a northern Federalist one of non-slaveholding "gentlemen." Tucker, in fact, stood philosophically with Virginia reformers on the social perils of uneven landownership. He also, in 1796, would advocate the gradual abolition of slavery in Virginia and propose that freed blacks resettle in the West.[36]

Finally, Tucker offered six recommendations for congressional land-policy makers: One, that the lands be divided, "as in Connecticut, into small townships," not exceeding 5,000, or at the most 10,000, acres, then subdivided into lots not exceeding 200 acres. Two, that each lot be settled or improved within a stated time or else forfeited back to the government. Three, that townships be numbered according to proximity to the areas already settled, so that "not a single township be sold, until the former is disposed of." Four, that the government sell no more than 100 townships—or a million acres—in any one year. Five, that lands in each township be surveyed and the lots "classed according to their value." Six, that no grant be made (title issued) until the terms of sale, settlement, and improvement have been completed.[37]

—✿—

In spring 1796, the government in Philadelphia finally addressed several of the land-policy questions that Hamilton, Tucker, and others had raised: whether to extend the 1785 Land Ordinance, how to accelerate sales and increase revenue for debt retirement, and in what ways to make the system more inclusive for ordinary Americans. Beyond those things remained the unrelenting conundrum of illegal settlement and the plight of those too poor to reach *any* minimum price and acreage levels. The House took up the subject of the price, some representatives arguing that continuing a high auction minimum would not bring ample sales, others insisting that it was the only likely deterrent to the "hydra" of land speculation. The latter view carried the day, and Congress settled on making the starting auction price $2.00 per acre. The most revealing part of the debate, however, centered on the acreage minimum. Barely submerged class conflicts surfaced here, as did increasingly passionate ideological differences between Federalists and their political opposition, most of whom would soon constitute an organized Jeffersonian Republican party.

On *both* sides, and not just the Federalist, fear of the "Democratic Societies"— and, with them, a crystallizing Jeffersonian opposition—seemed to permeate the exchanges, albeit indirectly. But newspapers revealed the intensity of rancor behind House members' more restrained words. A clear language of legitimate opposition had yet to form in national politics; instead, rhetorical conflicts between rival groups often assumed the attitude of a cosmic division between forces of good and evil. Less than a year earlier, during the fight over appropriations required by the Jay Treaty, the Massachusetts *Western Star* had referred to the "diabolical" intentions of "the Jacobin faction" in the House and "their beloved [Albert] Gallatins and [James] Madisons." Political conflict had become so ideologically sensitive that during the debate over the acreage minimum, Congressman John Van Allen of New York, who favored the sale of lands in lots no larger than 640 acres, struggled to avoid being lumped with the "Jacobin" crowd. Although "a friend of equality," Van Allen declared, he did not, "from anything he had said," wish to leave the impression that he supported an "Agrarian law"—a principle that he emphatically "disavowed."[38]

In the House on April 5, 1796, Jeremiah Crabb, an army veteran who had become a major landowner in Montgomery County, Maryland, proposed that half of surveyed 640-acre sections in new areas northwest of the Ohio River be sold in lots of 160 acres each. One day before, the idea that all of the sections be so divided had met extensive opposition. The reasoning was that 160-acre tracts—quarter sections—would better accommodate "real settlers," whom advocates preferred to those who bought only with the intention of selling again. The poor held more promise of going west than did the rich, as experience had now shown. Dividing land into small parcels, multiplying the number of independent small freeholders, would "have a tendency to make good Republicans instead of servile tenants dependent upon tyrannical landlords," argued Crabb. The "strength of the country," he added, consisted in "its compactness of settlements and the attachment of the people to the Government." Besides, the increased demand for land in the old states had caused both prices and rents there to rise beyond the means of poorer families. Few potential migrants, North Carolina's James Holland agreed, "would have so much money as would purchase" a minimum of 640 acres. Why not so assist "the poorer class," those "most valuable in a community," the ones called upon to fight in an emergency—they who would otherwise be forced to buy at higher prices from private sellers, or else "become tenants to others" without personal independence?[39]

But none of this rhetoric swayed Pennsylvania's Thomas Hartley, a lawyer who also had served in the Revolutionary War, nor did it persuade William Cooper, the land king of Otsego County, New York, who had been elected as a Federalist to the Fourth Congress. Hartley argued that further division of sections would delay the surveying and increase its expense, which could only reduce the vital net proceeds from sales. He suggested that would-be settlers "join together and purchase" a 640-acre lot. Cooper ranked among the most ardent and stubborn of Federalists, an uncompromising partisan of the Washington administration.

Privately, he condemned the Republican faction of the mid-1790s as a bunch of "hot-headed Lawyers, Bankrupts, mortified Politicians of our own Country mixed with the unfortunate Refugees & soured Sons of Europe." Republicans both in upstate New York and in Congress denounced him with equal contempt. As for land policy, he thought selling parts of the public domain in 160-acre tracts would do little to help poorer settlers in Ohio. Whether he *wanted* to help them stood open to question. He said that bargain-hunting speculators, not poor men, always bought up the smaller parcels. Nobody needed be told that Cooper's own landed interests—specifically, property values in Otsego County—might suffer if federal land only a little farther west were made more directly accessible to ordinary farmers. Meanwhile, some of the more frugal congressmen, like John Nicholas of Virginia, pointed to the governmental expense of the additional surveying that would be required: not less than $200 on every township, he estimated. Nicholas also thought it too much burden on a poorer buyer "to first go and explore the country" in order to find a tract to his liking. Most, he judged, "would rather wait till the sale was over, and the land come to be laid out and divided into farms." Abraham Venable, also of Virginia, disagreed. He believed many "farmers' sons" to be perfectly ready go west, but he noted that the purchase cost of 160 acres—perhaps $300 to $500—would still be no small sum.[40]

Both Madison and Gallatin favored the reduced tract size. By this time, the Geneva-born Gallatin, who spoke with a heavy French accent and represented recently settled Fayette County in western Pennsylvania, had emerged as a leading voice on land policy in the House. Many of his neighbors back home had, like him, immigrated to America, and many distrusted the centralized authority now emanating from Philadelphia. Two years earlier, Gallatin, like many of his constituents, had deprecated the Washington administration's handling of the Whiskey Rebellion as a gross overreaction by the federal government, only confirming their worst suspicions of Hamilton as a puppet of the northeastern privileged classes. While agreeing with Hamilton on federal lands in the West as a source of liquid capital, Gallatin wanted to extinguish the public debt as soon as possible and favored the $2.00 price minimum, not so much to dissuade speculators as to raise sufficient revenue to free the republic from the grip of wealthy creditors. No class of citizens would be "more benefited by this extinction" of the debt "than the poor," Gallatin wrote. With the debt retired, western lands might be made available to ordinary buyers on more generous terms. For the time being, he urged a credit program for actual settlers, and Congress in the 1796 law would allow purchasers one year's credit for the completing of payment.[41]

A majority in the House in 1796 favored the 160-acre provision, but Federalists in control of the Senate voted it down, leaving the minimum that one could buy at

TABLE 1
House Vote on Selling Half the 640-Acre Sections by 160-Acre Quarter-Sections, 1796

	Federalists		Republicans	
	For	Against	For	Against
NEW ENGLAND	0	20	0	4
Massachusetts	0	8	0	2
Connecticut	0	7	0	0
Rhode Island	0	2	0	0
New Hampshire	0	2	0	1
Vermont	0	1	0	1
MID-ATLANTIC	5	6	12	4
New York	2	2	4	1
Pennsylvania	1	1	6	0
New Jersey	0	1	0	1
Delaware	0	0	1	0
Maryland	2	2	1	2
SOUTH ATLANTIC	2	2	24	6
Virginia	1	1	14	1
North Carolina	1	0	6	3
South Carolina	0	1	4	0
Georgia	0	0	0	2
SOUTHWEST (Ky.)	0	0	2	0
Total	7	28	38	14

Source: Journal of the House of Representatives, 4th Congress, 1st session, 496–97.

640 acres (see Table 1 for a breakdown of the House vote). By the closest of tallies, the Senate struck down an amendment proposing that resident aliens (noncitizens) be allowed to purchase lands from the United States and pass such holdings on to their heirs; Vice President John Adams determined the outcome with his tie-breaking nay (see Table 2 for the vote). Although this question of the potential loyalty of western settlers had emerged before, it seemed more urgent as legislators contemplated an increasing foreign presence on the frontier and saw that as a condition to be distrusted, if not feared. Among the eleven opposition votes were arch-Federalists Rufus King, Caleb Strong of Massachusetts, and Connecticut's Jonathan Trumbull. Frederick Frelinghuysen of New Jersey, who had been commissioned as a major general to help put down the Whiskey Rebellion two years earlier, voted nay, as did John Henry of Maryland, who in 1787 had served on the committee that forged the Northwest Ordinance. Five Republican senators also joined the opposition, expressing their own concern for frontier loyalty as well as highlighting the Republicans' desire not to be labeled as radical "Jacobins." Among those voting in favor of the amendment were the four Federalist senators from

TABLE 2

Senate Vote on Allowing Resident Aliens to Purchase and Hold Federal Lands under the Land Act of 1796

	Federalists		Republicans	
	For	Against	For	Against
NEW ENGLAND	3	2	0	0
Vermont	0	0	0	0
New Hampshire	0	0	0	0
Massachusetts	1	1	0	0
Connecticut	0	1	0	0
Rhode Island	2	0	0	0
MID-ATLANTIC	4	4	1	0
New York	0	1	1	0
New Jersey	1	1	0	0
Pennsylvania	2	0	0	0
Delaware	0	1	0	0
Maryland	1	1	0	0
SOUTH ATLANTIC	2	0	0	4
Virginia	0	0	0	1
North Carolina	0	0	0	2
South Carolina	1	0	0	0
Georgia	1	0	0	1
SOUTHWEST (Ky.)	1	0	0	1
Total	10	6	1	5

Source: *Annals of Congress*, 4th Congress, 1st session, 83.

Pennsylvania and Rhode Island, states with long traditions of cultural diversity, ethnic complexity, and religious toleration.[42]

As to the administrative ordering of the land system, the law of 1796 adopted into federal statute much of the 1785 land ordinance. Federal lands were to be arranged in rectilinear townships of 6 square miles, with half of the newly surveyed areas organized for sale in quarter-townships of 5,120 acres each. The consecutive numbering of sections was to proceed east to west, starting in each northeast corner, in the manner the ordinance had prescribed. The law authorized sale of individual sections of 640 acres at land offices to be established in Pittsburgh and Cincinnati, while the quarter-townships could be bought only in Philadelphia.[43]

Over the next few years, however, the new law produced neither a spread of settlement nor significant public revenue. Fewer than 50,000 acres sold before 1800. In his "Sketch of the Finances of the United States," Gallatin, then in the House, argued that for most potential land buyers Congress had provided too little time in which to pay: "The credit is so short that the class of people who usually begin settlements will be nearly altogether excluded." To remedy this, lawmakers, at the urging of Ohio territorial delegate William Henry Harrison, produced the Land Act of 1800, which retained the price base of $2.00 but reduced the minimum purchase to 320 acres and allowed four years of credit, with a discount of 8 percent for cash payment. Also known as the Harrison Frontier Land Act, the law provided for additional land offices in the Northwest—at Chillicothe, Marietta, Steubenville, and Cincinnati. The majority rejected, however, an effort to include in the bill a preemption clause—one of many attempts between 1800 and 1830 to codify the "right" of migrants to occupy federal lands prior to formal auction and purchase.[44]

The credit "experiment" would succeed in its immediate purpose: to stimulate sales. Within the next year, nearly eight times as many acres transferred to private hands as had in the previous four years. But since payment could be deferred, the sales still did not bring much revenue. During the following two decades, the federal government proved benevolent to a fault in its capacity as land creditor. The four-year purchase period, generously extended time and time again to relieve both the poorer and the more profligate westerners, not only encouraged many more new settlers, but also gave rise to the rampant land speculation that eventually contributed to the Panic of 1819. As of the Land Act of 1820, which prohibited further credit purchases, the U.S. Treasury had received payment for little more than half the sale value of the lands discharged at auction, and by that time Congress had passed no fewer than twelve land relief acts for the benefit of buyers who had not met their obligations. The only other significant modification of the 1796 law prior to the Panic would come in 1804, when heavy Jeffersonian majorities in both houses agreed to a reduction of the land price minimum to $1.64 per acre and cut the minimum purchase amount to 160 acres. Revisiting and passing the quarter-section provision that the Federalist-dominated Senate had shot down in 1796, the Republicans established exclusive party control over the nation's land policy.[45]

—೦ᳵ

At his inauguration in 1801, President Thomas Jefferson described his fellow citizens as "possessing a chosen country, with room enough for our descendants to the thousandth and thousandth generation."[46] Indeed, America's vast territorial domain gave ample space for the extension and application of Revolutionary ideals—but, again, *whose* ideals? And if the new president stood ready to answer, *which* Jefferson would this be?

From his earliest days in colonial politics, Jefferson had espoused an agriculture-based vision of westward expansion. Unlike Virginia's most powerful planters, however, and in certain ways very much like Benjamin Franklin, he saw vacant lands in America as a vehicle of social and economic reform. In "A Summary View of the Rights of British America," his Revolutionary pamphlet of 1774, Jefferson had drawn a crucial distinction between landholding in America and in the Old

World of feudal tradition. This understanding represented, for him, as it would later for others, the foundation of republican political economy and an eventual spreading of population into unsettled territory—all part of an evolving concept that Jefferson and others would later call an "empire of liberty." The "liberty" to which this referred, however, would turn out to mean freedom from debt and protection against lawbreaking settlers just as much as it promised economic opportunity for legitimate small farmers and the expansion of republican principles.

Like the seventeenth-century "commonwealth men" of English political tradition, and also many of his fellow Virginia planters of the late eighteenth century, Jefferson had always feared the social and political implications of an extended public debt. Addressing the burdens of post-Revolutionary finance, he had recommended in 1784 that monies arising from land sales be "applied to the sinking such part of the principal of the national debt as Congress shall from time to time direct, and to no other purpose whatsoever." He also believed that, after the debt had been retired, the government should donate, not sell, western lands to individuals. Like Franklin, Jefferson hoped to confine industrialization and rapid urbanization to the Old World for as long as possible, celebrating the nature-based virtues of New World "agriculturists." In October 1785, to Dutch statesman G. K. Hogendorp, he wrote, "Whenever indeed our numbers should so increase as that our produce would overstock the markets of those nations who should come to seek it, the farmers must either employ the surplus of their time in manufactures, or in navigation." But, he quickly added, that day "would . . . be distant, and we should be drawing rough materials and even subsistence from America." Jefferson thought that Hamilton's vision of large, financially sophisticated urban centers and the growth of large-scale manufacturing would turn virtuous yeoman into an impoverished, unprincipled laboring mass, undercutting forever the dream of a liberty-preserving, fee-simple empire. The Jeffersonian alternative envisioned America's social and economic destiny as unfolding not only in farming but in a radically wide distribution of land. In the desirable event that western "husbandmen" might peddle their surpluses to Europe on a basis of free trade, Americans could restrict indefinitely their manufacturing to the rudimentary household varieties.[47]

As usual, these ideals collided headlong with the uncompromising realities not only of debt-management but also of governing a raw and distant frontier. By the time Jeffersonian Republicans assumed power after 1800, they still evinced more zeal than Federalists about territorial expansion but, having learned from experience of federal governance, they held no less concern about securing the West from chaotic and lawless exploitation. Although the Republicans had consistently opposed Federalist policies in the 1790s, their constituency had never been simply small farmers and old school antimodernists. It also included market-oriented larger planters, merchants, lawyers, and self-sufficient artisans who often disagreed politically with the more anti-statist "Old Republican" types like John Randolph, John Taylor, and Spencer Roane in Virginia, North Carolina's Nathaniel Macon, and George Clinton in New York. After 1800, Jefferson would cautiously lean toward the more commercial types in his party, a group that also included, among others, Gallatin, Robert R. Livingston, Alexander J. Dallas, Stephen Girard, and eventually Madison, who became Jefferson's secretary of state. Jeffersonian policy makers, especially the president himself and treasury secretary Gallatin, wanted settlement to proceed apace but in a restrained, orderly way—and without weakening the potential of western land sales to produce the federal revenue needed to lower the national debt and meet other expenses. In addition to contiguous settlement within the framework of the rectilinear survey system, the more commerce-oriented faction wanted to foster a spirit of business enterprise in new western towns and agricultural regions. Their goal was to build a nation of prosperous freeholders situated in close proximity to developing markets, preferably operating in harmony with Native American interests—as opposed to a scattered population of impoverished agrarians living in rustic desperation and at swords points with neighboring tribes.[48]

As treasury secretary under two Republican presidents, from 1801 to 1814, Gallatin prepared a new mixture of political economy that reflected the more commercial flank of Jeffersonian Republicanism. In land policy, he continued to envision sales to increase federal revenues and minimize taxes, and during his tenure under Jefferson and Madison the number of land offices in the West would grow from four to eighteen. In 1812, he oversaw establishment of the General Land Office, which afterwards lifted some of the burden of public-domain management from his successors. Abandoning some of the military-fiscal outlook of Hamilton and other Federalists, Gallatin would call for extreme frugality in defense expenditures, especially when little pressing need existed for much of a standing army or an extensive navy, while urging heavily increased spending on transportation projects to open interior regions for expanded trade. This spirit of internal improvement would take further expression in years following the War of 1812, first with the "Madison Platform" of 1815–1816, then in the politics of National Republicans like John Quincy Adams and Henry Clay, and finally in the form of projects funded at the state level for lack of adequate federal support. Republicans still united on rapid extinction of the public debt, with land proceeds being pledged to this end. In his early years as treasury secretary, Gallatin focused on that goal. "I am firmly of opinion," he wrote in November 1801, "that, if the present Administration and Congress do not take the most effective measures for that object, the debt will be entailed on us and the ensuing generations, together with all the systems that support it, and which it supports." He projected a final eradication within "fourteen or fifteen years." Revenue tariffs, internal taxes, and reduced government spending, combined with western land sales, lowered the deficit somewhat, before the Louisiana Purchase in 1803 added another $15 million to it.[49]

Yet, as soon as the early months of 1802, Gallatin's thoughts had turned to the long-range advantages of steadily increasing land revenue for projects other than federal debt retirement. As plans evolved within the administration to devote this revenue on a lasting basis to financing national internal improvements (preferably with a supporting constitutional amendment), it became more important to clarify restrictions on legislatures in territories soon to be admitted to the Union as the first states from the Old Northwest. In a letter to William B. Giles on February 13, 1802, Gallatin indicated what he believed were key public lands provisions: "1st, that the Legislatures of the Districts or new States shall never interfere with the primary disposal of the soil by Congress; nor with any regulations which Congress may find necessary for securing the title in such soil to the bona fide purchasers; 2d, that no tax shall be imposed on the property of the United States; and, 3d, that in no case shall non-resident proprietors be taxed higher than residents."[50]

Western states, then, had best appreciate the improvements—public education, roads, and canals—that sales of federal lands remaining within their boundaries made possible. The Ohio Enabling Act, signed into law on April 30, 1802, laid some groundwork for such projects while providing for admission into the Union of the first public land state. With this important legislation, Congress established the precedent of reserving to the federal government title to all ungranted and unsold public lands lying within a state's boundaries, except for a section of each township set aside for the support of education. As partial compensation for a new state's allowing federal tracts within its borders to go untaxed for ten years, Gallatin proposed that a tenth of the net proceeds of the land sales be "applied towards laying out and making turnpike or other roads, first from the navigable waters emptying into the Atlantic to the Ohio, and afterwards continued through the new State." Such roads might be laid out under congressional authority but not without the consent of the states. The result would be not only transportation improvement but also significant increase the value of the lands. The political intentions behind the proposal reflected a strong interest in minimizing the sway of sectionalism and tightening the appeal of the Jeffersonian party in western parts of the country—all contributing "towards cementing the bonds of the Union between those parts of the United States whose local interests have been considered as most dissimilar."[51]

The acquisition of Louisiana in 1803, adding some 828,000 square miles to federal territory between the Mississippi River and the Rockies, intensified the importance of issues surrounding public land disposition, including the question of intelligent uses for land revenue beyond eventual retirement of the public debt. For Gallatin and other commercially minded Republicans, "internal improvements" would now feature more prominently in their vision of a steadily expanding agricultural republic, a potential "world within itself," free of chaos and corruption, and durable beyond comparison beside any of the industrially modernized systems of Europe. Ideally, domestic manufacturing would serve only as "handmaid" to agriculture in this westward expanding society. Roads and canals would aid productive westerners—and, ideally, their Indian "partners"—by transporting their produce either to New Orleans or to the East Coast for export across the Atlantic, provided that somehow Old World mercantilist barriers might finally collapse. If those barriers remained, the North American continent provided ample room and resources for self-sufficient communities of republicans to thrive in the New World.

Visions aside, however, a sudden doubling of the country's size raised questions of practical governance that no one could answer, except in theoretical terms, until much later. While strengthening the security of the United States, the Louisiana Purchase increased the danger that illegal (and morally dubious) migrants might scatter too quickly throughout the newly acquired lands. Historians have always underscored the constitutional issues that arose with the acquisition of Louisiana, especially the interpretive about-face of Republicans from their earlier strict constructionist scruples. Even the ultra-traditionalist John Randolph supported the agreement, though he later would regret the constitutional stretching it required. The Federalist opposition, with equal irony, argued against broad governmental power to add territory. A less-often highlighted element of the debate on trans-Mississippi expansion, however, is one that in fact troubled *both* sides: the old question of whether government could possibly manage the dangerous centrifugal effects of such distant territorial possessions.[52]

In discussions of the Louisiana Treaty outside the capital, which had moved to Washington, D.C., in 1800, the specter of Montesquieu loomed ominously. A September 1802 newspaper editorial printed in Massachusetts pronounced the fears attending trans-Mississippi expansion to be "in the highest degree *chimerical*" but noted that such reservations, "expressed by most of the Federal and many of the Republican editors of the United States," permeated both parties. Far from putting anxieties to rest, news of the signing of the Louisiana Treaty in early May 1803 only intensified the discussion. Privately, Rufus King grumbled that the new region would be "too extensive" and "impossible to govern." For commercial reasons, Alexander Hamilton applauded American possession of the Mississippi River and New Orleans, but he looked upon the extensive lands beyond as a risk to national unity and republican stability. This apprehension was then—and had been since the Revolution—more widespread than most historians have noted. "The more extensive the territory of a state the greater is the difficulty of governing it AT ALL," declared "Fabricius" (Fisher Ames) in Boston's *Columbian Centinel* in summer 1803. A "pure republic," he instructed, could not last long even in a small country, "nor be long preserved from the most incurable extremes of democracy in one that is too widely extended." Ancient Rome had been unable to rule such an expanded domain without the kind of extensive, standing military force that would shock most Americans, Republicans and Federalists alike. Tiberius and Diocletian, Ames noted, had needed "the SWORDS OF FORTY LEGIONS" to hold a region just from the Elbe to the Euphrates. Short of that, how was a nation to "prevent the 'squatting' of hosts of renegadoes, and outlaws, and fugitives, who would laugh at our laws, and, when they became numerous, would defy our force and proclaim independence"? In another issue of the *Centinel*, Ames insisted, more succinctly, that Louisiana was just too much territory, for too much money, and too likely to "drain our people away" from manufacturing and commerce.[53]

The argument in both houses of Congress largely mirrored the one developing in the newspapers. Federalist warnings against overexpansion reflected not only political resentment that Jeffersonians had assumed power but also the earlier, and still legitimate, reservations about a too-rapid spread of population westward. On October 25, 1803, a rhetorical battle started in the House of Representatives over carrying into effect the Louisiana Treaty, which the Senate had ratified five days earlier. Judge Thomas Griffin, a Virginia Federalist representing Yorktown, declared his fears about the possible consequences of the Louisiana Treaty—the "effects of the vast extent of our empire," the increased value of labor, the decreasing value of eastern lands. Beyond that threatened the hazards of a far western climate widely suspected to be forbiddingly dry and barren. Griffin thought the West more likely to furnish not a "new Eden," but "a cemetery for the bodies of our citizens." James Elliott, a Federalist lawyer from Brattleboro, Vermont, who as a soldier in 1793 had fought Indians in Ohio, thought the advantages of acquiring Louisiana outweighed the possible evils that might result, but he cautioned, "The physical strength of a nation depends upon an aggregation of circumstances, amongst which, compactness of population, as well as territory, may be reckoned; our population may become too scattered." Harvard-educated Federalist Samuel Thatcher, who lived in the town of Warren, in Worcester County, Massachusetts, and who had read his Montesquieu, took a gloomier view. If the treaty went into effect, he predicted, "it would carry from its present centre a great portion of the population of the United States," would probably result in a removing of the seat of the federal government, and "might dismember the Union." Further, he noted, "all history showed that great empires, whether monarchies or republics, had been ultimately broken to pieces by their magnitude." Even in a short time, he warned, "The acquisition [and protection] of distant territory . . . will involve the necessity of a considerable standing army, so justly an object of terror."[54]

Meanwhile, a similar altercation in the Senate revealed legitimate apprehensions there, too. Federalist senators addressed the wisdom of further expansion; the negative side-effects, some thought, could not possibly be averted. Federalist Samuel White of Delaware thought it naïve to imagine that unwanted settlement could be contained: "you had as well pretend to inhibit the fish from swimming in the sea as to prevent the population of that country after its sovereignty shall become ours." The inevitable result, he reasoned, would be too many Americans living too far away from political authority: scarcely feeling "the rays of the General Government; their affections will become alienated; they will gradually begin to view us as strangers; they will form other commercial connexions, and our interests will become distinct." Apart from party identification, White noted, "Gentlemen on all sides, with very few exceptions, agree that the settlement of this [trans-Mississippi] country will be highly injurious and dangerous to the United States."[55]

The significance of Jeffersonian replies to these anti-Louisiana arguments consisted not in their unsurprising faith in westward growth but rather in their implicit *agreement* with their opponents' aversion to overly rapid expansion. Responding to Federalists in the House, John Randolph shared the concern that "so widely extended a country cannot subsist under a Republican Government," but if this be so, he continued, then "we have already far exceeded the limits which visionary speculatists have supposed capable of a free Government." Still, he said possession of New Orleans and commercial mastery of the Mississippi River were "inestimably valuable," as most Federalists would concede. As for the rest, Randolph counseled, "[T]he country west of the Mississippi does not reduce us to the necessity of settling it now, or for a long time to come. It will [meanwhile] tend to destroy the cause of Indian wars, whilst it may constitute the asylum of that brave and injured race of men." In the Senate, James Jackson of Georgia, a state with scattered settlements all along its Indian frontier, insisted that "frontier people are not the people they are represented." They would "respect the laws of their country; . . . it is not their interest to go to Louisiana, or see it settled for years to come." So what would stop them? Jackson's answer, that natural forces would suffice, sounded almost like what Federalists said *against* Louisiana. He doubted that a large migration would occur soon because "the settlement of it at present would part father and son, brother and brother, and friend and friend, and lessen the value of their lands beyond all calculation." If Jackson thought that filial ties would override the lure of distant lands, many Federalists—and not a few Jeffersonians as well—feared the reverse.[56]

The most optimistic support for Jeffersonian expansionism arrived, of course, with new-state senators, particularly Kentucky's John Breckinridge and William Cocke of Tennessee. And yet, their statements on the floor probably did as much to heighten as to dispel eastern distrust. Once a farmer and lawyer in Albemarle County, Breckinridge was one of many Virginia natives who found greener pastures in the West—in his case, a 1,600-acre plantation near Lexington in 1793, followed by rapid political advancement and then, in 1800, a Senate seat, thanks to Jefferson's long coattails. Jefferson, in fact, operated through Breckinridge behind the scenes during the Louisiana debate. In turn, Breckinridge no doubt spoke for Jefferson (and Secretary of State Madison) in contending that Montesquieu's "hackneyed doctrine" no longer applied. For an American republic, he announced in November 1803, "the more extensive its dominion the more safe and more durable it will be." Breckinridge did acknowledge the problem of social control, but he asked, "Cannot the General Government restrain the population within such bounds as may be judged proper?" It was enough, he urged, "for us to make the acquisition: the time and manner of disposing of it must be left to posterity." More hopeful than instructive, this advice could scarcely have inspired eastern confidence, given the repeated frustration in trying to govern the frontiers. As for the character of western people, Breckinridge assured his fellow senators that the "great proportion of them have emigrated from the Atlantic States, and are attached to them by all those ties which so strongly bind societies together." But then he delivered a chilling admonition: if Congress denied such people the western destiny they had come to consider theirs, it would be demanding "endurance beyond [that] which even the advocates for passive obedience and non-resistance . . . expect." Cocke proceeded to reinforce Breckinridge's caveat that rebellious westerners, if disappointed, could easily take law into their own hands. If Congress were to treat such people with "marked indifference, or injustice, as should rouse us to just resentment," Cocke agreed, "there is a point, beyond which we cannot go."[57]

The Jefferson administration, while eager to promote internal development and a westward future, expressed the same qualms about rapid expansion as their Federalist predecessors. The dominating fear continued to be that settlers would pour into the West too quickly, claiming vacant lands without regard for the systematic procedures of public land survey, organization, and sale. And especially, to let squatters reign on the public domain was to permit an undoing of the revenue-generating auction system, upon which other policies, including reduction of the federal debt, would depend. The earlier Federalist recourse to direct taxation remained ideologically anathema for Jeffersonians (and high tariffs not much less so). Jefferson's own concern about keeping unauthorized settlers off federal lands registered most strongly with the acquisition of the Louisiana Territory. At that time, while eager to promote agricultural expansion, he sought a carefully ordered, methodical filling of the frontier, with lands east of the Mississippi being settled first. "When we shall be full on this side," Jefferson wrote to John Breckinridge in August 1803, "we may lay off a range of States on the western bank from the head to the mouth, and so, range after range, advancing compactly as we multiply." Gallatin agreed, echoing cautious Jeffersonians in Congress: "our object should at present be to restrain the population and settlements on this side of the Mississippi . . . . [T]he acquisition of the country west of it enables us in fact better to regulate and control the progress of our settlements."[58]

What could government do, especially after purchase of the Louisiana Territory, to hold a potential tidal wave of migration within rational, policy-wise bounds? The Senate had approved the Louisiana Treaty by a vote of 24 to 7 on October 20, 1803, and the appropriations to put the bargain into effect followed quickly. But neither house, then or soon afterward, came up with satisfactory answers to this old, nagging question. Nor could the Jefferson administration and its "Virginia Dynasty" successors find a perfect solution. Their most sensible idea was to somehow coordinate western expansion with internal improvements so that settlement, commercial development, community building, and stable Indian relations might all go together.

In his Second Inaugural Address, on March 4, 1805, Jefferson urged a far-reaching commitment to improved transportation. With substantial sources of federal revenue coming in from moderate tariffs and regular land sales, direct taxation had been suspended during his first administration. Once the public debt disappeared, he projected, the revenue "thereby liberated" might, "by a just repartition among the states, and a corresponding amendment of the constitution," be applied in peacetime to river clearance, canal and road building, the arts, manufactures, education, and "other great objects within each state." In the same address and in other statements public and private, Jefferson expressed confidence in the possibility of "extending the sphere" of the republic without danger to the union, relying on Madison's "federative principle." "The larger our association," he declared, echoing Madison, "the less will it be shaken by local passions; and in any view, is it not better that the opposite bank of the Mississippi should be settled by our own brethren and children, than by strangers of another family?"[59]

Though he mused at times on the right of western America to determine its own destiny, separate from the United States, Jefferson really had no intention of letting the trans-Mississippi acquisition slip away. Socially, economically, and politically, the region remained too important both to the nation and to the future of Jeffersonianism. The Second Inaugural speech made this clear, as did his Sixth Annual Message to Congress, submitted December 2, 1806. In the latter, the president called for a reorientation in domestic policy, stressing again the capacity of federally sponsored internal improvements to bind the Union together. While conceding that the expenditures recommended were "not among those enumerated in the Constitution," he apparently believed the amendment needed only a little time to be passed. The message suggested continuing the impost on "foreign luxuries," in addition to its advice on selling western lands for the "great purposes" of roads, canals, river clearance, and public education. "By these operations," Jefferson declared, "new channels of communication will be opened between the States; the lines of separation will disappear, their interests will be identified, and their union cemented by new and indissoluble ties."[60]

The question of how to do all this fell into Secretary Gallatin's lap, and the answer shot back soon enough in his "Report on Roads and Canals" of April 1808. Despite President Washington's keen interest in the interior development of the country, Hamilton, with his Atlantic bias, had left the subject comparatively unaddressed. Gallatin's report advocated a federal outlay of some $20 million over a period of at least thirty years. Of importance to the frontier was the report's inclusion of four proposals: first, clearing for navigation the four great western river systems—the Alleghany, Monongahela, Kanawha, and Tennessee—and placement of canals parallel to them; second, building four "firstrate turnpike roads" from those rivers across the mountains, linking with corresponding rivers on the eastern side; third, constructing a canal around the falls of the Ohio River; and fourth, modification and repair of existing roads to Detroit, St. Louis, and New Orleans. These works would be in addition to the Cumberland Road, scheduled to commence in 1811.[61]

Gallatin's argument for this mammoth scheme again revealed the extent to which Republican political economy had evolved beyond the narrow agricultural contours of old school Jeffersonians. The "Report on Roads and Canals" urged centralized governmental assistance in areas of national development considered too risky or too daunting for private investment: "the great demand for capital in the United States, and the extent of territory compared with the population, are . . . the true causes which prevent new undertakings, and render those already accomplished less profitable than had been expected." Various transportation projects around the country—like Gallatin's proposed "intercoastal waterway" stretching along the Atlantic seaboard—involved commitments of such magnitude that only Congress could carry them out "as fast as the work itself can progress; avoiding thereby the ruinous loss of interest on a dormant capital, and reducing the real expense to its lowest rate." The acquisition of Louisiana and the prospect of more rapid migration made federal enterprise more urgent now than ever. "The inconveniences, complaints, and perhaps dangers, which may result from a vast extent of territory," Gallatin advised, "can not otherwise be radically removed or prevented than by opening speedy and easy communications through all its parts." Improvements reaching the frontier offered, he noted, increasing "value to the immediate forests of the Ohio," and the application of "national industry" in the West would "diminish the price of freights from New Orleans," the city destined to become the great "emporium" for western produce.[62]

For the whole range of national projects envisioned here, especially in regions as short on private investors as the West, public land proceeds were vital. "Amongst the resources of the Union," insisted Gallatin, the 150 million acres of arable public domain north of the Ohio River and south of Tennessee—lands expected to open for auction in the coming thirty years—seemed "particularly applicable to internal improvements." Despite its flaws in policy and administration, the treasury secretary held in high regard the land system he had helped to create: "For the disposition of these lands a plan has been adopted, calculated to enable every industrious citizen to become a freeholder, to secure indisputable titles to the purchasers, to obtain a national revenue, and, above all, to suppress monopoly." His chief regret was the higher prices that had been paid by "the first inhabitants of the frontier," but these had been necessary to prevent lands from "being engrossed by individuals possessing greater wealth, activity, and local advantages." In the future, however, nothing "could be more gratifying to the purchasers," thought Gallatin, "than the application of the proceeds of the sales to improvements."[63]

Meanwhile, official policy on squatters, despite exceptions here and there, remained as before. Gallatin regarded illegal settlers as "intruders," pure and simple; they threatened his treasury strategy of maximizing public land revenue. The Jeffersonian Congress added the Intrusion Act of 1807, which reinforced the ban against squatting on federal lands even if the rule would be hard to apply. The Federalists, understanding this provision as reinforcing the land policy that since 1804 had belonged exclusively to Jeffersonian Republicans, who enjoyed four-to-one majorities in both houses, voted nearly unanimously against this anti-squatter measure. This behavior reflected partisan opposition to the dominant party and not, of course, support for trespassing settlers (see Tables 3 and 4 for breakdowns of the votes). The only opposition in principle came from the few western members and from northeastern members of both parties who feared that rapid western settlement of any kind would drain population from, and destabilize, their own region. Even in his more radical agrarian days, Jefferson himself had expressed little sympathy for squatters. As governor of Virginia during the Revolutionary

War, he had not hesitated to order intruders northwest of the Ohio River to vacate, thus protecting those lands for Virginia officers and soldiers who had been promised much of that area. His 1780 proclamation on the subject specifically denied illegitimate settlers "any right of preemption or other benefit whatever from such settlement or occupancy." Ordering in ruthless "military patroles" to give clout to his words, Governor Jefferson wanted to avoid having to fight a squatter-inspired Indian war in western Virginia in addition to fighting the redcoats.[64]

Another reason to keep squatters at bay came with the Jeffersonian Indian policy of the early 1800s. Viewed sympathetically, early American "philanthropy" toward the western tribes provides a case of good intentions gone awry. The idea was for government to engage in the formal purchasing of Indian lands, offering money or goods in return for each plot of ground. The Indians, in turn, might become efficient cultivators of what remained, accepting a gradual, well-planned transition from "savagery" to "civilization" and contributing their part to develop-

TABLE 3
Senate Vote on the Intrusion Act of 1807

	Federalists		Republicans	
	For	Against	For	Against
NEW ENGLAND	1	4	3	2
Vermont	0	0	1	1
New Hampshire	1	0	0	1
Massachusetts	0	2	0	0
Connecticut	0	2	0	0
Rhode Island	0	0	2	0
MID-ATLANTIC	0	2	6	2
New York	0	0	2	0
New Jersey	0	0	2	0
Pennsylvania	0	0	1	1
Delaware	0	2	0	0
Maryland	0	0	1	1
SOUTH ATLANTIC	0	0	6	1
Virginia	0	0	2	0
North Carolina	0	0	1	1
South Carolina	0	0	1	0
Georgia	0	0	2	0
SOUTHWEST	0	0	1	2
Kentucky	0	0	0	2
Tennessee	0	0	1	0
NORTHWEST (Ohio)	0	0	0	2
Total	1	6	16	9

Source: *Journal of the Senate*, 9th Congress, 2nd session, 145.

TABLE 4
House Vote on Intrusion Act of 1807

	Federalists		Republicans	
	For	Against	For	Against
NEW ENGLAND	0	16	0	10
Vermont	0	2	0	2
New Hampshire	0	4	0	0
Massachusetts	0	5	0	6
Connecticut	0	5	0	0
Rhode Island	0	0	0	2
MID-ATLANTIC	0	1	24	12
New York	0	0	4	7
New Jersey	0	0	2	4
Pennsylvania	0	0	12	1
Delaware	0	0	0	0
Maryland	0	1	6	0
SOUTH ATLANTIC	0	1	31	1
Virginia	0	1	15	0
North Carolina	0	0	8	1
South Carolina	0	0	6	0
Georgia	0	0	2	0
SOUTHWEST	0	0	2	2
Kentucky	0	0	2	2
Tennessee	0	0	0	0
NORTHWEST (Ohio)	0	0	0	1
Total	0	18	57	26

Source: Journal of the House, 9th Congress, 2nd session, 637–38.

ing commercial activity in the West. As Jefferson told the Miami chief Little Turtle: "I have . . . always believed it an act of friendship to our red brethren whenever they wished to sell a portion of their lands, to be ready to buy whether we wanted them or not, because the price enables them to improve the lands they retain, and turning their industry from hunting to agriculture, the same exertions will support them more plentifully." Deception lurked here, too, as Jefferson eagerly imposed pressure on tribes east of the Mississippi to cede control of their lands to the federal government. He relied on Secretary of War Henry Dearborn and Indiana territorial governor William Henry Harrison to force the process, by military means if necessary, and get Indian lands into the hands of legitimate white settlers as soon as possible. The acquisition of the Louisiana Territory also opened further possibilities of Indian "removal," which to easterners seemed a humanitarian alternative to assimilation and to westerners, in years to come, a desirable form of ethnic cleansing.[65]

The administration's resistance to "squatter rights" reflected a desire to buy time for this "humane" Indian policy to work "by commerce rather than by Arms," as Jefferson fashioned it in 1804. Even so, survival of Native Americans rested ultimately on their willingness to make concessions to land-hungry white men. Sacrificing their traditional lands, of course, provided no real solution for them, as they faced continuing pressure not only from white squatters but also from competing refugee tribes. Native Americans would be the definitive losers in the War of 1812, just as they had after the American Revolution. The once-formidable confederation in the Northwest, under Shawnee chief Tecumseh, would crumble after his October 1813 death in the Battle of the Thames. It would have no chance of reviving without continuing British support, especially in the face of relentless white migration after 1815.[66]

As time passed, Jefferson's position on squatters softened only to the point of hoping the government could prevent illegal settlement from spreading; he wished to avoid having to drive "intruders" out at gunpoint. Better "to prevent than to exclude," as Gallatin put it. This was part of the strategy behind revising the land laws to accommodate smaller buyers. Ideally, illegal "tenants" might purchase the land they occupied and become legal freeholders—a way to make "honest" men and women of them. But the approach got muddied after the purchase of Louisiana, which provided for several degrees of illegal settlers, ranging from those who had arrived under previous (Spanish or French) title to those flocking in all the time. Making fair distinctions required "a hand as careful as firm," Jefferson wrote in 1804, with proclamations long in advance of any potential act of force.[67]

In practice, however, any specified penalties or (mostly empty) threats of force against unregistered occupants still proved insufficient to deter new squatters in years to follow. Jefferson seemed to be running short on patience by the latter years of his presidency. In March 1807, he told Gallatin that conciliation between Congress and the squatters on federal lands would be more promoted by general words than by (yet another) "higgling bargain with the tenant." Only a few days before, Gallatin had instructed the federally appointed registers at two Mississippi territory land offices on procedures for enforcing the Intrusion Act of 1807, "so that the settlers may know generally that they will be removed and exposed to penalties if they do not apply for permissions, and that new settlements are altogether prohibited." But prevention of extensive unrest, especially squatter insurrections, remained a high priority. Settlers with even the most dubious claims now heard that "cheerful compliance" with the letter of the law "would not certainly injure their cause."[68]

It complicated matters for Jeffersonian leaders in Washington that no one knew how squatter regulation could operate in practice, short of the least politically desirable (and most expensive) option of deploying troops. The reply Gallatin received from one of the land registers, Thomas H. Williams, who ran the office west of Pearl River in the Mississippi Territory, provided a window onto the actual process at ground level. Distance had its advantages not only for squatters but also, at times, for the federal agents who sympathized with them. It is perhaps telling that Williams delayed as long as he could before replying to his superior in Washington. Instead of sending a number of administrative deputies to canvass the country, confront inhabitants, and determine whose claims held legitimacy, he deemed it better to "appoint particular places" where he could "meet the people in person, and soften, as far as possible, the irritation this law had excited, and to explain away misrepresentations, if any were afloat." Apparently, such face-to-face communication skills had the effect of easing tensions and keeping frontier order, even if they did not persuade a single illegal settler to leave. Identifying, in truth, with his frontier neighbors but obligated to follow federal mandates, Williams— and probably many like him—walked a political tightrope. "So far from witnessing any irregularity," he assured Gallatin, "I found nothing but a disposition to comply promptly with the law." This he attributed not to his own "feeble efforts," but "to the good sense and temperance of the people, and above all, to that sound republican maxim, that a law, although it may be deemed a bad one, is, nevertheless, until repealed, sovereign."[69]

That was, of course, what Gallatin wanted and probably needed to hear. But Williams's response to federal authority also conveyed sensitivity to the alternative political universe that squatting settlers in distant reaches of the West actually inhabited. Many were "alarmed at some of the provisions of this law; and indeed, from their situation, it is impossible they should be otherwise." Some had "commenced their improvements" three or four years before, "under the impression that the lands would be open for sale in a short time," and now they faced a distinct possibility that speculators would "compel them to pay for their own labor." Not all who had settled outside the law were "intruders" in the strict sense of the word, Williams strained to argue. "In seating themselves on the land, their views were to purchase whenever the United States would sell, and they have been extremely anxious for the arrival of this period." The "only boon" they wanted was "to purchase for a bona fide consideration"; this was "little indeed," Williams added, "and it is to be sincerely regretted that this little should be withheld." In concluding, he could not hold back personal feeling: "I have been among those people. In them, I see industrious citizens, honestly and honorably engaged in the acquisition of a competence for their families, and firmly attached to the principles of our govern-

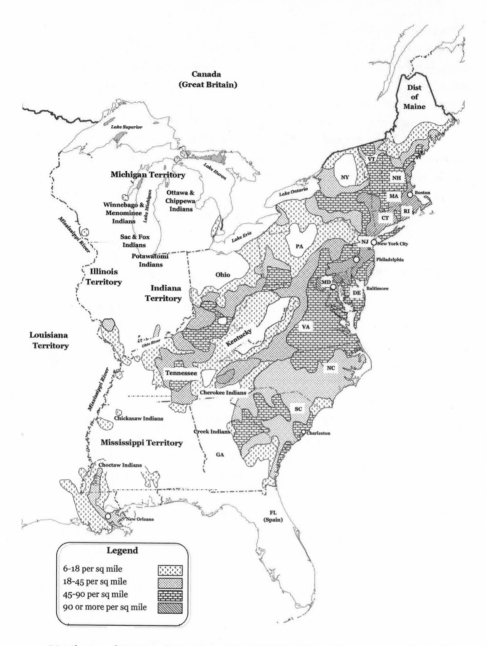

Distribution of U.S. Population East of the Mississippi River, 1810. Map drawn by Margot Gibson-Beattie.

ment." It would be a better policy, he insisted, "to quiet their fears, and put their anxieties to rest." A "right of preemption" remained the "only thing, under all circumstances, calculated to produce those happy effects."[70]

Even so, no serious answer to squatters' pleas nor governmental solution to the squatter "problem" came forth. The continuing flood of illegal settlers into frontier Indiana would help elicit from President James Madison a December 1815 proclamation once again threatening them with military removal, but given the performance of Madison's ill-prepared, underfunded army in the War of 1812, these brash Hoosiers scarcely trembled. John Badollet, the federal register at the land office in Vincennes, would complain that increasing numbers of squatters had been living under "the delusive hope of obtaining pre-emption rights." Indeed, in a January 1816 petition to Congress one such group entreated, "We still have hopes that surely the Guardians of our Liberties & rights will not suffer the farmes we have Made at such great inconveniancyes & riskes To bee Expose,d to publick Sail & the profits thereof Redownd to A welthy Republick."[71]

The congressional response to a petition from Amos Spafford in 1816 revealed the limited extent to which Jeffersonian lawmakers might consent to a "squatter's claim." Spafford had received a commission from President Madison in the spring of 1810 as collector for the port of Miami, on the Great Lakes. He had migrated with his family to the Miami Rapids of Lake Erie to assume the office. Once there, he purchased a tract near the foot of the rapids from a settler living, as it turned out, illegally, on federal land. He spent several hundred dollars to build a dwelling house and an administrative building where he performed his duties. Because the governmental "emoluments" for service in such a remote place had been "inconsiderable," he wrote, Spafford had turned part of his attention to "cultivation of the soil" to meet the needs of his family, and he made what he regarded as "considerable improvements" to the land over the next two years. With the surrender of Detroit during the War of 1812, he and his family had fled to the interior of Ohio, leaving "the greater part" of his property "to the mercy of the enemy." The British proceeded to plunder and destroy everything. Upon returning afterwards, Spafford went to the expense of rebuilding, and now he wanted a preemption right to a half-section of land to cover the costs of this second round of improvements.[72]

The House Committee on Public Lands finally took pity on Spafford and his beleaguered family, reporting him entitled to the relief he sought. "His appointment by the government, and the duties which by law he was required to perform was, if not an express, an implied permission to settle on the land of the United States," congressional lawmakers concluded. "The expenses which he necessarily incurred, and the losses sustained, distinguish the case of the petitioner from any of the numerous applicants for the right of preemption." Spafford's service to the nation, and the sacrifices his family had made therein, had placed him within the traditional profile of those deemed worthy to hold land by governmental favor. He had paid his dues as a citizen in a way that most others, by the social standards still in force, had not.[73]

—⁀ↄ—

If many settlers in the West, and their supposed Jeffersonian sympathizers, saw Federalists of the 1790s and early 1800s as aristocratic, arrogant, condescending, and unfriendly to democratic impulses, so too did many Federalists consider rapid settlement of the West by small, self-employed farmers as a threat to the community solidarity, prosperity, and economic potential in the East. Both groups recognized that westward expansion and the heavy, continuing influx of Celtic and central European immigrants strongly favored the Republicans. Overall, the differences between the two sides outstripped their similarities; most of the story lies in their conflict.

Still, on some issues of land policy Federalists and Jeffersonians agreed more than they disagreed. Both sides recognized that federal lands in general had to be sold and not given away, because servicing the national debt, paying the operating expenses of government, and possibly financing internal improvements projects required continuation of that source of revenue. Both sides understood that extending the territorial sphere of the United States far beyond the Mississippi River meant the considerable risk, under existing technology, that republican government might not work in a nation so vast. Both sides expressed anxiety that the settlement impulse could spin wildly out of the control of governing authorities, causing western lands to fill too rapidly, in haphazard fashion, and with men and women of too little economic means, questionable moral character, and dubious political loyalty. Neither side wanted the horror or the expense of a frontier held in check by Roman- or British-style military force. And, despite the lingering anti-statist impulses within Jeffersonianism, neither side thought in terms of letting society in the West develop free of influence imposed from the nation's capital.

As the United States moved beyond its "second war of independence" with Great Britain, the main philosophical and institutional contours of the national land system had become well established. Thanks to successful campaigns against Indian adversaries in the West during the War of 1812, the postwar period would bring the greatest westward migration in the early history of the republic.[74] But those new wilderness "seeds of population," similar to the ones that had worried George Washington, included not a few grains of class conflict. It needed only a jarring economic crisis to awaken the antigovernment radicalism that many of those seeds contained.

CHAPTER THREE

Rise of the Radical West

In early 1822, a letter to the editor from an anonymous writer in Worthington, Ohio, arrived at the ramshackle office of the Richmond (Indiana) *Weekly Intelligencer.* Just to show how scarce genuine, federally minted coin had become in the West, the letter said, "[T]here is but ONE quarter of a dollar in Worthington, and that has been borrowed so much from one to another to pay postages that it is worn smooth, and is now a twenty cent piece."[1]

Some say it helps to keep a sense of humor during hard times, but few westerners felt like laughing. "The situation of all the western country, as to monied matters, is truly deplorable," wrote a correspondent in Edwardsville, Illinois. Relief acts, newly established state banks, and scattered loan offices brought only temporary comfort. The private land market had collapsed. In Illinois and Missouri, public land sales nearly ceased. Federal auctions provided barely enough revenue to cover the expenses of surveying townships and running the land offices. The speculative profits for town developers evaporated. Smaller landholders dumped once valuable acres for small fractions of their earlier worth. The warning went out to any potential eastern investors: "hold as little property or make as few debts as possible west of the mountains, but more particularly west of the Ohio and Mississippi." Meanwhile, the fortunate few snapped up "valuable estates for trifles," the *Tennessee Clarion* reported. One example: in early 1820 a fine brick house in Cairo, Tennessee, that had sold a few years earlier at $1,500 fetched just a little over $100 in a sheriff's sale. Westerners on the short end of these events could easily agree that "extreme cases require extreme remedies."[2]

The ground-level impact on social relations and everyday behavior revealed the anguish. People accustomed to believing that some kind of rational order governed their universe could scarcely accept that profound adversity could befall truly innocent and virtuous persons. In matters of business, it strained popular credulity that "honest, industrious men" could encounter economic calamity through no fault of their own or defect of their personal character. "To be poor is the lot of many," a western columnist lamented, "but misfortune is apparently considered as a crime, and there is nothing more galling to a poor man of liberal mind than that kind of haughty arrogance which the rich and affluent assume towards him; more especially if he has once been in better circumstances, he feels it keenly—it sinks deep." For a poor man to be taken seriously by the more "respectable" people in the West, where opportunity supposedly abounded, had proven nearly impossible. "A man without money is a body without a soul,—a walking corpse, and a horrid spectre," observed the *Public Ledger* of Wayne County, Indiana, in its New Year's Day reflections for 1825. "His address is sad and awkward; his conversation tedious and troublesome. If he go to visit anyone, he never finds him at home; and if he open his mouth to speak, he is immediately interrupted, lest he should terminate his discourse by asking money."[3]

The Panic of 1819, the first major financial disaster of the early republic, devastated the fledgling economy of the West. The crisis also aggravated old fears that a far-reaching republic could not withstand the stress of factional squabbling and unrestrained economic growth. Western land promoter Edmund Dana said in 1819, "How large a range of territory, a free Republic, like that of the United States, can successfully extend its jurisdiction over, yet remains a problematical question; there being, in the history of man no parallel to our federal constitution." Republican experiments of bygone times—Greece, Carthage, Rome, and others—also had attempted "political confederacies," continued Dana, but "they were as ropes of sand, all rendered weak by their party patriotism, and their adherence to local interests." Abijah Hammond, on the other hand, saw the problem of size in far more personal and microcosmic terms. "I cannot refrain from repeating to you," he told his West Chester, Pennsylvania, neighbors in 1819, "that many of our farms are too large, and that the desire of working a large quantity of land without the means of fencing and cultivating it, has made many a poor man on a large farm, who might have lived in comfort, and acquired property upon a small one."[4]

The jarring depression that followed the financial catastrophe took several years to lift. Excessive speculation in public lands crowned the various forces that caused it. Many in Congress blamed the land-credit system both for the wild speculation and for encouraging westward expansion at a pace detrimental to the national economy as a whole. Federal credit had provided access to fertile government soil for men of moderate means, but it also had created a western society of people financially indebted to the federal government. With the onset of hard times, these people would be more likely than ever to resent the presence of such a government in their lives. The first efforts toward land reform during the Panic reverted to traditional and moralistic solutions. Congress aimed to eliminate frauds associated with credit sales and, assuming that insolvency denoted moral turpitude, to redeem the character of western settlers by selling only for cash on the barrelhead.[5]

When Congress went to work in 1820, lawmakers decided also to lower the minimum purchase to 80 acres and the minimum price to $1.25 per acre. The resulting Land Act of 1820, intended to encourage those deemed morally upright, left the advantage with middle-class buyers, including land speculators. Advocates of preemption, to legalize squatters' claims, still faced rigid opposition, as would proponents of Thomas Hart Benton's land price graduation proposal, formally unveiled in 1824.[6]

In the years that followed, however, a more radical reform position crystallized in the western states. Spurred as well by the economic crisis, this was one of several major manifestations of renewed sectional and ideological conflict in American politics. This radical belief indicted the early designers of the federal land system as wrongheaded: the role of auction sales should be greatly lessened, and government had no business playing such a paternalistic role in land distribution. Some advocates of this position, like Ninian Edwards in Illinois, insisted that central government relinquish its role almost entirely, ceding the public lands to the states where they lay. Most others, following the likes of Benton, asked that federal efforts be redirected toward building a more egalitarian society in the West, encouraging the poor to take lands quickly, at little or no cost, as opposed to favoring middle-class types who could pay auction prices. A memorial from the Missouri legislature in 1827 epitomized western radicalism: "Our country is peculiarly the asylum for the oppressed, and emphatically the poor man's home; every law then, which lifts him above the grade of tenant, which gives to him and his children a permanent resting and abiding place on the soil, not only subserves the cause of humanity, but advances and maintains the fundamental principle of our government." Reflected here again is the increasing confidence in the demands of squatters (or their sometimes less-needy spokesmen), who gained strength all the more, as in years to follow, from the power to vote.[7]

—co

Although the land bill of 1820 gave rise to the spectrum of reform approaches that would appear in the ensuing decade, historians have not fully examined its underlying rationale and political consequences. The traditional view of federal land policy makers that crystalized in the late 1780s and 1790s involved the belief that enlightened people, wisely placed in leadership roles, held an obligation to watch over the social and moral development of a fledgling national community, using political power as needed to set the proper course. The credit experiment introduced in 1800 had succeeded in stimulating sales and putting land into the hands of more farmers, but hard times had revealed credit to be more of a problem than a solution. "We cannot devote too much care to the revision of our land laws," the *Richmond Enquirer* counseled in October 1818, without specifying what fashion that revision might take, whose interests should benefit, and whose would suffer. The recent experience of war on American soil highlighted the need to tighten management of national revenue sources. Public lands—a huge potential source of that revenue—figured in the financing not only of transportation projects but also in building a navy and erecting forts, armories, and arsenals. The West, the *Enquirer* continued, would help to "discharge the public debts, and diminish the public burdens." But old school Jeffersonianism, which the *Enquirer* and its partisan, antinationalist editor, Thomas Ritchie, continued to espouse, taught that governance required "a sleepless vigilance, both in the executive and in congress, to detect all the frauds that may creep into their administration," implying that federal lawmakers had let down their guard against such corruption.[8]

As previous writers have said, opposition to excessive land speculation, and the corruption that went with it, at least partly inspired the land system reform in 1820. Various periodicals of the time charged the credit system with causing an economic tornado of "overtrading, luxury, and extravagance." It sounded like the old Harringtonian critique of burgeoning capitalism, the potential benefits and negative side-effects of which remained only dimly understood at best. Various suggestions for checking speculation, in addition to abolishing credit, included restriction of purchases to no more than 640 acres, on condition that buyers somehow demonstrate intent to settle on their land. Although such changes might have inhibited sales, they represented a determination to tighten policy and send westward more men and women of proven substance and social responsibility—"a much larger proportion of the most valuable classes of settlers," as *Niles' Register* tellingly phrased it. The financial assets of such citizens, and their presumed commitment to moral improvement, would foster a more concentrated population on the frontier. "Any further scattering of our people," the paper cautioned, "must tend to weaken the effective force of the nation without benefiting individuals."[9]

For perspective on intentions within the government, the best guide to the 1820 land bill might be its principal author, Senator Jeremiah Morrow of Ohio. Born in 1771 near Gettysburg, Pennsylvania, son of a Federalist farmer, young Morrow set out for the Ohio frontier at age 24, bought land in the Miami Valley, started his own farm, and became the proprietor of a flour mill. In 1800, as Ohio approached statehood, he won a seat in the territorial legislature and became associated with the antislavery "Chillicothe Junto." He sat also in Ohio's constitutional convention and later the state legislature. Morrow arrived in Congress as a commerce-minded Jeffersonian in 1803. During one of his toughest reelection campaigns, three years later, the opposing side falsely accused him of being a covert Federalist, an agent for speculators, and a believer in "aristocracy." Morrow replied that he stood for the "honest part of the community" and promised to keep "good old republican principles pretty much in fashion." Ohio legislators sent him to the Senate in 1813. As a Jeffersonian of the Gallatin mold, he promoted transportation development for Ohio, regarded the Cumberland Road and other internal improvement projects as "conducive to the interests of the western people," voted for the Second Bank of the United States in 1816, and aligned himself generally with the Ohio banking community. In years to come, he would support John Quincy Adams for president, voice Ohio's pro-tariff interests at the protectionist Harrisburg Convention of 1827, advocate Henry Clay's American System, serve as governor of Ohio, and eventually lead the state's Whig party.[10]

Morrow also became the chief specialist in Congress on land policy, sitting as chairman of the Public Lands Committees first of the House, then the Senate. Later, his Kentucky colleague John J. Crittenden would praise him as the man who had "long been our Palinurus in everything that related" to the public lands: "He has steered us safely through all its difficulties, and, with him as our helmsman, we have feared neither Scylla nor Charybdis." For some time, Morrow had favored reducing the acreage minimum and a further lowering of the minimum price per acre. Even before the Panic, he had urged that the government get out of the credit business that had produced an underclass of western debtors. Repeal of the 1800 provision would make land purchase more difficult for poorer men, but it would stabilize the frontier financially, a consideration all the more important in economically depressed times. Believing overspeculation in lands to be the cause of widespread private debt, he said his goal was a West dominated by the "independent landholder, secure and quiet in his possession."[11]

Morrow knew that land debts pulled capital away from areas needing it more. "In as far as the installments are collected," he argued, the system had operated "on the principle of rents collected, and withdrawn from circulation, or of a partial tax on that part of the community." Money that would otherwise have circulated in western localities drained steadily to the East. Under cash requirements, however, "the resources for payment would be drawn from other parts of the country, in as far as emigrants are the purchasers." Keep in mind that, apart from what they owed to the federal government, land buyers often borrowed further from private creditors, promising to pay in periodic installments, using whatever they did own as collateral.[12]

Morrow's intentions in land reform held consistent with earlier policy makers of the 1780s, which meant serving the interests of settlers who wanted to obey the laws, pay their bills, and do their best for their communities. One difference, however, was his insistence on reduced acreage and price minimums to accompany the end of credit sales. To institute the anticredit provision alone, he thought, "would virtually operate [as] an enhancement of the price, and lessen the facility of men of limited capital, of acquiring new lands for settlement and cultivation." But the phrase "men of limited capital" did not include the humblest migrants. Morrow's proposed changes worked to the interest of potential middle-class buyers with enough capital at hand to conclude purchases at the outset. He implied that men utterly lacking in finances, business sense, or farming know-how ought to stay in the old states. "The inducements of a long credit," Morrow contended, were "the principal causes of the failure of payment by purchasers of public lands." They had occasioned "purchases beyond the means of payment," owing to "the general disposition in men to anticipate the most favorable results from the products of their labor." Commercial fluctuations, unforeseeable by even "the most discerning," had made credit just too unreliable. He worried also about the passing of relief laws for previous credit buyers. Extending deadlines for payment without discontinuing sales would "produce an accumulation of the debt, and increase the difficulty in making final payments."[13]

One more dramatic, overarching consideration pervaded all of this: the political stability of the West. It was one thing for a government to be financially indebted to its people, as with Alexander Hamilton's funding program in 1790–1791, but something else indeed for citizens, especially those living far away, to be in perennial debt to the government. The history of frontier revolts in early America had shown the danger of creating whole districts where citizens owed tax collectors or creditors more than they could pay. All the more reason to make sure western settlers had a stake in their country while owing as little as possible for the privilege. As Morrow noted, "the principle of general policy required that charges on the people, for the necessary supply of revenue should be diffused over the whole society." By returning to cash sales, the injustice would be averted, and "the interest of subsequent purchasers would then be identified with that of the Government."[14]

The urgency of sidetracking frontier debtor unrest occupied the press as well. The *Kentucky Reporter* found the credit policy valuable in its capacity to "increase the scarcity of money [reduce the surfeit of bank-issued paper], and the embarrassments and bankruptcies of the speculators and banks." It had no sympathy for those "disappointed in their schemes of profit and monopoly." But the great danger of the policy, the writer observed, was that it produced debtors. This constituted "the most portentous evil that ever existed in America," one that even threatened a dissolution of union. Having more and more westerners indebted to government for their land recalled the scenario President Washington had feared in 1789, whereby western states and provinces, allying with Spain or Britain, could break off from the Union and go their separate ways. "Let numberless individuals of every description, from the most wealthy, intelligent and influential, down to those who are the reverse, be deeply indebted to the government of the Union, and will they not be in some measure disinclined to support it? " the *Reporter* asked. Moreover:

> Let nine-tenths of these persons reside in a particular section of the union; let that section be pre-eminently well situated for the formation of a separate government; let the existence of the debt depend on the continuance of the union; let the doctrine be advanced and enforced by every press and every orator in that quarter, that the other States had no just and natural right to the property for which the debt was incurred, while those States insist rigidly on an enforcement of the collection; and where will the bonds be found sufficiently strong to hold us together?[15]

What to do about excessive land speculation, a main reason for the Panic, raised a thornier problem. Morrow figured that the best remedy for this would be a reduced minimum price. "Experience has exploded the opinion," he said, "that injurious speculations might be discouraged, and monopolies prevented, by simply fixing a high price on the sale of the public lands." He thought the $2.00 minimum adopted in 1800 had prevented some of the more desirable farmers—"the industrious class, with small capital"—from purchasing. Like most in Congress, Morrow opposed a purely demand-based price strategy, like the price-graduation plan Benton would soon introduce. Yet, if farmers of "small capital" could not meet the government-imposed minimum, then the kind of social order he envisioned— one dominated by small producers and not speculators—could not materialize. "The demand for new land to bring into cultivation will in some manner be proportioned to the increase of population in the agricultural class of the community," he noted. "But the amount of sale will always depend (at any given price) on the capital destined to be so invested." In rural areas, the surplus product of agricultural labor ordinarily generated such capital, but if profits from farming proved insufficient to purchase new lands, then, Morrow concluded, it could "be fairly presumed that the price is excessive, and operates injuriously to the public industry."[16]

In short, Morrow thought the land system needed perfecting but not a lot of redesigning. Western society as he knew it was Ohio, the oldest public-land state, settled successfully enough under the old policies. If Congress refused to give lands away to settlers or allow preemption to accommodate "intruders," that was alright with Morrow. His outlook mirrored that of established, self-sufficient Ohio settlers—the sort he, himself, had typified twenty-five years earlier.[17]

Representative George Robertson, a lawyer who lived in Lancaster, Kentucky, championed the Morrow bill in the House. He, too, saw national interest as connected with the political and financial stability of the West. Robertson, then just 30 years old, had served in Congress since 1817. Like Morrow, he pushed for common school development back home, and, resigning his House seat in 1821 to return to the Kentucky legislature, he took a leading role in his state's anti-relief faction during the early 1820s. "[H]istory, and a knowledge of the nature of republican government," Robertson instructed fellow House members, taught that a "relation of creditor and debtor ought not to exist between the Government and the people." An indebted settler lacked personal independence. A "Pandora's box" of government largesse, he went on, had enticed him, stripped him slowly of dignity, and threatened the security of his loved ones. Union, community, family, and individual character—these, to both Robertson and Morrow, supplied the very foundation of a respectable, middle-class society.[18]

Also like Morrow, Robertson hoped those without the means to purchase western land, even at reduced price and acreage minimums, would stay in the East and maybe take up some occupation other than farming. Let it suffice, he thought, for settlers to purchase as little as 80 acres at auction prices starting at $1.25 an acre—attainable for many people of small means. This included "not that class of society who are in a state of pauperism, but those who are comparatively in a state of mediocrity, and are unable to purchase land for any other purpose than to occupy it." Many less-fortunate Americans, under these reforms, could still achieve enough financial substance to root themselves responsibly in a western community and pose no risk of dependence or threat of social disorder. "Neither the poor nor the rich have any right to complain, if credit should be refused," Robertson maintained. "If they are unwilling to purchase the public lands on the terms proposed, they will retain their money, and the public its land, and no injury is done to either."

Would ending credit stall population growth in the West? Robertson thought not: "If the cash system would prevent the emigration of any class of citizens," he argued, "it would be a class that would not be a very valuable accession to the strength, the morals, or wealth of the West; but who would only increase the Western debt, and diminish the real and substantial resources of the Western country." Should the federal government do much more than it had to accelerate western settlement? Again, Robertson's answer paralleled Morrow's: better to guide social development in balanced ways and a normal pace. "Let the principle of population and the rules that regulate and control it have their natural operation," he advised. "Do not endeavor to increase its fecundity or accelerate its results by artificial expedients. . . . Let it grow gradually and naturally, and it will be homogenous, and happy, and strong."[19]

—☙

Passing in April 1820—31 to 8 in the Senate, 149 to 23 in the House—the new land bill scuttled federal credit with overwhelming support from New England, middle Atlantic, and south Atlantic states. Western votes divided almost evenly, despite unanimous support from Ohio's representatives and senators. But the end of federal munificence would be long in coming. Between 1820 and 1832, Congress would pass eleven relief acts to aid pre-1820 buyers who could not meet payment deadlines. During congressional fights over relief legislation, western radicals expressed their increasing frustration with the historically restrictive principles of federal land policy. In the next ten years, these westerners, very different from Morrow and Robertson, would launch a strident, multifaceted campaign to undercut the national government's regulation of western social and economic development and dependence on public-land sales as a financial remedy.

While favoring generous relief to distressed settlers, Illinois senator Ninian Edwards, who had voted against the Land Act of 1820, condemned traditional land policy as designed primarily to soak the West for revenue. "Narrow considerations of interest, nice calculations of pecuniary profit, when the great question is one of legislative grace and relief, to a considerable portion of the community, seem to me to be out of place on this floor," growled Edwards. For him, a "just and liberal" policy meant more than financial indulgences to struggling buyers. But the breadth of Edwards's criticism implied far more than just alternative notions on land policy. He and other radicals on the geographical fringes of the country now voiced a whole different interpretation of republicanism, stridently antinationalist, more volatile and democratic than ever, and much more sympathetic with disaffected westerners. The system in place, he charged, had been designed to "suit the superannuated, corrupt, and tottering monarchies on the other side of the Atlantic." It never fitted "the dignity of a great, a youthful, a vigorous, and magnanimous Republic—a Republic founded on the affections of the people."[20]

In keeping with this inflammatory reaction, many westerners thought the Morrow-Robertson bill had ignored the real defects of the federal land system. Longer-settled Ohioans now seemed out-of-touch with the problems for settlers in the states and territories farther west than their own. Morrow's traditional perspective registered as incompatible with the developing radical outlook that reflected the banking and credit disputes, the fights for relief to victims of the depression of 1819, and a fermenting popular outrage against the perceived influence of privileged classes both in and outside of western society.

Robertson's Kentucky furnishes one of the best examples of how the Panic produced an eruption of class tensions. The Relief, or "New Court," Party pushed a radical program of currency inflation, stay and replevin legislation, and the dissolution of the state court of appeals, which had found many of the relief measures unconstitutional. Much of this reform activity targeted commercial interests and creditors, including groups connected with state banks and the Bank of the United States. The reaction to the Panic in Kentucky, and the conflict over economic remedies in the early 1820s, helped provide a foundation for Jacksonianism in the Southwest and gave notoriety to a pair of pro-relief journalists who would later play central roles in President Andrew Jackson's administration, Amos Kendall and Francis Preston Blair. Both identified with hard-money interests and approved of inflationary policies only as a temporary expedient to aid distressed small farmers and mechanics. During the same period, Henry Clay sided with the conservative "Old Court" faction and its anti-relief supporters, though the relief camp actually tried to claim him, too, until the autumn of 1826.[21]

Kentucky came along too early to be a public-land state, but the proximity of federal lands in neighboring states made land policy of pressing, though indirect, concern to Kentuckians. Largely because of pressure back home, both Kentucky senators, Richard M. Johnson and William Logan, and half of the Kentucky House delegation voted against the Morrow-Robertson bill. Yet, on May 11, 1820, during the early stages of the Panic and prior to the "relief war," the *Frankfort Argus*, Kendall's sheet, reacted favorably to the Land Act of 1820: "These changes it is believed will prove highly beneficial to the government, and not injurious to the people." Reflecting its editorial bias, the *Argus* singled out the possible benefit for lowly settlers but figured that it would be more for some, interestingly, than others: "The industrious and economical man with eighty acres, will soon find means to increase his farm without trouble to his government or embarrassment to himself."[22]

As the crisis for debtors worsened, however, the relief element in Kentucky complained that the Act of 1820 actually had stopped short of helping the poor, that its sponsors had addressed insufficiently the plight of public-land debtors in the states farthest west. Meanwhile, the movement for debtor relief gained momentum, and in December 1823, the *Argus* printed a sentiment more radical than its reaction to the 1820 Land Act: "one of the best means of perpetuating republican government, is the preservation of something like a general equality in the great body of the people, if it can be effected consistent with the right of property and the spirit of industrious enterprise." As in Virginia, entail laws had fallen by the wayside as relics of hierarchical aristocracy and an "overgrown wealth and opulence" incompatible with a republican revolution. But on the other end of the social spectrum, why not prevent extremes of agricultural poverty from occurring?

"Would it not be equally politic and just, to exempt from execution a small portion of a debtor's land sufficient to maintain his family by labor?" the *Argus* queried. Such a change "would in great measure, prevent the increase of paupers, convicts and delinquents in the collection of public taxes, promote habits of industry and love of country in the rising generation of the poor," Kendall added.[23]

Soon after the 16th Congress began its second session in November 1820, Senator Johnson introduced a resolution from the Kentucky legislature expressing views that would later appear in the *Argus*. The legislature urged that debtors be permitted to relinquish portions of public lands they had not paid for and receive outright title to the remainder as their legitimate purchase. As justification, the resolution pointed to "the unexpected depression in the price of labor and of property, the stagnation of trade and the derangement of the local currency in the Western States." In Kentucky, the Panic, its causes grasped only vaguely and its effects still uncertain, had "darkened the fairest prospects." Likely enough, this plea spoke, too, for Kentucky land speculators financially overextended when the Panic hit, but the resolution also criticized the Land Act of 1820 for not enabling debtors to sell any part of their purchases before paying for the whole. Those debtors often included ordinary settlers who, themselves, "speculated" on land other than their own farms.[24]

Few in Congress could have missed the significance of Johnson's being the senator who defended the Kentucky resolution most vigorously. As an affiliate of the relief cause, Johnson's state loyalty and desire for political advancement explained part of his political behavior. But his remarks in the Senate also anticipated the views he would manifest later in consistent support of Benton's land reform program. Johnson emphasized the harshness of the 1820 law toward settlers unable to complete their payments: "unless some person shall advance cash in hand for what is due, the land reverts to the United States, and the whole of the money paid upon it, improvements and all, are forfeited." Relief to land purchasers supposedly would rescue these debtors from the "grasp of penury and famine, in the land of plenty." Like Benton and eventually Presidents Jackson and Van Buren, Johnson stressed not the sectional but the nationwide benefit of policies to assist lower-class westerners: "To them we owe our national safety and prosperity. Virtue and independence, when exiled from every other class, find an asylum with them."[25]

―⁂―

"INTERNAL IMPROVEMENT, being one of the chief objects of this Journal, we have with pleasure recorded Mr. Maxcy's report on PUBLICK SCHOOLS," the *American Farmer* told its readers in Baltimore, March 1820. "If all Legislators possessed his public spirit, enlightened and directed by equal intelligence—*Maryland* would no longer shut her eyes on the example of New-York, Pennsylvania, Vir-

ginia, and other States." The subject was education, which all states and communities needed. But within a few years, coming across a westerner with so high an
opinion of Maryland's Virgil Maxcy might be harder than finding hair on a frog.[26]

The controversy arose in early 1821, when a committee of the Maryland state legislature, Maxcy its chairman, issued a report urging federal appropriations of public lands to encourage educational improvement throughout the nation. Maxcy,
a noted legal scholar, born in Attleborough, Massachusetts, in 1785, graduate of
Brown University and the Litchfield Law School, had made his mark in the Maryland Senate as a champion of rural districts, where funding public schools proved
difficult. His report of January 30, 1821, contended that the public domain had
been, under terms of the several deeds of cession, intended for the "equally liberal"
and "common benefit" of the Union. It violated principle, then, to set aside a section of each surveyed township—a one thirty-sixth part—for western benefit only,
as provided in the Ordinance of 1785. These specific educational grants, Maxcy
argued, benefited exclusively the new states and territories, not the "national" purposes embodied in the precedent-setting Virginia Cession of 1784. "Whether as acquired by purchase, conquest, or cession," the report contended, all federal lands:

> Are emphatically the *common property of the union*. They ought to enure, therefore,
> to the common use and benefit of *all* the states, in just proportions, and cannot be
> appropriated to the use and benefit of any particular state or states, to the exclusion
> of the others, without an infringement of the principles, upon which cessions from
> the states are expressly made, and a violation of the spirit of our national compact, as
> well as the principles of justice and sound policy.[27]

The Panic of 1819 had hit Maryland with particular severity. The crash of the
Baltimore financial firm of Smith and Buchanan had staggered the city, ruining in
turn more than a hundred merchants and putting thousands out of work. The state
had tried to prop up its banks by prohibiting the exchange of specie for Maryland
bank notes at less than par. The law was easy enough evade. Besides, protecting
inferior money could only drive specie out of the state and worsen the crisis. Eager
to raise public revenue, Maryland lawmakers also had levied a tax on any bank not
chartered by the state legislature, primarily targeting the Baltimore branch of the
Second Bank of the United States. That move led to the controversial Supreme
Court ruling in *McCulloch v. Maryland* (1819), which vindicated the Second Bank of
the United States. Following sometimes dubious advice, Maryland had lent enormous sums of public money over the years to various private contractors who had
subsequently defaulted. One of these, the Potomac Company, chartered in 1785 to
improve the navigability of the Potomac River, owed the state about $40,000 that
it could never repay. One editorial assessment in 1822 held that "upwards of three

hundred thousand dollars of the State's capital" had been lost this way during the previous five years, enough "to awaken investigation among the people of Maryland in regard to their financial affairs."[28]

Providing for Maryland's future appears to have been the primary intent of Maxcy's committee. In years before 1819, the state's legislature had hoped to establish a common school fund, but after the Panic that possibility looked remote. Maxcy figured that an alliance including most of the sixteen non–public land states would be enough to push an otherwise reluctant Congress to act in their favor, despite enraged western opposition. The principle "too plain and too obviously just to be disputed," he said, was "that the *common property* of the *union* ought to be applied to *national purposes* only, and that when it is appropriated to the use and benefit of any *particular* state or states, to the *exclusion* of the others, the spirit of our national compact and the principles of justice are violated." With the prospect of state appropriations for education dimming by the day, his Maryland committee recommended that Congress earmark public land grants for each of the older states, corresponding to one thirty-sixth part of their individual land area. In addition to the allotment for common schools, he urged another one-fifth of every thirty-sixth part for new eastern colleges and academies. According to *Seybert's Statistical Annals*, Maryland contained 8,960,000 acres of land. Under the Maxcy plan, the state would be entitled to 248,888 acres of land in the West to support its local school system, along with an extra 49,777 acres to assist the public financing of higher education.[29]

The report anticipated the protest of westerners that these lands lay situated within jurisdictional limits of the newer states and territories. This made them no less the common property of all states together, Maxcy insisted. As he saw it, "the interest which a citizen of an Atlantic State has in them, as a part of the property of the Union, is the same as the interest of a citizen residing in a State formed out of them." Federal lands had been as legitimate a source of national revenue as tariffs on foreign commerce, but land grants to encourage learning, like the one thirty-sixth provision in surveyed townships, had gone only to the West. What if Congress were to appropriate one thirty-sixth part of the revenue collected from foreign commerce in the ports of Baltimore, New York, Boston, Norfolk, Charleston, and Savannah to support common schools only in those six states? That would be no more unjust, argued Maxcy, than the current policy of appropriating one thirty-sixth part of the public land in Ohio, Indiana, Illinois, Tennessee, Mississippi, and Alabama for the exclusive benefit of *their* schools.[30]

Proceeds from land sales received into the federal treasury had always been applied to national projects of some sort—debt retirement, military expenditures, funding for the Cumberland Road, and so forth. But Maxcy's plan went much further, asking that Congress distribute the actual lands for education and allow the states receiving them to carry out sales themselves, on terms of their choosing. "It is undoubtedly true," he justified, "that emigration is injurious to the Atlantic States, and to them alone." Indeed, if eastern population emptied too rapidly, the value of property, goods, and services left behind would plummet. Not that westward emigration should be restrained, but why should not eastern states enjoy the same revenue provision for education that western states had received?[31]

The Maxcy report had seized upon one of the most glaring ambiguities of the federal land system. The one-thirty-sixth provision in the 1785 Ordinance exclusively benefited the public land states, an act of favoritism that contradicted the whole "common good" principle. If states coexisted on an "equal footing," then any advantage extended to one, by ordinary rule, had to be offered to all. If the "first duty" of any government was to encourage a "general diffusion of knowledge," Maxcy argued, then Congress should allocate impartially the national resources available to that end.[32]

Other eastern states, weakened by the Panic and just as eager to finance their common schools, quickly followed Maryland's lead. After adopting the report and the resolutions accompanying it, the Maryland legislature sent copies to governors of other states, asking them to seek approval from their respective legislatures. Like Maryland, the smallest state in the Union, Rhode Island, had never held a public domain of its own. One newspaper in Providence, calling the Maxcy plan "intimately connected with the best interests of the State," excitedly calculated that Rhode Island's share would be 33,705 acres—28,088 of that for common schools and 5,617 for academies and colleges. Virginia stood to receive the most—1,493,332 acres. By the end of January 1822, a year after publication of the Maxcy report, the legislatures of New Hampshire, Rhode Island, Connecticut, Vermont, Maine, New Jersey, Delaware, Georgia, North Carolina, and Kentucky—along with the *North American Review, Niles' Weekly Register,* and the *National Intelligencer*—had all thrown complete support behind the Maryland plan. Secretary of War John C. Calhoun, who frequently corresponded with Maxcy, also liked the scheme.[33]

Unsurprisingly, no new state would ever favor the plan, but it dismayed Maxcy to encounter opposition in the Northeast, first in New York, then Massachusetts. Both saw Maryland's actions as stirring dangerous sectional jealousies too soon after rival sides in Congress had agreed to compromise on the admission of Missouri in 1820. New York, in a counter-report drafted in mid-1821 by Gulian C. Verplanck, expressed substantive reservations. Verplanck, born in 1786, a King's College graduate known as a newspaper writer and lawyer, served in the New York Assembly from 1820 to 1822. There, educational policy became his chief interest, too; however, his reputation as a free trader, which would earn him a seat in Congress in 1824, probably accounts most for his opposition to the Maryland proposal. Distributing lands among the old states, as Maxcy had urged, or just land revenues among all the states, could be an antiprotectionist's nightmare. That would leave only high tariffs to carry the burden of national treasury needs.[34]

The first of Verplanck's objections contended that the older states had already received due consideration for the lands appropriated for western education. The additional revenue accruing to the federal treasury as a result of the increased value of those lands in the West, Verplanck said, was compensation enough for the East. The increased value not only induced sale at a higher price but also made the lands attractive to financially responsible types of settlers who would be more inclined to make "prompt payment." "The [western land] reservations complained of," he concluded, "ought therefore to be regarded, not as a partial donation, but as a judicious arrangement calculated and intended to increase the value" of that common fund held for the benefit of all.[35]

Anticipating that objection, Maxcy had already cautioned that the argument would not address his central point: that the benefits of public lands were not being divided equally. "This increase of value," Maxcy wrote, "has not been an *exclusive* benefit to the Atlantic states, but a benefit *common* to all the states, eastern and western; while the latter still enjoy exclusively the advantage, derived from the appropriations of land for literary purposes." The West had gained directly from land disposition, the East only indirectly. Increases in land worth that resulted from emigration and settlement provided "peculiar benefit" to citizens of the new states—in building local tax bases, for example.[36]

A second Verplanck complaint, however, reflected the concern of eastern moralists for the developing character of the West. "It is surely of the deepest interest to the welfare, the peace, and good order of the whole union," he wrote, "that the states every day springing up in the west should not hereafter be peopled by a race possessing nothing of civilization, but its vices and its arts of destruction." In this way, too, the common fund of public lands already served the national interest. Thus, by providing a section of each western township for public education, founders of the land system had wisely made an exception to the principle of equal benefit. In Verplanck's view, it was not for the betterment of the West alone that these "liberal and judicious donations" were made, but for the good of all citizens "who should, from time to time, be induced to seek happiness and competence in the new territories." At the same time, the older states would be relieved the "evils always, in some degree, attendant on a crowded population."[37]

In truth, of course, eastern profit from western growth was tangential and impossible to measure, and no one could prove that current policy had saved the West from barbarism. In any case, the Senate Public Lands Committee rejected the Maryland proposal without waiting for all states to weigh in. The Senate committee majority, guided by a westerner, Jesse B. Thomas of Illinois, agreed that such grants to the non–public land states would damage the West too much. In Thomas's words, the new states "would have an excessive proportion of their superfices taken up with such donations, leaving but a small part of the land in each subject to taxation or to settlement, except at the will of other sovereign states." The report noted Verplanck's observation that educational grants to the new states immediately enhanced the value of remaining lands, whereas grants to older states did not assure this. And yet, Thomas conceded that it might be "just and expedient" to grant a "per centum" of the revenue from public land sales to the older states, the amount to be apportioned according to population. A certain redeeming value had been found in Maryland's idea after all: the hint that Congress might agree to distribute land proceeds, but never the actual lands.[38]

Still, the western states boiled with rage. Thomas warned against empowering eastern states to control the terms of sale and settlement in any part of the new states. In his annual message of December 1821, Ohio governor Ethan Allen Brown denounced the Maryland initiative in more extreme terms, as would the Ohio legislature, even suggesting a sovereign right of its own to federal lands lying within state limits. Many westerners already had reified the federal land system as an implacable villain, wielding authoritarian control over the amount and location of lands offered for sale and the minimum purchase restrictions, setting auction-price requirements higher than the market value of many tracts, being stingy with funding for internal improvements, stalling on school grants, prohibiting the states from taxing federal land, and so on. The Maxcy plan seemed to add further insult to the series of perceived injuries inflicted by an insensitive, eastern-led policy-making establishment. "Is it not uncommon," an Illinois newspaper queried in January 1822, "to see an elder child squander away the property given him by an indulgent parent, and at the death of this father come in and boldly claim an equal share of the inheritance with the younger children who had received nothing?" The analogy seemed to apply: "The old states have sold their land for little or nothing, and in many instances given it away to whoever would settle it."[39]

Even though its failure to win over Massachusetts and New York already had bled much of the steam from the movement, passions erupted again when the Maxcy scheme came up for debate on the U.S. Senate floor early in 1822. There, Ninian Edwards launched a two-hour harangue against a resolution by Maryland's Senator Edward Lloyd that had favored the Maxcy position. Furthermore, Edwards would hear nothing of any alternative schemes, such as distribution of land proceeds as opposed to the actual lands.[40]

In Edwards's view, the several cessions that constituted the public domain carried three crucial stipulations: first, that Congress alone regulate the granting and settling of open lands; second, that the lands be settled and not deliberately withheld; third, that after settlement they be admitted to the Union as "distinct republican states." Land disposition had to reflect these aims. Congress made land regulations, but it was in no way empowered to exploit the public land states for the benefit of the old states. Any division of proceeds among members of the Union would only bring the higher land prices that westerners dreaded; it would reflect no common purpose that he could see. "If ever the day shall arrive," Edwards roared, "when the authority of this Government shall be admitted to extend to such objects, then adieu to all State sovereignty. It will be completely swallowed up in the great vortex of a grand consolidated National Government."[41]

Six years later, Edwards, by then governor of Illinois, would extend this logic to a more radical conclusion: the East was no more entitled to *any* proceeds from western land sales than it was to shares of the actual soil. Western states had exclusive right to lands within their borders. Others had voiced this idea, but Edwards meant to champion it. Maxcy's reasoning had helped to define his objective. The new West had been promised an "equal footing" in the Union, but the existing arrangement mocked that principle, the Illinois governor would argue. As long as the national government retained control over lands inside new states, extracting revenue from emigrants' pockets, there could be neither true equality nor real economic freedom for westerners. The only real corrective, then, was denationalization of all public lands lying within state limits.[42]

—◦—

While western resentment simmered, other new-state leaders contemplated different kinds of changes to the increasingly despised federal land system. While Kentucky illustrated some of the class-based and ideological connections between local relief issues and land policy revision, its neighboring state of Tennessee became the testing ground for one of the most hotly debated reform concepts to appear in Congress during the 1820s: the land price graduation scheme, politically synonymous with Senator Thomas Hart Benton of Missouri. While both Tennessee senators had voted for the Morrow-Robertson bill in 1820, four of its six House representatives joined in the 23 nays. Represented here, again, was a strong western belief that the basic structure of the federal land system needed not just a little tweaking but a radical overhaul in both theory and application.

Benton was born in 1782 near Hillsboro, North Carolina, the oldest son of Jesse Benton, a lawyer and plantation owner, who died in 1791, leaving a widow, Ann Gooch Benton, and eight children. Ten years later, the family moved to a 40,000-acre tract of undeveloped land that they owned 25 miles south of Nashville, Tennessee. With the aid of about twenty slaves, they farmed 3,000 acres of this semi-wilderness at West Harpeth; the rest, eventually known as Benton Town, they parceled out among a small colony of tenants. In Tennessee, Benton studied law and became an attorney, a state senator, and an advocate of judicial reforms. In 1815, he moved to St. Louis, Missouri, where he practiced law, edited the *Missouri Enquirer*, and built a popular following by promoting lead mining, fur trading, and slaveholding interests. Selected as one of the state's first two United States senators after Missouri's admission to the Union, Benton advocated western interests as he saw them. That meant supporting small farmers by pushing for internal improvements and cheap land, opposing paper currency, and condemning banking practices in general. Like others in the West who would join the Jacksonian movement, Benton favored a society based chiefly on agriculture and populated as rapidly as possible by whoever might come, regardless of their economic means or status and, perhaps most critical, free from governmental restraint.[43]

Benton's political alignments before the depression of 1819, as a spokesman for elite French merchants in St. Louis and their fur trade, made him an unlikely defender of poor men's interests. By the time he left for Washington, however, the Panic had ravaged Benton's personal finances and those of many Missourians. Bank failures converted him to his "hard money" position and gave him the moniker that historians have carried down the ages: "Old Bullion." His agricultural constituents blamed their distress not only on Missouri's men of means but also on eastern creditors, particularly the Second Bank of the United States. With the Panic quickly eroding his own and Missouri's shaky faith in federal authority, Benton grew increasingly sympathetic to the agrarian, strict-constructionist perspective of the "Old Republicans," like that of his close friend, Nathaniel Macon of North Carolina. Benton now gained repute throughout the West as advocating a new wrinkle in land policy—"graduation," or a radical lowering of the price of federal lands according to their length of time on the market, with an annual reduction of 25¢ per acre before finally being offered free to actual settlers.[44]

However much it lightened his own pocketbook, the Panic provided the key event of Benton's career. It produced the "hobby"—graduated land prices—he would ride for the remainder of his time in national politics. According to the Missouri senator, the federal relief laws passed in the wake the 1820 Land Act lacked two crucial features: "*first*, a pre-emptive right to all first settlers; and, *secondly*, a periodical reduction of price according to the length of time the land should have been in market, so as to allow different prices for different qualities, and to accomplish in a reasonable time the sale of the whole." Benton griped that preemption had been rejected in 1820 without due consideration, preventing so much as the prospect of eventual success. "Not even a report of a committee could be got in its favor," he complained, "nothing more than temporary provisions, as special favors, in particular circumstances." This, of course, had been true since the beginning of the republic. Unlike most federal policy makers in previous years, Benton saw no danger in the concepts he advocated. He thought settlement before purchase an "equal advantage" to both the migrant and his government. With preemption, he argued, "the settler gets a choice home in a new country, due to his enterprise, courage, hardships and privations in subduing the wilderness: the government gets a body of cultivators whose labor gives value to the surrounding public lands, and whose courage and patriotism volunteers for the public defence whenever it is necessary."[45]

Unlike preemption, which various westerners had urged since the 1780s, the graduation idea had scarcely been mentioned at the national level before the 1820s. It had come up briefly in the Confederation Congress, but no one picked up on it. The exact origins of Benton's graduation scheme remain unclear, but one version of it seems to have developed as a result of legislative trouble in the disposal of state lands located in the Hiwassee (River) District of southeastern Tennessee. After acquiring title to this rugged, barely arable 40-mile block in 1819, the state adopted a rectilinear survey procedure similar to that of the federal government. Despite more liberal alternatives, including an initial graduation proposal, the legislature finally instituted a credit sales plan like the federal one in operation until the Land Act of 1820. Thus, thought Benton, Tennessee repeated the mistake of Congress and produced its own class of public-land debtors. In late 1820, with the Panic spreading, the state Assembly searched for a way to relieve indebted purchasers and terminate its credit system, as Congress had done. During consideration of possible solutions, James C. Mitchell of Athens, Tennessee, a resident of the Hiwassee District and a member of the joint land committee of the legislature, proposed a graduated reduction of land prices to replace credit sales. The idea probably made sense for the Hiwassee area, one of the most rugged and inaccessible in all of Tennessee, where inferior parcels of potential farmland would not have been appealing enough to attract many buyers.[46]

Mitchell found policy makers of his era "too much prone to stick to old precedents, and to follow long-settled practices, without troubling . . . with an inquiry into the propriety of either," and he viewed the national land system as "erroneous in its inception and ruinous in its practices." He had worked out and proposed the Tennessee graduation plan in 1819. The idea was simply to lower the minimum prices on unsold tracts in proportion to their length of time on the market. This assumed that desirable lands naturally sold for high prices, protecting the value of choice tracts already in private hands. More important, the concept allowed men of small means to acquire lower-grade lands at little cost, avoiding the burden of credit obligations to any government.[47]

The scheme met strong opposition from critics in Tennessee who feared that such a system would prevent land from selling except at the lowest allowed rates, causing heavy speculation. Time after time, graduation failed in the Assembly. Meanwhile, Mitchell retired from the Tennessee House to practice law until his election to the United States House of Representatives in 1824. Finally, in 1823, with the help of Mitchell's friends in the Assembly, the graduation bill became law in Tennessee, applying to lands in the Hiwassee District that had remained at market since the opening of sales in 1820. The law gave settlers already occupying the district a six-month window in which to purchase land there at $1.50 per acre. For a three-month period after that, Tennessee was to offer the lands for general sale at the same price. It would then lower the price to $1.00 per acre and offer it first to occupants for three months, then to general buyers. Gradual reductions would continue until reaching a final minimum of 12½¢ per acre on remaining tracts.[48]

Benton's proposals in the U.S. Senate substantially resembled that of Mitchell and his cohorts in Tennessee. It is uncertain exactly how and when Benton's interest in land policy began, but he wrote much later that his concern about land questions antedated his migration to Missouri in 1815 and had sharpened during the period he spent as a member of the Tennessee Assembly. Although he did not attribute to others any credit for the graduation idea, Benton later introduced correspondence from Tennesseans, including Mitchell, to advance his Senate case for the scheme. A February 28, 1828, letter from Nathaniel Smith, an entry-taker for the Hiwassee District, described the impact of the graduation law in his state. "I have no doubt," wrote Smith, "that, if the Congress of the United States could witness the good effect that this law has had on the citizens of our little district, . . . your bill would pass almost unanimously." He reported that graduation had stimulated the desire of "all classes of citizens" to own land in the area. The policy also seemed to have had a regenerative effect economically and morally. Smith said he could identify many residents of his district who, before the reductions, "were not worth fifty dollars on earth," but as soon as land came within their means, they demonstrated enough "industry and good management" to purchase land, build good homes, and become "respectable members of society." Robert Baird, in an 1832 advice tract for would-be emigrants, one of many published in this period, came to the same conclusion about the Hiwassee district, calling it "the Switzerland of the United States," containing by that time "an active, industrious, frugal and moral population."[49]

In a March 29, 1828, letter to Benton, Mitchell in Tennessee agreed with Smith's basic assessment. No federal system of land disposition could "make as many freeholders united to the soil of the country that they have to maintain and defend, without being burdened and oppressed, and at the same time yield so much to the treasury, as a well-digested graduating system," Mitchell contended. "It will in a short time bring all the refuse lands into usefulness." This, he thought, had proven true in Tennessee: "[T]he refuse hills and mountains which lay north and east of the congressional reservation line for half a century, and viewed as worth nothing, have been appropriated by the people under the graduating system of that State." Interestingly, Mitchell thought the liberalization of Tennessee law for these marginal, if not worthless, lands had not undermined the revenue dimension of state land policy. The boost to land sales from reduced prices had brought a "handsome sum of money" into the Tennessee treasury. Smith's February 28 letter had estimated that sum at $276,200. Once in private hands, the same lands would provide further state revenue by way of annual land taxes.[50]

Benton could as easily have noted the need for a graduation of land prices in parts of his adopted state of Missouri, where the idea appealed for the same reasons and to the same sorts of people as in Tennessee. The non-Indian population of the Missouri Territory had tripled in the decade following the War of 1812, most of the new settlers avalanching in from Kentucky and Tennessee. These newcomers at first detoured around both the New Madrid lowlands and the high ground of the Ozarks, the former ravaged by the massive earthquake and aftershocks of 1811–1812 and the latter too rough, remote, and infertile for lucrative commercial-type farming. In neither case could the lands justify the federal minimum price of $1.25 an acre. The Ozarks held appeal to at least one group, however: migrants from the Appalachian highlands of Tennessee, who found there an environment much like the mountain ways they had known. Even if residents on Missouri's "refuse lands" would more likely squat than purchase, a graduated price scheme might coax some of them back within the law—and activate them politically in Benton's Missouri constituency. Besides, Benton would take any edge he could to undercut Missouri's other senator, David Barton, who not only opposed the graduation-donation concept but favored the nationalist political economy of John Quincy Adams and Henry Clay.[51]

The graduation idea quickly drew supporters also in the Northwest, where the Panic had brought desperate pleas for congressional relief to buyers of government land. The economic crisis especially devastated Indiana, a public land state, admitted to the Union in 1816. The value of grain, the state's main product, had declined precipitously. Hoosier land values had plummeted, sometimes wiping out entire towns. Under pressure from the Bank of the United States, Indiana's vital Farmers' Bank, at Madison, suspended specie payments in the autumn of 1818, then finally closed its doors in 1820. The three branches of the state bank at Vincennes, which had grown rapidly during the postwar boom and held the federal deposit in Indiana, also put specie payments on hold during the Panic, causing the federal government to withdraw its deposits in July 1820. Despite efforts of financial and political notables from southern Indiana, including Governor Jonathan Jennings and congressional leaders James Noble and William Hendricks, opposition to the Vincennes bank grew, eventually contributing to the Jacksonian movement.[52]

In the Hoosier state, opposition to the Land Act of 1820 reflected, in part, a rivalry between state and national views in political economy. The traditionalist approach of Morrow and company with regard to land reform did not suit Indiana financial interests. Indiana's Senator Noble, of Brookville, and the state's only member of the House of Representatives, Hendricks, from Madison, voted against Morrow's land bill. On February 2, 1820, Noble presented in the Senate a petition from the Indiana General Assembly requesting that Congress retain the credit system, which would leave debtors borrowing from Peter to pay Paul, a situation indirectly beneficial to state money-lending interests more than federal cash sales. As a member of the House Public Lands Committee, Hendricks steadfastly opposed the Morrow-Robertson position for the same reason; in 1827, he would advocate cession as an alternative to congressional land management. Noble and Hendricks saw Congress as pulling the financial rug out from under western creditors at a crucial time. The result in Indiana was that, by late 1820, the widespread failure of banks brought intensified appeals from the state for congressional sympathy toward western land debtors. On November 28, Governor Jennings urged Indiana legislators to implore Congress "to relieve actual settlers from the forfeitures of their homes, their money, and their labor, which without relief must be inevitable."[53]

In 1824, Benton introduced his graduation bill on the premise that, for much western land, a price of $1.25 per acre, the 1820 minimum, could not be justified. Like Mitchell of Tennessee, he assumed that more productive lands would always sell before poorer lands. While preemption allowed poor men access to unused land with the right to purchase later at the minimum price, graduation would open much unclaimed land to migrants at levels far below the minimum price. "It is certainly a fair principle that land, like every thing else offered for sale, should be sold for what it is worth, Benton wrote in reply to a private correspondent in April 1825, "and as all individual settlers conform to that rule, it is difficult to conceive a reason why the Federal government, the greatest of all land sellers, should not do the same."[54]

In theory, graduation also encouraged compact settlement, proposing to keep an already huge and diffuse western population from spreading too widely. Benton said the plan offered "strong motives to many a parent to enlarge his domain in such a manner as to provide for the settlement of his children around him." It would, he claimed, "check a spirit of avarice which severs the dearest ties and blood friendship in quest of remote wilds" and instead "foster the spirit of fellowship and kindred feeling by uniting in harmonious neighborhoods friends and kindred and enable them to realize in a much shorter time, the rich advantages and social enjoyments of our parent States." According to graduation advocates in the Illinois legislature, selling all land only at market prices had caused the "tide of population" to be "diverted into a thousand channels, and suffered to roll over immense regions, creating feeble and thinly scattered settlements, and leaving extensive tracts of wilderness behind." In a scattered population, the Illinoisians contended, "public institutions are seldom established; systems of education cannot be matured; moral restraints are tardily enforced; laws are feebly executed; and revenue raised with difficulty."[55]

After Benton's bill appeared in the Senate, western anticipation of land price reductions began to approach fever pitch; leaders in the new states envisioned vast political, social, and even military benefits. As Finis Ewing, a Presbyterian minister in Kentucky, wrote to Henry Clay in August 1825,

> There is one particular subject which the people of the West, particularly the States of Missouri, Illinoise, Indiania &c. feel a deep, very deep interest in—. That is the graduation of the price of publick lands— I am persuaded that nine-tenths, perhaps more, of the people are exceedingly anxious that such a law should pass and I am persuaded Sir, if the president could make personal observations on the situation &c, of the several States & Territories in which the Gov ment hold lands, he would think that such a measure would be *wise, humane, & Just.*

In 1827, Indiana Governor James B. Ray expressed a related view on the security advantages of a compact, contented, and landed population: "The government being composed of the people in it, will be strong and effective in proportion to the number of free holders it contains. Where the citizen, the soldier and the land owner are combined in the same person, you will find him defending his pass against the encroachments of the enemy like Leonidas at Thermopolae." Ray also favored donating refuse lands to the poor "as a gift, in preference to tenancy."[56]

In the Senate, Benton claimed his land policy to be in perfect sync with republicanism—but hardly that of the republic's founders. His professed social concern operated from bottom-up, as opposed to their top-down. "Tenantry is unfavorable to freedom," the Missourian told his still-cautious 1820s colleagues. "It lays the foundation for separate orders in society, annihilates the love of country, and weakens the spirit of independence." The farming tenant had no stake in society—"no country, no hearth, no domestic alter, no household god." A freeholder, by contrast, was "the natural supporter of a free government; and it should be the policy of republics to multiply their freeholders, as it is the policy of monarchies to multiply tenants." The way to advance and maintain a republic, then, was to "multiply the class of freeholders; pass the public lands cheaply and easily into the hands of the people; sell, for a reasonable price, to those who are able to pay; and give, without price, to those who are not."[57]

Meanwhile, western demands for preemption legislation to legalize squatters' behavior also had gathered momentum during the years just after the War of 1812, becoming more insistent as a result, again, of the Panic. Between 1815 and 1819, district land offices in Illinois and Indiana reported influxes of "intruders" at a faster clip than ever. This trend disconcerted land system administrators in the West, who could not do their jobs, short of military intervention, if settlers would not honor the law. Thomas Sloo, land officer in Shawneetown, Illinois, reported in 1815: "There are nearly a thousand improved places in this District that are not located—And if the Government does not adopt some energetic Measures to nip this Conduct in the bud—it will retard the sale of all those places." A writer for the *Illinois Intelligencer* in 1830 estimated the population of that state at 100,000, half of them settlers on federal land they could not afford to purchase—and in Missouri and Arkansas, another 50,000 in the same condition. At prevalent growth rates, he guessed, there would be 300,000 squatters in those three states by 1840. The same story unfolded throughout the public land states and in federal territories. In Florida, another newspaper reported, "[T]he people as well as the government, are great losers in consequence of the squatters, who are cutting and carrying away the fine oak timber in that territory, which will never be of value until the titles are settled." Typically, squatters moved in, picked favored sites, felled the great forests, built wooden dwellings, erected fencing, and made commercial profit on timber that remained. In 1835, the *Daily Commercial Bulletin* in New York would half-jokingly advertise an "important new invention" that would "prove of incalculable advantage to the western farmer, and more particularly that class of farmers known in the west by the appropriate epithet of 'squatters.'" It was a machine for the felling of timber of any size, featuring "cranks, levers, wheels, &c." sufficient for one man to "cut down a tree three feet in diameter in the course of a few minutes."[58]

Squatters themselves, of course, took a brighter view of their activities. One group of Hoosier settlers, petitioning Congress in February 1816, believed that their "intrusion" on public lands had promoted economic growth:

> we flatter ourselves that when the true Situation of Our Country is understood that some Modifications will be made in favour of those who have Settled on the old purchase or in the Settled parts of the Territory—We are confident that instead of an

injury that they have been of advantage to the revenue of the United States the land
ocupied by Such is of the poorer kind and such as would not be entered perhaps for
many years but in Consequance of their improovements.

The argument would gain rhetorical polish, if not greater cogency, in the hands of
crafty politicians. Years later, Indiana Jacksonian John Tipton would achieve popularity among his constituents by characterizing "squatters' rights" as a protection
of lower-class settlers from wealthier westerners who coveted the land claims and
productive labor of others. Preemption, he would declare in 1834, "shields the poor
from the grasp of the speculator and secures to him his improvements upon the
public land."[59]

Along the same line, Territorial Delegate Joseph M. White of Florida, in an 1828
letter to Benton, argued that preemption and graduation, taken together, promised
a general moral improvement in America. He thought that a heightened chance
for a stake in society could turn the poorest men quickly into virtuous, productive
citizens—from a supposed liability to an asset in the body politic. He described the
potential beneficiaries in Florida and in neighboring states:

> This kind of population is extremely numerous in the southern States. They have no
> slaves to aid them in their labor; they have no means of purchasing, and the system
> of tenantry used in the northern States is scarcely known. This is the class of poor but
> industrious people who labor the earth with their own hands, and whose wives man-
> ufacture their own cotton clothing, and who go to seek better fortunes in Florida and
> Alabama, and become squatters on the public lands. A cart, a horse, and a few cows
> are . . . the only property they bring with them; they sit down on the public lands,
> and make small improvements to furnish them the means of temporary subsistence.

As White saw it, opening public lands to the least fortunate amounted simply
to smart political economy. A Florida newspaper reported in 1825 that only 361,000
acres of land had been surveyed there, compared to many millions of acres in
other states and territories. Florida "had as yet made but little progress; she had
a most exposed frontier; and it was necessary not only to bring a large quantity of
lands into the market, but of such lands as would induce purchasers." Much of
the territory was already "covered with squatters." White believed that the worst
lands would be least attractive to speculators. It would increase the value of inferior
tracts to make them readily available to nonprivileged families, who would be most
willing and eager to cultivate them. He told Benton that a tract "passed by with contempt by the man who had one or two hundred dollars to spare would be viewed
with delight by one of these poor settlers if he could call it his own."[60]

White's view, like Benton's, reflected the sharpest radical indictment of old policies: the traditional land system had been wasteful and incapable of meeting the needs of a rapidly expanding republican society. Historically focused too much on revenue, it neglected the human resources of the country. Doing away with credit sales, without making other structural changes, ignored the worst deficiencies of the system. Representative Joseph Duncan of Illinois, a member of the House Public Lands Committee from 1827 to 1834, thought the traditional structure not only had impeded the poorer migrants but had actually retarded the social and moral advancement that President John Quincy Adams and his National Republicans constantly stressed in the middle to late 1820s. As organized, he concluded, federal land policy deprived westerners of "the advantages of well settled neighborhoods, so essential to the education of youth, and to the pleasures of social intercourse."[61]

At the same time, anti-radical traditionalists both in Congress and outside—including some westerners—quickly registered doubts on all this. Their perspective, they said, held the merits not only of being rooted in late-eighteenth-century wisdom but also of having been tested for more than a generation. And so, drastic changes in the basic structure of the land system would subvert public virtue, subsidize frontier lawlessness, tarnish government's reputation, and encourage disrespect for policy makers. In the event that federal legislation might pair preemption with graduation, both would backfire, further undermining orderly settlement and systematic development of the West as originally planned under a benevolent, guiding force of federal power.

Hostility to illegal settlers continued strong throughout the 1820s. As an 1826 letter to the editor of an Arkansas newspaper complained, there remained "among the Members of Congress, and with the Officers of the Government" a strong prejudice "against what they call *squatters* upon the Public Lands." The federal government still threatened intruding settlers on Indian lands in the South and Southwest with conviction, fine, and imprisonment, even though little coercive action followed. If government were to encourage squatters, said one congressman, "a certain description of our population" would locate even more freely "upon the public lands without much regard to lines or boundaries." Samuel F. Vinton, an Ohio lawyer and member of the House Public Lands Committee from 1823 to 1829, still insisted that preemption contradicted "enlightened" principles of land policy. Removing legal prohibitions against trespassers, he thought, would obstruct, to public detriment, any further sales of western land. In his words, "those who would otherwise become purchasers would, instead of purchasing, be induced . . . to settle down upon the lands of the public with the intention . . . of purchasing when compelled to do so, but not before." Radical changes, then, would only produce an undesirable class of settlers that more-respectable westerners would resent. The legitimate purchaser would find himself unwelcome in the West, as squatters soon would employ any "combination, violence, and artifice" in their power "to prevent his ingress into their neighborhood, or to drive him from it."[62]

Just as important, would men who had honored restrictions under the old system calmly accept radical changes in policy? Expressing the dominant view of the House Public Lands Committee in 1827, John Scott of Missouri insisted that offering special privileges to squatters would fix "a dangerous precedent, awarding a premium for the violation of the law, and holding out assurances" that "future rewards" would be given for "similar transgressions." Concurring, Vinton added that such an "impolitic and inexpedient" shift might reduce faith in government. The public good therefore required that law-breaking squatters be evicted swiftly and efficiently, not sanctioned and pampered by government. Other critics of the radical program agreed with Virgil Maxcy that western lands should remain a "common fund" for the continuing encouragement of education and internal improvements throughout the United States. Representative James Strong of New York, a one-time Federalist who favored parceling federal lands for the financing of schools, reflected the frustration of many eastern congressmen when he noted the "apathy in the public mind in regard to the value and importance of these lands."[63]

As for Benton's graduation scheme, the *National Intelligencer* warned in 1825 that "the plan of selling at a very *reduced price*, and *immediately*, would throw all the government lands into the hands of speculators, who, though they might pay taxes, would nevertheless make actual settlers give an enormous price for their farms." The western people themselves would be more injured than aided, "inasmuch as the effect of every reduction of the market price of an article must be to reduce its value in the hands of individual holders." Other opponents of land price graduation in the West developed what might be termed a Gresham's Law of land settlement—an argument that poor settlers tended to drive out the middle class. A group of citizens in Michigan Territory, petitioning Congress against graduation in 1828, reminded the lawmakers that earlier western settlers, not desperate latecomers, had laid the necessary social foundations for republicanism in the West. Better, then, to avoid policy changes destined to entice "the dregs of community from the old States" and "drive every respectable man" farther west. The same Michigan group cautioned that large-scale speculators would snap up "immense quantities of land" at Benton's reduced prices, leading only to another destructive credit system, this time a private one, where land prices could soar "from twenty-five cents to two or three dollars per acre."[64]

⸺◦⸺

The government policy of credit sales, most in Congress came to believe, had not fostered a "moral population" in the western states and territories, but instead a dependent, in some cases irresponsible, class of debtors. Still, the majority of lawmakers also agreed that the original land system, with its auction component, remained the best policy for dispensing public lands and ensuring conscientious settlers a "respectable neighborhood." The comparatively radical political economy of Benton and others, however, implied more than just the opportunity for lower-class settlers to acquire government lands. It argued a labor theory of value that gave highest recognition not to capital investors but to the "actual producers" of wealth—the "humbler" classes of farmers and workingmen. Poorer men and women, supposedly, would benefit most from the policy changes that the more radical westerners advocated. Whatever its merits, the philosophical appeal of the Bentonites would later help unite western voters with the Jacksonian coalition of the 1830s and, over the course of political development, contribute also to the free labor ethos of the Republican Party in the 1850s.

In January 1829, after National Republicans had been vanquished at the polls, *Niles' Register* disapprovingly referred to the Missouri senator as chief among the "*new sect* of politicians." That referred to western strict constructionists, brash and vociferous, anti-statist, scornful of tradition, and dedicated anew to unfettered individual enterprise.[65] Benton ultimately would throw his reputation behind the free homestead principle—160 acres to western migrants who had settled and improved tracts of their choice for at least five years. His support of homestead legislation would signal a new, free soil (and antislavery) tendency in the Missouri senator's politics that would cost him his seat in 1851. But during the 1830s and 1840s, especially in the western-most public land states, Benton and his cohorts would make a mountain of political hay with graduation and preemption.

CHAPTER FOUR

"A World within Itself"

Thomas Hart Benton faced a prodigious rival for the sympathies of westerners—another crafty new-state politician, equally charismatic, with a vastly different economic agenda and a desire for power that burned even hotter than Benton's. Some people referred to Henry Clay by his nickname, "Harry of the West." He, not Benton, had received credit for the congressional compromise that brought Missouri into the Union as a slave state in 1820–1821. Whether in an increasingly populist political culture Clay could muster enough voter support in the West to trump the Missouri senator's growing influence—and, greater still, that of war hero Andrew Jackson—only time and the unfolding of events would tell.

For generations, the "American System," a nationalist program that aimed to unite the country economically and make Clay president, has been standard fare in history books. But historians have seldom viewed the public lands element of Clay's "system" in relation to the political economy and social circumstances that generated it. In his time, economic doctrines that glorified agriculture held sway with many in Congress and throughout America, threatening the tariff protection that Clay urged. Also, as James Madison warned, the tendency of vacant lands to draw away the laboring class could frustrate any protectionist approach in the United States. "This is the great obstacle to the spontaneous establishment of Manufactories, and will be overcome with the most difficulty wherever land is cheapest, and the ownership of it most attainable," cautioned Madison. The apparent dilemma of reconciling a manufacturing policy with the promoting of western interests nagged Clay through much of the early nineteenth century. From 1824 on, Benton's political dramatizing of the land question, with various proposals to reduce progressively—or graduate—the minimum price of federal lands according to their length of time unsold, challenged Clay's image as a western leader and questioned his economic affinity for his own section. Alternatively, Ninian Edwards's agitation in the late 1820s for Congress to cede the lands outright to the new states, within whose boundaries they lay, posed no less of a problem for Clay.[1]

Could the federal government promote manufacturing without pegging federal land prices so high as to stem a free flow of westward migration? And if Congress were to balance growth of the West against that of manufacturing, would this choice undermine the cherished Jeffersonian vision of an expanding agricultural republic in America? During the 1820s and early 1830s, Clay and his followers answered a strained "yes" to the first question and a cautious "no" to the second. These responses came when economic events after 1815 had called for much rethinking of Republican political economy, not only in light of foreign trade prospects, but also to accommodate an increasingly diverse and more fluid domestic society. Understanding the evolution of Clay's position on unsettled lands clarifies both his role as a leader from the West and how his economic views helped shape the varied landscape of Jacksonian-era politics.

Perhaps because historians have seen the American System chiefly in terms of protective tariffs, federally funded internal improvements, and a national bank, they have understated the importance of public land policy to Clay and other nationalists. As if swayed by Benton's egalitarian rhetoric, many writers have assumed the Kentuckian's advocacy of the "revenue theory" of the national domain to mean that he stood against rapid settlement. In fact, the actual filling of lands mattered to him as much as revenue because of its impact on the social structure, economic stability, and moral character of the West. In his mind, no serious conflict ever existed between revenue and settlement objectives; both could be served well enough in a system that kept lands reasonably cheap but did not give them away. More broadly, the Panic of 1819 presented a moment of reckoning for Clay, as it did for other westerners—and other protectionists. Much of the American System emerged in reaction to the social and economic chaos of the Panic—not just the need for national self-sufficiency after the War of 1812. While historians have long considered the effect of the Panic on Jacksonian ideology, its role in the political economy of Jackson's opponents, Clay and the National Republicans, has attracted much less attention.[2]

—◦—

Prior to the 1830s, the American System looked far less like a united economic program than it did a host of compatible nationalist concepts, representing both eastern and western interests. The wealth-generating potential of vacant lands gradually would become integrated into the larger theoretical picture. Clay admired, built on, and also influenced the work of prominent eastern journalists of the 1820s, particularly Mathew Carey and Hezekiah Niles. In February 1845, six years after both of these friends had died (and a month before James K. Polk's inauguration as president), Clay despaired, "If we could see the pens of two such men as Hez. Niles & Mat. Carey employed, as their pens were, in upholding the

American System, firmly, perseveringly but moderately, I should have great hopes that it would survive the blow meditated against it." Their protectionist views, like those of economists Daniel Raymond and Friedrich List, had gained force after the War of 1812, when British merchants dumped their surplus manufactured goods in American markets. That, along with the desperate lack of capital and factory-type labor in the Northeast, had prostrated competing American manufacturers before a flood of lower-cost imports. Britain's trade restrictions also denied a vital foreign market for American products, leaving nascent firms localized and underdeveloped.[3]

Western input to the American System, by contrast, reflected conclusions very different from Benton's that Clay drew from the West's troubled financial condition after 1819. In areas vital to Clay politically, where commerce was tied to the Ohio and Mississippi Rivers, the Panic brought acute distress after a period of misleading prosperity. Reckless expansion in western bank notes between 1815 and 1818 had fueled grossly excessive land speculation. Capital resources needed for roads and canals to funnel agricultural produce cheaply to eastern markets went to waste. Despite thriving steamboat traffic on the major rivers after 1810, westerners remained trapped in a limited trade that cheated their labors, depressed their incomes, and stunted town growth. Lacking an expanded market, many growers of foodstuffs in the Northwest languished near subsistence, even before their banks collapsed. Reduced demand in 1819 sent wholesale farm prices plummeting to roughly half what they had been a year earlier. Without adequate capital resources to weather the crisis and rebuild quickly, the depression devastated the more heavily populated western areas.[4]

"The West" in the post-1815 period was, in truth, an increasingly diverse expanse, complicated by regional variations and competing internal interests. By the mid-1820s, the first group of trans-Appalachian states—Kentucky, Tennessee, and Ohio—had become suppliers not only of goods and services but also of migrants to the newer states farther west and southwest. Their economies, like those of the eastern states, had progressed sufficiently to be hard-hit by the Panic. Their landholders stood well enough settled to distrust policies that could subvert the value of the property they had worked so hard to develop. Especially after 1819, frontier farmers in states farther west, Benton's stronghold, could appear as a very different political constituency from rural producers in more settled areas. In Ohio, where Clay had strong support, the more fertile federal lands had already sold by 1821. Four years later, the state embarked on an ambitious canal-building program that would further transform its commercial life and stimulate economic groups already sympathetic to the American System. Ohio no longer represented the cutting edge it had been just a generation before and, in some senses, could now lose as much as it might gain from further westward expansion. Ohio politicians voiced significantly less enthusiasm for Benton's steep land-price reductions than came from Illinois, Indiana, Missouri, and Michigan Territory. Even so, Clay's program held greater appeal throughout the Northwest than in the newer southwestern states. The latter region divided internally on federal aid to internal improvements, but throughout the South, save for Louisiana's sugar lobby, the tariff looked like an ugly manufacturers' conspiracy to trample states' rights and intrude on the cotton kingdom. In general, Clay and his allies sought to capitalize on the emerging divisions between—and within—the "old" and the "new" West, hoping to tap rich veins of support in the more established and commercially advanced sectors.[5]

Whether based in East or West, formal advocates of an American System viewed post-1815 America as a potential "world within itself," well suited for self-contained prosperity—a home market. Although relying heavily on Alexander Hamilton's 1791 "Report on Manufactures," many advocates, like Clay, identified with the commercial side of Jeffersonian Republicanism. While they deplored Old World "luxury" and "corruption," they adhered to important vestiges of eighteenth-century republican ideology. As nineteenth-century nationalists, however, they also saw an antidote to social decay in a federally monitored development of America's vast interior. They argued throughout the 1820s that the public domain made it possible to avert the social ills that many Americans believed to exist in Europe. They believed, as *Niles' Weekly Register* asserted in 1827, that England in particular was "overburthened with population, because overburthened with taxes and monopolies—but we have room enough for the 'thousandth generation.'" The gloomy European forecasts of Thomas Malthus and David Ricardo seemed inapplicable to the United States. Population increase could never outstrip food supply while there remained a carefully guarded outlet of western lands. American protectionists contended that domestic industry would not violate the economic innocence or corrupt traditional morals of republican communities—not while the West offered viable alternatives. Manufacturing employment could give workers a chance to avoid the abandonment of family and community for the uncertainties of the frontier. Or it might provide some with the means of going west and buying the 80-acre minimum (after 1820) for as little as $1.25 per acre.[6]

In the early years of the movement, protectionist writers tended to worry that hasty western settlement would delay the growth of manufacturing by draining the East of population. When the Panic of 1819 brought a clamor in newer parts of the West for dramatically reduced federal land prices, easier terms of sale, and preferential treatment of squatters, an implied threat to manufacturers' intentions showed clearly. These provocative demands helped push protection advocates toward a defense of their position that took western interests more into account. Various members of Congress, including Clay, joined publicists like Carey and Niles in warning against policies that might not just divert too much from manufacturing but also diminish the value of settled lands, squander the West's economic potential, and destabilize communities in all sections.

A prolific writer, Mathew Carey was one of the earliest proponents of economic nationalism. Before 1825 he had organized both the Philadelphia Society for the Promotion of National Industry and the Society for the Promotion of Internal Improvements. He rejected much of Adam Smith's emphasis in *The Wealth of Nations*, writing in 1829 that as the Jacksonians—whom he distrusted—assumed power, the likely effect of free-trade would be to "paralyze our industry" and "render the United States virtual colonies of the manufacturing nations of Europe." Throughout the 1820s, Carey had thought that the Panic revealed how vulnerable America would stay without a balanced economic system. "A nation peopled only by farmers must be a region of indolence and misery," he declared in 1820. While many placed increased emphasis on public lands as an eventual outlet for excessive industrial population, Carey did not want the West to become an automatic refuge for the unproductive. Better for new eastern factories to provide uplifting places for labor cut adrift by the Panic.[7]

Carey's recoiling in 1820 from a wholesale opening of new lands to the poor revealed a lot. He thought the shock of depression had masked one of the more disturbing economic maladies of the East, the growing presence of people without motivation to work. His presumed cure: a self-sufficient, manufacturing-based economy. Factory work supposedly would limit cases of actual poverty to men of debauched character and little economic potential. As Clay said also in 1820, no advantage lay in luring decadent easterners westward. Merely changing their environment could not cure beggars' bad habits, make them productive, or give them wherewithal to consume factory-made goods. The vision of a home market could not be realized that way.

Carey spoke for most protectionists in repudiating the traditional, or "country," critique of industrial development and rejecting the notion of agriculture as a panacea for social and economic troubles. The antinationalist "Old Republicans" of the now-fragmenting Jeffersonian Party continually sang the praises of agricultural simplicity and noninterventionist government. Inspired by the likes of Taylor of Caroline, Randolph of Roanoke, and Macon of North Carolina, they would see Clay and the National Republicans as not extenders but betrayers of the economic and political legacy of the American Revolution. Fearing a loss of influence in the Southeast, they also opposed frontier growth far more than most nationalists did. "The changes have been rung," Carey noted in 1820, "on the depravity, corruption, and pauperism inseparable from large assemblages of men, women, and children, collected in small compass, inhaling a pestiferous atmosphere, both moral and physical." Granted, it would be "folly and insanity" for government policy to lure too many of "the Arcadian cultivators of the soil into the business of manufacturing." But why not make agriculture, manufacturing, and commerce work together in harmony? "In so wide a country as this," he argued, "if manufacturers were degraded and oppressed by men of great wealth in one district, they would be able to resort to establishments in another." When factory life no longer afforded sufficient opportunities, then "the western lands would afford an asylum for the oppressed." After all, the lack of manufacturing enterprise, rather than the presence of it, often caused poverty, idleness, and immorality. The depressed condition of the West seemed to support his view that "paupers" and delinquents numbered as heavily in farming as in commercial and industrial areas. The dissipation of youths in agricultural districts owed to "their early years in total idleness and in the contraction of bad habits," he concluded.[8]

If social virtue could actually *depend* on manufacturing, then arguments for delaying industrialization stood open to attack. Why wait for vacant lands to fill before encouraging industrial development? Carey insisted that southern tariff opponents, who often were guarding slavery as much as suspecting manufacturing, labored under "ineffable delusion." But the battle against them seemed like trying "to arrest the cataracts of Niagara with a mound of sand." A political economy rooted so heavily in agriculture, reminiscent of French physiocratic doctrines, seemed to Carey more like a vestige of medieval thought, likely to bring with it all the "debasing and depraving influence of feudal obligations." Instead of reverting to a social order of the past, America could demonstrate "the genial and invigorating influence of manufacturing industry" and release productive energies like "darkness yielding to the day-dawn."[9]

It followed that a multitude of settlers scattered at random across a massive domain—the result seemingly implied in proposals to undo the federal land system—would be a poor foundation for a republican society. "A numerous population, in a state of wretchedness," Carey declared in 1822, "is rather a symptom of debility than of strength." Any widely dispersed people would be "ripe for treason and spoil," but dense settlements, "usefully and profitably employed" in manufacturing, could represent "the pride and glory of a statesman" and the "power and security" of the nation. Industrial opportunities would draw America's share of foreigners "possessed of useful talents." Virtuous people presumably would attract others like themselves—another point that Clay, too, would argue repeatedly. With a frontier settled in compact communities and a growing demand for factory labor in the East, the nation would appeal more than ever to "the eyes and longings of that active and energetic class of men" from abroad.[10]

In Carey's view, manufacturing would ensure prosperity, elevate workers, and attract desirable immigrants. But also, if encouraged in the West as well as in eastern regions, it might enhance the social and economic stability of frontier communities. He admired the settlement of Harmony in western Pennsylvania—a productive example of "placing the manufacturer beside the agriculturist." The well-known German settlement, founded in 1805 by George Rapp and his communitarian followers, seemed to verify in microcosm the advantages of a home market. These "Rappites," who expected to proliferate their model throughout the Northwest, had "made a more rapid advance in wealth and prosperity" than had settlers in parts of the country that still depended on foreign markets.[11]

Carey saw advocates of land price reduction and further indulgences in credit for government land buyers as clinging naïvely to the notion of the West as a "sovereign and infallible" refuge from complex social and economic problems. The worst advice being offered to victims of the Panic, he had complained in 1820, was " 'to go back' [westward] and cultivate the soil, where there is ample field for their industry." Given the economic instability of western communities, desperate easterners would gain little by going there. A better short-term solution for them lay not in the West but in the East, where plenty of unused labor waited for factory work. "Believe me," Carey implored James S. Garnett of the Fredericksburg Agricultural Society, "there is a sober reality in this picture. Would to heaven that you could visit our cities, and see the distress and the misery of thousands . . . who are able to work, . . . but are utterly unable to procure employment."[12] The idea, then, was to promote the creation of manufacturing jobs, thus providing these workers the steady employment and economic security they needed.

So, for Carey, those who would "remedy" the Panic with easier access to western lands had raised, by implication, two basic questions. First, would manufacturers in general have been capable of cultivating vacant lands? Second, if the thousands of employed workers were to take up agriculture, was there "any chance of a market for the surplus of their produce"? The first query was easier to answer. Shifting people from urban trades to western farming was not simple: "a man who has spent the prime of his life in making watches, cabinet ware, hats, or shoes, or weaving cloth, would be nearly as much out of his element at agricultural labor as a farmer would be in a shoemaker's or hatter's workshop." A rapid fruition of manufacturing, not a wild settling of western regions, would better occupy those who were "wholly unfit for farming."[13]

The second question pointed to the need for a national home market. Surplus produce had been the bane of American agriculture since the end of the Napoleonic Wars and was one of the reasons for economic hardship in the early 1820s. The solution lay not in multiplying the number of rural producers, as agricultural theorists wanted, but in enlarging the domestic market for farm goods. In Carey's analysis,

> It is palpable that so far from an increase of agriculturists being necessary in the interior of this state [Pennsylvania], and in the whole of the western states, that they are too numerous for their own prosperity, and hence agricultural productions are almost constantly a drug, and afford a very slender remuneration for the labours of the field. Increase the number, and you increase the evil. Increase the number of manufacturers, you diminish it.

A balanced economy, bolstered by protective duties on crucial products, would ensure growers and merchants higher prices at home than they could obtain in ruinously competitive West Indian and European markets. Such a policy would eventually benefit every section of the country. In addition to repaying production, it would raise the value of America's unsettled lands, securing full economic benefit of westward expansion. "I might cite the cases of Brandywine, Wilmington, Pittsburg, Providence, Lancaster, and a hundred other places in the United States," Carey said, "where the establishment of manufactories, by affording an extensive and advantageous market to the farmer, doubled and trebled the price of lands in their neighborhood."[14]

Hezekiah Niles, too, advocated the home-market idea and recognized the need to frame western land policy around it. He and Carey knew each other and frequently traded ideas. Niles also exchanged correspondence with Clay. By 1820, he had spent just nine years building his *Niles' Weekly Register*, published in Baltimore, into one of the preeminent magazines of its time. During the Panic of 1819, it claimed 10,000 subscribers, including many members of Congress and state legislatures, Clay among them.[15]

The War of 1812 first impelled Niles to the cause of American self-sufficiency. He later picked up on the home-market arguments of Carey, Raymond, Clay, and others and participated heavily in the protectionist conventions at Harrisburg, Pennsylvania (1827) and New York City (1831). Niles identified particularly with Clay. In 1822, while the Kentuckian was temporarily retired from Congress, Niles told him: "In times like these *national* men must not all quit the field. The liberality & broadness of your views . . . are inestimably valuable just now. The legislation or direction of the public affairs seems to regard a quintal of codfish, a hhd. of tobacco *or* a bale of cotton, instead of keeping an eye to the whole." Like many other protectionists, Niles applied nationalist elements of Jeffersonian Republicanism to the new social and economic problems of the 1820s. He thought the public good had to be "divested of local partialities and sectional prejudices." More surrounded by southern influence than was Carey, Niles worried about the worsening sectionalism of the 1820s and 1830s, and he considered the separatist talk in the West to be as troubling as any he was hearing around Baltimore. Preserving the Union, he wrote in 1816, depended on "the political wisdom of the people," their "reciprocity of interests," and "the compactness of our population."[16]

Without a careful federal policy, he believed, farming would expand out of control and out of balance with manufacturing and commerce, as Madison had said it would. In 1819, Niles observed, "Agriculture is the noblest and best occupation of man, and in a country like the United States, where land is plenty and labor is scarce, it will always be pushed to the extent which a profitable market demands." For expansion to continue at a constant pace was fine as long as it did not progress beyond the country's capacity to absorb western goods. But by the time of the Panic, it *had*. Economic distress would lead him to expand arguments he had started earlier. By coordinating manufacturing with agriculture, Niles had observed in 1817, "[l]ands are improved and property rises in value," a reward not just to speculators but also to settlers who owned the land they lived on. A home market would benefit industry and farming mutually, securing outlets for capital investment and the enhanced worth of vacant lands. "I well know a district of country in a neighboring state," he wrote, where "by the extension of one manufactory and the establishment of one (or two) new ones, the land, for *several* miles round, has trebled its price within the short period of about eight years"—and numerous fields, once considered worn out, were seeing "the most luxurious productions."[17]

For Niles, the economic goal was "'equilibrium' between manufacturing and agriculture." Such a balance would protect well-established economic groups, "the middle class—'the bone and sinew of every country'—from annihilation." Concerned about social order as well as economic harmony, Niles often stressed, as he had in 1817, the averting of destructive class tensions:

> A nation of pure agriculturists cannot be numerous unless there are lords and peasants, masters and slaves;—a nation of manufacturers must abound with nabobs and paupers;—and a nation of merchants, to the misery of these two would superadd a degradation capable of trampling upon the cross and dealing in the scalps of men to make money. But each balances, regulates and refines the rest.

This amounted almost to a "theory of factions" in political economy, the economic equivalent of Madison's formula for political stability in a large nation. Both aimed at preserving republicanism as it expanded westward. The farming potential of the United States enabled the balance envisioned here; nations without such land resources could not match it. The Panic seemed to highlight the possibility that manufacturing would bring a degree of social stability unknown in Britain, Niles said, "where the making of one rich man sends thousands to the poorhouse."[18]

Like Carey, Niles did not necessarily see western development as an enemy of manufacturing, but he did fear that rapid, uncontrolled expansion might further destabilize the West and undermine national economic growth. A large part of the problem was the land-credit system that had produced such a sizeable class of debtors to the federal government. Although the Panic had forced new buying to tail off precipitously after 1818, unpaid credit purchases in the Northwest alone amounted to 8 million dollars—part of an overall total of 22 million dollars by September 1819. Western land purchases had dried up by then, after roughly 4 million acres had sold for an average of $3.37 per acre the previous year. In the early 1820s, Niles thought western lands ought to be settled more methodically and compactly than they had in the past. "No one has been more anxious for the gradual expansion of the people than myself," he wrote in January 1824, "but the march west has been more rapid than the public good has justified—weakening the force of the population, embarrassing the government, and inflicting misery on thousands, seduced, as it were, to purchase land without the means of paying for it." Continuing agitation for easy land terms, including the first introduction of Benton's graduation idea in the Senate, provoked Niles to reinforce the point in 1825: it had been a mistake "to *force* the sales—whereby an unprofitable dispersion of our people was made, and thousands of them embarrassed by premature purchases."[19]

Dismissing southern objections to the American System, Niles's protectionism stressed not only the rise of manufacturing alongside agriculture in the new western communities but also the spread of free labor throughout the Union. No state could set a more compelling example by shifting from land-based, slave-dependent practices than Virginia, where Thomas Ritchie's *Richmond Enquirer* espoused a free-trade position similar to Adam Smith's in *The Wealth of Nations*. From a protectionist point of view, the Chesapeake region already showed the dismal results of Ritchie's economic perspective: "Virginia should have a numerous and efficient population. . . . but this cannot be obtained while free labor is discouraged or disgraced, and disfranchised," Niles wrote in 1825. Southerners had long suffered the ill effects of widely scattered settlement—plantation agriculture supported by slavery—with devastating impact on poor whites: "They are wretched and miserable, . . . and you may visit whole families, not one member of which can read and write." "Are these," asked Niles, "the legitimate fruits of the republican system—such as we should hold up to the world for its imitation and respect?"[20]

Tariff advocates in Congress, including Clay, often muted free-labor sentiments for fear of antagonizing slaveholders, but editor Niles operated under no such restraint. Southern leaders dreaded attacks upon slavery, but they also feared the potential draining of their white population westward—just as New Englanders did. In 1827, Niles thought the South could avert such depopulation simply by introducing domestic industry into tobacco- and cotton-producing regions: "It is especially important to the south that manufactures should grow up among them, to increase, or retain, the free laboring classes." He assumed that slave labor and manufacturing stood at odds. Niles expected the 1830 census to show "an unprecedented acquisition of population in the eastern states, because of manufactures," adding, as an appeal to both southerners and westerners, that "like causes will everywhere produce like effects."[21]

While protectionist writers like Carey and Niles pushed in the direction of a coherent philosophy, it remained for politicians in Congress to convert ideas into policy. Banking, tariffs, internal improvements, public lands—all received intense congressional scrutiny after 1815. While votes usually followed sectional or regional interests, arguments in committees and on the floor reflected lines of ideological conflict as well. Throughout the 1820s, Clay and other protectionist members worked to establish a long-range home-market policy against the arguments of free traders and promoters of agriculture who contended that rushing manufacturing in America would be like compelling an orchard to yield ripe fruit before its time. Representative Thomas Montgomery, a fellow Kentuckian, not only summarized the anti-protectionist view in 1823 but pinpointed its relation to unsettled lands: "[W]e have an immense, unexplored, and unfelled forest, affording occupation or employment to very many indeed. . . . Can it be true, then, that it has become necessary to legislate, in order to provide employments for our people?"[22]

No one in Congress articulated the protectionist side better than Clay, who also became the most frequent target for opposition attacks. In his House speech of March 30–31, 1824, Clay acknowledged Carey's influence, commending him as "entitled to the greatest attention." Scores of Carey's political economy essays, written all through the 1820s under the pseudonyms "Hamilton" and "Colbert," appeared in two Washington newspapers that Clay read with regularity, the *National Intelligencer* and the *National Journal*. From time to time, the Kentuckian also received copies of Carey's latest work from the author directly. And yet, Clay was less indebted to Carey and other protectionist writers than he was philosophically *related to* and *involved with* them. Although a second-generation Jeffersonian, he obviously owed as much as they did to Hamilton's seminal "Report on Manufactures." His own interest in protectionism originated well before 1824. In 1810, he had argued publicly that a manufacturing system would prevent, not accelerate, the "indigence, vice and wretchedness" that urban Europe had experienced. Abundant land made all the difference. Advanced manufacturing and a home market would keep an economically independent America from becoming a poverty-ridden industrial colossus. "If we [like the British] were to become the manufacturers of other nations," declared young Clay, "effects of the same kind might result. But if we *limit* our efforts by our own wants, the evils apprehended would be found to be chimerical."[23]

By 1820, the Panic had considerably disrupted Clay's personal economic world and would soon transform political life in his home state. There, as an attorney and legislator, he almost always had done the bidding of the financial establishment. His marriage to Lucretia Hart in 1799 had tied him to a socially prominent Kentucky family and to the so-called Bluegrass gentry, which included the most influential merchants and bankers in the state. He had, like many Kentuckians, invested in hemp-growing and sheep-raising and, by 1805, held several thousand acres of land, much of it speculative property in neighboring states. He owned a hotel in Lexington and part of a salt mine, sat on the board of the Bank of Kentucky, and helped to found the Madison Hemp and Flax Spinning Company. As a member of the state legislature from 1803 to 1806, and again from 1807 to 1810, he promoted internal improvement, manufacturing, and financial causes, including the Kentucky Insurance Company. But the crisis resulting from wild land speculation and reckless banking now exposed his family and other leading Kentuckians to mounting debts. During the Panic, Clay's personal obligation to creditors approached a staggering $20,000, forcing him to leave Congress and resume law practice between 1821 and 1824.[24]

Westerners in general faced a shortage of capital, made worse by the decision of the Bank of the United States in 1819 to forbid western and southern branches from issuing notes and to accept no remittances eastward except in specie or bills of exchange on eastern or European banks. As a result, hard money drained uncontrollably from the West, leaving regional bankers and indebted land purchasers holding the bag. Clay informed National Bank president Langdon Cheves in April 1819, "It is a great mistake to suppose that the money is supplied by emigrants from the Eastward wholly to purchase the public lands. Kentucky Ohio & Tennessee are and long have been parent states."[25]

In Kentucky the Panic's impact was worst for small farmers. Their shrill appeals for relief fell on receptive ears in the legislature. Stay laws against immediate foreclosures, abolition of imprisonment for debt, and the chartering of the Bank of the Commonwealth, with power to issue unbacked paper currency, kept creditors at bay for a time. The crisis split Kentucky's Jeffersonians into two rival factions, divided along economic lines. The relief element supported the radical steps of the legislature and included many future Jacksonians, like William T. Berry, Amos Kendall, Joseph Desha, and Thomas P. Moore. The anti-relief group, representing merchants, manufacturers, lawyers, and the more secure planters, condemned the measures for debtor rescue. Their leaders, men like Robert Wickliffe, George Robertson, John Pope, and John J. Marshall, challenged the relief laws before the Kentucky court of appeals and won, triggering a squabble that animated the state's politics for a decade.[26]

Although he tried to stay aloof from this political fight in his home state, Clay privately sympathized with the anti-relief position and the economic interests behind it. As chief counsel for the Bank of the United States in the Ohio and Kentucky region, he (lucratively) sued hundreds of debtors for default in 1821–1822. Western voters who had suffered at the hands of the federal bank would remember him bitterly for this involvement. But in larger terms, Clay thought the Panic had exposed the essential problem for the commercial West: insufficient capital. Even the most trusted banks lacked sufficient specie reserves to weather the crisis, especially with hard money flowing steadily eastward. Lacking a base of surplus capital, western states had gone without the transportation improvements needed to widen market horizons and stimulate urban growth. The growth rate of Clay's Lexington, though the city was still one of the largest in the West, had dropped over 40 percent from what it had been ten years earlier.[27]

In addition to the Panic itself, the deluge of protectionist literature gave the Kentuckian's position greater persuasive force than it had ten years earlier. Making one of the same arguments as Carey, he proclaimed in 1820 that pauperism in the nation was "the effect of an overflowing population" and an excess of commerce and agriculture in comparison to manufacturing. Economic distress now made unemployment the issue of the day, and it drew Clay's attention to the coordination of manufacturing and frontier growth as a remedy for idleness and crowding:

> The unseated lands will draw off the redundancy, and leave the others better provided for. If an unsettled province, such as Texas, for example, could, by some convulsion of nature, be wafted along side of, and attached to, the island of Great Britain, the instantaneous effect would be, to draw off the redundant portion of its population, and to render more comfortable both the emigrants and those whom they would leave behind.

While some critics saw an open West as undermining the low wage levels considered necessary for capitalist profits, Clay believed this objection failed to account for innovations in manufacturing technology. Machinery had reduced labor's role as the principal factor of production, leaving no economic need to chain workers to the East.[28]

It is important to distinguish Clay from *anti*-western figures of the 1820s—like Treasury Secretary Richard Rush of Pennsylvania and Connecticut Senator Samuel A. Foot, author of a resolution offered in December 1829 that would anger westerners by proposing a sudden restriction of public land sales and would lead to the famous Webster-Hayne Debate. Probably influenced by Rush, who wanted to prevent population diffusion, President John Quincy Adams would hint at similar views in his Annual Message of 1827. Clay never advocated limitation of new settlement or a braking of western economic growth; he was not an intellectual descendant of northeastern Federalists like Rufus King in matters of the frontier. Although among the strongest proponents of domestic manufacturing, Clay did not fear that western development would drain away eastern workers. The rising tide of European immigration by the 1830s made that a moot concern, anyway. He never suggested raising the minimum price for public lands, as President James Monroe had in December 1817. Unlike some nationalists in 1820, he opposed abolition of the credit system for public land sales, possibly to avoid the political ostracism at home that reportedly threatened other Kentucky members who supported the repeal. As House Speaker, he refrained, however, from voting on the bill. He did vote for the February 1821 measure that extended the credit period for distressed land debtors.[29]

As a westerner himself, Clay eagerly sought development of his section, while also promoting the self-sufficiency of the republic as a whole. At this point, he thought the natural checks against a flood of emigration to the West were enough to make artificial, government-imposed barriers unnecessary. The vast travel distance alone imposed a deterrent to pulling up stakes in the East. He also saw a "natural repugnance," as he put it, toward abandoning one's place of nativity. The frontier, no matter how wide open, would be insufficient to absorb the post-1815 explosion of eastern population. And whatever the lure of western lands, the East would still contain a residue of "women and children, who could not migrate, and who would be comparatively idle if manufactures did not exist." In 1820, social stability in the older parts of the Union required a more sophisticated plan than mere reliance on the West as a safety valve. As Clay moralized, again like Carey, "Those who object to the manufacturing system should recollect that constant occupation is the best security for innocence and virtue, and that idleness is the parent of vice and crime."[30]

Although eastern protectionists easily could have matched the Kentuckian's views on the danger of surplus produce, Clay saw better than they did the advantages of a home-market economy for the West itself. In an August 1823 letter, Clay told Virginia jurist Francis T. Brooke that America's westward progress, as well as world events, had made the free-trade perspective archaic:

When this Government was first adopted, we had no interior. Our population was inclosed between the Sea and the Mountains which run parallel to it. Since then the West part of your State, the Western parts of N. York & Pennsa. & all the Western States have been settled. The Wars of Europe & the emigrants to the West consumed all the surplus produced on both sides of the Mountains. Those Wars have terminated; and emigration has ceased. We find ourselves annually in the possession of an immense surplus.

The problem affecting western farmers and eastern manufacturers with common severity was the lack of market for these excess goods. Even if it meant higher prices for manufactured goods, an American home market remained to Clay the most sensible scheme for all sections at once: "There can be no Foreign market adequate to the consumption of the vast & growing surplus of the produce of our Agriculture. We must then have a Home market. Some of us must cultivate; some fabricate."[31]

Clay in the 1820s responded to agitators like Benton of Missouri and Edwards of Illinois that changes in policy had to consider the interests of the economy as a whole. He would elaborate this position in the 1830s, as commercial development, along with population, spread farther westward. While politically invested in this frontier growth and supportive of a West more open than not, he thought that merely luring the unemployed westward could bring no security from future panics and no guarantee to westerners of a more productive population. Manufacturing represented as much a safety valve for developed parts of the West as fresh lands meant, in theory, for the manufacturing states. A radical liberalizing of federal land laws—undermining of the land auction system and the price minimum per acre—would only waste the public domain as a revenue resource and populate the new states with the undesirable poor. "The great desideratum in political economy," Clay said, was "the same as in private pursuits; that is, What is the best application of the aggregate industry of a nation, that can be made honestly to produce the largest sum of national wealth?" The West offered no simple answers for economic problems, and an ill-considered frontier policy could only detract from national wealth and well-being.[32]

Clay's House "Speech on the Tariff" of April 1820, shortly after the Missouri Compromise vote, provided specific clues to his idea of economic stability for the West. Arguing the virtues of home manufacturing, he paid tribute to his friend Isaac Shelby, the commerce-promoting former governor of Kentucky. "If you want to find an example of order, of freedom from debt, of economy, of expenditure falling short of rather than exceeding income," Clay told fellow House members, "you will go to a well regulated family of a farmer. You will go to the house of such a man as Isaac Shelby." Here was not the type of westerner one found "resorting to taverns, engaged in broils, prosecuting angry law suits." Shelby illustrated, rather, a traditional middle-class work ethic in action: "You will behold every member of his family clad with the produce of their own hands, and usefully employed, the spinning wheel and the loom in motion by day-break." Clay wanted to see the capital-generating Shelby virtues spread across the nation as a whole.

If Shelby embodied the westerner of highest character, Clay knew the other types just as well. "If you want to see an opposite example," he continued, "go to the house of a man, who makes nothing at home . . . . He is engaged with the rum grog on the table, taking depositions to make out some case of usury or fraud. Or perhaps he is furnishing to his lawyer the materials to prepare a long bill of injunction in some intricate case. The sheriff is hovering about his farm to serve some new writ. On court days (he never misses attending them,) you will find him eagerly collecting witnesses to defend himself against the merchants' and doctors' bills." These sentiments resembled Clay's harshest condemnations of unruly frontier westerners, the invective he later reserved for squatters who stood to benefit from preemption laws. Such claimants, he later insisted, were no more than trespassers or, as Gallatin said, "intruders." Apparently it did not offend many rural voters in the older western states when he deprecated shiftless or "lawless" farmers in frontier areas. Clay had always tended to wave aside the rhetorical smokescreens that glorified every actual settler and condemned every land speculator. Like the federal land system's founders in the 1780s, he believed that no shortcut to land ownership could miraculously transform the behavior of irresponsible men.[33]

Understanding Clay's reaction to the Panic of 1819, then, reveals his political economy of the 1820s in the light of that day. He regarded the home-market idea as the main thrust of the American System. His vision for the West fit nicely into the overall conception of an economically balanced, self-sufficient nation. He advised in his April 1820 speech that frontier land be kept "easily accessible to all who wish to acquire it" and that Americans' predilection for agriculture be countervailed "by presenting to capital and labor motives for employment in other branches of industry." Tariff protection could easily appeal not only to western producers of sugar and wool but also those of "Hemp, Cotton bagging, Iron and Spirituous Liquors"—interests Clay knew well and courted for support. In addition, he would prove in 1824 his ability to win majorities in western areas where commercial prospects, often tied to the hope for transportation improvements, loomed brightest.[34]

Did the American System offer nothing to struggling farmers or itinerant laborers in the newer states who more likely wanted preemption or graduated land prices? Poor workers and farmers, too, could gain from transportation improvements and secure values on whatever lands they owned or might someday attain the means to purchase. Would federal encouragement of manufactures inhibit agricultural expansion? The moderate land-price levels provided by the federal auction system did not deter westward migration and land buying between 1815 and 1830, a time of protective tariffs. Clay thought a carefully conceived disposition of western lands, together with other elements of the home-market vision, could reconcile conflicting sections, classes, and interests. This meant land prices low enough for men of average means yet sufficiently high to protect the West from a flood of lower-class easterners and impoverished immigrants. Clay argued consistently that an oft-changing or radically generous policy would disrupt western social order, endanger land values, and threaten the economic harmony of the Union. As for squatters on the public domain, he viewed them in the traditional way: as land thieves who thumbed their noses at federal authority. Appeals for preemption, cession of public lands to the states, and Benton's land-price graduation scheme would receive not a shred of sympathy from him.[35]

If the West held promise for an expanding middle-class commercial society, along lines of Clay's American System, it also remained a continuing source of national revenue, vital to "the spirit of improvement" that President John Quincy Adams wished to pursue after his election in 1824. As Kentucky's George Robertson had observed in April 1820, the public land system originally served revenue *and* "the substantial interests of society." National Republicans like Adams and Clay agreed that the second purpose could be achieved partly through the first. Since the 1780s, sales of public land had provided revenue toward the retirement of the national debt; but the Louisiana Purchase, the War of 1812, and the Panic had swollen the government's obligation to its creditors more than ever. The war also exposed an even more desperate need for internal development of the country than in Albert Gallatin's days as treasury secretary, when he first heavily promoted it. In the mid-1820s, public land sales again drew attention as a way to supplement the capital that states and private investors might contribute for that purpose.[36]

Still, a fundamental question remained: under whose authority would the primary initiatives come? One option, President Adams's preference, required land sales to remain completely under federal control, with Congress funneling the proceeds directly into the advancement of transportation and education throughout the nation. Another possibility, like the Maxcy plan, would allocate shares of public domain to both the western states and the eastern, with further disposition as state legislatures might direct. A third proposition arising at this time, and attractive later to Clay, was for the federal government to distribute not the actual lands but the proceeds from land sales among the states. And finally, the most radical idea was for Congress to cede the federal lands now under its care to the states where they lay, fully denationalizing public land ownership and control over land development and leaving to only new states the direct benefits of western land resources.

When politicians and pundits of the 1820s (and later) used the phrase "internal improvements," they referred to a wide spectrum of activities, public and private, ranging from the clearing of rivers to the broadening of minds. Transportation advances, whether by federal, state, or private efforts, promised to make a lasting impression on the American landscape, converting subsistence farming areas into proto-commercial regions prepared for systematic settlement and growth. The "spirit of improvement," as John Quincy Adams would fashion it, could include support for education, as well. National Republicans, following Adams, aimed to develop and implement a policy in which "every dollar expended would have re-paid itself fourfold in the enhanced value of the public lands."[37]

If improving transportation (and market access) in the new states and territo-ries mattered so much, then perhaps government should stimulate the building of western roads and canals, instead of waiting for it to occur by state or private initiatives, if at all. In his Seventh Annual Message, on December 5, 1815, Presi-dent James Madison had called for a limited commitment of national energies to improvements in transportation. "No objects within the circle of political economy so richly repay the expense bestowed on them," he advised. And in 1816, most of Congress agreed. Ohio senator Jeremiah Morrow immediately praised Madison's idea of an internal commercial system—new turnpikes and improved inland nav-igation—reminiscent of the Gallatin Plan: "Such a commerce will, in its natural tendency, create interests and feelings, consonant with the great interests of the community."[38]

Clay, as a House member in 1818, had already prepared a no-nonsense answer for "Old Republican" strict constructionists, like John Randolph, who still thought that federal action held more potential for internal corruption than for improve-ment. In a new country, Clay suggested, "the condition of society may be ripe for public works long before there is, in the hands of individuals, the necessary accu-mulation of capital to effect them." Apart from the unavoidable truth that some special interests would benefit and others suffer, both undeservedly, everyone realized that local political opposition often impeded change as much as capital shortage. "Sometimes the interest of the place of the improvement is adverse to the improvement and to the general interest," Clay observed. One example close to his own experience was in the town of Louisville, at the rapids of the Ohio River, where the local interest was "more promoted by the continuance, than the removal of the [natural] obstruction." National power offered a solution—congressional appropri-ations to do what state and local governments lacked the resources to accomplish.

The result, in Clay's words, would be to authorize and execute projects "fixed to the soil," becoming "a durable part of the land itself, diffusing comfort and activity and animation on all sides."[39]

There was no separating the political implications of national improvements projects from their economic value to the republic. Congress had always struggled with the question of how to unite remote western parts with the rest of the Union, and the acquisition of Louisiana had complicated that picture exponentially. Back in March of 1806, as he contemplated the social issues inherent in settling the trans-Mississippi region, Kentuckian John Breckinridge, the U.S. attorney general, had considered it vital that the Senate pass a bill to encourage emigration to the "Orleans Territory" by allowing a bounty of land (some 160 acres) to any able-bodied militiaman agreeing to settle there. "Should this measure be adopted," he then scribbled to Clay, "it will not only effectually protect that, at present, very defenceless & vulnerable part of the Union, but enable the people there to carry out their civil government with more ease & harmony, by infusing among them a more general knowledge of our laws, customs, &c." In a similar spirit, Clay pleaded with his House colleagues in March 1818: "Look at the line of the Atlantic, and that of the Mississippi—look how nature invites you to make perfect the geographical advantages which she has granted to you; and, keeping in view the great principle of preserving the union of the states, see how essential is the power, how important its exercise, of connecting these two great lines by means of roads and canals."[40]

A young South Carolina congressman, John C. Calhoun, then an ardent nationalist, agreed. In 1816 he had advocated a permanent endowment for internal improvements, taken from the bonus fund of the Second Bank of the United States and the stock dividends accruing to the federal government. "We occupy a surface prodigiously great in proportion to our numbers," Calhoun said. "It is our duty, then, as far as in the nature of things it can be effected, to counteract this weakness." President Madison on March 3, 1817, vetoed this "Bonus Bill," disagreeing not in principle but for other reasons, including its free construction of the general welfare clause. But Calhoun's congressional defense of the measure captured the essence of nationalist concern for a controlled political and moral development of the West: "No country, enjoying freedom ever occupied anything like as great an extent of country as this Republic." Abundant land had exempted the United States from the "causes which distracted the small Republics of antiquity," but it had also exposed the nation "to the greatest of all calamities, next to the loss of liberty, and even to that in its consequence—*disunion*."[41]

Congress, of course, had already established the precedent for federally aided road building in the West. Authorized in 1806 with a $30,000 appropriation to get it started, the Cumberland Road by 1818 stretched from Cumberland, Maryland, to

Wheeling, Virginia, where it met the Ohio River. For many thousands of Americans, this improvement served as an avenue out to the frontier and a route back for eastbound grain, livestock, and other western products. But to nationalists, even the economic value of the road came second to its expediting of an extended republican community. In Clay's words, "settlements had been multiplied—buildings of all kinds erected—villages had sprung up as if by enchantment; . . . the road resembled one continued street, almost the whole way from Cumberland to Wheeling." It was the beginning of an imagined network of turnpikes that would diffuse law, liberty, and intelligence throughout the wilderness, making Americans masters of their continental empire, just as sturdy ancient roads had spread Roman influence throughout Europe.[42]

Other than a vague reference to "the spirit of improvement" in his First Annual Message of December 6, 1825, the New Englander John Quincy Adams had not displayed much sympathy for western interests. How much of that "spirit" might in his view apply to western development remained unclear. It may have helped the West's cause a little that the westerner Clay, despite the "corrupt bargain" election controversy in 1824, had become Adams's secretary of state, but many who lived in the West would find little of comfort in the president's language or background. They expected him (correctly, it turned out) to favor continuing high public land prices, buoyed by the auction system and the minimum price restriction. Adams held a low opinion of Benton's land reform ideas, as did most New Englanders in the middle to late 1820s. The *Boston Courier* said of the Missourian's graduation scheme, "It is one of Col. Benton's clap-traps, in which he catches the 'sweet voices' of the ignorant by promising them farms free of expense . . . exceedingly captivating to the squatter portion of Mr. Benton's constituents." Adams agreed. Allowing western lands to go for so little money could mark a dangerous precedent in the relationship between national government and the historically unruly settlers on the frontiers. "Benton has been the first broacher of this system," Adams wrote privately in November 1826, "and he relies on it to support his popularity in the Western country." The real purpose of the scheme, Adams thought, was "to excite and encourage hopes among the Western people that they can extort the lands from the Government for nothing."[43]

Adams's treasury secretary, Richard Rush of Pennsylvania, son of the Philadelphia physician Benjamin Rush, mirrored the president's economic views, including his aversion to newest-state westerners. The mid-1820s would be a period of escalating controversy between protectionists and free traders, a dispute that more and more involved land policy as much as internal improvements did. Rush sided with the protectionists. He admired the German home-market advocate Friedrich List, praising List's political economy as "original thought." Among Rush's close

friends and most frequent correspondents was Charles Jared Ingersoll of Philadelphia, a fellow Princeton graduate and former member of Congress, who had
become an ardent supporter of federal transportation improvements and tariff
protection. Rush also identified with Mathew Carey, who had been inundating the
Treasury Department and Congress with his writings and those of other protectionists. Shortly after receiving Carey's latest protectionist offering in late August
1827, the treasury secretary exclaimed, "It contains a distinct and to my mind con-
vincing condensation of facts and views in favor of the manufacturing policy."[44]

Rush shared Carey's interest in the country's potential for diversified production and internal consumption. Also like Carey, he lived in a different philosophical universe from the agrarianism that Benton had found (or made) increasingly
popular in the West. American agriculture could never reach its full potential,
Rush wrote, "but under the constant and various demand of the home market,"
and that required the "full encouragement and success of domestic manufactures." Like many easterners, Rush saw America's westward expanding empire as
both valuable and worrisome. The size and fertility of a country needed the "provi-
dent" hand of government to "second these gifts." Adams had said the same thing
in his 1825 Annual Message: "To give perfection to the industry of a country rich
in the gifts of nature, and blessed in the beneficence of its Government" ranked
"amongst the highest ends of legislation."[45]

Rush's attitude on western lands lacked the political finesse that Clay might
have employed had *he* been treasury secretary. In a move that many westerners
rightly took to represent Adams's opinion—and, wrongly, that of the whole Northeast—Rush decided in late 1827 to treat the public lands question as subordinate
to tariff policy. "It will be of a nature to draw down attack in congress," he confided
to Ingersoll that November, as if hankering to lay down the sectional gauntlet. He
knew the pro-tariff lobby had gained encouragement from a recent protectionist
convention in Harrisburg, Pennsylvania. Woolen interests had been unhappy with
the Tariff of 1824, and after the defeat in Congress of a new Woolens Bill in 1827,
a hundred friends of protection from thirteen states had met in Harrisburg at
the end of July and drawn up a forceful memorial to Congress. "I shall probably
attempt some developments this year under this most fruitful head," Rush continued, "and in connexion too with the manufacturing question, in ways which, if
done before, I have not seen."[46]

That was an understatement, considering the magnitude of political indiscre-
tion he now contemplated. Rush's report to Congress in December 1827 explicitly
contradicted Benton's view, but it offered little reassurance to westerners of their
advantage in supporting the American System. It damaged the home market cause
by emphasizing too much the *supposed* contradiction between western growth

and the encouragement of eastern manufacturing. "There is an inducement to increase legislative protection to manufactures in the actual internal condition of the United States," argued Rush, "which is viewed with an anxiousness belonging to its peculiar character and intrinsic weight. It is that which arises from the great extent of their unsold lands." The secretary proceeded to outline a distinctly pro-eastern political economy, with a capital-intensive emphasis on manufacturing. This included a passage that seemed almost calculated to jolt westerners, repudiating the Jeffersonian agricultural vision that had inspired many of them:

> The manner in which the remote lands of the United States are selling and settling, whilst it may possibly tend to increase more quickly the aggregate population of the country, and the mere means of subsistence, does not increase capital in the same proportion. It is a proposition too plain to require elucidation, that the creation of capital is retarded rather than accelerated by the diffusion of a thin population over a great surface of soil. Anything that may serve to hold back this tendency to diffusion from running too far, and too long, into an extreme, can scarcely prove otherwise than salutary.[47]

Rush's point was that national government should provide special inducements to domestic industry to counterbalance the natural encouragement that America's open lands offered for agriculture. Assuming that the West had benefited enough from gradually liberalized federal land laws, the secretary offered nothing for expansionist western interests.

Like Adams, Rush had placed policy for its own sake ahead of political considerations, rather than finding a way to balance the two. Exclusive focus on principle precludes compromise and was a style ill-adapted to a burgeoning era of vigorous party competition. Before the report appeared in public, the secretary had written to Ingersoll, on December 3, 1827, "The difficulty in my station is, to present views of it not found in the discussions of every day"; and then, two weeks later, "You will, in good time, find my report attacked fiercely. . . . This is what a public man must expect." But Rush's report did win the approval of President Adams, who wrote, "the policy that it recommends will outlive the blast of faction and abide the test of time."[48] Andrew Jackson and his allies thought differently. So would the nation's voters in 1828.

—◦—

The move bore all the earmarks of political blackmail: early in 1829, the Illinois Assembly sent to Congress a memorial calling for the cession of national holdings within its sovereign limits and intimating an eventual seizure of the lands unless federal authorities met their request. The document questioned whether federal tenure to the public lands was really "valid and binding on the new States" in the first place. Illinois legislators had rallied behind their governor, Ninian Edwards, who had chosen even more provocative language in his annual message to the legislature that previous December.[49]

Ironically, the Illinois governor hailed originally from Virgil Maxcy's state, born in Montgomery County, Maryland, in March 1775. At age 20, he settled in Kentucky, took up a law practice, and wound up in the state legislature—en route to becoming chief justice of the Kentucky court of appeals in 1807. Young Edwards's meteoric rise reflected the sudden ups and downs of frontier politics. In 1809, President Madison appointed him territorial governor of Illinois. He served in that capacity until his territory became a state in 1818. Early on, Edwards established a reputation for strong-willed behavior that earned him both loyal friends and staunch opponents, particularly after he landed right in the center of the factional infighting that preceded the emergence of distinct parties in Illinois.

Often more focused on personality than issues, the pro-Edwards versus anti-Edwards division in Illinois continued well into the 1820s and generated political animosities that would follow Edwards over the years. Friends in the legislature (or perhaps enemies who wanted him out of the state) sent Edwards to the United States Senate in 1818. There, he took stands for swifter western growth and the admission of Missouri as a slave state. In 1826, Illinois voters returned Edwards to the statehouse, where he went to work against Indians, state banking, and federal control of public lands.[50]

Despite his support of western internal improvements, which Illinois needed, Edwards condemned the Adams administration for its position on public lands— that is, Rush's 1827 report. Of that document, he said, "[T]here has been nothing so well calculated to awaken our apprehensions, as certain principles which it has recently avowed and acted upon." The indictment of federal land policy in the governor's message of December 2, 1828, aimed its appeal to all shades of western radicalism. The new states, he maintained, had been "seriously injured" by the system, which, he declared, "prohibits settlement and cultivation without previous purchase" and "refuses to sell, but upon terms far more exorbitant" than had ever been set by any of the states or, for that matter, "the Powers of Europe that have held land on this continent." Moreover, he continued, the federal government "exacts the same price for all land, good, and bad and indifferent." Year after year, westerners had implored Congress to address these grievances by granting "small donations out of the public domain, to poor, but meritorious and useful citizens who are unable to buy; and by reducing the price, and apportioning it to the quality of the land." Not only had such petitions been fruitless, "but an aggravation of the evils, already so severely felt, is seriously threatened," Edwards protested. Referring again to Rush, the Illinois governor continued, "A high Functionary of the government, sensible of the magnitude of the interests at stake, but unappalled by it, in an elaborate and eloquent official report to Congress, at the last session, in glowing colors, depicts even the present poor encouragement afforded to the settlement and cultivation of the public lands, as an evil to the nation."[51]

The message could be understood on two levels. Directly, Edwards was making a case for the agricultural political economy of "Old Republicanism," once the ideological bailiwick of Taylor, Macon, and Randolph, and now championed in the West by Benton. He capped that argument with a daring assertion of the right of western states to all territory lying within their sovereign limits. Embedded in the message was a point that would shock the East, especially after being repeated as a constitutional doctrine only a few weeks later by John C. Calhoun (turned anti-national) in the *South Carolina Exposition and Protest*, of 1828, and also, a few years thence, by South Carolina nullifiers in the most threatening sectional standoff since the Missouri Crisis of 1819–1821. Edwards sarcastically referred to "a new discovery" that, in a nation abounding with "waste lands" of unparalleled fertility, "any vocation is better calculated to increase its capital, or promote its welfare, than agriculture." Yet the treasury secretary in Washington had recommended a "legislative discountenance" of agriculture in favor of promoting more modern industrial interests. For his agricultural political economy, Edwards drew selectively from Emer de Vattel, the Swiss natural law philosopher of the eighteenth century. To Vattel, as Edwards fashioned him, agriculture was "the nursing father of the State," the source of public virtue and social order. He quoted Vattel that "government ought carefully to avoid every thing capable of discouraging the husbandman, of diverting him from the labors of agriculture." It was equally agreeable "to the dictates of humanity" and to the advantage of government, Vattel had written, "to give these desert places to strangers who are able to clear the land and to render it valuable."[52]

Federal title to the public domain, Edwards said, distorting history, "primarily derived from these principles, and must forever remain subject to the obligations they impose." From the time Europeans discovered North America, he continued, the "law of nature," required that "thinly scattered" aborigine hunters be replaced by white pioneers devoted to cultivating the soil. It was the duty of any American government to subsidize this destiny above all, providing through agriculture any needed "boon to a poor and dependent, but faithful and useful citizen." Colonial Virginia law had served this end, said Edwards, by requiring a speedy seating and development of lands granted to individuals. Through the conditions of the Cession of 1784, he claimed, Virginia extended this principle to the new public domain. Any political economy for the nation therefore should value land development above and apart from capital accumulation. This was, he avowed, the true aim referred to in Virginia's stipulation that public lands be disposed of for the "common benefit of all the states." Similarly, the stipulation for the admission of new states into the Union "on an equal footing with the original states" contemplated "all usual and ordinary inducements to settlement and cultivation" and "their accomplishment within a reasonable period."[53]

This overstrained (not to say *mistaken*) view of Virginia's intentions led Edwards to a bold conclusion: if the national government would not manage lands situated within new states without violating original principles, and if it refused to cede the lands to those states, then western state legislatures had a political option to "nullify" federal laws applying to the lands. The admission of a state to the Union, he asserted, "ought to conclude all question as to the expediency or duty of permitting, if not encouraging, settlements coextensive with its limits." But those presently responsible for national policy thought that government was bound only to sell western lands, said Edwards, "for the payment of the public debt; that, in reference to every other object, it may or may not dispose of them, as the particular interest of a majority of the states may seem to require." The question came down to whether national policies seen to be working "oppressively" against a minority of states still warranted the obedience of that minority. Because powers not delegated to the United States, nor prohibited to the states separately, were reserved to the states or to the people, each state of the Union had sovereignty within its own limits, as Calhoun also would say in the *Exposition and Protest*. From the same proposition followed Edwards's view of the Constitution, which echoed ones expressed during the 1819–1820 Missouri Crisis: "a union of coordinate, sovereign, and independent states, in which each yields, and retains precisely the same powers; and in authorizing the admission into the Union of new states, could not have intended that they should be admitted upon any other, than terms of perfect equality." Therefore, any actions or "bargains" restricting the "equal rights" of sovereign states stood "not only voidable like civil contracts made during infancy, but absolutely null and void as being incompatible with, and repugnant to the fundamental law."[54]

Following Illinois's, Indiana's legislature endorsed Edwards's position, on January 9, 1829, claiming for itself an "exclusive right to the soil and eminent domain" of unappropriated lands within its boundaries. Between 1828 and 1833, three other states—Alabama, Louisiana, and Missouri—called for outright cession of federal lands to the states. None of this found much favor in Congress. Representative William S. Archer of Virginia, although he opposed distributing public land proceeds around the Union, condemned the Illinois doctrine as merely feeding "a relation of war, between States." James S. Stevenson of Pennsylvania agreed: "[I]f any States have, in reality, an unhallowed desire *to get*, it may be useful to them to reflect that the other States have the power *to keep*."[55]

By the end of 1829, it would have been hard for any member of Congress—

or those outside its halls—to miss the parallels between land cession demands and the nullification issue. South Carolina extremists had been promulgating the concept of nullification at least since 1825, linking it with the Virginia and Kentucky Resolutions of 1798. Edwards's message came only seventeen days ahead of South Carolina's passage of eight new resolutions declaring the 1828 "Tariff of Abominations" unconstitutional, oppressive, and unjust. Calhoun's *South Carolina Exposition and Protest*, published anonymously, accompanied the South Carolina statement. Within two months, Georgia, Mississippi, and Virginia had registered similar tariff protests.[56]

Given the potential of public land policy to provide federal revenue and—more important—to influence the structure, direction, and values of western communities, any fundamental alteration of the original land system would carry profound ramifications. Such change would reverberate across the entire spectrum of economic issues, including tariffs and internal improvements. Those who thought land proceeds crucial for subsidizing roads, canals, and public education—whether for the West alone or for every state in the Union—had reason for alarm over radical proposals that attacked the traditional land system. As western radicalism continued to spread, defenders of that system, including certain New Englanders, grew far more nervous—and more vocal as well.

CHAPTER FIVE

Foot's Resolution and the "Great Debate"

In the small western town of Indianapolis, population roughly 1,900, the February 11, 1830, issue of the *Indiana State Gazette* reported, "A debate of immense interest to the people of the west, in relation to the public lands, has been going on for some time in both houses of Congress." Under discussion in distant Washington, D.C., were "measures, more injurious to the west" than any others the writer could imagine—so much that the "bare discussion of the propriety of adopting them" would "doubtless meet with the unqualified animadversion of the western people."[1]

The 21st Congress had just begun its work in December 1829 when Senator Samuel A. Foot of Connecticut, on Wednesday the 30th, introduced a resolution that sales of public land be restricted temporarily to tracts already surveyed and on the market. He also suggested abolishing the office of surveyor general as a way to promote governmental retrenchment. Meanwhile, in the House of Representatives, Jonathan Hunt, a Vermont protectionist, had entered a resolution for the distribution of western land revenue throughout the Union, eastern and western states alike, for purposes of internal improvement (and to justify continuing high tariff rates). Because these propositions came from easterners—in Foot's case, one known for antipathy toward the West—they carried implications certain to incense many in the newest states. Some westerners in those states saw a frightening, increasingly aggressive attitude against their interests. Thomas Hart Benton, more animated than ever, claimed that Foot's proposed restrictions reflected an eastern conspiracy to stunt the agricultural growth of the new section, strangling its fragile farm-based economy. Others claimed that any halting of surveys and sales would threaten a multitude of land investors in the West, thriving again since the Panic of 1819 had run its course. The vitality of many trans-Appalachian towns and cities depended on such investors.[2]

The hyperbolic responses of western lawmakers and journalists to Foot's initiative smacked of overt sectionalism and a desire to advance radical politicians in the new states. But were they unfounded? In fact, the resolution represented the views of resentful, anti-Jackson northeasterners who not only opposed Benton's graduation plan but also feared their region's loss of status and influence in favor of the rapidly emerging West. In no way, however, did the resolution speak for Daniel Webster, senator from Massachusetts, who had nothing to do with it and no prior knowledge of Foot's intentions. He preferred to avoid the subject if possible, leaving the land policy of the nation undisturbed. True, Webster would side with Foot in opposing Benton's graduation scheme in May 1830, but by that time Benton seemed to be courting supporters of Webster's rival, John C. Calhoun of South Carolina. Meanwhile, the wily Missourian would seize upon Foot's resolution as a silver-platter opportunity to build a coalition of westerners and southerners in Congress—enough, if the strategy worked, to get the graduation plan passed—and possibly more.[3]

· Outside Washington, Foot's resolution no more reflected a broad consensus in the Northeast than the overheated rhetoric of Benton and his allies represented the views of all westerners. The dramatic—and misleading—appeal of the great Senate debate on the resolution naturally draws attention to Benton's provocative objections and to the actions of Calhoun's protégé, Senator Robert Y. Hayne, also of South Carolina, who underscored Benton's words and supported the radical West. Historians usually focus on Webster's two legendary replies to Hayne, especially the oft-quoted second one. At stake in these exchanges appeared to be nothing short of the balance of power in Congress and, with that, the political and economic destiny of the Union. Much about the situation justified this impression, and yet any account that concentrates too much on the speeches alone will miss at least half of another complex and interesting story, the public lands part.

On December 24, 1829, the *Boston Courier* declared that the public lands question that had commenced this debate was "destined to produce . . . more heart-burnings, more recriminations, and more quarrels, than any other subject which could at present be brought before Congress." Other commentators said the same. The reason was not simply that land sales generated federal revenue, which gave the national government power. More disturbing was the truth that radicalism in the West constituted as great a threat to social order, and perhaps even union, as South Carolina's nullification doctrine, which is generally regarded as the most grave and, in many accounts, the *only* serious challenge to federal authority at that time. Seen a different way, the federal government could contain South Carolina radicals or, if necessary, crush them, but exerting governmental control in the far West had always been more problematic than in the East. The "untold power of Selfishness," the *Courier* added, "must be, with narrow minds, a barrier against the assaults of Argument, Reason, and perhaps Justice." No less revealing than the contest in the Senate was the cultural debate going on throughout the country, a discussion that had involved tariffs, internal improvements, and—always indirectly—slavery. But hinging more and more on this battle, and on the outcome of the fight between disparate regions, sections, and interests, was the future of the West and what that could mean for everyone.[4]

—◦—

The election of Andrew Jackson over John Quincy Adams in 1828 had shaken the East at its foundations. Around mid-1827, National Republicans, advocating domestic manufacturing and internal improvements, had counted their odds strong of winning several western states, including Ohio, Kentucky, Indiana, Missouri, and Louisiana. All five went to Jackson. Although Old Hickory's public policy vision remained somewhat vague, the strong southern and western elements in Jackson's electoral coalition foretold little of promise for Adams's New England, the only secure stronghold of National Republicanism. Henry Clay, "Harry of the West," remained the party's best hope for the presidency in 1832, but he had retired temporarily to Lexington. Webster therefore bore the burden of saving nationalist principles from those who regarded "union" secondary, if not irrelevant, to "liberty."[5]

To some contemporaries—and most historians—the rhetorical battle on the Senate floor between Webster and Hayne registered as being somehow separate from, and more important than, the subject of land sales and the immediate welfare of the new states and territories. It was not. The wider implications of western land policy, all of which connected vitally to the future of both liberty and union, heavily influenced all the debate's participants. In its largest sense, the antagonism between Foot and Benton, East versus West, in the last days of 1829 reflected more than sectional conflict; it was a clash of rival economic beliefs and world views. At the same time, more narrowly, the battle revealed divergent regional and local perspectives, too. The ostensible purposes of Foot's resolution smacked of New England's most conservative ways of thinking, especially the reluctance of some parts to accept the legitimacy of an explosively growing, increasingly assertive West. The gradual loss of New England's stature in national politics after the War of 1812 roughly paralleled the advance of the new states. The Hartford Convention, a source of subsequent humiliation for New England nationalists like Webster, had exposed the sense of isolation and futility in the region. And later, struggling to escape the shackles of traditional seagoing commerce, many New England manufacturers resented the tendency, however exaggerated or wrongly perceived, of the frontier to drain away precious industrial labor.[6]

The Adams administration, and especially John Quincy Adams's treasury secretary, Richard Rush, had expressed little sensitivity to western interests. To Rush, the "common good" of all states together in a consolidated union meant federal support for protective tariffs, high land prices, and a controlled growth of agriculture in the new states. Many westerners read that as a continuing suppression of their rights in favor of the East. Whenever public lands became the precise subject of discussion after 1828, Jackson's election triumph notwithstanding, it was Adams, Rush, and anyone associated with them who remained easy marks for radical western criticism.[7]

Somehow, historians have always figured Samuel Augustus Foot to have been clueless about the implications that westerners would find in his resolution. The opposite more likely was true. His personal history does not suggest a man who could have been so naïve politically. Born in Cheshire, Connecticut, on November 8, 1780, he was the seventh son of John Foot, minister of the Congregational church of Cheshire. Graduating from Yale in 1797, young Foot studied at the well-known Litchfield Law School. Shortly afterward, though, he gave up law in favor of the lucrative New Haven shipping business, soon building a successful trade with the West Indies. Nearly ruined by Jefferson's embargo and the War of 1812, Foot turned to politics. A Republican probably for lack of a viable party alternative, he rose through the Connecticut legislature, winning election to Congress in 1819 and to a Senate seat in 1826. During the 1830s, he would migrate to the Whig party. Aside from the resolution carrying his name, the high point of Foot's political career would come in 1834, with his election as governor of Connecticut. Devoutly religious, he believed that a free government could "be sustained only upon the principles of the Christian religion." Ardently against slavery, he considered the institution an "abomination in the sight of God," a "foul reproach to a Christian nation" that could "probably never be exterminated, unless in blood."[8]

Foot's career in Congress prior to December 1829 may have been undistinguished, but it was hardly dull. Serving first on the House Committee on Enrolled Bills and then on the Revisal and Unfinished Business Committee, he became known as an opponent of slavery expansion and an advocate of governmental frugality. In February 1820, before the compromise decision to admit Missouri as a slave state, which he supported for the sake of sectional harmony, Foot introduced a resolution to bar slavery from the remaining territories. He also insisted that the Missouri constitution be altered to allow the presence of free blacks and mulattoes, following the effort of the proslavery Missouri constitutional convention to ban those potentially disruptive groups from the state. These views undoubtedly drew the attention of Missourians like Benton, who wanted their new state to decide such things for itself. As for government spending, Foot believed the military too expensive and not sufficiently accountable to the public. He focused on officer salaries, as he would later on the expense of public land surveying. Escalation of these, he declared in February 1821, represented a growing evil inconsistent with the republican simplicity of an earlier era in America. Deaf to pleas of the more desperate westerners during the Panic of 1819, Foot supported the Land Act of 1820, favoring the repeal of the credit system for public land purchases; he also in 1821 voted against the Relief Act that extended payment deadlines for indebted buyers, and he urged restoration of the $1.64 per acre minimum price following the 1820 reduction to $1.25.[9]

During his second stint in the House, Foot added federally funded internal improvements and protective tariffs to his growing list of political interests. Apart from objecting to their cost and disproportionate benefit to westerners, he scorned transportation subsidies as reaching beyond the powers expressly granted to the federal government; let it be the business of the new states themselves to undertake such projects, he thought. Showing what Benton would consider the traditional hostility of New England toward westward expansion, Foot (*un*like Webster) even voted against extensions of the Cumberland Road. Although willing to consider "judicious" tariff revision, he warned against the "taxation of agriculture" and opposed Clay's 1824 tariff bill on grounds that people can be "legislated into adversity" but not into prosperity. As the economic destiny of Connecticut came to lie with textile manufacturing, however, so did Foot's political sympathies. After 1828, he supported major tariff bills.[10]

In the 1820s, Foot regarded himself as an "Adams man," even if some of his earlier economic views fell short of Adams's nationalism. In an election that reflected an emerging ideological cleavage in Connecticut politics, the legislature chose him for the U.S. Senate in 1826 to replace Henry W. Edwards, who would soon become an organizer of the Jacksonian movement in the state. Foot viewed Jackson and his party with nothing but contempt from the start—an "unprincipled & malignant opposition." As a senator, he would condemn Indian removal, support the Bank of the United States, lament the corrupt rewarding of Jackson administration favorites, and disapprove Jackson's seemingly personalized use of the veto power. Foot accepted party competition as a way of venting "honest difference of opinion" and exposing "unchastened ambition," but after Jacksonians had more or less revealed their true colors, he wrote: "when the spirit of party degenerates into a mere scramble for power and place;—sacrifices principle to interest—distributes the honors and emoluments of office to purchase votes;— and pledges the '*spoils of victory*' as the reward of servile devotion to men, without regard to their measures; it corrodes the very vitals of the republic, and paves the way to despotism!"[11]

More than once in the Senate before December 1829, Foot had crossed swords with the powerful Democrats, including Benton. Surrounded by southerners and southwesterners, he was the lone New Englander—and a dissenting voice—on Benton's Indian Affairs Committee in 1827–1828. In May 1828, it was Foot, then antiprotectionist, who attacked the Missouri senator for attributing to New England all responsibility for the "Tariff of Abominations." For some time Benton and other Jackson sympathizers had taunted New England, hoping to provoke a confrontation detrimental to the Adams administration. This tariff episode, in addition to Foot's earlier views on the Missouri question and Indian policy, undoubtedly would influence the exchange between Foot and Benton on the land issue a year and a half later.

It bothered Foot that the most recent report of the commissioner of the Land Office had shown 72 million acres of public land remaining available at the federal minimum of $1.25 an acre. The market was glutted. So, in terms of land values and settlement needs, it made no sense for the government to put any more land up for sale. Benton saw this differently. To him, slow sales meant that the government had not done enough to encourage them. At the same time, opening still more acres would further enhance the western appeal of Benton's graduation plan and make him even more the heroic provider of cheap lands for his fellow westerners.[12]

Foot implicitly attacked Ninian Edwards's view along with Benton's. Connecticut, he went on to note, like every other state in the Union, held a stake in the public domain because the lands were "the common property of the United States." This referred to the earlier quarrels over the Maxcy proposal and the land policy fights of more recent sessions of Congress, including the controversy still brewing in the House regarding distribution of public land proceeds. The public domain, he concluded, "was a subject which involved important interests; the whole United States have a deep interest in it."[13]

Other northeasterners agreed. In 1830, the *North American Review* reported that the federal government held property rights to 1,065 million acres of land in the American West. Of this amount, Congress retained authority over roughly 170 million acres *within* the states of Ohio, Indiana, Illinois, Mississippi, Alabama, Louisiana, and Missouri. This included some over which Indian title still applied. Add to that another 85 million, again including Indian lands, in the organized territories of Arkansas, Florida, and Michigan. As the writer noted, it required "no very prophetic spirit to perceive, that whether surveyed in its economical or its political connexions, this question of the public domain of the country is prodigiously momentous." Without question, some northeasterners thought that more of the benefit from sales of this land should already have accrued to the old states. Whether by federal or state choices, the internal improvements once promised had not materialized. A columnist in Pittsfield, Massachusetts, would complain in early 1830, during the debate on Foot's resolution: "Where are our Western lands? . . . What do we have to show for them? Nothing." Differently managed, the western soil that once belonged to the Bay State could have produced the sums needed to finance common schools. Instead, he wrote, "all that we have received from them has been dissipated in some favorite project or squandered away upon some favorite minion, or lavished upon some sectarian institution, or has been expended in furthering the views and interests of a party, or in the resistance of the National Government."[14]

As westerners scrambled their defensive forces, Senator John Holmes of Maine spoke up, confirming not only that Foot had allies in New England but also that Benton was their target. The curmudgeonly, 57-year-old Holmes, a controversial figure in Maine state politics, had a reputation for verbally abusing his adversaries (and, some said, for being frequently inebriated). Rising on December 30, 1829, to endorse Foot's resolution, he declared that he had no wish to "check emigration to the West" or advocate "exclusive or sectional legislation." He then proceeded to irritate Benton as much as he could. The fact remained, Holmes continued, that "there are seventy-two million of acres of land at present in the market, of which it appears that only one million a year can be sold"—enough, he figured, "to supply the market for seventy-two years to come." Benton and his cronies had argued that some land in the West remained unsold because of quality too inferior to justify the $1.25 minimum. "Suppose," Holmes went on, "according to the reasoning of the gentleman from Missouri[,] that it is all refuse land—all poor land; then certainly there is much need for inquiry indeed. How . . . has it happened that these surveyors have surveyed land which is good for nothing?" Provoking still further, Holmes also questioned the federal expenditure of many thousands of dollars to pay for the extensive surveying of tracts "which no one will inhabit." In other words, it looked to him, too, as if further surveying ought to be suspended to prevent such a wasteful (and perhaps corrupt) expenditure from continuing.[15]

Because Foot's resolution had caught Benton off guard, his reply on December 30 may have revealed more than did the prepared speech he would deliver three weeks later. Determined to equate western interests with his own agenda—and not Clay's—he had trumpeted all over Missouri that the whole Northeast opposed western interests and Clay acted only as a puppet of its manufacturers. Foot's resolution would prove even more an opportunity for him than for Hayne or Webster. Although the resolution called only for Senate inquiry, nothing more, Benton anxiously stripped the matter of pretense. To stop surveys and suspend sales of fresh lands was "an old and favorite policy with some politicians," he replied. That "old policy," by his account, only victimized the West for the benefit of the East. Foot promptly denied that, but the Missourian's resentment had only started to crest.

"The Senator from Connecticut shakes his head," Benton sniffed, "but he cannot shake the conviction out of my head, that a check to Western emigration will be the effect of this resolution. . . . The West is my country; not his. I know it; he does not." The resolution, Benton charged (correctly), resembled the Adams administration's attitude. "The idea of checking emigration to the West was brought openly at the last increase of the tariff," Benton recalled. "The Secretary of the Treasury [Rush] gave it a place in his annual report upon the finances. He dwelt openly and largely upon the necessity of checking the absorbing force of this emigration in order to keep people in the East to work in the manufactories." What lands would be left for sale if Foot's resolution should take effect? "Scraps; mere refuse; the leavings of repeated sales and pickings!" Benton cried. Would any "man of substance" remove to the West only to offer his family such "miserable remnants"?[16]

Foot's antiwestern reputation caused the resolution to be seen as hostile and confrontational to the new states. But did his attitude toward the West speak for New England generally? By 1830, the answer was certainly "no." New Englanders opposed Benton's graduation plan but were otherwise divided on western policy, even though in some parts of the region, including much of Foot's Connecticut, westward expansion loomed as far more of a threat than it did elsewhere.

In addition to the more traditional—and still compelling—desire to shape the West in the cultural image of the Northeast, budding manufacturing interests had started to see the new states less as a threat to eastern prosperity and more as a potential home market for manufactured goods. Property that was declining in value because of an overloaded land market would not lure westward the prosperous settlers who had money to buy those products. In early January 1830, the Hartford-based *Connecticut Courant* reprinted an anonymous letter to the editor of the *New York Daily Advertiser* arguing that Benton's position did the West far more harm than good and that Foot's resolution, despite its pro-eastern bias, actually made better economic sense for the West than Foot himself might have realized. "No greater injury can be inflicted on the western country," the *Advertiser* contended, "than to open other land for sale." The reason was "obvious":

> The quantity of land in market is so great, that improvements will not sell for one half the money it costs to make them. The depression in the price of western lands, prevents thousands of persons from emigrating thither, who otherwise would be disposed to go into the western country. People in the old states learn, that if money is vested in western lands, it cannot be realized on a resale. . . . What prudent man will invest his money in any article with which the market is glutted?

Moreover, putting additional land up for sale just to please Benton's "deluded" constituents made bad cultural sense as well: "By continuing the surveys, the consequence will be, that other large tracts will be offered for sale, and emigrants will be spread over the western regions, destitute of the conveniences of life, and of literary, moral, or religious instruction." Thus, if Benton really wanted more compact settlement, which his graduation plan had promised, then to further increase the amount of land in market would only thwart his own purposes.[17]

New Englanders in Congress overwhelmingly had voted for the Land Act of 1820 that repealed government credit sales. All ten New England senators supported it, along with 37 (all but one) of its House members. This did not, however, denote the kind of hostility toward western interests and resentment of its growth that Benton and other westerners understood Foot to express. After all, half of the western-state senators and representatives in 1820 wanted the credit system to end as well. Further, as Webster would emphasize in his Second Reply to Hayne, the legislation had provided a sizeable reduction in the minimum price of public lands—from $2.00 an acre to $1.25. Indeed, had Foot's resolution come in 1820, it might have gained wider support on grounds of its being in the best interests of westerners themselves. Noting that purchasers of public land owed the federal government a total of nearly 12.5 million dollars, the *Connecticut Courant* in August 1819 had posed the land policy question that would soon resound in Washington, during the early months of the financial panic: How could the debtors of the West ever pay such a vast sum? "We consider it far better for the nation that no sales should be made for years to come," the *Courant* writer declared, "than that this ruinous speculating system of selling them on credit should be persisted in." Further, in 1821, when Congress passed the relief bill allowing public-land buyers to relinquish credit purchases that hard times had rendered them unable to pay—more liberation from debt than any private creditor would ever grant—a large majority of New Englanders, and the Northeast generally, had supported the measure.[18]

Although people interpreted economic policy issues through widely varying lenses, the eastern frame of reference remained the experience of the Panic of 1819. The governor of New York, DeWitt Clinton, in his 1827 message to the legislature expressed the hope "that learning wisdom from experience and moderation from adversity, we will never again witness a recurrence of a spirit of overweening speculation and over reaching cupidity, equally injurious to good morals and social prosperity." While Clinton's preventative for anarchy—economic and otherwise—remained faith in internal improvements, Connecticut governor Gideon Tomlinson in May 1828 sensed a greater threat to public order in the brewing tariff crisis in South Carolina. By this time, the South Carolina legislature had passed a resolution that protective tariff laws created without the intention of raising revenue

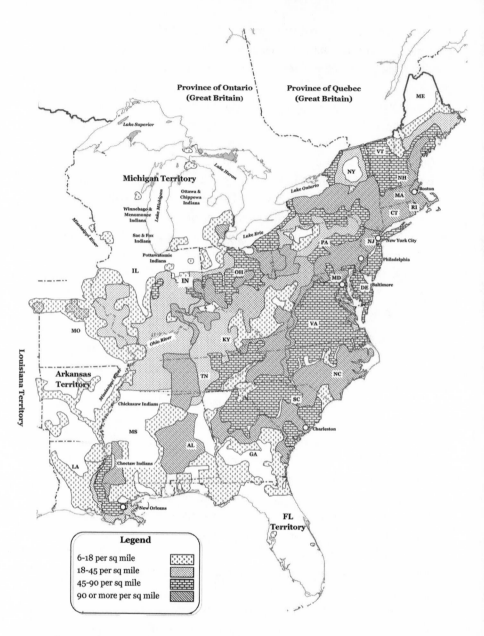

Distribution of U.S. Population East of the Mississippi River, 1830. Map drawn by Margot Gibson-Beattie.

or regulating foreign commerce were "violations of the constitution in its spirit" that "ought to be repealed." It also declared that Congress lacked the constitutional power to construct internal improvements in the states, whether or not the states in question assented to them. The Georgia Senate had followed suit with a similar declaration. Tomlinson stoutly disagreed: The framers of the Constitution meant to facilitate the commerce of the nation—"roads shortened; interior navigation on our eastern side opened, and the communication between the Western and Atlantic districts, and between the different parts of each, would be rendered more easy" via an interlocking system of roads and canals. "The dangers anticipated from the exercise of the powers, are imaginary," he insisted.[19]

If any part of the Northeast had reason to fear western growth, however, Connecticut did. In 1830, Foot's home state had a population of approximately 298,000, third highest among the six New England states, trailing Massachusetts's 610,000 and Maine's 399,000. More significantly, however, Connecticut was *by far* the slowest growing state in the region and, for that matter, the entire Union at this time. Its population had increased only 13.7 percent since 1810 and 8.4 percent since 1820. Massachusetts, by contrast, had multiplied by twice this rate: 29.2 percent in the previous 20 years and 16.6 percent in the preceding decade. By further contrast, Ohio, the oldest and largest state in the Northwest with a population of about 938,000 in 1830, had grown 306.1 percent since 1810 and 61.5 percent since 1820. The migration of easterners into Indiana and Illinois over the same period had helped to fuel an explosion of population at a rate roughly three times greater than Ohio's. Settlement processes that before had taken generations to develop seemed to whiz out-of-control across the historical landscape. Benton's Missouri, with something close to 140,000 inhabitants in 1830, had grown 109.0 percent in just the preceding decade. For the people of Connecticut, where many investors now pinned their money-making hopes on textiles, a continuing drain of labor westward could indeed have meant serious economic difficulty in the near future.[20]

But the rest of New England felt less cause for alarm, and cultural perspectives throughout the region pointed strongly to the need for a more complex understanding of rapid western growth. The lingering effects of the Panic of 1819 may have dampened easterners' inclination to take risks but not their *own* western prospects. Daniel Webster wrote to the wife of a friend in 1829: "The *times* have *pinched* New England, like a vise. We hope we are getting over the hardest of the *screwing*, & if this should turn out to be so, our emigrants to the West would be more likely to be able to possess the means of business & credit, wherever they might fix themselves." Showing that people in the Northeast paid attention to census returns, the Amherst, New Hampshire, *Farmer's Cabinet* noted early in 1829 the "astonishing" fact that "although during the last half century the Atlantic coast has suffered such a steady and powerful drain, it has itself continued to advance in population, wealth, and arts, with no perceptible diminution in the ratio of progress." Meanwhile, under the "patronage" of the federal government, the West had grown more "in fifty years than the Atlantic coast was able to do in three times that period." As this writer saw it, the inhabitants these North Atlantic states had sacrificed included few of low character or poor economic potential: "The young men, who have emigrated from the Atlantic coast to the West, did not, like the emigrants from Ireland and the Palatinate, leave potato-fare and six pence a day behind them. On the contrary, they left a country of high wages and hearty diet." Such was the benefit of keeping the western "safety-valve . . . calculated to open at a very low pressure," thus averting "the most disastrous explosions."[21]

Rather than fearing the damage western growth might cause to the manufacturing economy of the Northeast, other writers there worried more about the kind of western world that might be developing—whether it would become a place of civilization, order, and community and its culture one of virtue, refinement, and restraint. Or would the West of the future degenerate into a venue for anarchy and mayhem; its people destitute, illiterate, and selfish; its economy languishing; its politics corrupt; its leaders unprincipled? More broadly, what kind of *nation* would result from unrestrained westward expansion? Many northeasterners saw a road to perdition in the whole of Jacksonian governance, while especially deploring Benton's proposal that lands in the West be dispensed not to those with the means to buy but for practically nothing to anyone who wanted them. Still more frightening was the sectional crisis that might ensue if western states defied federal authority and just seized the public lands lying within their limits, as Edwards of Illinois had suggested.

If the American frontier could not be settled according to New England design, it mattered to northeasterners at least that it not follow the lead of Benton, Edwards, or—worse than both—the political economy of slavery. Here, of course, the "patronage" of federal policy makers mattered vitally. Only the federal government, they believed, not the states separately and not entrepreneurs operating privately, could possibly engineer a western society closely compatible with eastern interests and concerns. While some public figures in the East, Clinton and Tomlinson for example, had referred to western policy by implication, others addressed the challenge of the new states more directly, noting the implicit political advantages of a western home market. One of the latter was Boston's Edward Everett.

If no one in 1820s New England could rival Daniel Webster's growing eminence as a politician who spoke from both the cultural heart and the political head of the region, Everett came a close second. A kind of role model for rising New England intellectuals—Ralph Waldo Emerson dubbed him "the American Cicero"—Everett managed to combine public lecturing with a professorship (in Greek literature) at Harvard and the editorship of Boston's *North American Review*, the country's leading literary magazine of that day. A former Federalist turned National Republican, Everett also made his way into politics, in the 1820s, and, as an Adams man, served in the U.S. House of Representatives from 1825 to 1835. Often in his travels he made the case for the salutary social and economic effects of industrialization in the Northeast. One occasion when he did so was at an inn on June 29, 1829, in Yellow Springs, Ohio—in the west-central part of the state, near Dayton and about 10 miles south of the National Road. The speech glorified the westward advance of New England's civilization and political values, the worth of community development in the West, and the importance of fortifying the Union against impending sectional strains. Parallels in Webster's reply to Hayne little more than six months later—and the stark contrast with Samuel Foot's more narrow outlook—are hard to ignore.[22]

That night, standing before an audience of propertied and economically contented Ohioans, Everett found in the progress of the "western country" more than just a numerical multiplication of its citizens. It was "civilization personified and embodied" that had gone forth to "take possession of the land." The *"principle* of our institutions," he said, had advanced along with large numbers of New England migrants onto the rich Ohio lands, "through the vacant regions of space, but scattering hamlets and villages and cities in its path." This urban pattern of expansion would cement the "ties of interest, which connect all the states of this union," adding "all their strength to the compact," helping "to merge, in one comprehensive feeling"—as "ought to be the desire" of "every true patriot"—"all discordant sectional preferences." There could be little doubt, in this place so friendly to nationalist feeling, that Everett's reference to "discordant sectional preferences" meant the cessionist impulses of Edwards's Illinois no less than the radical doctrines in Calhoun's South Carolina. Because New England settlers had built so many of the "foundations of Ohio," carrying "the high traits of character" that linked the best of western development with eastern origins, Everett said, "we cannot be insensible to the prevailing affinity, between your population and ours," like "the ripening of a fruit, which our fathers planted." The system of public schools in Ohio, providing the "diffusion of intelligence" that "binds the different members of the body politic, by the strongest ties"; the state's canal policy, resulting in "a system of artificial navigation of nearly 400 miles rapidly advancing to its completion" and tying the commerce of the Old Northwest with that of the Northeast; and the political legacy of the 1787 Northwest Ordinance, modeling the "efficacy of public and private virtue" and principally the handiwork, Everett claimed, of a fellow Massachusetts man, Nathan Dane—all of this proved New England's historic commitment to a strong, stable western world. And, he added, that aegis far exceeded the earlier, pathetic, and comparatively disengaged policies of the British Empire.[23]

By contrast, on the same western tour, Everett had visited another local inn about three weeks earlier, in Nashville, Tennessee—the guest of honor at dinner in a "numerous and respectable company of citizens." On this occasion the audience had been one of "strangers" and, with few exceptions, Jackson supporters. To this audience he had made far more measured and conciliatory remarks: Everett took care not to offend producers of the cotton that Massachusetts textile manufacturers needed. In Nashville, it had not been good schools and transportation improvements that sparked his awe; the Southwest featured too few of these. And, of course, the Northwest Ordinance, with its territorial ban against slaveholding, applied only to the region north of the Ohio River, so that topic was best avoided.

Instead, Everett cited the natural endowments of the countryside: "the prodigious extent of the territory; the magnitude of the streams, that unite into one great system the remotest parts of this boundless region;—the fertility of its soil." With regard to the social fabric, he observed, "the scene presented by our western country, is not that of a barbarous race." But the credit for this, he reminded listeners, belonged to easterners: Daniel Boone, a cultural icon, "whose flight from wilderness to wilderness" had formed "a sort of Hegira in the west," and men for whom counties had been named: Lincoln, Greene, Knox, Warren, and Perry. He praised the "substantial yeomanry" (not the planter elite) who had produced highly cultivated farms, lauded the spectacular growth of towns and cities, and highlighted the importance of western loyalty to "the perpetuity of the Union." Although met with "tremendous cheering," this speech, like the one he would give in Yellow Springs, celebrated far more the West of Henry Clay than that of Jackson, Benton, or Edwards. Interestingly, the concluding part of Everett's Nashville remarks conveyed a thinly veiled cultural anxiety about the West generally, a worry that many northeasterners, including Webster, still shared and one not limited to the intellectual elite: "We feel happy in the belief, that in your further advancement you will not forget the cradles of the American race, and that you will bear in kindly remembrance the men and the deeds, which are among the dearest titles of our glory."[24]

A correspondent for the *Boston Recorder*, passing through Ohio a few years before Everett went there, stumbled upon what he recognized to be the very best kind of western settlement—the fulfillment, in microcosm, of a New England vision for frontier America. "I was introduced to a family," he wrote, "whose history I have no doubt will truly illustrate that of many an emigrant in that flourishing State." The head of this household was "honored with the highest political confidence of his fellow citizens"; his house "large, commodious, handsome; well furnished; surrounded by gardens, out-houses and fruit trees; and so located on a swell of land, as to overlook a large village." The village itself, no less impressive, featured "a meeting-house, court house, academy, many stores and mechanical shops, taverns and numerous dwellings"—its population nearly a thousand. Twenty years before, this family had come from Connecticut, through western New York, their belongings loaded on packhorses. After purchasing the land, they had felled the first tree in their township, built the first cabin, commenced the town by measuring out and selling lots, and secured for themselves as much property "as any good Christian should desire." Their children evinced "health, intelligence and contentment." A "republican independence of spirit beamed in their eyes."[25]

Such descriptions permeated newspapers and magazines of the Northeast and compared closely to the renderings of certain New England artists, especially Ralph Earl. Living in New Haven, Connecticut, Earl painted mostly portraits—solid citizens like Roger Sherman, Oliver Ellsworth, and Abigail Wolcott Ellsworth—epitomizing the dignity and simplicity of republican New England. But his landscapes, somewhat foreshadowing the Hudson River School, also drew attention among the cultural elite of the region. Earl's "View of Bennington" (1798) depicted handsome, well-ordered dwellings of prosperous settlers and civic leaders in that western Vermont town and conveyed a sense of man's ability—better yet, his obligation—to improve the natural and social environment around him. The background of the scene features Bennington County's first courthouse, symbolizing good citizenship and the rule of law, despite still-rough surroundings. "Looking East from Denny Hill" (1800) featured Earl's idealized vision of a rural village (in this case, near Leicester, Massachusetts), showing virtuous men and women variously engaged yet all contributing in unison to securing a bountiful harvest. In the distance, at least sixty-five structures, including white steeples, meetinghouses, family dwellings, and various outbuildings, complete this purposeful landscape and provide a sense of community mission and social continuity.[26]

—∽—

If Benton glorified hardscrabble settlers scratching a meager living from submarginal lands that other buyers had passed over, then his idea for the building of a good society diverged in almost every way from that of Ralph Earl, Edward Everett, and many others in New England. Not surprisingly, Benton could count about as few close friends in the Northeast as Samuel Foot could beyond the Appalachians. New England senators had voted unanimously against his graduation bill in 1828, providing nearly half the total of nays, and were joined by all but one of the mid-Atlantic votes as well. Except for a few southern yeas, support for graduation came entirely from the West.[27]

By contrast, Foot did not have to travel outside New England to find the Jacksonian types he despised. One of them, Levi Woodbury of New Hampshire, further inflamed the debate on Foot's resolution a few days after it started. He proposed an alternative resolution calling for hastening western land sales and increasing the surveying—the opposite of Foot's proposal and supposedly a test of *real* eastern empathy toward the West. To no one's surprise, Webster, while more pliable than Foot, declined this bait, refraining from comment. Afterwards, the *New Hampshire Patriot* would call Woodbury "the Champion of New-England Democracy," praising him for exposing the truly antiwestern motives of Foot and other "federalists" and for looking to the "new republican States in the West to protect the Democracy of the North, and to crush its Aristocracy." Back in New Hampshire, vibrant party conflict, drawing partly on class resentment, had supercharged the political atmosphere.[28]

By 1830, Benton felt more empowered than ever in the Northwest. The popular appeal of graduation there, especially in Indiana, had helped to force John Quincy Adams's political demise. Now, if the Missouri senator could lure southern free traders into a lasting alliance with radical Democrats of the West, National Republicanism, along with its pro-government overtones, might be smashed for good. The political basis for such an arrangement was easy enough to imagine. Benton supporters obviously would deliver antitariff votes in return for southern backing of radical public lands bills. The *New York Commercial* reported, "It is generally believed that the attack on the East by Mr. Benton, was the commencement . . . of a settled design to make wide and deep and impassible the gulph of separation between the East and the West. It is believed that the understood compact which the South are disposed to form, was to give the public lands to the West, provided the West could go with the South in producing some modification of the tariff." Indeed, the anticipated coalition might restore the traditional affinity between South and West that went back to the early years of the republic. Former president John Quincy Adams glumly wrote that "Benton and Hayne . . . proposed to break down the union of the Eastern and Western sections, . . . restoring the old joint operation of the West and the South against New England." Benton's object, he surmised, was "personal advancement" in the West, South Carolina's control over tariffs and internal improvements, "and Calhoun's[,] succession to the Presidency."[29]

A postponement of debate on the resolution had given Benton time to prepare a carefully considered answer to Foot. Rising again on January 18, 1830, he outlined to his fellow senators four ways Foot's resolution, if carried from mere inquiry to

legislation, would injure the West. The first point elaborated on his earlier contention that any limiting of sales on lands of lesser value then on the market would
stifle interest in westward migration (and undermine the graduation scheme). In
his own state, such lands were "the refuse of forty years picking under the Spanish Government and twenty more under the Government of the United States."
Second, confining purchases just to tracts already for sale would inhibit the normal settlement process in the newer states. "These lands in Missouri," Benton
explained, "only amount to one third of the State. By consequence, only one third
could be settled." He complained that it would take several decades for residue
lands in the West to sell at the minimum of $1.25 an acre.[30]

The Missouri senator's third point reminded Senate colleagues that Indian title
had already been extinguished and native inhabitants long removed from many
lands not yet up for sale. Doing what Foot wanted, Benton argued, would "deliver
up large portions of new States and Territories to the dominion of wild beasts."
Aside from squatters' claims (which most easterners also still rejected philosophically), these vacant lands, ready in large part for proximate use, would go to waste.
Such lands in Missouri amounted to "about forty thousand square miles, covering
the whole valley of the Osage River, besides many other parts." Benton's fourth
contention focused on the administrative impracticality, and danger to orderly settlement, of abolishing the surveyor generalship. "The abolition of these offices,"
he bellowed, "would involve the necessity of removing all their records, and thus
depriving the country of all evidences of the foundations of all the land titles."[31]

And so, as Benton would have it, Foot had proposed to repudiate the West and
undermine its development. "I will vote for no such inquiry," Benton proclaimed.
"I would as soon vote for inquiries into the expediency of conflagrating cities,
of devastating provinces, and submerging fruitful lands under the waves of the
ocean." Extensive, unrestrained, and immediate use of the public domain by all
classes of settlers, especially the least privileged, was the "great moral principle"
that radicals struggled to win, and Benton stood ready to lead them. Even more,
if the conventional lawmaking process did not provide the desired result, there
remained the thinly veiled threat, now increasingly heard from South Carolina and
Illinois alike, of taking law into their own hands:

[T]his inquiry, if it goes on, will have the greatest dissatisfaction to the new States in
the West and South. It will alarm and agitate them. . . . It will connect itself with other
inquiries going on . . . in the House of Representatives—to make the new States a
source of revenue to the old ones [Hunt's resolution]. . . . These measures will go
together; and if that resolution passes, and this one passes, the transition will be easy
and natural, from dividing the money after the lands are sold, to dividing the lands

before they are sold, and then to renting the land and drawing an annual income, instead of selling it for a price in hand. The signs are portentous; the crisis is alarming; it is time for the new States to wake up to their danger, and to prepare for a struggle which carries ruin and disgrace to them.[32]

Benton's argument implied that the very rules of the federal republic stood up for grabs. Could a single state, acting on its own concocted authority, simply seize the federal lands lying within its boundaries or refuse to enforce a protective tariff that did not serve its interests? Could a president repudiate a congressional or a court decision that did not please him, or a western settler take any tract he wanted, declining the legal formality of bidding at public auction? If so, then federal authority and the rule of law no longer meant anything.

—◌

A risky game now unfolded in both the West and the South, and as Tomlinson had cautioned in his governor's address, political opportunists of every stripe sat in the wings, curious to see where it might lead. Aggressive leaders in both of those sections had issued direct theoretical challenges to the federal government, although so far no action had followed. Connecticut's Samuel Foot had stirred a political hornet's nest, and Benton of Missouri had stung him in return. Now it was the South's turn.

Robert Y. Hayne's speech of January 19, 1830, accepted the Missouri senator's invitation to the South, as historians have said. But Hayne, like his political mentor, Calhoun, also took interest in Illinois governor Edwards's argument for the cession of public lands to the western states, because of the concept of state sovereignty that underlay the idea. Both public lands approaches, Benton's and Edwards's, promised considerably less federal control of western settlement and, certainly in the case of the Illinois proposal, far less federal revenue from land sales. To Benton, cession held a less important place than other options favoring lower-class settlers individually; graduation, land donations, and preemption all carried with them potential free-soil implications likely to disturb southern slaveholders.

In 1830, the 39-year-old Hayne spoke for some of the wealthiest and most influential planters in the South—the prominent "aristocracy" of the low-country region along the Atlantic coast. He had grown up on the family rice plantation in the Colleton District of South Carolina. In lieu of college, Hayne had studied law in Langdon Cheves's office in Charleston. He acquired his share of lowland South Carolina wealth and influence through his two marriages. Linked closely to Calhoun early on, he won election to the United States Senate in 1822 and again, without opposition, in 1828. Sharing Calhoun's newly found sectional outlook,

Hayne did his best to stem a rising tide of tariff protectionism, which he regarded as both unconstitutional and unnecessary. He feared that the South might become both economically and culturally too dependent on the North, which he saw as boding ill for the southern way of life, namely slaveholding. That worry led him in 1828 to help establish the *Southern Review*, committed specifically to the shoring up of southern literary identity.[33]

Hayne's South Carolina in 1830 had the smallest white population of all the southeastern states—only 258,000 compared to the largest, Virginia's 701,000—and it was the only one whose slave population (roughly 323,000) still outnumbered whites. The Palmetto State, like Connecticut, was losing influence, in its case as much to the North as to the West. South Carolina in the early 1800s had sacrificed a large number of its people to western Georgia, Alabama, and Mississippi. Its white population was increasing more slowly than those of all the other southern states; growth rates were 20.6 percent in 1810–1820 and just 8.7 percent in 1820–1830. Quite a few of those westward migrants had been up-country Piedmont planters who, increasingly indebted because of the steadily decreasing price they received for their short-staple cotton, produced in overabundance, had left South Carolina in the mid-to-late 1820s. By contrast, more specialized markets for rice and Sea Island cotton, used for luxury garments, had safeguarded low-country planters from the growing competition presented by southwestern cotton producers. But in the opinion of most low-country residents, nothing except resistance to federal power guarded them against protective tariffs to benefit northern manufacturing, rising abolitionist agitation in the North, and a mounting suspicion of slave unrest in their own backyard, seemingly justified by Denmark Vesey's chilling slave conspiracy of 1822.[34]

By the mid-1820s, South Carolina had assumed intellectual leadership in the national discussion of states' rights and in opposition to centralized government. This held particularly true in its cultural capital, Charleston, and at South Carolina College in Columbia, where scientist and political philosopher Thomas Cooper dominated the scene. South Carolina's interest in public lands sprang in part from its worry about further tariffs that would raise costs of imported manufactures and threaten the future of the southern exporting trade. Public domain issues connected to federal revenue, too, and revenue meant power. National Republican political economy, as defined by Adams and his administration, stressed a direct connection between American protectionism, restrictive federal land policies, and hostility to ceding lands to the western states. The 1827 Harrisburg (Pennsylvania) convention, as visible evidence of a pro-tariff affinity in New England, the Middle Atlantic States, and the Northwest, had fortified nationalist views, inspired demands by woolen manufacturers and others for higher duties, and appalled antitariff cotton growers all the more. Southern radicals answered swiftly. Robert J. Turnbull's series of newspaper articles, published in pamphlet form as *The Crisis*, and Thomas Cooper's *Consolidation* both condemned the calls for increased federal power, which both authors associated with antislavery forces in the North. Cooper especially shocked Yankee readers by saying the South would soon have to "calculate the value" of a union so indifferent to southern interests. It might have to choose between "submission or separation."[35]

Although Hayne, like Calhoun, had been a post–War of 1812 nationalist, he followed the current of ideological change in his native state and now identified with the nullification faction of his low-country peers. This prompted him to seize the opportunity to criticize Foot's resolution as a way of attacking the pro-statist social and economic theory he *assumed* to underlie it. In only a few years, he realized, the long-standing public debt finally would disappear. With that event, bringing an end to any immediate need for the public domain as a sinking fund, Congress would have to reconsider its western policy. Hayne bore in mind the approach of that moment and the subsequent decisions sure to affect all parts of the Union— though perhaps not in equally beneficial ways.[36]

Oversimplifying northeastern motives as much as he slanted the history of federal policy, Hayne told the Senate that the real long-term choices for public lands amounted to only a pair, the preferences of "two great parties" in the country— "very opposite opinions in the relation to the character of the policy . . . in relation to the public lands." One opinion contended that Congress had already pursued too far a "liberal course" of "extraordinary kindness and indulgence"; the other, held by much of the West, accused Congress of acting as a "hard task-master," promoting "selfish [eastern-based] interests" at western expense. As to the future, one side envisioned the western public lands as a permanent reserve, a "fund for revenue and future distribution among the States"; the other campaigned for their relinquishment to "States in which they lie." Hayne did not refer to any possibility of reform without yoking it to denationalizing the disposition of public lands. He sided with Benton but *agreed* with Edwards—two westerners, both radical, but very different in the changes they proposed.[37]

Hayne objected to the land policies of the Union as differing from the way he understood the handling of unclaimed lands during earlier periods of American history—especially prior to 1785. The English, French, and Spanish colonizers in the New World had, according to him, "all adopted the same policy," one that "had always been found necessary in the settlement of new countries." This was the granting of lands on a free basis, "without money and without price." Hayne saw the original thirteen states as having been settled for "a penny or a pepper corn." Under such a system, the English colonies grew up to an "early and vigorous manhood," enabling them "in a few years to achieve their independence"—an example of generous policy yielding the most abundant and desirable results possible over a relatively short time. The colonial system, Hayne said, afforded "the only certain means of building up in a wilderness, great and prosperous communities."

Born of early needs for public revenue, the federal land system had evolved into something "diametrically opposite" from the old settlement principle, Hayne contended, and nothing could have been less consistent with either the national good or the most essential purposes of westward expansion. An obsession with finance, he charged, now threatened to quickly undermine western prospects: "Lands, which had been for fifty or a hundred years open to every settler, without any charge, . . . were, the moment they fell into the hands of the United States," held up for sale at public auction. And so, the spirit of mammon had taken over; Congress had lost sight of the settlement needs of the country and the formation of new states, making "the cardinal point of our policy, not to settle the country, and facilitate the formation of new States, but to fill our coffers by coining our lands into gold."[38]

To continue this revenue system beyond the purposes justifying its inception would not only perpetuate an unnecessary practice but endanger public liberty. "Will it promote the welfare of the United States," Hayne asked, "to have at our disposal a permanent treasury, not drawn from the pockets of the people, but to be derived from a source independent of them?" Not that he wanted any further revenue drawn from the pockets of Charlestonians, of course. The real danger, therefore, was "corruption," and the best preventative, denationalization. An ongoing fund based on public land proceeds—or any other source—would entail temptations to financial wrongdoing beyond the ability of the citizenry to identify or prevent. Hayne would preclude this evil by limiting the federal treasury "to the means necessary for the legitimate purposes of the Government." This comment was, in part, a reply to Hunt of Vermont and any others who then or later might favor some way of distributing land proceeds to benefit the states generally. To adopt the fiscal policy that National Republicans advocated would be to "enable Congress and the Executive to exercise a control over States, as well as over great interests in the country, . . . even over corporations and individuals—utterly destructive to the purity, and fatal to the duration of our institutions." Hayne equally opposed any scheme for the distribution of the actual lands, by any ratio, among all states of the Union. Anything like the Maxcy plan of 1821 could only evince, he said, "the interested and selfish feelings of our nature," forecasting "many and powerful objections" to the revenue principle. The same went for Rush's Treasury Department report of 1827, which he saw as embodying the views of both Adams and Henry Clay:

It is supposed, . . . by the advocates of the American system, that the great obstacle to the progress of manufactures . . . is the want of that low and degraded population which infest the cities and towns of Europe, who, having no other means of subsistence, will work for the lowest wages, and be satisfied with the smallest possible share of human enjoyment. And this difficulty it is proposed to overcome, by so regulating and limiting the sales of the public lands, as to prevent the drawing off this portion of the population from the manufacturing States.[39]

And so, what Hayne saw as shared among National Republicans was a desire to "consolidate" the nation, expand its powers over states and individuals, govern by distribution of "favors," create a "spirit of dependence," and "sow the seeds of dissolution to produce jealousy among the different portions of the Union." Political safety for both the West and the South therefore lay in Americans' remaining "essentially an agricultural people." A speech that had started as a review of conflicting opinions on federal land policy ended as a full-fledged condemnation of nationalist political economy. While Hayne's words brought rejoicing in much of the West and South, they intensified the worries of people still determined to realize the dream of a union of states tightly bound in a nationalist "spirit of improvement." Anti-statist, sectional views on key economic and social issues—tariffs, internal improvements, banking, and public lands—threatened this dream and weakened the "spirit" that former president John Qunicy Adams had hoped would become the great theme of his administration and of public policy generally. And, still intertwined dangerously with each economic question, there remained the most delicate issue of all, potent enough to devastate and finally end the Union: slavery.[40]

From the outset of the republic, and especially since the Missouri Crisis of 1819–1821, the problem of slavery and its extension to the frontiers had cast its shadow over Congress. Realistic statesmen on all sides regarded the Missouri Compromise, with its 36°30' division between areas of slavery and those of freedom, as no more than an imperfect, temporary solution. Opponents of the American System, along with South Carolina's nullifiers, had called into question the extent of federal powers over the states and territories. Although South Carolina claimed tariff policy to be the primary issue, none could miss the potential ramifications for slavery. As Governor Edwards and Senator Hayne both had by this time intimated, the debate on federal powers and their effects had not begun with the present tariff controversy and would not end with public lands.

⁓

Legend has it that Daniel Webster had never before paid much attention to land policy—that his impressive grasp of the subject resulted from just a few long evenings of study as he prepared to face Hayne. In fact, neither his knowledge nor his enthusiasm about western growth could possibly have been so new.

Even in his younger days, Webster had pondered territorial expansion and a commercial policy to sustain it. In December 1800, while freezing at Dartmouth College in New Hampshire, he concluded that the United States ought to acquire the Floridas. "It is true, on general maxims," he mused, "that our country is suffi-ciently large for a Republican government, but if, by an inconsiderable extension of our limits, we can avail ourselves of great, natural advantages, otherwise un-attainable, does not sound policy dictate the measure[?]" Moreover, he observed, the export commerce of the interior depended at that time on commercial access to the entire Mississippi and its tributaries, emptying into the Gulf of Mexico. Spanish power in the West still threatened that. As long as this remained so, an un-desirable war with Spain loomed. Anticipating the foreign policy of the Jefferson administration, 18-year-old Webster wrote: "Here then we are under necessity of extending our territories, by possessing ourselves of all the country adjacent those rivers, necessary for our commerce; or of giving up the idea of ever seeing Western America a flourishing country." Later, during the War of 1812, Webster thought that the expansionist impulse had gotten off track by focusing more on Canada than the West. In February 1814, he wrote to Boston manufacturer and businessman Isaac P. Davis: "The truth, is Mr. Madison & the Western People will carry on the War, tho' it should be five years, till they get Canada, Quebec & all, unless the Peo-ple, by their strong disapprobation, oblige them to make Peace."[41]

Western interests within the Union as a whole had crossed Webster's mind often enough in the years immediately prior to his 1830 encounter with Hayne. At a June 1828 dinner given in his honor at Boston's Faneuil Hall, he declared: "If there be any doubts, whether so many Republics, covering so great a portion of the globe, can be long held together under this Constitution, there is no doubt in my judgment, of the impossibility of so holding them together by any narrow, contracted, local, or selfish system of legislation." Hoping to build a National Re-publican voting base in the Northwest, Webster in the House of Representatives a few years earlier had spoken in favor of extending the Cumberland Road from Wheeling, Virginia, to Zanesville, Ohio. He believed that the good of the nation de-pended on a balancing of favors accorded to all sections: "While the Eastern fron-tier is defended by fortifications, its harbors improved, and commerce defended by a naval force, it is right and just that the region beyond the Alleghany should receive fair consideration and equal attention in any object of public improvement, interesting to itself, and within the proper power of the Government."[42]

Like Clay, Webster in his Senate career had found no incompatibility between settling the West and using frontier lands for the revenue needed to fund transportation improvements, thus binding the Union more closely together. While advocating federal subsidies for state and national improvements, he at first refrained from taking up the causes of preemption, graduation, or free homesteads. But later, unlike Clay, he would see preemption as consistent with settlement-driven home-market considerations—as well as advantageous to himself politically in appealing to westerners.[43]

In private, Webster's impressions of the West, where he had yet to travel, reflected the same social order concerns that other New Englanders expressed at the time. The image he formed from some of his correspondence with westerners remained one of frontier lawlessness, dishonesty, cheating, blatant opportunism, and political dirty tricks. A National Republican friend, John Test of Brookville, Indiana, who in 1826 had lost his reelection bid for a House seat to Jacksonian Democrat, Oliver H. Smith, reported in March 1827 that Jackson's friends there had become polished at winning elections by undercutting their opponents with lies. With Adams's campaign for reelection on the line, Webster a month later cautioned John C. Wright of Steubenville, Ohio, on the urgency of putting "proper means of forming right judgments into the hands of the People; the opportunity must not be lost." Wright responded by confirming Webster's distrust of western politics: "our opponents are active & unprincipled. They stop at nothing. We must be vigilant." In 1830, Webster thought Benton the epitome of the "unprincipled" type, and he welcomed Samuel Atkinson's assurance that he had "many friends" in the western country—"real friends. No Bentons among them."[44]

For all of that, it was Calhoun, not Benton, who worried Webster the most. If Calhoun's doctrine, as outlined in the *South Carolina Exposition and Protest*, could destabilize federal authority in the Southeast, what might it do in the West? Webster realized that a Calhounite alliance between the South and West might destroy National Republicanism. When he rose on January 20, 1830, in his first reply to Hayne, people knew Webster primarily for his appearances before the Supreme Court and for having endorsed Adams administration goals, including federal subsidies for roads and canals—which Calhoun had once supported but now opposed. About a month after the debate, Webster wrote privately that his own participation had been "quite unexpected." True, he had not anticipated Foot's resolution or the reaction to it. Even so, in January 1830, the public lands question offered an ideal platform for a nationalist of stature to refute not only the view of state sovereignty in Calhoun's *Exposition and Protest* but also, indirectly, the Illinois memorial and Ninian Edwards's argument. In so doing, Webster deliberately avoided any reference to slavery. In his mind, national unity always trumped abolitionist principle.

Hayne employed a similar tactic, assailing northeastern attitudes by addressing the West rather than framing the question as South against North.[45]

Other commonalities between the two orators furnished their clash with touches of irony. Both of old English stock and farming families, each had struggled to secure a basic education before reading law. While Hayne could afford no college at all, financial burdens troubled Webster as he moved through Phillips Exeter Academy and Dartmouth. Both, after studying law privately, had entered government only after building a successful law practice. Both men had catapulted to the Senate during the 1820s. Each saw the value of an economic kinship and, if possible, political alliance between his region and the developing West. For Webster and Hayne alike, the "Great Debate" would surpass earlier personal glories. At this point, however, the parallels fade. After that Senate term, Webster would stay in Washington, remaining in the national limelight until his death in 1852. Hayne would retreat from the national arena, serving as governor of South Carolina during the Nullification Crisis of 1832, mayor of Charleston, and promoter of a southern rail system, before dying in 1839.[46]

Webster's January 20, 1830, speech turned out to be only the first of two memorable replies to Hayne; the second, on January 26–27, carried more dramatic language and fully transcended the immediate subject at hand. Drawn by the emotional impact of the famous "second reply," scholars have comparatively passed over the shorter prelude to it. The "first reply" contained the constitutional theory Webster wanted to articulate, while buoying an eastern pride that had suffered under the tide of Jacksonianism.[47]

Although the first speech started with a soft-pedaled view of Foot's proposal and ended with a mild vindication of Rush's 1827 report, it also entreated western sympathy toward the Northeast. Webster argued that any existing prosperity and social stability in the West owed nothing to the South's recent attentions, and certainly not to any limiting of constitutional powers, but to the continuing benevolence of New England, as reflected in the economic paternalism of traditional federal land policy.

"I rise to defend the East," Webster proclaimed, but not the East that Benton had associated with Foot. He denied that New England had "at any time shown an illiberal policy towards the West." The whole "accusation" was "without the least foundation in any facts, existing either now or at any previous time." The East, he claimed, had provided a land system ordered well enough to guarantee security of title, as opposed to the spectacle of conflicting claims. Adapted from New England practice, the federal way of land survey and disposition represented a clever solution for managing "those immense regions, large enough almost for an empire" yet destined for appropriation to private ownership. This "Northern mode," contrasted with the southern-style "shingling" of claims that had led, south of the Ohio River, to so much "speculation and litigation,—two great calamities in a new country." Webster said he hoped to witness an eventual extension of the "Northern system" throughout the West, as a monument to New England's "intelligence in matters of government and her practical good sense."[48]

As it had been for Edward Everett, the thriving state of Ohio served as Webster's *prima facie* evidence for the effect of New England's enlightened supervision. In 1794, Webster reminded the senators, the entire Northwest was "one vast wilderness, unbroken except by two small spots of civilized culture"—Marietta and Cincinnati. Since then, over a period of just thirty-five years, steady settlement and rational development had converted this state of nature into an independent member of the republic, with a population greater than of "all the cantons of Switzerland." In numbers of well-ordered, industrious inhabitants, Ohio now rivaled Virginia and Pennsylvania, only shortly to "admit no equal but New York herself." The advance had taken place under the same national policies that Benton and Hayne called unjust and destructive to western growth. "For my own part," Webster confessed, "I also look with admiration at the wisdom and foresight which originally arranged and prescribed the system for the settlement of the public domain. Its operation has been, without a moment's interruption, to push the settlement of the western country to the extent of our utmost means."[49]

The great anathema, then, was the idea of ceding the property of the nation to the western states—and, of course, Edwards's radical addendum, the theoretical right of western states to seize the lands if the government would not cede them. Here, Webster pinned his argument on the "common benefit" provision of the 1784 Virginia Cession, which had defined the public domain as a "common fund" for the mutual "use and benefit" of the United States generally. Massachusetts and Connecticut had relinquished their western claims on similar conditions. Two other "substantial conditions or trusts" had accompanied these agreements. First, territories had to evolve into "republican" states with the assurance of admission to the Union and, second, public lands contained within those territories or states had to be sold and settled "at such time and in such manner as Congress should direct."[50]

All of this evidence constituted, in Webster's view, the legitimate and inviolable basis of the national land system. In refusing to relinquish the public domain to the western states and reserving it instead for the "common good," Congress had honored the "solemn conditions" of the founding fathers. Because they had organized the land system to correspond with mutually agreed republican principles, any fundamental changes altering the system could only carry the most radical implications. For Webster, those original principles imposed an "earlier mortgage" on the public domain, a contract that honorable legislators could not, and would not, breach. "For the fulfillment of all these trusts," he insisted, "the public faith was, and is, fully pledged."[51]

Webster revisited this view of the land system's origins and inviolabilty at length in the second reply to Hayne, defending federal policy in terms similar to those of Clay and other National Republicans. Before the speech, he had asked Joseph Gales, the most skilled shorthand reporter in the country, to record the speech, which would, in February 1830, be published in Gales's *National Intelligencer* and thereafter reprinted as a pamphlet that would circulate widely—multiple later printings would follow the initial production of 40,000 copies. A key point in the speech was that he—and the East—cared not just about public revenue but also how the new regions would be settled. "The country enjoys a benefit as well in the sale of the lands as in what it receives from the sale," Webster asserted. "And, though I have said that the public lands are held by us as a common fund for the common benefit, yet I have always considered that the sale of the land was also a common benefit." His view, he explained, had not changed since 1825, when he had advocated westward extension of the Cumberland Road: "the land should be brought into market as it is needed and sold at prices so low as to secure, to every man who is able to cultivate it, a comfortable and sufficient farm, but not so low as to throw it into the hands of speculators."[52]

Finally, Webster moved from his answer for Edwards and the cessionists to a rebuttal of Calhoun. Hayne regarded "consolidation" as the greatest threat to liberty. For Webster, "consolidation" referred to policies that held the Union in one "common interest"—basic National Republican political thought. His opponents, Hayne and Calhoun alike, were showing "no deep and fixed regard" for the Union, Webster said. They considered everything associated with it, including the public lands, as "a mere question of present and temporary expediency; nothing more than a mere matter of profit and loss." For them, it sufficed for the Union "to be preserved, while it suits local and temporary purposes to preserve it; and to be sundered whenever it shall be found to thwart such purposes."[53]

—◌

Nearly five months after provoking all of this acrimony, Samuel Foot finally made *his* reply. As he sat those weeks in the Senate, marveling at the fireworks bursting around him, Foot believed that his resolution had "exposed the machinations and plots" that had been forming against the government—and "their latent causes." The debate had revealed "with what perfect ease the majesty of the laws has been maintained, and the Constitution preserved from every insidious as well as open attack." The republic was safe, he trusted, thanks to its real tribunes, like Webster.

Then Foot spilled forth his sarcastic contempt for Benton, who had "entered the field with his bloody standard, with this motto—'*War to the knife, and the knife to the hilt!*'" As for himself, Foot announced, "the *mover*" had "not been much *moved*" by Benton's attacks. After culling yeas and nays over forty years to prove the hostility of the East toward the West, Benton had only discovered northeastern men "voting upon principle, honestly and consistently—men who did not change with every wind: votes which ought to make none but political trimmers and demagogues blush for inconsistency." Would Benton's own record show "as much purity of intention, and patriotism, and as much consistency in his political course"? And as for Hayne, who had mounted such "a furious attack upon the Federalism of New England," Foot challenged, "If the Republicans of South Carolina will make the same disposition of their rash and imprudent men, as the Republicans of New-England have done of those among them, the union of the States will be in no danger."[54]

On the subject of land policy, Foot had heard nothing to change his mind: "neither the interests of the United States, nor the best interests of the new States will be promoted by forcing such immense quantities of public lands into the market." He did not believe that Benton really spoke for ordinary settlers in the first place. Given that few tracts now sold for more than $1.25 an acre, Foot queried, what would happen if the price of some land were reduced to, say, 10¢ an acre? Under market forces in operation, with the current excess of land up for sale, he answered, even the choicest land ultimately would sell for no more than 10¢—and at that only to combinations of speculators. Another very practical reason to preserve the existing land system, he added, was the danger that even more illegal settlers would scatter "a very sparse population over an immense tract of country, wholly destitute of the means of either literary or religious instruction, . . . incessantly calling on the government for protection." The history of white-versus-Indian conflict in the West, he noted, would "shew that most of these wars have been produced by unlawful encroachments upon the Indians." The cupidity of whites would never be satisfied while Indians possessed even "an acre of land which is thought to be better than the lands in our possession."[55]

The October 1830 number of Everett's *North American Review* told its readers that "the welfare of the country, the happiness of our children to the end of time, and the cause of free government and liberty, throughout the world" lay at stake in the controversy that Foot had started. At that time and in the months shortly preceding it, this declaration did not seem a gross overstatement. "If Col Hains answer is received as the true construction of the Constitution, our government is at an end," predicted Jeremiah Mason, Webster's friend and fellow lawyer. Some southerners actually thought the same. Were the "new doctrines" of South Carolina to prevail, declared Alabama nationalist Charles Tait in a letter to Webster, "there will be, sooner or later, an end to this Union." Webster, too, expressed his greatest fears in private, using language that applied as much to western radicals as to southern firebrands. Either way, allowing any state to define its own obligations to the larger community—or to withdraw at will—would mean ruin for the republic. "It is plain to me," he told Hayne supporter George Hay of Virginia in March 1830, "that secession is Revolution. It may be more or less violent: it may be bloody or not bloody: but it is fundamental change of the political system: it is Revolution: and the Constitution does not provide for Revolution. As in other cases, so in this. Revolution, if it comes, must bring its own law with it."[56]

Webster could not directly attack Ninian Edwards's version of the South Carolina doctrine because he dared not be branded as an enemy of the West the way Foot, Rush, and Adams had been. It was Everett, another close friend and political disciple of Webster's, who publicly noted the bearing of cession on the argument in the Senate. The "circumstance" that had made the contest "as delicate as it is important," Everett wrote in the *North American Review*, was that so much of the public domain in the West remained "included within the limits of the state sovereignties." Some of those states, Illinois and Indiana particularly, had "advanced the claim, that the State governments have a jurisdiction unshared by the United States, over all persons living within their boundaries," despite the proposition's being "obviously groundless." It distressed him that "[i]n like manner, in several of the States, the claim has been set up, that the States, as an incident of sovereignty, possess the title to the soil of all the lands, not held by individuals, within their limits."[57]

With a West of uncertain proclivities growing in political strength and one of its most powerful sons, Jackson, in the White House, no one knew how the impending drama—apart from but related to the one in South Carolina—might finally play out. In the years to come, an association—but not a true political alliance—between cessionists and Calhounites would solidify. Writing to Ninian Edwards in January 1831, Duff Green, the Calhoun-supporting editor of the *Daily Telegraph*, found the public lands question "daily attracting more attention." He assured the Illinoisian that "the anti-tariff party of the South anticipates that the West will unite in some modification of the entire system so as to give to the West the fund arising from the sales of public land as a permanent appropriation for the purposes of internal improvement." Though it differed from cession, promising the western states all proceeds of federal sales still would radically denationalize the land system.[58]

The following year, on January 14, 1832, expressing to Edwards the hope that his "doctrine must ultimately prevail," Green again stressed the then-certain link between southern tariff opposition and western discontent on public lands:

> The next few years are to decide the fate of this Republic. I am well satisfied that if Congress does not take the alarm and modify the tariff, . . . the South will nullify, and the result will be the adoption and acquiescence in the doctrines of the South or a civil war.
>
> The new states stand in much the same relation to the gen'l Government, and must ultimately combine against the project of *selling* the public domain to them.

On November 10, 1832, *Niles' Register,* strictly opposed to nullification and cession alike, noted how closely related the two really were: "The stand taken by South Carolina against the tariff may be taken by Illinois concerning the *public lands* and so on, by other states, through the whole catalogue of their *supposed* interests. Counties may nullify the acts of states—and Nantucket proclaim her port a 'free' one. THERE IS NO END TO THE DOCTRINE."[59]

Among various plausible conclusions in the aftermath of the Great Debate, the New Haven *Columbian Register* hit the nail on the head: The speeches had as much bearing on the subject of "the next presidency" as they did on anything else. Webster probably figured his National Republicans could not get substantial support against Jackson from the South, especially the Southeast, but they could win a national election if they had the help of the Northwest. After Clay's defeat to Jackson in 1832, Webster set off in mid-1833 on a westward tour of his own—a two-month trip to Ohio and western parts of New York and Pennsylvania—sampling the mood and letting as many western voters see him as possible. He returned feeling both heartened and a little surprised by his experience. "I was much delighted with that part of the Western Country which I saw," he enthused. "An excellent spirit, social & political, at the present moment pervades The People. . . . [T]he public mind is in a very favorable state to receive just impressions, respecting the great public interests of the Country." Ohio, he said, would prove to be "a strong link, in the chain of the National Union"; it was "full of enterprising People . . . far, very far, exceeding my anticipations." The voters there, unless "cajoled & cheated," would "do *right*, in all political matters."[60]

The support that Webster encountered in Ohio, western New York, and western Pennsylvania might have justified nationalist optimism. Also, the irascible, unpredictable Jackson by this time had pleased nationalists by standing firm against South Carolina in a major test of federal authority: the Nullification Crisis of 1832–1833. Cessionist agitation in the West, given pause perhaps by presidential saber-rattling directed elsewhere, had subsided a little. Meanwhile, the ringleader of the cessionists, Ninian Edwards, at age 58, had died of cholera in July 1833, after being defeated in a bid for election to Congress the previous fall.

The Great Debate had addressed the viability of the Union, the future of the West, and the very right of the federal government to hold parts of the public domain. In the background loomed issues that eventually would divide North and South: state sovereignty, nullification, and slavery. The Webster-Hayne quarrel had voiced not only the sectional but also the ideological differences over public land policy. Who had won the debate? First, Webster's combination of eloquence and moderation set the tone for opposition to cession. And yet, the politics of Thomas Hart Benton gained most from the controversy. No power at Webster's command could dispel western distrust of the traditional East or ease eastern qualms about the radical rumblings heard from the West. And second, Benton, not Webster or Hayne, captured the unfolding narrative. His political allies, such as Arkansas congressman A. H. Sevier, went on to advance the same thesis Benton had argued: Foot's resolution had really proposed an inquiry into "stopping the settlement of the western country" with the intent of keeping "a host of paupers to carry on the extensive factories of the east." The real purpose of the resolution had been to array "one portion of this Union against the other," creating "what ought never to be encouraged—sectional jealousies and prejudices." This being true in a way, Foot had blundered in his boldness, and even the powers of Webster had failed to make things right.[61]

Benton's graduation scheme remained stalled in Congress, and the grand alliance he sought between the West and the South never fully materialized. And yet, a coalition of the two sections did pass the nation's first general preemption bill, a one-year measure allowing every "settler or occupant" on a piece of public land in 1829 to purchase as much as 160 acres of that claim, including improvements, at the minimum price of $1.25 an acre. The measure had navigated the Senate, carrying by a vote of 29 to 12, without opposition by any senator south of Maryland or west of the Appalachians. The House passed it 100 to 58, with more opposition coming from the Middle Atlantic states than from either New England or the South—and all westerners voting in favor except for five Ohioans. Jackson promptly ushered the bill into law as a temporary but significant victory for western forces—those identifying far more with the "Magnificent Missourian" than with "Harry of the West."[62]

CHAPTER SIX

Whose West?—Alternative Visions

If Clay and Webster could have structured society as they wished, based on the nationalist political economy of the American System, there might have been far more westerners like Dr. Daniel Drake and more profusions of capital growth like that of Cincinnati. Drake was one of the premier physicians in the West, if not the entire country. The English travel writer Harriet Martineau met him when she visited Cincinnati during her mid-1830s tour of the United States and was charmed right away. "He is a complete and favourable specimen of a Westerner," she gushed.[1]

Drake, born in New Jersey, had moved to frontier Ohio in the late-1780s when the region that would become the "Queen City" was languishing—as just "one expanse of canebrake, infested by Buffalo," Martineau wrote—and populated by little more than one hundred white settlers, mostly French. During the following four-and-a-half decades, he had witnessed the rise of a river metropolis—35,000 people, marketing annually some six million dollars' worth of produce and manufactures. Cincinnati was a place as distinguished for its economic and cultural institutions as for its rapid population growth. For the year 1835 alone, Martineau reported, the city could boast more than a dozen common school buildings, the new Church of St. Paul, two new banking houses, and 150 "handsome private dwellings," recently constructed. It featured four daily and six weekly newspapers, a bustling street life encumbered neither by "the apathy of the South nor the disorder consequent on the presence of a pauper class," and a vibrant river commerce spearheaded by craft of every type, including steamboats moored "six or more abreast" at any given time. Bostonian David Henshaw found the booming Ohio River city "beautiful," its private homes "furnished as sumptuously as the best houses in the Atlantic cities." Still another traveler in the mid-1830s, Frederick Hall of Washington, D.C., exclaimed to his wife back home: "I must say, that Cincinnati, so far as related to refinement of manners, intellectual culture, and hospitality to strangers, is more like Boston than any other city." The same was true, he added, of "the attention it pays to the education of its youth, and the diffusion of useful information among the different classes of its citizens."[2]

Before 1850, Cincinnati would be the sixth-largest city in America, and during Drake's time there its growth outstripped them all. German immigrants accounted for most of the swelling of its population, but the Irish, driven by a series of potato famines in their native land, would quickly surpass the Germans in number: 14,000 sons and daughters of Erin crowded the city by 1850, and many more settled throughout the Northwest. About half of all manufacturing in the West centered in Cincinnati, and half of all capital investments. Cincinnati became famous for its pork-packing industry—"Porkopolis," the locals called it. Herds of swine constantly infested the streets, on their way to slaughter from the rich farmlands of Indiana and Ohio. Residents could scarcely go out for a stroll without bumping into a hog or two, allowed to roam freely, consuming the scraps of garbage dumped every day from peoples' doorsteps into the roads and alleyways.[3]

Physicians on the frontier spent a lot of time traveling to see their patients. While doing so, Drake reflected on what he saw and the people he met. Amid the plethora of Welsh, Irish, English, Germans, New Englanders, and others transplanted to southern Ohio, he knew and treated all types. As his reputation increased, so did invitations to speak publicly. Drake knew Clay personally and believed in the American System, especially as it might apply to the West. Asked to speak before the Literary Convention of Kentucky, Drake presented a vision of western unity scarcely distinguishable from speeches Clay had made before similar audiences in the early 1830s. Differences between slave and free states notwithstanding, the people of the trans-Appalachian "commonwealths" shared much in common: "the hills of Western Virginia and Kentucky cast their morning shadows on the plains of Ohio, Indiana, Illinois, and Missouri. . . . Thus connected by nature in the great [Ohio] valley, we must live in the bonds of companionship," he declared. There was no "middle destiny." Therefore, the West's people of culture— "teachers, professors, lawyers, physicians, divines, and men of letters, from its remotest sections"—shared a common duty "to mould a uniform system of manners and customs out of the diversified elements" and to "foster Western genius, encourage Western writers, patronize Western publishers, augment the number of Western readers, and create a Western heart."[4]

—☙

Drake represented the most fortunate people in the West—educated, cultured, respected, and propertied. Could a poor, landless migrant aspire to the same—even achieve what everyone sought first and foremost: landownership? Some historians turn to census evidence showing the growing numbers of landless individuals and families who permeated the new states by the mid-1800s. No "free" land existed in the West before the Civil War. And so, did the vaunted Jeffersonian vision fail as wildly impractical in the first place? Did the harsh truths of actual settlement spare only a few of the poor from a European-like dependence, denying their dream of an independent freehold?[5]

Reading the observations of travelers, commentators, and settlers of that day, a somewhat different picture emerges, one murkier and more complex than the usual one. Much depended, of course, on when, how, and where one settled. Poor white squatters in the Southwest after 1830 faced much longer odds against land speculating companies, more numerous and powerful there than in parts of the Middle West, where speculators usually bought smaller tracts and encountered squatters better organized in vigilante "claims clubs" to protect themselves. What, if anything, mattered more than timing, circumstances, and location of settlement? Many witnesses answered: preparation, prudence, and, above all, the character of the settlers themselves.[6]

"Again, wealth depends upon economy," emphasized one of many 1830s advice tracts for aspiring western settlers. "It is the prudent, saving man, and not the prodigal, who acquires a fortune;—a penny saved is a penny earned, was the maxim of a wise philosopher, and its truth has been fully tested." The same traveler, passing through the "flourishing" town of Alton, Illinois, cited the community's "busy appearance." Obvious reasons for that included the "enterprize of its citizens": "no loungers—no idlers—no 'loafers' to be seen." Another descriptive sketch of Illinois in 1837 included an extract from *Peck's Emigrants Guide*, asking potential settlers to consider matters of "plain common sense," such as "facilities for obtaining all the necessaries of life" along with the selecting of "farms and wild land" where "others of similar habits and feelings live." The author, John Mason Peck, a Baptist missionary who in the 1820s had worked as the general western agent of the American Bible Society in Indiana, Illinois, and Missouri, knew firsthand the difference between popular myth and hard-bitten experience. Above all, he said, the realistic settler should bear in mind "that there are difficulties to be encountered in every country, . . . surmounted with reasonable effort, patience, and perseverance," and also that "in every country, people sicken and die."[7]

Some unsuspecting new settlers simply bit off more than they could chew. Finding $1.25 an acre to be "thundering cheap," some migrants from rocky, land-exhausted parts of the East could not resist buying up all they possibly could and then, when it came time to cultivate, found their purses empty and the costs of farming higher than anticipated. "Reader!" announced an 1838 guide for those headed for Wisconsin and Iowa, "I request you, for the sake of your family, and your own welfare, . . . no man should buy lands that he does not intend to improve, for although the prospects are inviting, he will generally be the loser." Robert Baird, born in the West in 1798 and resident there most of this life, cautioned Illinois settlers in 1832 to restrain their ambitions. Starting on unimproved land, they could not "expect to have costly homes for a few years," while "cultivated" land purchased from private sellers would cost between $2.50 and $8.00 an acre.[8]

One friend to aspiring settlers, James Hall, a judge in Cincinnati and founder of the *Western Monthly Magazine* in 1833, actually calculated what it took for a hardworking landless person to own land west of the Ohio River and concluded that "any industrious man may buy a farm." As of the mid-1830s, federal land in that region sold in tracts of 40 acres for the government minimum of $1.25 an acre—$50 for an unimproved tract. In the free states of the Northwest, Hall figured, a top laborer earned 75¢ a day. From that, his living might cost 25¢. Therefore, in a hundred days, or about four months, he should be able to purchase a 40-acre farm— and after a year, one twice that size. An ordinary laborer, by contrast, might receive $10 per month along with his board—$120 per year. After deducting $20 for clothing, he too could purchase a 40-acre farm in six months' time and a larger one after a year. Mechanics, blacksmiths, and shoemakers made higher wages, enough to pay for 80 acres in six months. A school teacher, Hall thought, received $2.50 or $3.00 per quarter for each pupil, and so a school for thirty students could bring in $360 per year. The federal government did not tax these westerners or preclude them from voting or holding office, Hall noted. Few were starving, "houseless," naked, or imprisoned for debt; no standing armies quartered among them, nor did "myrmidons of government eat out their substance"; seedtime and harvests did not fail; nature rewarded the "labor of the husbandman"; earnings seldom fell prey to "fraud or violence"; oppressors did not "grind the poor"; life and property remained secure; and no one bothered a man who sat "under his own vine."[9]

In the *Western Monthly*, Hall promoted the West any way he could. Others, however, restrained their boosterism and considered the actual costs of building a prosperous farm on undeveloped land. Baird, taking a more cautious view, advised beginning with not 40 but 160 acres for planting, at the lowest possible price of $1.25 per acre ($200), then adding 160 acres of "timbered land" and adjoining prairie for pasture (another $200). He calculated the expense of breaking 160 acres with a rented plow as $2 per acre (add $320 more) and the construction outlay for cabins, stables, fences, corncribs, and other necessary structures amounting to still another $200. And so, by Baird's reckoning, the likely total for a good farm would come to at least $920. Beyond all that came the expenditure for a few horses, some cows, hogs and sheep, plus the eventual purchase of two or three plows, harrows, wagons, and other supplies. Granted, few emigrants went about everything in this way; most relied on their own labor instead of purchasing or hiring. Could an "industrious" man of ordinary ability succeed? Yes, and many did. Still, not every laborer, mechanic, blacksmith, shoemaker, and teacher—even if lucky and self-disciplined enough to accumulate the money—possessed also the aptitude, skills, and experience to build a farm of his (or her) own. The opportunity for the poorest, least credit-worthy sorts loomed much slimmer still.[10]

Farming lent itself even less to people with dissolute habits or a lack of ambition. And yet, plenty of those types found their way westward too. Judge Hall in 1834 could not resist mentioning the "loose individuals" he had seen on the frontier, those "who, if not familiar with crime, have very blunt perceptions of virtue." The genuine woodsmen, that is, "the real pioneer" he regarded as "independent, brave, and upright," but in that person's footsteps too often followed a crowd of "miscreants destitute of his noble qualities." These degenerate settlers, Hall said, resembled "the poorest and idlest of the human race—averse to labor, and impatient of the restraints of law and the courtesies of civilized society." They modeled "sheer laziness." He dismissed them as "helpless *nobodies*, who, in a country where none starve and few beg, sleep until hunger pinches, then stroll into the woods for a meal, and return again to their slumbers." This kind of behavior could not be attributed to the vicissitudes of the market, but in times of distress the West also attracted people no more likely to find refuge there than in the East. During the early months of the Panic of 1837, another travel writer lamented the sight of "the miserable beings we have seen on the road—men, women, and children—whom these disastrous times have thrown out of employment, and thus deprived them of the means of subsistence, and who are urging their way on foot, and starving, to the West."[11]

—◦—

From a postmodern perspective, it might seem a little quaint to cite the "character" factor, but many Americans of the early nineteenth century believed nothing to be more important or influential. By the mid-1830s, another transplant to Cincinnati had become obsessed with the building of character in westerners: the widely known minister Lyman Beecher, whose influence on the shaping of Christian institutions, education, and public attitudes in the Old Northwest would prove important but also ambiguous. "There is no danger," wrote Beecher in his 1835 *Plea for the West*, "that our agriculture and arts will not prosper: the danger is, that our intelligence and virtue will falter and fall back into a dark minded, vicious populace—a poor, uneducated, reckless mass of infuriated animalism, to rush on resistless as the tornado, or to burn as if set on fire of hell." Such concern, less about the quantity than the *quality* of population growth in the new states and territories, had compelled many religious people of the 1820s and 1830s to embark on an evangelical mission. It prompted Beecher in 1832 to abandon Connecticut in favor of Cincinnati, where he would spend nearly two decades as president of the Lane Theological Seminary. Daniel Drake would become the Beechers' family physician.[12]

Beecher liked to sprinkle into his homilies some of his own reflections on political economy, combining Christian morality with arguments for a balanced home market system. By 1818, he was advocating protective encouragement of domestic manufacturing. Like many, he believed that the West's capacity to absorb the discontented would help perpetuate republican society. But in December 1819, as part of a sermon at Litchfield, Connecticut, Beecher spoke out against unbridled westward expansion and its disordering effect on both East and West: "The rapidity of our migration, and extension of our agricultural territory, is itself a national evil, demanding a remedy, instead of an increase." He meant to suggest not an end to westward growth but a cautious national supervision over it. Steady, systematic expansion would lay the best foundation for the social morality essential to well-regulated republicanism. "The prosperity of a nation depends on the moral qualities of its population, the vigor of its institutions, the relative proportions of its materials, and the compactness of its organization, by means of which, one heart may beat the pulse of life to every extremity, and one arm extend protection and control to every member," he affirmed. But how could that happen in a raging fever of emigration, which, he said, sapped the "older settlements" of population and energy and extended to the new ones "the bones and sinews only of society, without flesh and skin to cover them"?[13]

Thomas Hart Benton celebrated the restless energy of the West. Beecher feared it, believing that the filling of unsettled lands could proceed safely only if accompanied by institutions of civilized society. Family and community relationships had to be the core of an honest, vibrant political culture. A civilized nation was one that nourished virtue and order in its people, generation by generation. "This nation, so extensive in territory, so powerful in resources, so energetic in enterprise, so high minded in independence, cannot be held together and governed by force merely. Ties of blood and kindred, institutions and interests, must lend their amalgamating influence" Beecher contended. Rapid emigration threatened to unravel those ties. "Had this nation been peopled at first by adventurers who rushed upon our shores in quest of land and agriculture, leaving schools and religious institutions to lag after them," he thought, Americans could scarcely have been rescued from "barbarism." And if settlers were to "push prematurely a vast population into distant wilds, in a state of half formed society," they would "create a nation for our neighbor and rival, fierce, heady, high-minded, to teach us our folly, by eternal wars, and a protracted frontier of desolation and blood."[14]

Closer to land policy, Beecher's recommendations encouraged industry, and a "regular growth" of all the constituent parts of society. The results would contribute not only to sound morality but to elements of vigorous internal commerce: increased capital, a sound currency, and "a steady demand at home, for the product of the field." The older states should offer "the helping hand of charity" to their brethren who emigrated, inspiring a western gratitude to the East that "no ordinary convulsion" could destroy. And the occupation of new lands should occur "as the surplus population of the old settlements shall demand, and with such rapidity only, as that the hand of charity, the favor of government, and the exertions of the emigrants themselves, shall enable them to carry with them the elements of a good state of society."[15]

The danger of western heathenism, raised more by the *white* settlers than the Native American population, had troubled Beecher and many other northeastern clergy for some time. In Ipswich, Massachusetts, at the ordination of two young missionaries to the American frontier, Pastor David T. Kimball in 1815 declared, "*[O]ur beloved country* has stronger claims on her own sons for missionaries, than any other region under heaven." French and Spanish influence had given Catholicism a head start in the West, he feared. Was it not so, Kimball asked rhetorically, that in Louisiana, a state with "a population of more than seventy-six thousands," there was "not a single protestant minister of any denomination?" The rapid filling of the new states above the Ohio River only compounded the issue. In 1826, Anglican bishop Philander Chase, eager to build Kenyon College as a place to train clergymen for frontier America, hoped the federal government also would designate a permanent fund in western lands to promote schools, colleges, churches, and ministers of the gospel. The progress of settlement in the West had "far outstripped the means of religion and learning," he feared. Deterioration "too painful to describe" already showed in young people growing up in Ohio: "The son, save in very few instances, knows not, nor unless something more is speedily done, is he ever likely to know what his father knew." By 1826, Charles Grandison Finney, thanks to the newly opened Erie Canal, was dispensing his own message of regeneration to ever-growing throngs of listeners in western New York State—in Rome, Utica, Auburn, and Troy, and just a few years later in Rochester.[16]

In those places, ironically, the appeal of heaven rang strongest for those who had succeeded on earth. As historian Paul Johnson has noted, "free agency, perfectionism, and millennialism" constituted "middle class orthodoxy" in much of the "Burned-Over District" of New York by the 1830s. Some of those middle-class converts, aided by marvelous new technologies—the steamboat, canals, steam-powered printing, and eventually railroads—soon would carry the flame of faith on westward. The religious influx included Quakers and Baptists, Mormons, Millerites, Methodist circuit-riders, Campbellites and countless others. Joining them was a growing flock of auxiliary Protestant organizations—the American

Education Society, the American Sunday School Union, the American Tract Society, the American Home Missionary Society, and all the rest—mostly bankrolled by eastern philanthropists. Often enough, these godly zealots competed, quarreled, and persecuted one another. Beecher and Finney, engaged in the same work but not in the same way, could not get along. But on one thing they all agreed—the need to subdue "impiety" on America's frontiers. Privately, in an 1830 letter to his daughter Catherine, Beecher stated the issue better than anyone: "The moral destiny of our nation, and all our institutions and hopes, and the world's hopes, turns on the character of the West." That especially included the education of the rising generation, where the "Catholics and infidels" had already advanced. "If we gain the West," he concluded, "all is safe; if we lose it, all is lost."[17]

A phalanx of religious publications entered the fray as well. One of many examples, the *Quarterly Journal* of the American Education Society, in April 1828, conveyed the sense of alarm among many Protestant intellectuals at the sudden growth of the West. With the shifting center of national population went the civil and moral destiny of the American people. Between 1790 and 1828, the population of the western states and territories had risen from fewer than 150,000 inhabitants to nearly 4,000,000—an average of seven persons per square mile. "Before the present generation shall have passed off the stage," declared the *Journal*, "the 'star of empire' will have taken 'its way westward,' and the consequence will be either a blessing or a curse, just in the degree that virtuous or vicious principles prevail among the people." Not only might an ignorant and corrupt populace overrun America's frontier, but control of the national government would soon belong to representatives, senators, and presidents from those new states. Without proper care, the *Journal* predicted, "Vices will spring up like weeds in an untended garden, and despotism will come in the might of the strong man armed." From the "hot beds of luxury, and the sinks of pollution," a "pestilential smoke" would rise and blot out the light of prosperity forever. By now, Christians, should have had this "engraven on their hearts, and 'burnt in on their memories' by the terrific scenes, the blood and conflagrations of the French revolution."[18]

The unidentified author of those words could easily have been Lyman Beecher, who often said that individual agency without a moral compass, like an unbridled populace without governmental restraint, would undercut the principles of community he considered to be the foundation of society. From pulpits in New England, from Litchfield to Boston, he inveighed against intemperance and tobacco use, condemned dueling, bashed Unitarians and Catholics alike, promoted the American Bible Society and other reform associations, and lamented the moral "decline" of the republic, the ebbing of public virtue, and the eclipse of the common good. Substituting the inclusive language of individualism for the more distressing, less persuasive tenets of original sin and predestination, he also scorned Jacksonianism and all its liberating tendencies. "The purpose of God as to the wisest and best scheme in the government of the natural and moral world by general and uniform laws, must be maintained," Beecher declared in a sermon delivered early in 1831, comparing the laws of the early Judaic tribes to a federal system of republican government. "Infidels," whose "only law is licentiousness," by contrast, could not know the "true liberty," that derived from "wholesome law." Further, the "most unparalleled trait of republicanism" in the Jewish system of law was, as he saw it, "the equality of condition secured by a distribution of the land, which constituted every adult male a landholder." This "exempted them," as it might also any morally grounded landholders in a westward-expanding America, "from the two extremes of overgrown wealth, and sordid, vicious poverty."[19]

Beecher's philosophy highlighted both sides of the same coin: the necessity that citizens be willing to submit to law, both holy and temporal, and the importance of laws being balanced to serve the needs and interests of all, the privileged and humble alike. Thus, for Beecher, who had once been a student disciple of Timothy Dwight at Yale, the republican institutions that governed New Englanders had derived not from Greece, with its "tumultuous democracies," and not from Rome, whose object was "to plunder the earth," "subjugate provinces," and squander the wealth of the world on "luxuries," but, in truth, from the orderly and socially just teachings of the Bible. Moral reformers of the 1830s often invoked a biblical political economy, one rooted in a radical notion of noncoercion and stressing communitarian virtues of compassion, brotherhood, and fairness to all. That perspective blended Christian morality with a censuring of unfettered self-interest and a degree of ambivalence about free-market capitalism. But how did it apply to economic relationships and the developing social order of the western regions? The answer borrowed from the image of "weeds in an untended garden": infant societies needed to be governed, restrained, and regulated, if not by governmental force, then by the initiative of individual members themselves.[20]

Beecher wrote that when he first visited the Ohio Valley he felt "overpowered" by its vastness and the "uncontrollable greatness" of the trans-Appalachian West—a region half as large as Europe, four times the size of the Atlantic states, and twenty times that of New England. In just forty years its population had ballooned from a mere 150,000 to nearly 5,000,000. What could be done, he asked, "to educate the millions which in twenty years Europe will pour out upon us?" Like Finney and other evangelists of the Second Great Awakening, he worried that moral authority had lost its basis in everyday experience. A wild, undirected growth of the West could only facilitate the devil's work. The danger of the "uneducated mind," Beecher fretted, was "augmenting daily by the rapid influx of foreign emigrants, the greater part unacquainted with our institutions, unaccustomed to self-govern-ment, inaccessible to education," and susceptible to "sinister design."[21]

When the Beechers moved to Ohio in 1832 so that Lyman could become the first president and a professor of theology at Lane Seminary in Cincinnati, it began a stormy tenure that would last until 1851. Lane had been established in 1829 as a western outpost for the schooling of Presbyterian ministers—"the great Ando-ver or Princeton of the West." But some interested parties, like Theodore Dwight Weld, insisted that the seminary should play a more comprehensive role in mold-ing the consciences of westerners than its president expected. Abolitionists at Lane pressured Beecher to abandon his support for the American Colonization Society, which assisted free blacks in returning to Africa, and embrace instead their radical immediatism toward the ending of slavery, but he stubbornly resisted, seeing other social issues in the West as more pressing.[22]

For one thing, Beecher by the 1830s had become fixated on the "threat" posed to America by the Roman Catholic Church. In his mind, the wellbeing of the West depended as much on subverting Catholicism as it did on extending republican-ism. At the time he arrived, Cincinnati had started to feel the effects of massive immigration, still more southern Germanic than Irish, but mostly Catholic in both cases. Even though the Irish numbered only about a thousand in Cincinnati as of 1835, their very presence—their poverty, their propensity for strong drink and other amusements, and their presumed blind allegiance to Rome—did enough to alarm western evangelicals, who, along with Beecher, branded them especially as "infidels." Beecher had already gone to war against Catholics as a pastor in Boston. His inflammatory speeches, writings, and sermons about "popish plots," allegedly carried forward by Irish immigrants and others from central Europe, may have inspired the Protestant mob that attacked and burned the Ursuline convent in Charlestown, Massachusetts, in August 1834. His *Plea for the West*, published in 1835 and filled with such inflammatory warnings, originated as a discourse given in several Atlantic coast cities that Beecher toured to raise funds for Lane and other such institutions.[23]

Wherever Beecher went on his travels, he thundered away on the political im-plications of leaving to their own natural devices "a million of voters without in-telligence, or conscience, or patriotism, or property." As the number of Catholic immigrants to the West began to skyrocket in the mid-1830s, he fulminated that "unprincipled, reckless voters, in the hands of demagogues, may, in our balanced elections, overrule all the property, and wisdom, and moral principle of the nation." How did he know that the "potentates of Europe" had evil designs on American liberties? What else could explain paying the passage of and "emptying out upon our shores such floods of pauper emigrants"? This human refuse represented "the contents of the poor house and the sweepings of the streets." On they came, "multiplying tumults and violence, filling our prisons, and crowding our poorhouses, and quadrupling our taxation, and sending annually accumulating thousands to the polls to lay their inexperienced hand upon the helm of power."[24]

Beecher targeted not just Catholicism but the cultural diversity of the West. Catholics happened to challenge his evangelical "norm" more than any other people around. When he spoke of the need for "the first order of minds in the ministry . . . to command attentions, enlighten the understanding, form the conscience and gain the heart" of their congregations, and supply the land with "all the apparatus for the perpetuity of republican institutions," what he meant was the imposition of cultural sameness. In this respect, Beecher thought the one-time-frontier settlements of his native New England had a great advantage; they had been "few in number, compact in territory, homogeneous in origin, language, manners and doctrines." Settlements there had taken shape more deliberately. Not so with the population of the West, "assembled from all the states of the Union, and from all the nations of Europe."[25]

For the Beechers, educating and converting the West became a family enterprise. Daughter Catherine, having earlier established the Hartford Female Seminary, founded Cincinnati's Western Female Institute in 1832. Son Edward trekked on to Jacksonville, Illinois, where he served as president of Illinois College. But for Lyman, apart from his contributions at Lane, the great mission to reform the character of westerners and mitigate the appeal of Rome would fall considerably short of expectations. To some westerners, his revivalist zeal, moral absolutism, and lack of tolerance for differences, cultural as well as religious, proved a little too much. "Like a mighty locomotive engine," quipped one of his Lane students, "he had leaped his track in coming to the West." If frustrated temperance crusaders had proved one thing, it was that eastern workingmen often simply tuned out middle-class preaching, and the same held true of many "humbler-class" westerners. For that matter, some of the more established types in the West resented eastern religious fanatics coming around to find fault with the new society they proudly touted. Drake eventually had a falling-out with Catherine Beecher and others in the family. After hearing enough pyrotechnic criticism of western habits, tastes, and behavior, Judge Hall excoriated Lyman in the pages of the *Western Monthly*. Hall liked stories about self-made westerners who followed their own drummers and built their own empires in their own ways. In that respect, Beecher's overly emphatic message of self-restraint and higher moral authority ran against the frontier grain.[26]

When the economic depression of 1837 dried up half of his financial backing, primarily from lenders and donors in Boston, New York, and Cincinnati, Beecher wondered whether his work in the West had been in vain. "Thus has the ground of my support failed, and the considerations which brought on me a sense of duty to leave Boston and my people have, in a degree failed also," he reflected. But Lane Seminary had taken root under Beecher and would survive various reincarnations over the years, eventually merging with Chicago's McCormick Theological Seminary, in 1932. In the end, Beecher would find solace, as always, in the "confidence that God was well pleased with my coming, approved of my motives, and will sustain me as through my life of dependence on him."[27]

—☙—

Twenty-five-year-old Robert John Walker moved to Natchez, Mississippi, in 1826 because his older brother, Duncan, who lived there already, had tempted him with a lucrative law practice and the promise of a land speculator's paradise in the burgeoning Southwest. Walker's idea of the West had formed within the classic paradigm of the plantation South, built on the twin pillars of cotton and slavery. But for reasons perhaps more self-serving than visionary, he also wanted to make this planter-dominated world more open, rewarding, and inclusive for lower-class whites. Robert Baird described the southwestern elite in 1832 as "distinguished by high-mindedness, generosity, liberality, hospitality, indolence, and too often, dissipation," their character "a noble one, when moulded by good influences." If so, then perhaps it is owing to both Walker's northeastern roots and his experience in the new West that he, as well as Benton, would become, by the late 1830s, a premier champion of squatters' rights in the United States Senate.[28]

The Walkers were ambitious people. The family patriarch, Jonathan Hoge Walker, a Whiggish lawyer and judge, cut a prominent figure in Northumberland, Pennsylvania, where the north and west branches of the Susquehanna River converged. A domineering man, over six feet tall, he contravened traditions of his day by opposing capital punishment and favoring the participation of women in politics. If he instilled a few iconoclastic views in his children, he likewise demanded that they make something of their God-given talents. Of English and Scottish descent, the family had been mostly farmers, land speculators, and lawyers. Some, by Robert's later account, may have once been squatters on their land. They had borne arms in times of crisis: one ancestor died in the French and Indian War, and Jonathan had fought against the British and their local allies in the American Revolution.[29]

Young Robert excelled at the University of Pennsylvania and then went to Pittsburgh (his family having moved there) to read law under Judge Walker's exacting tutelage. His marriage, in 1825, to Mary Bache of Philadelphia connected him to the financially important Bache and Dallas clans. Thereafter, he might easily have risen within the urban moneyed elite and followed an inside track into Pennsylvania state politics, but Robert insisted on cutting his own path. Contemporaries described him as an odd-looking man, only five feet two inches tall, with a large head that seemed out of proportion with his diminutive frame. Even in middle-age he would weigh little over 100 pounds and often appeared to be frail in health. But a nimble mind, polished oratorical skills, and graceful prose compensated for what he lacked in physical presence. His principal biographer described him as possessing "turbulent energy which he devoted to a restless struggle to achieve honor and wealth," even if those the two goals often clashed. Robert Walker's penchant for independence manifested itself not only in his choice of the sweltering Mississippi low country over the refinements of the urban Northeast but also in his support of Andrew Jackson in the presidential campaign of 1824—a personal commitment to the Old Hero and the Jacksonian movement that would scarcely waver as the years passed.[30]

Between 1798 and 1820, the population of Mississippi had advanced from fewer than 9,000 to more than 222,000, most of this increase coming in a great wave after the War of 1812. That was more than enough for the territory to qualify for statehood in 1817. Drawn by a seemingly endless supply of high-quality, inexpensive, cotton-growing land, settlers spilled in from Georgia, the Carolinas, and the declining tobacco regions of Virginia. This migratory phenomenon occurred in large part thanks to a technological breakthrough in 1793, the cotton gin, credited to Eli Whitney, which made economically feasible the short-staple type of cotton that grew inland, away from the low-lying Atlantic coast. The problem with growing this variety of cotton before mechanical ginning was that the numerous and troublesome seeds, annoyingly interspersed in every fluffy boll, were too time-consuming to pluck out by hand. The Natchez District pioneered short-staple cotton growing in the Southwest, preparing the way for an agricultural boom that made the fiber by far the number one export of the United States by the 1830s.[31]

Families of ample means brought with them coffles of plantation slaves and purchased the most fertile lands in the Mississippi Delta, leaving other regions of the state, at first, to the poorer classes of settlers. This inequality among whites hallmarked society in the early Southwest as much as cotton growing or slaveholding. In a cotton economy, the greatest advantage always went to those who could purchase larger acreages and command sufficient slaves to make a plantation-scale enterprise work. In Mississippi, as in the rest of the South, yeoman farmers persisted, even though their political influence steadily ebbed in favor of the planter elite, while poor whites exerted little agency at all. In fact, historians today incline to believe that most poor white emigrants to the Southwest failed to become landowners there and would have found their chances more promising north of the Ohio River.[32]

During the early years of the southwestern frontier, squatting settlers—those without any legal claim and too poor to purchase for themselves—often lived undisturbed on lands that either belonged to wealthy speculators or that the federal government had yet to clear of Indian title. This lasted until the cotton bonanza animated the legitimate owners and brought increased pressure on Washington to remove the native tribes, primarily the Chickasaws and Choctaws. At that point, the wealthy men who owned or quickly bought up these lands usually sent the white interlopers away too, claiming the improvements left behind. Studies of census records support the conclusion that a large class of white, rural, and poor people developed in the Southwest—men and women who had no land of their own and far fewer opportunities to live by wage-earning than did their white counterparts in the free states. Some of the displaced rural poor traveled northward, to the southern regions of Indiana, Illinois, and Missouri—places where slave competition threatened them less. Others remained, too desperate, too weak, or perhaps just too beaten down to move on. It has been estimated that by 1830 at least a third of white household heads in Alabama and Mississippi were landless and relegated to the plantation-economy margins, as seasonal employees and hired help on smaller farms, taking what few laboring jobs they could find, and with few nearby kin to help out.[33]

The great planters are familiar to historians, their records plentiful and well-preserved. Not so for the poorest whites, including the thousands of squatter families who filled the Mississippi interior and would later constitute a large segment of Walker's Jacksonian political constituency. Among the most comfortable Mississippians, such as the Natchez elite, the backwoods settlers tended to be viewed with condescension and contempt. A letter printed in the Natchez *Ariel* in 1826, for example, ridiculed a certain candidate for local office, John H. Norton, for his inelegant speech and prose—and for having "made a settlement" ten years earlier without the ability to pay, thus thrusting himself into the "predicament" of being "a squatter." More revealing, however, were the accounts of John James Audubon, better known, of course, for his portraits of birds. Audubon frequently encountered this squatter population in the early 1830s while tracking ornithological specimens in backwoods Mississippi, and he found these folk different from what he had expected. The first impression he had received of them came from European travelers gliding down the great river. What "sallow, sickly looking," and "miserable" sorts of beings these rootless poor whites of Mississippi were, according to some accounts he had heard or read. The desperate men and women sometimes spotted on shore survived by "living in swamps, and subsisting on pignuts, Indian corn, and bear's flesh." Granted, that was one type, those perhaps already displaced and now trying to endure from day to day. But the squatters Audubon actually met in the interior included people who, thus far, remained on the soil they hoped to claim: "They mostly remove from other parts of the United States after finding that land has become too high in price; and they are persons who, having a family of strong and hardy children, are anxious to enable them to provide for themselves."[34]

On one of his rambles, in 1831, Audubon stumbled across a squatter's cabin on the banks of Coldwater River in northwestern Mississippi, a tributary of the Tallahatchie. Taking supper that evening with the owner of the hut, his wife, and two sons, he learned that they had migrated from Connecticut. What had induced them to move to this "wild and solitary" place? Audubon learned simply that "the people are growing too numerous now to thrive in New England," whereupon the conversation quickly turned to the comparative richness of the hunting and fishing in the Mississippi wilderness. In many other cases, the migrants started as land-less people from Virginia or the Carolinas who likewise had heard enticing reports of the great streams in the West, the rich soil, the growth of timber, the abundance of game, the market access for their commodities. To these "recommendations" was added another, Audubon explained, "of ever greater weight with persons of the above denomination, namely, the prospect of being able to settle on land, and per-haps to hold it for a number of years, without purchase, rent, or tax of any kind."[35]

These landless families, usually in small groups, tended to start their journeys in May. Each carried only the most essential belongings, the few items of value they had—an axe, a rifle and ammunition, fishhooks, small bundles of seeds, a little bedding, some flour, a few pots, kettles, and pans. They moved by foot or wagon along uncertain roads for three or four grueling months before reaching a desirable forest location within commercial reach of the Mississippi River or one of its various tributaries. After clearing a small swathe, they erected makeshift cab-ins, staked out pens for any livestock they might have brought, planted a few tur-nips and other vegetables, and hunkered down against the "hoarfrosts" of the "un-healthy season." As years passed, with luck, they gradually improved their material wellbeing and accumulated a small stock of horses, cows, and hogs. Larger, more solid buildings eventually replaced temporary shanties. Corn patches and fruit trees filled places where timber had been removed. Soon enough, tiny backcoun-try villages emerged, with modest warehouses, stores, and workshops. Daughters married the sons of neighboring squatters, betting their future on little but "the bounties of Providence" and the flimsy aspiration that a benevolent government in Washington might, in time, offer them title to the ground beneath their feet. "Thus are the vast frontiers of our country peopled," Audubon concluded, "and thus does cultivation, year after year, extend over the Western wilds."[36]

Walker, upon his much more fortunate arrival in Mississippi, quickly added his shingle to the frontier law practice his brother had already launched in Natchez, the old territorial capital. Bordering the Mississippi River, in the extreme south-western part of the state, Natchez would boast a population of 2,789 by 1830. In Pinckney's Treaty of 1795, the Spanish had surrendered to the United States all claims to the site. The town, fixed on high bluffs overlooking the eastern bank of the Mississippi, offered an ideal location for a river port. By the time Walker settled there, steamboats were making regular landings to load cotton en route to New Orleans or sometimes upriver to St. Louis or Cincinnati—and from those places to the busy spinning mills of early industrial New England or on to Great Britain. In Walker's time, thanks to the cotton boom, the Natchez bluffs would become dotted with the opulent mansions of the wealthy cotton-planting elite. Within a few de-cades, the city would be home to more millionaires per capita than any other place in the United States. For generations, the spot had been known as the end point of the Natchez Trace, first an Indian trail and then a route from Nashville through southwestern Tennessee, across Alabama, into the heart of the old Mississippi Territory. Meanwhile, flatboatmen and keelboatmen made a living by carrying multivariate goods downriver to Natchez or New Orleans, and then, with delivery completed, made the long trek on foot either back home—usually Kentucky—or perhaps to plant themselves on unsettled lands in the upcountry forest.[37]

As for Walker and other entrepreneurial southwesterners of all classes, nothing could have delighted them more than Jackson's Indian removal policy of 1830. Cotton merchants and aspiring planters exulted. So did many of the poorer inhab-itants. In defiance of law, thousands more land-hungry whites, mostly squatters, poured into regions that more properly belonged to the Choctaws and Chickasaws. In frontier Natchez, financial confidence abounded. Expecting land values to soar, creditors prepared to dish out loans practically for the asking. The long-anticipated Mississippi bonanza was about to arrive full force. "All classes of our community will feel the benefits of the new purchase," Walker gushed at a public dinner at Parker's Hotel in Natchez, held on October 10, 1830, to celebrate the impending departure of the state's victimized native inhabitants. "The taxes will be dimin-ished, and the means of paying them increased—the wealth, the industry, the population, the influence and prosperity of our state greatly augmented, and from the centre, to the extremities, the pulses of the body politic will beat, with new life and new vigor." A more generous federal land policy that put the formerly Indian lands into white, private hands as quickly and cheaply as possible would make this imminent market miracle complete. Walker knew just how this could happen in a way that would open his own political horizons as well. He continued: "Next in order, and perhaps of superior importance, would it be, to secure a preemption of one section, to the enterprising settler of this new country. The hardy pioneer of settlements, the Daniel Boone of the forest, deserves the aid of a paternal government." The Mississippi Constitution of 1817 gave all adult white males the right to vote if they had met the length of residency requirement and paid their taxes. That would include an already considerable, ever-growing, increasingly vocal contingent of poor white squatters.[38]

Indian removal usually did not mean squatter removal also. Prior to 1830, an estimated thirty thousand white settlers had invaded Creek territory "in violation of treaties, laws, and the rules of justice," as one New England newspaper put it. Indeed, the Treaty of Cusseta of March 1832, which provided the Creeks new land west of the Mississippi River but also permitted individual Indians to stay in the ceded territory if they so chose, required that all illegal white settlers vacate the area (or be forcibly removed) to make way for systematic land surveying. Unlike its conduct toward the Cherokees in Georgia, the Jackson administration in spring 1830 issued a proclamation calling for the removal of these white intruders, ordering the United States marshall near Huntsville to clear the Indian lands, with the help of federal soldiers if necessary. When the federal marshal took action in 1833, violence erupted. By the end of that year, state authorities in Alabama had "bristled up" in opposition, "with as much spirit as the South Carolina Nullifiers." A dispute ensued between the War Department and the governor of Alabama, John Gayle. A graduate of South Carolina College who had migrated west in 1813, Gayle condemned South Carolina's nullification ordinance in 1832 and had been a friend and ardent political supporter of President Jackson—until *now*.

Asserting states' rights (and probably speculators' interests), Gayle published a proclamation countering Jackson's, calling upon state authorities to resist operations of the federal government upon the Indian lands and organizing the state militia to perhaps shoot the federal troops who got in the way. At the same time, Gayle upheld the squatters' presumed "right" to remain on the land. His reasons for doing so remained unclear, but after 1830, when Congress enacted the first in a series of temporary and limited preemption laws, speculators often employed some squatters as "floats," that is, people who agreed to live on valuable tracts long enough for their fraudulent employers to purchase the land for themselves at the federal minimum of $1.25 per acre. Gayle also dismissed as irrelevant the Treaty of Cusseta, claiming that Alabama held precedence in determining policy for any land within its territorial bounds, and repudiated Jackson's squatter removal policy as an unconstitutional intrusion into the state's internal affairs. Ninian Edwards in Illinois had never acted so boldly. Before the year was out, the audacious Gayle easily won reelection as governor; no Alabamian wanted to oppose him.[39]

Eager to end the controversy, Jackson dispatched the Washington lawyer Francis Scott Key, author of the lyrics to "The Star Spangled Banner," to Alabama to patch things up. In October 1833, Secretary of War Lewis Cass instructed Key "to preserve the proper ascendency of civil authority," "let all legal process . . . be submitted to without resistance and without hesitation," and avoid the option of military force. "The supremacy of the civil over the military authority is one of the great features of our institutions, and one of the bulwarks of the constitution," Cass reflected, adding that "the President is particularly solicitous that no act should be done to violate this great principle."

Key did what he could to soothe Gayle. He quickly ordered the rapid surveying of the Creek lands, protecting the claims of the Indians who wished to remain. Then, he negotiated favorable terms for the white settlers, requiring only those sitting on lands reserved for the Creeks to vacate, and arranged for titles to other squatters' claims to be purchased at minimal cost from the Indians. Yet another Jacksonian collision between federal and state authority thus ended without further saber rattling. "It has now become evident that there will be neither war, secession, nor nullification in Alabama," reported the New York *Commercial Advertiser* in November 1833. "The squatters will triumph, and be left in possession of the lands they occupy." What of Jackson's vaunted pledge to uphold the operation of federal law? It played out this time with more of a whimper than a bang. All whites who had illegally set themselves down upon Creek lands happily remained, "except perhaps some dozen or two of the family of Lacklands, too poor in wealth, or political interest, to raise opposition or excite sympathy." Jackson incurred at least one political casualty, however. Still embittered, Governor Gayle left the Democratic Party and became the leader of the states' rights–oriented Alabama Whigs.[40]

As for Mississippi, the story would prove less dramatic but not less interesting. The Jackson administration needed no replication of the fiasco occurring in Alabama. From their base in Natchez, Walker and other land-grabbing whites went traveling around the interior to find the most promising areas for speculative purposes. The federal land Walker scouted, and much that he would later purchase, teemed with squatter settlements. "I saw the hard pioneers who had entered and were subduing the forest, and had selected a home they had hoped to secure by a pre-emption," he told Natchez residents in the October 10 speech. Many had already been disappointed in their expectations and now faced distress. Speculators had taken their lands "and fixed upon them a price in many instances, far beyond their ability to pay; a price enhanced by the grounds they had cleared, the improvements they had made, and the houses they had erected." Earlier in life, some of these unfortunates had been, he said, volunteers in the War of 1812, when they "rallied to the rescue of our common country." It is possible these hapless settlers called to mind an image of his own ancestors in Pennsylvania—or perhaps they registered only as a future political constituency for him to cultivate. In any case, Walker chose to remind his wealthy Natchez neighbors that some of *them*, living

now in the older-settled counties of Mississippi, had enjoyed the fruits of "gratu-
itous grants" conferred long before by the British and Spanish governments—or
in the case of some favorites, special donations by Congress. To oppose the pleas of
the present settlers, he declared, was to resemble the sentiments of "an avaricious
and unfeeling aristocracy."[41]

All during this time, Walker increased his involvement in Democratic Party
politics and built his public reputation in Natchez. He campaigned ardently for
Jackson's reelection in 1832 but failed that year in his own bid for a U.S. House
seat. Meanwhile, with J. F. H. Claibourne, he launched a pro-Jackson periodical
in Natchez. He was one of a small clique of transplanted Pennsylvanians in Mississippi who recognized the political benefits of exploiting the class conflict between self-styled Natchez "aristocrats" and resentful lower-class whites, the "piney
woods" people, who were multiplying a lot faster than the wealthy elite who lorded
over them.[42]

Invited to speak at a local meeting in January 1833, Walker took the occasion to
address some major national issues, particularly the Nullification Crisis in South
Carolina, the tariff, and public lands. Although he espoused the southern partiality
to states' rights and the antifederal attitude of most Jacksonians, Walker expressed
no sympathy for Calhoun and the Nullifiers. Nor did he demonstrate interest in
the cessionist rumblings around the West. He wanted the Union kept intact, and
in years to come he would identify himself with coast-to-coast "Manifest Destiny."
Massachusetts had once threatened disunion, he reminded his audience, and now
South Carolina was doing so; but "if permitted in one state, it will be exercised
by all." Ironically, it was the same fear that had animated Webster in his debate
with Hayne. Federal "consolidation" might not have seemed to foster Mississippi
interests, especially the security of its heavily invested slaveholders, but neither
did South Carolina's radicalism. "If we hold Southern Conventions," Walker cautioned, there would be "Northern, Eastern and Western Conventions, and they will
overthrow the Union."

Turning to protective tariffs, however, he envisioned a serious danger to southwesterners. Protectionism, he told his Natchez listeners, "would reduce the revenue, from imposts on imports so low, that more than two millions of dollars must
be raised annually from the sales of public lands, all taken from the cultivators
of the soil of the West." With the federal debt soon to be (temporarily) retired, he
observed, there should no longer be any need to price public lands any higher than
the expense to the government of survey and sale. Mississippians would be interested in this for an obvious reason: more than 27 million of the 32 million acres of
territory within its boundaries, though heavily occupied by squatters, still belonged
to the federal government. This "onerous system," as Walker put it, which "arrests

the cultivation of the soil and growth of our country," would be perpetuated as long as a federal protective tariff policy remained in force. "Let the tariff be reduced to the wants of the government," shouted Walker, "but let it derive *no revenue* from the sales of the public lands."[43]

Still, Walker had every intention of deriving maximum *personal* revenue—and political benefit—from his own investment in public lands. Rising land values, easy credit, and the introduction to market of the now-vacated Indian lands made a perfect climate for speculators. In 1833, when the former Choctaw region—roughly a million acres—went up for sale on the south side of the Yalobusha River in northwestern Mississippi, Walker and his agents made sure to be on hand. He, along with William M. Gwin, Henry S. Foote, John A. Quitman, and Joseph Davis—fortune seekers, all—had established a land syndicate that eventually came to include about 150 speculators from Tennessee and Alabama as well as Mississippi. So many land buyers flocked to the land office in tiny Cocchuma that by 1835 the once-obscure frontier village had become a small boom town, with five thriving businesses, a saloon, three hotels, and five boarding houses to accommodate them. Walker succeeded in buying up "a considerable body of land, thereby identifying my fortunes and interest with the future growth and prosperity of Mississippi," he rationalized. Even that was an understatement. His purchases at Cocchuma for himself and in partnership with other speculators totaled 76,597 acres, much of it snapped up at the minimum federal price of $1.25 an acre.[44]

Similar events unfolded when the former Chickasaw region north of the Yalobusha went up for sale in January 1836. Here, as in the area once belonging to the Choctaws, the federal government did not allow squatters to file preemption claims. Five land speculating firms financed largely by northern capital, the most extensive being the New York and Mississippi Land Company, managed to engross more than 750,000 acres of former Chickasaw lands, about a third of the whole district up for sale. Buyers for the companies had snatched up many of the best tracts even before the sales officially opened, purchasing directly from the Chickasaws or illicit small traders at prices well below the government minimum. Often the government's own land office appointees—the registers and receivers who conducted the sales—used their positions to line their own pockets, executing various tricks and selling inside information to make sure the speculators who bribed them got special advantage.[45]

In years after, some of Walker's neighbors and political adversaries—including the politically inspired, anti-Jacksonian Senator John Poindexter of Mississippi—questioned the compatibility of Walker's extensive land speculation and his flaunted compassion for backwoods settlers. In fact, the state's poor white population included a sizeable contingent of squatters living illegally on the tracts he had just acquired. Walker replied, "It is true that these lands have advanced, and are advancing in value, but I have yet to learn, that it is criminal in me to exercise a privilege that is common to every other citizen." He also produced (or perhaps hired) a host of "witnesses" to give depositions attesting that Walker had made his purchases with the intention of protecting the squatter inhabitants against rival speculators from Alabama who would be less sympathetic toward them. Walker, they all swore, had acted by faithful, "fair and honorable means" to "secure the lands to the settlers at the minimum price" and "without any reward or compensation whatever."[46]

Keeping a number of squatters around rather than sending them packing had been, in fact, the comparatively unorthodox policy of Walker's syndicate. There is little cause to attribute this to altruism; their motivation combined economic and political interest. On the economic side, some large-scale speculators in the Southwest saw commercial benefit in having industrious sorts of squatter families remain on the land the investors had purchased. A "good quality" neighborhood tended to lift the value of adjoining and surrounding lands. Public-spirited Mississippians eagerly promoted settlement in their state, a cause that speculators, of course, supported. Mississippi congressman William Haile expressed this attitude in an 1828 report to his constituents, regretting the administrative slowness of the federal government in confirming land titles for legitimate settlers in Mississippi. Until that confirmation occurred, such people remained technically squatters, therefore vulnerable to speculators. "Many valuable citizens have abandoned the country from this cause: an event greatly to be deplored, as it checks the population of the state, retards its settlement, and deprives it of many who might have been its ornament and strength," Haile complained. "While such a danger continues," he went on, "owners of the most valuable tracts will find it impossible to procure for them settlers of substance and character." Some southwesterners worried that such "desirable" types of settlers would abandon their part of the country in favor of the free states. And in terms of social order, keeping poor whites attached to the soil, even illegally, could seem far preferable to augmenting a potentially unruly element of "miserable" landless whites.[47]

As for political intentions, Walker and his cohorts encouraged their squatter residents to purchase, at cost (usually $1.25 per acre), the lands on which they lived, up to a limit of a quarter-section, 160 acres. This arrangement matched the federal preemption policy in place since 1830, which provided a window of opportunity for public land squatters to secure claims at that price without having to bid at auction for them. But this policy did not apply to the former Indian lands of northern Mississippi, meaning that squatters on Walker's land who did not cooperate with his syndicate faced the likelihood of losing everything, including their improvements.

More generally, Walker made a point of siding with squatters in the district, sometimes defending them in claims disputes against speculators other than Walker's
business partners. Everyone, of course, expected the squatters who had benefited
from syndicate largesse—or Walker's legal prowess—to prove politically grateful.[48]

And indeed they did. Come late summer 1835, in the hamlet of Madisonville
just north of the state capital at Jackson, Walker launched his campaign for a seat
in the United States Senate. He had changed his official address from Natchez to
Madisonville in order to appear more local in the eyes of "piney woods" voters.
An uneasy mood hung over Mississippi at the time; rumors circulated of slave
insurrections, fueled, many thought, by northern agitators, whom southerners
most often associated with the Whig Party in the North. Mississippi Democrats
sensed their chance to dislodge George Poindexter from the Senate. Walker, with
his Natchez connections, carefully cultivated image, and the support of his Cocchuma District friends, the lower-class country whites, looked like just the man
Democrats in the state legislature wanted for the U.S. Senate.[49]

Although at one-time a Jacksonian Democrat himself, the incumbent Poindexter had called down upon himself the wrath of President Jackson by defending
South Carolina during the Nullification Crisis, then by opposing the Force Bill,
and finally by questioning White House patronage decisions for Mississippi. His
chances of reelection had steadily ebbed. But Walker's most serious challenge
during the campaign came from Congressman Franklin E. Plummer, a one-time
Democrat turned Whig, who also courted the "piney woods" vote. Plummer accused Walker of being a "wolf in sheep's clothing"—his Pennsylvania origins, his
activities as a speculator, his lack of formal experience in politics. Walker answered
in language that had by now become a classic Jacksonian formula: "I have no
banks, state or national, to sustain me. The aristocracy and their organ at Natchez,
and the enemies of Andrew Jackson, are all arrayed against me." In campaign-
ing, Walker pledged to support Benton's bill to graduate public land prices, along
with donations to actual settlers, and to oppose "any protective tariff, any Bank of
the United States, all local improvements by the general Government, and any
interference by Congress with the question of Slavery in any State, District, or
Territory."[50]

And so, Walker in January 1836 received his "solemn" political mandate from
Mississippi's legislators to return east at last and replace the politically willful
Poindexter. The specific nature of that mandate Walker perceived clearly enough.
Speaking from the Senate floor a few months later, he would boast that he "was
descended from squatters" and that "squatters [had] sent him to the senate." In
addition, he asserted that, "[a]lmost all great men were squatters. The pilgrims of
Plymouth were squatters; Columbus was a squatter; Benton's American people

were all squatters—(therefore the squatter party) . . . . The squatters defend our frontiers from the Indians; and if there had been squatters enough at Bladens-burgh [during the War of 1812], they would not have hopped away from the British. They would have nobly squatted out their ground." Still only thirty-four years old and a neophyte to public office, he would soon occupy the position that Jacksonian Democrats believed appropriate for a Mississippi land speculator and friend of western squatters whose voting influence had come to matter so much, the chair-manship of the Senate Committee on Public Lands.[51]

The Lexington, Kentucky, to which Henry Clay returned in 1829, after his four-year stint as John Quincy Adams's secretary of state, remained one of the largest cities west of the Appalachians, with just shy of 25,000 inhabitants. In late 1805, a traveler, Josiah Espy, had written that Lexington was then "the largest and most wealthy town in Kentucky." The main street had "all the appearance of Market Street in Philadelphia on a busy day." During Clay's time, Lexington turned into a western manufacturing center, drawing on the hemp production from the country-side, good for rope and bagging. Although landlocked, the city became an import-ant trade center because of its central location in Kentucky, accessible to travelers from surrounding smaller towns looking to purchase imported goods along with other articles and services to be found only in an urban place.[52]

A more troubling situation lurked in the background, however—one that many Lexingtonians probably did not sense because they took it for granted. This con-sisted in the fate of the slaves who lived there but also the fate of some poorer whites subsisting in semi-squalid conditions, whose chance of advancement in a slave-labor economy barely exceeded that of the chattels. Frederick Hall, a Wash-ington physician who had just visited Pennsylvania and Ohio, could not help not-ing the comparative social inequality he witnessed in central Kentucky. When he arrived in Lexington, the difference between poorer whites in the slaveholding states and those in the free states became starkly visible, especially in "their habits of industry." "In the former," he said, the white population looked "vastly more indolent"; on the day he arrived, in June 1837, there were "hundreds of idlers—or men, who seemed such—sitting in the public places, lounging in the bar-rooms of taverns and coffee houses, collected in squads at the corners of streets, lolling on benches in front of the houses, or balancing, Yankee fashion, on two legs of a chair—all apparently at a loss how to get rid of the time." Hall's impressions are borne out by statistics. Property records show that fewer than one in five of Lex-ington's white inhabitants, and fewer than one in ten of its craftsmen, held land by the 1820s. Moving on to Harrodsburg, a town maybe a day's ride from Clay's plan-tation, Hall saw again the "capacious and handsome" mansions of several large planters but also the "indifferent" habitations of the lower-class whites—"slightly built," their appearance "shabby," and "not kept in good repair."[53]

Although one of the most famous, privileged, and ambitious residents of the state, Clay mostly contradicted the northern antislavery stereotype of the haughty planter, surrounded by luxury, untroubled by the sufferings of others. "Mr Clay, although one of Nature's noblemen, has nothing, in his deportment, of the aristocrat," Frederick Hall reported. "He is easy of access, and remarkably urbane and friendly in his manners." Inspired by his father-in-law, Thomas Hart, young Clay invested in a variety of commercial and manufacturing ventures, as well as speculative land purchases and Ashland, his hemp-growing estate of more than 600 acres near Lexington, worked by varying numbers of slaves, somewhere between 30 and 50. He assumed that his own road to economic self-betterment, though fortuitous in marriage and aided by chattel labor, lay just as open to other white men who lived within the law and exerted similar ambition.[54]

Like George Washington and other post-Revolutionary leaders, Clay believed that a stable society had to be rooted in the fundamental virtue and loyalty of its citizens, and he respected westerners who contributed to the building of secure, prosperous (and republican) communities. In his ideal world, the West would be dominated by the sorts of people—the middle-class planters and slaveholders, lawyers and businessmen—who supported him in and around Lexington and with whom he identified personally, as well as those in western cities, like Louisville, Cincinnati, and St. Louis, where economic growth had been most rapid. Clay, like many of his neighbors, took enormous pride in Lexington. As he once described it: "The City is paved and watched and well built. The population occupies itself with Commerce, Manufactures, the Mechanic arts, the learned professions, and with Seminaries dedicated to the education of the youth of both sexes. . . . Society is good, hospitable and intelligent."[55]

With the American System, he courted such a constituency throughout the West—along with others, whether landed or not, whose economic interests somehow connected to the development of commerce and manufacturing. One westerner of this sort, fellow Lexingtonian Hector P. Lewis, observed that "a people to be free must be virtuous," and a virtuous community emphasized personal independence and industry. It included, as Lewis put it, "the shepherd upon our mountains who tends his little flock—the mechanic and manufacturer, who by their constant toil and labor, sustain and cherish a family, full of hope, though without comfort—the agriculturalist as he joyfully transports the fruits of his yearly industry to the markets." Even if not all men owned land, all could be morally upright and support themselves by honest work, whether on the land or by a trade. Like Clay, Lewis had been born in Virginia; he had attended Transylvania University, and he owned a farm of about 1,000 acres outside Lexington. With Lewis's letter to Clay came the signatures of twenty-three other leading citizens of the Lexington area, well-educated men, War of 1812 veterans, public office holders, and respected people of property—a small microcosm of Clay's natural constituency.[56]

Clay would return to Washington in 1831 to serve in the Senate, where the following year he proposed a comprehensive plan for the distribution of public land revenue among the states for purposes of internal improvement, one that might have invigorated idle Lexingtonians and many others like them. Although often underemphasized by historians, like the political economy it contained, this 1832 scheme aimed to spread around the country—and especially in the West—the middle-class, market-oriented success Clay had seen in more prosperous parts of the new states. The plan revised earlier renditions of the American System by tying together the protectionist economic vision of National Republicans and the more specific lessons for western land policy Clay had taken from the Panic of 1819—all within a somewhat denationalized constitutional framework that he hoped could satisfy states' rights advocates. He believed, moreover, that a new proliferation of capital would stimulate investment in the West, thereby increasing the range of employments and, in so doing, help to lift the character of poorer westerners, too.

In the early 1820s, the Maxcy proposal had raised searching questions about the equity of federal land policy. Now, a growing federal treasury (and ultimately a surplus) from the combination of tariffs and land sales gave proponents of revenue distribution—Clay's forces—an opportunity they needed. Regrettably for them, the ever-increasing variety of ideas and interests involved in land questions would make distribution that much harder to sell, but similar ideas had surfaced before. In December 1824, Senator Henry Johnson of Louisiana had recommended creation of a "permanent and perpetual fund, for Education and Internal Improvements." Two years later, Mahlon Dickerson, a strict-constructionist senator from New Jersey, had argued that using federal revenue only to pay the national debt, owed mostly to foreign creditors, excessively drained America of potential investment funds. Although he thought direct federal subsidies unconstitutional, distributing portions to states could stimulate domestic "industry and enterprise" in proper style. Also in 1826, Rhode Island had petitioned Congress for a proportion of the public lands to finance local education, but nothing came of the request. In February 1829, a select committee of the House claimed that the time had arrived "when the community should be awakened to a protection of their rights; when measures should be adopted . . . to give the States a direct interest in the income arising from the sales of the public lands." The same year, Representative Jonathan Hunt of Vermont had pushed for distribution of proceeds during the twenty-first

Congress when Foot's resolution came up. At that time, Spencer Pettis of Missouri had retorted that Hunt's proposal would only delay other policy changes that interested westerners more, including preemption, Benton's graduation of land prices, donations of tracts to actual settlers, and additional grants to western states.[57]

In the early 1830s, the conflict between crystallizing political parties turned more and more on questions tied to western land disposition. In a major Senate speech on May 16, 1826, Benton had revised the graduation proposal to include reducing the price minimum within four years to 25¢ an acre on lands remaining on the market unsold, along with donations of frontier tracts to impoverished settlers. Western interest in graduation had mushroomed wildly in the late 1820s, even though Benton's graduation bill had yet to survive beyond the Senate. There, a watered-down version had passed in 1830, by a slim margin of 24 to 22 and with the help of six anti-tariff South Atlantic senators, but it then failed in the House 68 to 82 despite the nearly unanimous support of western members, excepting Ohio's. Still, to nationalists at the time, the Senate vote bore the early look of a prospective—and to them, ominous—South-and-West coalition.[58]

Meanwhile, Andrew Jackson's election in 1828 had ended both Clay's service as secretary of state and an association with Adams and Rush that had hurt him politically in the West. When the Kentuckian joined the Senate in 1831, his primary goal was to forge a North-and-West alliance and win the presidency himself in 1832. But many westerners, even in Clay's Kentucky, now found Jackson more appealing. Clay needed to redeem his reputation among voters in the older western states and throughout the Northwest, where, despite the groundswell for graduation, there remained ardent support for internal improvements at federal expense and tariff protection of rural products—such as hemp.

After the sprawling debate over Foot's resolution, protectionists, too, had become more respectful toward the West, more solicitous of western support, and readier to acknowledge a pivotal role for western interests within the political economy of domestic manufacturing. No better example appeared than the published statements of the October 1831 Friends of Domestic Industry Convention that assembled in New York City—509 participants, representing every New England and Middle Atlantic state (including Maryland), plus Ohio, Virginia, and the District of Columbia. The more prominent members in attendance included Mathew Carey, Daniel W. Coxe, Charles J. Ingersoll, and William Wilkins of Pennsylvania; Abbott Lawrence and George Blake of Massachusetts; Hezekiah Niles of Baltimore; James Tallmadge of New York; Joshua Pierce of New Hampshire; and Charles Paine of Vermont. Distancing themselves as far as possible from the shrill statements of Samuel Foot and Richard Rush, they made sure to regard the great quantity of western land as a blessing and not a curse. "The peculiar advantage of the United States consists in the abundance and cheapness of fertile lands, affording an easy subsistence and high remuneration to labour," declared the convention report.[59]

Like the vociferous crowd that had flocked behind Benton, the protectionists now emphasized a more distributive vision: greater equality and economic justice, but through manufacturing and internal improvements—as opposed to a doctrine of capital growth with benefits primarily to the East or Benton's idea of agricultural expansion, chiefly helping the West. The New York convention's system of "manufactures and the arts" recommended "distributing and equalizing these peculiar advantages [of the West] through all the departments of industry and through all classes of society."

By this time, transportation improvements already in place (and others contemplated) had linked the interests of East and West more closely than before—and a pro-manufacturing policy would help to maximize that northeastern advantage. "The states of New-York, Pennsylvania and Ohio have invested a capital of enormous amount, which may be reckoned as at least fifty millions, within the last ten years, in . . . canals, rail-ways, and other facilities," the New York convention observed. "This capital depends entirely upon domestic industry for its fruits. It would be a loss to the four millions of people who have expended it, and might as well be abandoned at once, without the protected products of domestic industry for its returns." Transportation advances also enabled a geographical proliferation of manufacturing, which, the convention suggested, would *include* ordinary westerners rather than exploiting them (as Benton had charged), expand the range of employment in the new states, generate cultural as well as economic gains, and furnish farmers with more extensive market opportunities and richer lives all around. "A rapid increase in population, dwellings, culture, and the comforts of life and the value of property, wherever manufactures prevail, bespeak their capacity to diffuse happiness and wealth," the New York assemblage contended.[60]

A March 26, 1832, memorial to Congress on behalf of the New York Convention elaborated with intellectual force on all of these points. The author, Alexander Hill Everett of Boston, was the brother of Edward Everett. Addressing specifically the Senate Committee on Manufactures, which Henry Clay now chaired, Everett, too, cited the "boundless abundance and variety" of the western regions—an endowment "which we are ourselves scarcely beginning to realize." The spread of manufacturing not only throughout the East but also into the West promised "an accession of wealth, population, and political importance, exactly proportioned to the whole amount of capital, and the whole number of persons which they employ." The argument offered, in essence, a reformulation of the American System, more western-inclusive than in the early 1820s—all the more potent for Clay politically. "[A]n agricultural village, town, and country, which obtains its supplies of manufactured articles within its own limits, is, in the same proportion more wealthy, populous, and flourishing, than one, in other respects similarly situated, which sends for them to a distant city," Everett stressed. The symbiotic exchange between the agricultural and manufacturing "classes" would be one of "the means of subsistence for the products of art." The cultivator "supplies the manufacturer with food and materials," collecting in return "the articles of use, comfort, and luxury, into which these materials have been fashioned." The result would be a narrowing of economic and cultural differences between farmers and laborers and the emergence of a unified middle class of mutually prosperous, interdependent producers—and, by obvious implication, a supremely powerful political base for an economically nationalist politician. "But this exchange can never take place to any great extent," Everett continued "excepting when the two classes are situated in the neighborhood of each other, and belong to the same political society," making their public policy interests more similar to than separate from those of the Northeast.[61]

Everett, knew he dared not lean so far westward as to lose support from *eastern* manufacturing investors and promoters, who liked the American System when it seemed to offer more exclusive benefit to them. But for protectionists, a new, and in their view more volatile, political world had emerged, especially with the congealing of Jacksonian strength in the West. The strict constructionist, anti-logrolling implications of Jackson's Maysville Road veto on May 27, 1830; southern objections to federal consolidation now being voiced by Hayne, Calhoun, and, by extension, Benton; the brewing, soon-to-explode nullification crisis in South Carolina; the uncertain future of the Second Bank of the United States; Martin Van Buren's partisan, party-building machinations behind the scenes; and the possibility of Old Hickory's reelection in fall 1832—none of this could be seen as boding well for the protectionist cause. Add to that the pro-squatter agitation throughout the West that Walker of Mississippi, among others, hoped to harness, at whatever cost to the revenue-generating potential and market value of public lands.

Everett's words exposed the thinning political tightrope that protectionists now had to walk. For the benefit of nervous eastern allies fearful of losing their labor force to the West, he repeated the promise that domestic manufactures would continue "in restraining emigration from the settled to the unsettled parts of the country." But for suspicious westerners, sensitive to any scheme to stunt frontier growth, he wrote: "These remarks are not made under impressions in any way unfavorable to the character of interests of the younger members of the union. . . . [T]he sudden expansion of our population over the unsettled territories of the union, has been thus far productive of good. It has thrown open a broad and ample field for the national industry." And to court possible favor from Jackson, who had taken a stand on nullification and the Union but not on tariffs or land policy, he pointed out that the new states had also furnished "a new political element, which serves as a sort of mediator between sectional interests, which might otherwise have proved to be irreconcilably hostile."[62]

Although Clay's basic political economy had changed little since his days in the House, he, like the Friends of Domestic Industry Convention, began adjusting to new circumstances. Clay, too, had begun thinking more in terms of distributive, as opposed to accumulative, economic development. Still committed to protective tariffs, he turned increasing attention to federally encouraged internal improvements as a way of opening less-developed areas of the West, binding them more securely—and more commercially—to the Union, and fostering socially stable western communities along much-needed transportation lines. Land policy for the sake of *both* revenue and settlement, and with an eye to internal improvements, became more crucial than ever in Clay's vision. These things were "due [owed] to the American people, and emphatically due to the Western people," he avowed in the Senate on January 11, 1832. The impending retirement of the public debt raised a new prospect: surplus federal revenue. Clay favored approaching this situation not by reducing land prices, as Walker and the Bentonites urged, but by modifying the tariff and somehow allocating land proceeds for internal improvements throughout the country, yet with special consideration to the capital-starved West.[63]

The steady decline of the national debt also was inspiring adherents of the graduation and cession ideas to intensify *their* demands for fundamental changes in federal land policy. They hoped that antinationalist southerners would join them. On April 1, 1832, Illinois Jacksonian John M. Robinson confided to Ninian Edwards his anticipation of a basic shift in the Senate:

> Now is the favourable time for us of the new States to make a stand for the reduction in price or a transfer to the States of the Public Lands. Now that the public debt is good as paid, and a new system . . . of revenue to be formed, if that system be formed barely for the exigences of the Government, without any change as to price or disposition of the public domain, it will be a kind of estoppel to any future relief on this subject. I say relief, for the present land system is a burthen of the most onerous character to all the new States.

Southern opposition to protective tariffs constituted only *one* threat to Clay's economic nationalism. The growing political clout of these "new States"—meaning, to Robinson and Edwards, those *west* of Ohio, Kentucky, and Tennessee—demanded attention, too.[64]

Given the nationalist role Clay envisioned for the public lands, anyone could have predicted his reaction to cession. He condemned "certain portions of the

South" that might exchange denationalization of federal lands for western anti-tariff votes. "A more stupendous, and more flagitious project was never conceived," the Kentuckian declared to Francis Brooke on March 28, 1832. "It will fail in its object, and it ought to be denounced." As for Edwards in Illinois, Clay raged on, "there are about forty millions of acres of public land, and about one hundred and fifty or one hundred and sixty thousand people. What think you of giving that large amount of land to that comparatively small number of people?" While congressional interest in cession had waned somewhat by this time, the radical lowering of land prices that Benton demanded also could derail the American System. If the land were only "nominally sold," Clay added contemptuously, "it would, in the end, amount to a mere donation." Meanwhile, like Edwards in Illinois, Benton had to address his own problem of shifting factional politics back home. Having outlasted one rival for influence in Missouri, former Senator David Barton (who had opposed graduation), he now faced Clay supporters trying to organize there.[65]

As the only westerner on the five-member Senate Committee on Manufactures, Clay prepared to withstand a calculated offensive against what he hoped would be an impenetrable fortress within the American System, his land program. Political enemies wasted little time forcing the matter into his lap. In March 1832, the Senate had referred to Manufactures a resolution for inquiry into land-price reduction and cession. Because such a resolution normally would have gone to the Committee on Public Lands, Clay rightly detected a strategy to embarrass him and damage his presidential chances in the autumn of 1832. He assumed that the ploy represented a Senate majority "composed of all the anti-Tariff Senators and some of the Jackson Tariff Senators." Jackson supporters dominated the Senate and its Public Lands Committee, headed by a foe of the American System, William R. King of Alabama, and influenced behind the scenes by Benton. These enemies of Clay figured that he could not endorse the resolution without losing needed support in the East and contradicting his personal beliefs. To report unfavorably, however, would be to risk being branded a traitor to his own section, jeopardizing his political stock in the West. By this time, trying to hold back the movement to dismantle the traditional land system seemed like "sitting upon a volcano," Clay confided to John Ewing in 1832. "There is no safety or certainty with the Jackson party; and as they are in the majority in both houses they can do as they please."[66]

Although he protested the "incongruous association of subjects," Clay embraced home-market theory regarding domestic manufacturing and public lands. Again he would advocate a government policy devoted simultaneously to industrial modernization and systematic western development. Having recently reported on the tariff, the Manufactures Committee turned exclusive attention to land policy. Perhaps because much of the financial and intellectual community of the

Northeast by then endorsed a home market, Clay aimed his report at commercial westerners—planters, lawyers, and businessmen resembling his own Lexington coterie. Like Daniel Webster, another National Republican presidential aspirant, the Kentuckian needed to forge political bonds between Northeast and Northwest, but Clay counted on having greater western sway than Webster. He also hoped to disarm the cessionists for good by offering their states a large share of public-land proceeds in place of the actual lands.[67]

His public lands report, dated April 16, 1832, refuted cession in principle, just as Webster had done two years earlier in his debate with Hayne. Rigidly opposed to any denationalization of the public domain, Clay based his case on the "common fund" theory, an argument redolent of Revolutionary days in that it placed the general good above selfish private interests. When the original states ceded their western claims to the Confederation, he recalled, they created "a great, public, national trust." The purpose had been to help Congress keep peace within the Union, "to check the progress of discontent, and arrest the serious consequences to which the agitation of this question might lead." The former colonies supposedly gave up their territorial claims "for the *use* and *benefit* of all the States," as opposed to releasing massive quantities to states, companies, or individuals. Therefore, Clay contended, Congress had a mandate against making radical changes: "[T]o divert the lands from the general object; to misapply or sacrifice them; to squander or improvidently cast them away; would be alike subversive of the interests of the people of the United States, and contrary to the plain dictates of the duty by which the General Government stands bound to the States and to the whole people."[68]

Apart from centralized control, compelling advantages of the land system, to Clay's mind, included its uniformity and its careful rationality. Although modified through the years as practicality warranted, the methodical surveying and auctioning of public lands, divided and subdivided in precise rectilinear units, had brought order upon the West. To denationalize public lands, as cession advocates demanded, would invite chaos. Moreover, Jackson on April 5 had signed a new law to allow the "poorer classes" 40-acre tracts at $1.25 per acre, a provision sufficient, in Clay's judgment, to bring ownership within reach of any man of honest ambition. Federal policy already had enabled a proliferation of responsible landholders in the western states. Radically reduced land prices would only encourage more of the desperate, dishonorable, and unworthy to go west. From a commercial perspective, he assumed that early western development required men of proven financial responsibility, able not only to acquire land but also bring out its full value, building on it, investing resources, and contributing quickly to the aggregate capital of emerging communities. While Benton sided with the poorer classes no matter what types that category included, Clay saw no one more likely to stabilize new areas than the men of trade on whose favor he depended.[69]

Further, the systematic organization of federal lands—a feature so easily ruined by careless pro-squatter policies—would avert the disaster of overlapping claims. Clay knew firsthand of such dilemmas often faced by litigants in his home state. Without the regularity of federal townships and sections, Kentucky landowners once lived in fear of losing holdings rooted in capricious Virginia statutes and claims records. As a young Lexington attorney, he himself had made a small fortune on such cases. For landholders, these disputes raised "the worst of all species of litigation," Clay said. By securing titles and boundaries more tightly, federal policy had guarded the "foundations of useful civil institutions" for both present and future generations of settlers.[70]

Within this constraint of traditional policy, Clay stood not less but *more* enthusiastic about a speedy settlement of the West in 1832 than he had been in 1820. Then, he had looked to "natural checks" against emigration: the West's distance from the original states, the strength of familial ties, the "natural repugnance" of leaving one's birthplace. Now, he gladly stressed that federal policy had not obstructed a massive westward movement; the auction system had neither inhibited extensive sales nor dampened enthusiasm for migration. According to Treasury Department records cited in the report, revenue from land sales had tripled—from one to three million dollars—between 1828 and 1831. As for surplus revenue, Clay modified Virgil Maxcy's 1821 idea in Maryland: congressional distribution of public-land proceeds (and not the lands themselves, as Maxcy had proposed) among all 24 states, according to population, with an additional 10 percent earmarked for the public-land states. States, in turn, were to apply their shares "to education, internal improvements, or colonization [of former slaves], or to the redemption of any existing debt contracted for internal improvements." The slaveholding Clay probably hoped the "colonization" provision might shore up his standing among antislavery voters north of the Ohio River who had pilloried him for the 1820 Missouri Compromise.[71]

While Clay's distribution proposal urged central direction of land revenue, finance was only one of its objectives, along with protecting the existing system of land-price determination. In effect, Bentonites wanted to eliminate the $1.25 minimum and let prices fall, hoping to induce the most rapid population growth possible in new areas within a short period of time. Clay defended the existing minimum and insisted that the federally controlled supply and auctioning of government tracts served propertied interests (and stability of land values) in all sections of the country. That view particularly served the older western states—Kentucky, Tennessee, and Ohio—where rates of population growth no longer could match Indiana, Illinois, Missouri, Alabama, Mississippi, and Louisiana. For the western non–public land states—Kentucky and Tennessee—distribution would offer an unexpected windfall. Clay, a Kentuckian as well as a nationalist and a presidential contender, found no "cogent and conclusive reasons" for a sudden government reduction of land prices, which "might seriously impair the value of property." Preventing devaluation mattered to the "yeomanry" of responsible landowners, "decidedly the most important class in the community," the most "patient" and "patriotic" group, whose support he coveted.[72]

Differing further with the Bentonites, Clay saw also in auction competition and the $1.25 minimum the best possible protection against speculative land grabbers. He thought Benton-style price reductions, making land acquisition easier for everyone regardless of character or status, would not only devalue property but also "excite and stimulate the spirit of speculation." "If the price were much reduced," Clay contended, "the strongest incentives to engrossment of the better lands would be presented to large capitalists, and the emigrant, instead of being able to purchase from his own government . . . might be compelled to give much higher and more fluctuating prices to the speculator." Clay recalled the disaster of bounty lands granted during the War of 1812. These had been "thrown into the market at prices below the Government rate," and they "notoriously became an object of speculation." Falling into the hands of unscrupulous investors, many of these areas had remained socially and economically undeveloped.[73]

With this committee report, Clay reasserted himself as a protectionist with a broad, West-inclusive policy vision. Its strong subtext held that basic economic nationalism—both that of earlier days and of the 1830s—adhered to traditional republican values more than the Jacksonians' proposals did. Those values, Clay implied, had once translated into a policy commitment to "the common good," not just a libertarian unleashing of individuals to pursue their private interests as they saw fit. He aimed that argument—in vain it would turn out—to lessen Benton's influence in the West. On May 18, 1832, King's Public Lands Committee reported a competing bill that endorsed Benton's graduated lowering of land prices, the concept that would compete against Clay's distribution bill for popularity among western voters.[74]

The distribution idea quickly became *the* featured proposal in the American System, its implications extending to the major economic issues of the age: tariffs, internal improvements, banking and finance, and public lands. With stubborn reliance on the federal land auction system, governed by the minimum-price stipulation, Clay's stance reinforced his popularity with middle-class commercial and propertied interests in the West and nationally. Those types worried most about the stability of value on lands they already owned. The Kentucky senator made sure his public lands report circulated widely, and he sent personal copies to his friends. Many pro-Clay newspapers extolled it. *Niles' Weekly Register* judged the subject to have been "grappled by a fearless and a master hand" and proclaimed the whole matter "*subdued*." Richard Rush, probably believing the report too generous toward the western states, gave measured approval: "[Y]ou have established in an irresistible manner all the main points of the policy you recommend." But some of the western feedback foretold the plan's fate. William F. Dunnica in St. Louis told Clay in June 1832 that the report did "not meet the approbation of a majority of Our State. They have heretofore been so entirely devoted to Benton's [land-price graduation] scheme that every thing that comes in opposition to his views are rejected." He added that Clay's proposal struck most Missourians as just "a favorable scheme for the Eastern states," but later Dunnica remarked, interestingly, that "the reading part of Citizens have expressed themselves decidedly in favor it."[75]

Clay's 1832 land bill passed in the Senate by a vote of 26 to 18, but the House postponed action on it. Reintroduced in 1833, it passed in both houses, only to be pocket-vetoed by the newly reelected President Jackson. Allowing the congressional term to expire while the bill sat on his desk avoided any possibility of an override. Old Hickory, who as a United States senator in 1824 had voted for internal improvement and tariff bills and who, in his first two Annual Messages, had endorsed an eventual distribution of surplus revenue among the states, now fell in step with Benton and graduation. He claimed to be protecting the states against excessive federal government meddling. Arguably, Clay's land bill constituted one of the most comprehensive and far-reaching pieces of legislation ever rejected by an American chief executive; it should be regarded among Jackson's most critical vetoes.[76]

Despite the land bill's failure in 1832–1833, and that of his presidential campaign against Jackson, Clay had articulated what would become the Whig view on public land issues. Although pressure at home later forced most western Whigs to break ranks and support preemption, land policy votes still tended to follow party lines during the Jacksonian period, with Whigs favoring distribution and Democrats advocating land price reduction or cession. Beneath this conflict of parties lay fundamental alternatives in political economy and social philosophy.

Although certainly never of one mind, the Jacksonians tended to envision a West of agricultural regions populated as rapidly as possible by enterprising producers of goods for export, regardless of their economic means or status and without much governmental restraint. Whigs, while no less diverse than their political adversaries, leaned toward a different view, anchored in home-market theory and a belief in active government. They imagined an agricultural West of economically balanced communities dominated by men of established capital means and social responsibility.[77]

Between 1819 and the mid-1830s, economic nationalists applied in a variety of ways the central idea of the American System, that a diversification of employments in a home-market economy was the best insurance against what Clay termed in 1824 a "demoralization of society," that is, an unraveling of social order. Daniel Drake and Lyman Beecher agreed, while Robert J. Walker embraced a radical alternative. Clay, Beecher, and Drake, such different men in many ways, all regarded development of manufacturing as essential. They also identified careful development of western lands as vital not only to manufacturing but also to a full economic integration of East and West, North and South. Jeffersonian political economy had prescribed making frontier land available on terms easy enough to prevent a class of desperately poor citizens from appearing in America. Clay's American System advocated not a departure from this idea but a modification to include domestic manufacturing and make allowance for a more complex and rapidly changing economic scene than that of Jefferson's day. The 1830s modification of that policy relied on federal government power, operating in concert with the states, to reconcile new commercial realities with the older, "country" predilections of many states' rights people. Clay had asserted all along the compatibility of agricultural, trading, and manufacturing pursuits and had always favored a harmonizing of increasingly diverse, often conflicting sections, classes, and interests within the Union.[78]

CHAPTER SEVEN

"A Lawless Rabble"

When subscribers in Chautauqua County, New York, opened the *Jamestown Journal* in late April 1836, they read that a United States senator from faraway Mississippi wanted to give preference in public land sales to people who had settled illegally, characterizing *them* as "the finest portion of republican citizens!" Should this proposition find favor, the article continued, "the whole public domain will be at the mercy of adventurers of every sort, who may prefer taking rich lands to buying them." Several months later, readers in Portsmouth, New Hampshire, another place where traditions died hard, were advised to brace themselves for the inevitable, "a grand national ordinance in favor of *squatters*." To benefit from this new policy, the column went on, "a man must be a violator of the laws. He must trespass upon lands that do not belong to him." He must "out-travel the honest emigrant, and squat ahead of him, driving off the Indian, if the Indian is in his way." The "old States of this Union" were thus to be "drained of population" in order to build a new nation of citizens and voters such as these.[1]

Meanwhile, squatting settlers continued to flood western regions in overwhelming numbers. In a news item entitled "TROUBLE BREWING," the *New York Commercial Advertiser* in July 1837 announced the presence of 14,000 illegal residents in "the Iowa district"—the part of Wisconsin west of the Mississippi River—where no federal land had yet been opened for sale. Another estimate held the entire number of squatters on public lands throughout the United States to be "not much short of 50,000 souls!"—20,000 in the Wisconsin Territory alone.[2]

Historians should consider the 1830s political response to news of this kind from the perspective of those who opposed "squatters' rights," not just the more familiar viewpoint of those who favored them. Either way, people at the time well knew that the manner of western lands settlement would profoundly influence the character of American society. It made a difference what kind of government policy lawmakers adopted toward that end. Over the generations since, many writers have assumed that the Jacksonian Democratic Party, by advocating policies such as the gradual reduction of federal land prices and preemption rights, cared more about the actual populating of the West than Henry Clay and his fellow promoters of the American System. That view overlooks the importance of western land settlement in the political economy of Clay and other nationalists. The National Republican—and, later, the Whig—side of the land policy argument merits far more attention than it has received.

Today, Clay is often noted for advocating the distribution of federal land revenue among the states in the 1830s, but the actual filling of lands mattered as much to him as the raising of revenue because of the impact of settlement—by men of average means—on the social structure, economic stability, and moral character of the West. This vision, however, provided no room for squatters and no sympathy for "squatters' rights." Although never tested as policy in Clay's own time— categorized then, and later, as elitist and undemocratic—the Whig land program may well have held greater potential for a West of economic opportunity, individual advancement, and basic regard for law than any of the alternatives of the day.[3]

The idea of distributing land proceeds among the states (with special benefit to western states) became a distinct part of Clay's agenda in 1832–1833, when Congress passed—and President Andrew Jackson pocket-vetoed—the bill that would have instituted that plan, to go along with the Compromise Tariff of 1833. As Whigs and Democrats continued to debate the distribution of land revenue, an equally difficult part of the western lands question lingered throughout the 1830s: preemption, the legal recognition of squatters' claims on the public domain. Preemption had challenged lawmakers since the Confederation era: Could the national government safely allow individuals to occupy vacant tracts of their choice—prior to registration and purchase (and perhaps even before official surveying)? Might such an approach be reconciled with the planned order and precision of the land system and the avoidance of frontier chaos? Clay's consistent answer to these questions, especially after 1834, was an emphatic, almost fanatical *no*. As he saw it, to legitimize squatting was to encourage people of the worst character to inhabit the West, just as lawmakers had thought back in the 1780s. He stated in 1838 that squatters on federal territory constituted a "lawless rabble" that "might as well seize upon our forts, our arsenals, or on the public treasure, as to rush out and seize upon the public lands." Clay's vehemence—and eventually his strategy—in opposing squatters helped his enemies (and some Jackson-period historians) to brand the American System as more pro-eastern and pro-elite than it actually was. And yet, by the late 1830s even some of the most conservative Whig statesmen, Daniel Webster in particular, had accepted squatters' rights as a *fait accompli*. By 1841, a large majority of westerners in Clay's own party sided with their Jacksonian adversaries on preemption.[4]

Why did Clay, a westerner himself, a man of political sagacity known for centrist leadership and famed for willingness to compromise, so persistently resist this tide? The complex answer to this question has much to do with who Clay was—as a person, politician, and policy maker, but also as an economic thinker and promoter of ideas. There is more to be said about the political economy of the American System, especially the place of Clay's land policy views within that framework and the larger vision of western development that he saw as key to the strengthening of the Union and the steady enrichment of its citizens. Beyond the American System and its implications, however, this is a story of how an aging Whig statesman, one who still longed for the presidency, tried to confront the shifting cultural politics and social beliefs around him. It also shows why he and others resented Jacksonian democracy so intensely.

Clay's fight with Democrats over land policy provides good insight into the cultural politics of the period. His vantage point reveals how much public lands legislation, and the perspectives that shaped it, really *did* change during the Jacksonian years—far beyond the shrinking of the purchase minimum from 160 to 40 acres and the reduction of the cash-sale minimum to $1.25 per acre from the pre-1820 credit-sale price of $2.00 per acre. While Congress did not in this period give away the lands or cede them generally to the western states, the triumph of preemption still jarred traditionalists like Clay who had invested so much faith in the stability of law and so much confidence in the ability of government to control—and even prescribe—the course of development for society. The popular, "new democratic" language that legitimized squatters rights was an idiom the venerable Kentuckian did not speak, understand, or accept. But his opponents did. A "cultural gatekeeper," to borrow a phrase from historian John Brooke, Clay saw the traditional foundation of federal land policy—the land auction system—as not only providing market value for federal lands but also guarding against a moral debasement of the western population. Competitive bidding for land, which preemption circumvented, had served an important purpose beyond just that of filling the federal treasury; it also governed what types of people and what elements of culture would—or should—be drawn westward.[5]

—⟡—

A negative view of unauthorized settlement had dominated policy making during the early years of the republic. Many late-eighteenth-century intellectuals believed that extensive land in the West provided insurance against an ultimate corruption and decay of American society, but this view included a less-recognized understanding that overly rapid and haphazard settlement could impede balanced economic growth and a spirit of community. The Land Ordinance of 1785 had introduced a congressional policy designed to control and consolidate settlement, as well as raise needed revenue from land sales, with the intention that illegal settlement should be prevented. That same year, Congress even embraced the undesirable option of sending a military force, under Colonel Josiah Harmer, to drive out squatters in the Northwest Territory. That expedition had failed to secure its objective.[6]

Federalist leadership after 1789 had tried to regulate the pace and character of westward settlement and ensure the political loyalty of settlers. The decision two years earlier to sell hundreds of thousands of acres, at just $1.00 per acre, to the Ohio Company, its organizers being former Continental Army officers, served as a prime example of the socially elitist concept that Federalists were following. When Clay's original political party, the Jeffersonian Republicans, assumed power after 1800, they shared the Federalists' concern about securing the West from lawlessness. President Jefferson, while eager to promote agricultural expansion, wanted a carefully ordered, methodical filling of the frontier. The official policy of his government, reinforced by the Intrusion Act of 1807, had continued to ban squatting on federal lands no matter how difficult the strategy was to enforce. Clay, as a young senator in 1807, had followed pressure at home to vote against that anti-squatter law; but like most other Jeffersonians in Congress, he did not in principle oppose the early federal land system.

Apart from the lessons of traditional policy, Clay's view of how the West should be settled apparently came from his experience in Kentucky. While he, like many settlers, purchased and sold land speculatively to augment his income, he did not care for land buyers who lived far away and whose profits did not benefit the western economy directly. In his Kentucky, where no federal-style system of prior surveys and rectangular grids had furnished clear boundaries, the late-eighteenth-century flood of settlement included a large number of farmers who took up residence on lands to which, as it turned out, they held no clear title. An ambiguous patchwork of Virginia land legislation, including an ill-designed preemption policy, had led to a morass of overlapping claims, the same tract being, as Clay put it in 1814, "frequently covered by two or three or more original patents granted by the State [of Virginia]." He added, "[I do] not much like the character of the persons through whose hands the titles have passed; most of them being Land Speculators"; he would make similar statements about nonresident speculators later in his career. Humphrey Marshall's 1824 *History of Kentucky* echoed some of Clay's concern; it recounts that the whole mess had "retarded" the state's population, "obstructed her improvement—distracted her people—impaired her morals—and depreciated the value of her rich soil." At the end of all the land claims litigation, occupiers of land often found themselves unseated not by neighboring settlers but by absentee claimants. As a result, when Kentucky entered the Union in 1792, half of the adult male inhabitants owned no land at all, and 90 percent owned less than 500 acres.[7]

Between 1797 and 1820, the Kentucky legislature tried to enact a system of occupying claimant laws to protect these unsuspecting settlers from being dispossessed with nothing to show for their improvements. The state sent Clay, along with George M. Bibb, to defend these laws when the Virginia legislature challenged them and also later, when the United States Supreme Court, in *Green v. Biddle* (1823), ruled them an unconstitutional violation of the contract clause. "Of all evils which can afflict an unhappy country, scarcely any was so aggravated as that of having its soil, the source whence all our riches flow, and all our wants are supplied, the subject of endless litigation," Clay told the Virginia General Assembly in February 1822. "The system supposes that innocent men have mixed their property together, the one, believing it to be his own, having improved it; and the other being ascertained by judicial investigation to have the best title." Clay's position on the occupying claimant laws implied contempt for absentee speculators who sought unfair gain at the expense of settlers. Still, he did not sympathize with those who *knowingly* settled on another's land, nor had Kentucky's laws defended that behavior.[8]

The chaos of land claims in Kentucky forced thousands of good settlers to migrate, as Clay put it, "to more favored states and territories where they could enjoy in peace and tranquility their beloved homes." But what if some refused to abide by the Supreme Court and defied speculators who wanted to take up their claims? Clay's answer in a letter to one Virginian in 1823 empathized with Kentucky's victimized settlers, almost endorsing the frontier radicalism he normally condemned: "[I]f the people . . . [upon the lands] should happen to exhibit . . . some little spirit, in the maintenance of what they believe to be their rights, it will be a misfortune resulting from the blood descended to them from their ancestors." Even if political necessity inspired in him more compassion for these Kentucky squatters than he would express later for those on federal lands, Clay had made a key point in his legal work for Kentucky, as had the state with its occupying claimant laws: no land program should work *against* the interests of innocent, law-abiding settlers.[9]

While in Congress, Clay aided poorer westerners, as he had in Kentucky—if they respected legal authority. Although employed by the Bank of the United States during the Panic of 1819 to prosecute unresponsive Ohio Valley debtors, and although privately sympathetic with the anti-relief faction at home, Clay also tried to help legitimate settlers pay for their land during hard times. The Land Act of 1820, with its repeal of the credit system for land purchases and reinstitution of cash sales, worried cash-poor settlers in general, not just those who hoped for preemption rights. Clay had opposed this repeal (though as House Speaker he did not vote on it), siding (perhaps out of political necessity) with the widespread pro-credit sentiment in the western states, while going along with subsequent bills for the relief of federal land debtors. Some relief applicants in the mid-1820s believed Clay, by then secretary of state, to be more sympathetic to their appeals than President John Quincy Adams, and Clay's influence may have caused Adams in his Annual Message of December 1827 to urge extension of the time allowed for payments.[10]

As for land policy in general, a succession of legal adjustments had opened western landowning considerably by 1830—without a general ending of the ban against unauthorized settlement. Then, in 1832, Congress enabled non-squatters to purchase as little as 40 acres, at a time when the auction price rarely exceeded $1.25 per acre. Clay thought this more than sufficient to bring ownership within reach of most honest, hard-working citizens. It meant that anyone with $50 might acquire such a farm in the West without settling on land that did not belong to him. The "forty-acre law" marked three-and-a half decades of steady modification in federal land law to accommodate individual buyers of modest means—quite a difference from the 1796 purchase minimum of 640 acres for no less than $2.00 per acre. This pattern of legislative change shows that, in the half-century after 1780, most policy makers, including Clay, had come to accept land policy that encouraged virtuous citizens of middling status, as opposed to the earlier policy, which favored the privileged and well-connected.[11]

—⟡—

Although Clay's anti-squatter mindset would place him more and more out-of-fashion in the West during the 1830s, there had been—and remained—a wider cultural context for it. The concern about illegal settlers on the part of Clay and others, of various political inclinations, related to larger anxieties about the effects of the frontier on "civilized" life. To some early observers, the ways of squatters had seemed so incompatible with refined behavior as to constitute an entirely distinct and much inferior strain of culture. Among more sophisticated Americans, the word "squatter" itself held an uncomplimentary connotation: one who sits unproductively on property not belonging to him, making no commitment to improving it, doing nothing to uplift his community. Congregationalist minister and future Yale president Timothy Dwight, traveling through western New England and New York in the late eighteenth century, declared that such men and women could not live in regular society: "They are too idle; too talkative; too passionate; too prodigal; and too shiftless; to acquire either property or character. They are impatient of the restraints of law, religion, and morality." The *North American Review* in 1827 categorized squatters as settlers on other people's land who were "afraid of being brought to account." A writer for the Boston-published *New-England Magazine* in

October 1835 called them "a transient company" of people, "indulgently suffered to pick a living" off the earth. In general, those who disapproved of squatters tended to portray them in terms antithetical to the emerging "middle-class values" of the period—deficient not just in economic means but also in qualities of character that distinguished the "middling" sort from the "lower" types, qualities like frugality, self-restraint, genteel manners, social responsibility, and a diligent work ethic.[12]

Some westerners, too, observed behavior that corroborated the uncouth and lawless reputation of squatters. A correspondent in Missouri in 1831 referred to such people as a "semi-barbarian population, which is constantly pressing on the heels of the retreating savages." With regard to religion and moral culture, they were, he said, "most deplorably ignorant, having little concern about a future existence." And yet, when news of impending preemption started to circulate, a hell-bent scramble often followed. Indiana resident John B. Chapman reported in March 1834 that "a predatory warfair was commenced," with settlers launching into a mad frenzy to claim the best available lands, even "pulling down houses, over peoples heads; killing cattle; burning haystacks;—and a distruction of every thing that would prevent another from a settlement." A few years later, Thomas Osborn and 270 unnamed supporters lobbied Congress against squatters' rights and price reduction by delineating the kind of subterfuge that went on: "hundreds of small pens, from 10 to 15 feet square, . . . built upon the public lands, and a few carrots or peppers sowed in them, and perhaps a few trees felled together to form a shelter for a short time; and from that small piece of improvement, a deed has been obtained for a good tract of land."[13]

Contrary to the long-standing auction system that Clay favored, proponents of preemption in its most radical form asserted a belief that settlement, even before lands had been surveyed, and then purchase at a guaranteed minimum price, offered greater benefit to society than a policy that prohibited settlement prior to survey and required competitive bidding upon sale. While Congress had passed many narrowly targeted preemption acts between 1800 and 1830, none had established a consistent policy or a long-term commitment to squatters generally. Federal administrators in the General Land Office condemned the idea of preemption; inviting squatters to roam the public domain would greatly complicate their jobs. But far more than that, making preemption a systematic feature of the federal land system would endorse what previously had been regarded as "illegal settlement." Congress would be giving in to behavior that many still considered morally questionable and bound to undermine federal control.[14]

The Preemption Act of May 29, 1830, passed with a blend of western, southern, and Jacksonian Democratic support, offered settlers who occupied and improved tracts of surveyed public land in 1829 a preferential right to purchase, before auction, 160 acres at the minimum price of $1.25 per acre. Although antedated by various special grants for settlers—and earlier, more limited preemption laws—this statute offered a temporary expedient, restricted to just one year, and not an adoption of principle. Congress supplemented the 1830 law with two-year extensions in 1832 and 1834. After returning to the Senate in 1831, Clay voted for the 1834 preemption bill—favoring not the principle, he said, but the specific focus, the restricted duration, and the guarding "against violence as well as corruption" in frontier regions. His presidential aspirations for 1836 also made this vote politically expedient. But after 1834, preemption looked as if it might never end; Democrats featured their support of it all the more, and squatters' rights became a direct challenge to Clay, his presidential hopes, and the American System.[15]

Clay's enemies would use land policy against him because he had staked so much on the idea of distributing federal land revenue, a program more basic to his economic nationalism than historians have acknowledged. His June 20, 1832, Senate speech on the distribution scheme stressed careful management of the public domain and avoidance of sharp reductions in the price of federal lands, both strategies crucial to the proper development of transmontane regions. Price reductions, he argued, would depress the value of all land in the new states and territories. Clay thought that tracts offered to transients on nearly give-away terms would almost inevitably fall to the worst sorts of speculators, resulting in higher prices for settlers, who then would be forced to buy the better land from private sellers: "It is a business, a very profitable business, at which fortunes are made in the new States, to purchase these refuse lands, and, without improving them, to sell them again at large advances."[16]

More important, in Clay's view, was distributing federal land proceeds among the states, with an extra 10 percent for the new states of Ohio, Louisiana, Indiana, Mississippi, Illinois, Alabama, and Missouri. Such a policy would promote capital growth in the West, rather than continuing the capital drain from western states to the East—especially during hard times. Democratic land policies like preemption and graduation, Clay thought, offered little to benefit the western poor, adding less to markets and the tax base of the West than a systematic fostering of internal improvements would. In addition to justifying high protective tariff rates, the disbursement of federal money for transportation, education, colonization of free blacks, and payment of state debts would help bind the West to the Union, elevate the intellectual and moral condition of western people, promote commercial development, and help the public-spirited, middle-class types Clay favored (who, in turn, would vote for the Whigs). Considering the stakes in the distribution plan, for Clay politically and for economic progress in the West, Jackson's killing of Clay's 1832–1833 land bill mattered hugely, as Old Hickory knew perfectly well. Clay believed that the American System could have provided the West a broader, more stable middle-class population, richer capital market, and steadier commercial development. He later thought it would have lessened the impact of the Panic of 1837, as well, and made subsequent western growth faster, more diversified, and more widespread than what occurred under Jacksonian leadership.[17]

While Clay attempted to revive the distribution program that Jackson had vetoed, pro-squatter interests in the early to middle 1830s swamped Congress with pleas for a revamping of federal land law. Few such petitions expressed any faith at all in the guiding hand of central government, which alone made them antithetical to Clay's political economy. Since Congress had half-opened the floodgates to preemption in 1830, many contended, why not complete the process and let nature take its course without federal interference? The clamor for change included the expectation that President Jackson and the Democratic Party would deliver on promises made or implied to the West in 1832–1833 in the scuttling of Clay's land bill. On January 11, 1833, for example, the House Public Lands Committee received a memorial from Illinois arguing the interest of a general class of people in the West, including "many worthy heads of families," who had "entered upon the public lands and made openings in the forest, thereby attracting others of more capital and enterprise to the neighborhood, and . . . furnished inducement to others to vest capital in land." In February 1833, Alabama urged a general reduction of public land prices to assist its "poorer, but not less meritorious" citizens against "wealthier neighbors" who pushed them from their "original homes" to find subsistence on "comparatively sterile tracts." Later the same month, Missouri legislators asked their representatives to support a general preemption law, graduation of prices, land donations to poor settlers, and cession of federal lands to the states—changes philosophically meant "to smooth down those inequalities which are apt to grow up in a society, and which are so baneful to the principles of republican government." Another Missouri petition, of February 22, 1833, contended that nothing benefited the nation more than for every freeman to possess property and a home, "from which spring all those endearing attachments both to a country and society."[18]

Jacksonian politicians around the country attuned themselves to such appeals, mastering the rhetorical claim that open land, with easy access for all, fostered essential traits of American democracy. Many petitions implied that broad cultural forces were at work, that democratization required a general opening-up of society and the ending of traditional restraints, especially governmental ones. This combination of political and cultural enfranchisement had moved squatters from beyond the fringes of civil life into the mainstream, from political nonentities to people of importance. Preemption, redefined as vital to a new society of liberated, self-directing, enfranchised individuals, now could seem much less disruptive than it once had—except to those, like Clay, who still saw respect for law, basic property rights, and social order as threatened by it. Indeed, the more extreme ideas for social reform now promoted by George Henry Evans, Thomas Skidmore, and other eastern egalitarians made squatters' demands look milder and more reasonable by comparison. In the early 1830s, Evans urged a complete abandonment of the land revenue concept in favor of free grants, in small parcels, to the landless, with a limit on the amount any one individual could hold. Skidmore in 1829 had questioned much of the very foundation of private ownership, advocating an agrarian redistribution of property to all citizens equally.[19]

In the new political vernacular, preemption aspirants had not only argued their merits as enterprising individualists but also claimed cultural identity as members of the middle class—worthy, meritorious people who scratched an honest livelihood by the sweat of their brows. According to Jacksonian rhetoric, rapid settlement of the West by ready availability of federal lands to poorer migrants would regenerate the republican virtue that commercial development had endangered and renew the simple, village-based agricultural society then disappearing in the East and the longer-settled parts of the West. Thus fashioned, preemption not only assisted poorer men and women who had settled on the public domain but also stymied "land speculators," identified more and more as the scheming equivalent of eastern corporate monopolists. As they had in the controversies over banking, Jacksonian Democrats asserted the cause of equal rights against a supposed nationwide threat of economic consolidation, with western settlement as part of their vaunted battle to cleanse society of "corruption" and advance the fortunes of its less-privileged members.[20]

—⌒—

In the political economy debate of the 1830s, "squatters' rights" operated against Clay's economic vision and in favor of the Jacksonian one. Clay would later surmise, "In the opposition to distribution, we find associated together the friends of preemption, the friends of graduation, and the friends of the cession of the whole of the public lands to a few of the States"—all united in "throwing away the public lands." Looking, in 1834, at the fragmentary state of internal improvements and manufacturing development in his own section and considering the ever-more-strident calls for preemption, Clay felt that "the people of the Western & especially N. Western States" had "erred in sustaining the present [Jackson] Admon upon these subjects." More broadly, he cited the "wound" that Democratic politics had "inflicted upon the moral sense of the Community." Venting privately in June 1834, Clay complained, "What looseness of principle, what scandalous abuses, what disregard of moral and political rectitude have been quickened into life by the predominance of Jacksonism!" About a year later, still lamenting "degeneracy" in the political community, he mused, "History records long periods, in the progress of Nations, during which depraved & wicked men obtained the sway, and sometimes they have been finally displaced by the revival of public virtue and public spirit."[21]

In public, however, he could not wait for the wheel of history to turn. The land-policy dispute flamed anew in 1836, when Mississippi's Robert J. Walker sponsored a land bill that tied preemption to Benton's land-price graduation scheme. Walker, chairman of a Democrat-controlled Senate Public Lands Committee, meant his legislation to conflict with Clay's distribution plan. In March, the Kentucky senator called the Walker proposal "a bill to give every thing to the new States [the ones farther west than Kentucky and Ohio], and leave nothing for distribution among the older States of the confederacy." With its graduation, donation, and preemption clauses, Clay sneered, "it might as well be called by its true name—a bill to give the whole of the public lands to the new States, or to the settlers that would roam over them." When Clay referred to those would-be settlers as "squatters," Walker objected vigorously; they were "actual settlers," he insisted, the types of people who should be extolled rather than denigrated. Had 1,000 of these "much-abused squatters" been riflemen under Andrew Jackson's command in 1814, Walker continued, "never would a British army have polluted the soil where stands the Capitol." At that, spectators in the crowded Senate galleries erupted in applause. Walker's rhetoric drew on the "new democratic" image of preemption claimants—their cultural and political rehabilitation from degenerate trespassers to new-fashioned republicans—and caught Clay off guard. The exchange made the Kentucky senator look anti-western (the same strategy the Democrats had tried in 1832). Clay offered a quick, albeit qualified, apology for using the term "squatters," replying that although he had meant no "intentional disrespect," such men hardly "would have saved the Capitol unless they had given up their habits of squatting."[22]

In his letters during this period, Clay began to express escalating anxiety, which coincided with an approaching presidential election. "I believe . . . the present period in the affairs of our country is imminently critical," he wrote to Ohioan John Patton in April 1836. "It requires all the wisdom, the virtue and the energy among us to avert impending danger." Two weeks later he informed Philadelphia journalist Robert Walsh, Jr.: "We have been in the midst, during these late years, of the most exciting scenes in our public affairs. I did not much underrate the power which I was opposing—certainly not its disastrous tendency. I felt that I was struggling for the Country, for its civil liberty, its institutions, its property, its virtue."[23]

Although the Senate did not act on the 1836 Walker bill, the acrimony it generated, not to mention Martin Van Buren's election in 1836, foreshadowed further controversy, as did President Jackson's Specie Circular in July of that year, requiring specie only as payment for federal lands. Intended to brake inflationary land speculation, the circular in fact compounded the central problem that Clay's distribution idea had aimed to solve in the West—a shortage of capital. "One rash, lawless and crude experiment succeeds another," Clay protested, expecting that Jackson's move would only subject banks in the western states to "perpetual drafts of specie to meet the wants of purchasers of the public domain." Presciently, he added in January 1837 that the policy would cause banks to hoard specie, make it disappear from circulation, and bring on a general panic throughout the country.[24]

In early 1837, another such "experiment" did come, in the form of the revised Walker land bill, offering easier terms and fewer legal barriers for preemption claimants. "The Senate is no longer a place for any decent man," Clay grumbled to Robert Letcher. "It is rapidly filling with blackguards." The new preemption system, if instituted, would open unsurveyed as well as surveyed lands to squatters' advances—a further release of federal control over public lands that brought a greater risk of Indian conflict than ever. "Pass this bill, and the national domain is gone," Clay persisted on the Senate floor. Within a few years, it would "require a search-warrant and corps d' armee to find any part of it." He would vote against this radical departure from all earlier forms of preemption even "if no one else did." Among those who agreed with him was Hugh Lawson White of Tennessee, who advocated internal improvements and had supported Clay's tariff and distribution bills in 1832–1833. White opposed any "radical change" in land law—especially one that could depress land values—unless "the people of the whole Union" approved it. Another, staunchly anti-squatter senator, Thomas Ewing, an Ohio Whig who had preceded Walker as chairman of the Public Lands Committee, praised the middling, more honorable types of western speculators, whose "honest mode of acquiring property" provided a "resource in after life, or an outfit for their children." By a vote of 27 to 23 the bill passed in the Senate in February 1837 but later failed in the House.[25]

As economic crisis loomed, the drumbeat for reform intensified. On January 23, 1837, Wisconsin applied for an extension of federal preemption laws, complaining that without such a "wise and humane system of protection the occupant may be easily deprived of his home, and his family reduced to wretchedness and despair, by being placed in competition with the speculator." Such speculators, if left unchecked, could "monopolize a great part of the public land, . . . retard the settlement and improvement of the country, and create the relation of landlord and tenant, or an unlimited money aristocracy, both of which are dangerous to civil liberty." Some memorials came from private groups akin to the so-called "squatters' protective societies" that had arisen during the 1830s to prevent outsiders from bidding on members' claims. A "committee" of Illinois citizens, on February 21, 1837, appealed for preemption on unsurveyed public lands by refuting the depiction of squatters as men without personal responsibility and public virtue: "[W]hile struggling with the difficulties ever incident to new and frontier settlements, we have not lost our regard for the maintenance of good order, nor our respect for the laws of our beloved country."[26]

Encouraged by the Jacksonians, the movement to undo the traditional land system reached a climax during the Panic of 1837. Following another period of widespread prosperity and wild monetary expansion, hard times devastated the West again, notwithstanding its phenomenal economic gains since the previous depression of 1819. The opening of cotton lands in the Southwest and a rapid increase in the value of cotton exports had largely accounted for the soaring prices there—until 1837. From 1819, western cities and towns had grown rapidly, creating a commercial and manufacturing infrastructure that complemented flourishing agricultural areas—also until the Panic of 1837 hit. Drawn into this once-booming economy, western farmers had enjoyed the inflationary benefits of flush times, as had speculators in western lands, who took advantage of the prosperity of the early 1830s and helped generate a five-fold advance in public-land sales between 1834 and 1836. Then the bubble burst. By March 1837, business in New Orleans had stalled. New York City banks suspended specie payments on May 10 of that year, and banks elsewhere quickly did the same. With the Panic taking its toll in the Northwest, thirty-five "citizens" of Medina County, Ohio, issued a petition for reform on December 22, 1837, protesting against "rich speculators" with "ready money to spare" who engrossed huge portions of frontier territory to sell later, "at high prices, to their poorer and less favored countrymen."[27]

Democrats tried to use the Panic for political advantage, as would the Whigs, and that meant wooing as many westerners as they could. In July 1837, William Cullen Bryant's *New York Evening Post* tried to sweeten eastern perceptions of squatters by calling them "our old friends and neighbors—men who have emigrated from the Atlantic states—men who are perhaps a little more adventurous and restless, but quite as moral and intelligent as those they have left behind." More important, the crafty new president, Van Buren, fashioned part of his First Annual Message in December 1837 to cast the party's political net over squatting settlers, hoping to snare their votes: "They ask that which has been repeatedly granted before. If the future may be judged by the past, little harm can be done to the interests of the Treasury, by yielding to their request." The *Richmond Whig* protested that even surrendering the lands to the states where they lay would be better than to adopt Van Buren's "propositions." If his "wicked Administration" were to succeed in this, it declared, the federal domain would "constitute a standing fund for corruption," engendering "a brood of innumerable demagogues and speculators, to prey upon the substance of the people, and cheat them of their liberties."[28]

Meanwhile, Clay's irritation mounted as he endured the unfolding of events that he had predicted and believed his distribution program and Whig leadership could have prevented. Already convinced that a "spirit of lawlessness and violence" had gained a foothold, with squatters "gathered in great numbers" and "organizing themselves into companies" in defiance of the law, Clay heard on December 29, 1837, from his Ohio agent, Joseph Vance, that his own property there had fallen prey to local robbers: "the timber is being very much destroyed on your land [in Ohio] by the persons in the Neighborhood." Having his own resources stolen, by unruly westerners perhaps emboldened by Jacksonian ideology, could only have sharpened the Kentucky senator's contempt for the political hypocrisy he saw lurking behind the rhetoric glorifying squatters and the policies threatening the security of *both* public and private lands. It also, no doubt, heightened his belief that squatters' protective societies and other such groups were just vigilantes with no regard for property rights. He saw in other reports of lawlessness and disorder, in the West and elsewhere, the beginnings of a social nightmare that he had hoped peace and prosperity under the American System would avert. Told in mid-December 1837 of a "parcel of giddy and ambitious young men" in upper New York readying to march into Canada to aid a revolt there, Clay answered: "No lover of his Country can fail to be afflicted by the too numerous manifestations of personal violence and lawless proceedings of which our Country is the theatre. They throw obloquy on our free institutions. They ought to be put a stop to."[29]

The efforts of organized squatter groups to intimidate "honest purchasers" and prevent fair competition in western land sales had been well publicized. In one instance, reported from frontier Chicago in June 1835, travelers who had gone some distance to purchase government lands received a blunt warning from the former and present governors of the state, John Reynolds and Joseph Duncan, "not to bid against the worthy and industrious yeomanry" of squatters who, in some cases, had done no more than pile up a dozen logs for a "house" or merely cut the grass off an acre of prairie to justify a preemption claim. Add to that a further "terror," that *no man's life was safe who should bid against a Squatter*"—a threat reinforced by the "ferocious appearance" of squatter thugs circulating through the crowd of once-hopeful buyers. "These are gross abuses," the unidentified reporter complained. "The public lands cease to be public, except in name, so long as this vile monopoly is countenanced or permitted." Some of the preemptive claimants, another witness said, actually operated as "agents" of speculators who "had combined to cheat the government," and these "same squatters and their employers were ready to play off the same game in any other region where a sale [was] soon to take place." Two years later, a Milwaukee editor reported that a group of "settlers or squatters" at Green Bay (Wisconsin Territory) had "set up a government of their own" to defend themselves against the so-called "oppression of the proprietors" of the lands where they lived. The *Cleveland Herald* later referred to this same Wisconsin bunch as operating on "the principle that might makes right" and "combining their exertions to put down interlopers at the land sales where their claims will be offered." Also in 1837, a Detroit newspaper gave its account of another "society who have taken possession" of certain public lands, threatening "Lynch Law to Uncle Sam, Governor [Stevens T.] Mason or any person who shall dare to disturb them." The *Alexandria (Virginia) Gazette* later concluded that the day of "wholesome competition" for federal lands was over. It no longer mattered whether Congress passed preemption laws or not, for "the combination of the squatters to deter adverse bidders, either by persuasion or threats . . . discourages adventurers from a distance."[30]

The 25th Congress focused intensely on preemption during its second session in early 1838, following unsuccessful attempts by Benton and Calhoun, respectively, to revive proposals for the graduation of federal land prices and cession of lands to the western states. Despite the objections of auction system defenders and regardless of speculative frauds linked with "squatters' rights," preemption had gained considerable support after 1830, especially in the West, among both Democrats and Whigs. On the Democratic side, part of this resulted from Van Buren's continuing entreaties.[31] Also, by the late 1830s, increasing numbers of easterners, including some who speculated heavily in western lands, had come to favor settlement without governmental restraint, as opposed to Clay's policy of keeping settlement in balance with capital development in the West.

On December 28, 1837, Walker's committee reported a new preemption bill, this time only retrospective in scope, with no promise of extension for future migrants. Still, the bill came to represent not simply another renewal of the 1830 law but a test of preemption's acceptability as a distinctive—and permanent—feature of federal policy. On January 25, 1838, Walker presented the bill in the Senate, igniting a debate on the political economy and social justice of a full commitment to squatters' rights. The Washington *Globe* described the controversy that followed as "one of the most interesting debates which has ever been witnessed here." On January 26, Clay again proclaimed the whole idea of preemption to be unjust because it rewarded squatters for violating the law and encouraged "a fraudulent, heartless, scandalous, abominable speculation." He would speak against it, he vowed, "as long as God gave him strength to do so." Arguing, as usual, that preemption attracted the wrong kinds of settlers, Clay quoted one recent communication from a Louisiana district attorney: "If reckless and unprincipled men can succeed in cheating and defrauding government, . . . [then] corruption and venality must and will become the order of the day."[32]

Western supporters of preemption still suspected easterners of coveting the public lands for their own use, and Clay hoped to refute this to his advantage, as he had done with his distribution bill in 1832–1833. He promised to "repel the imputation of the senator from Mississippi [Walker] against the old States." "It was not the old States," he insisted, "but some of the new, that were grasping at the public domain." Delaware Whig Richard Bayard agreed, contending that the preemption system, if continued, "would drain the old States of their agricultural population and advance the new at the expense of the old." Calhoun, more against frontier anarchy than supportive of Clay, warned that preemption "would operate, in the end, to the almost exclusive benefit of the rich, the strong, and the violent"—such as in the "Ioway country," which, someone told him, "had been already seized on by a lawless body of armed men."[33]

Hostility to the anti-squatter side developed quickly in the Democratic press. The Washington *Globe* argued that preemption would help secure public order on the frontier instead of enhancing disruption, that existing violence came only as the result of desperate groups of settlers combining to save their claims and improvements and that frauds under preemption had been greatly exaggerated. "If the honorable H. CLAY would conciliate the New England people by his hostility to pre-emption laws," the *Globe* writer avowed, "he will fail in his object. The old men of New England begin to find that the benefits of liberal legislation, in respect to our public lands, are partaken of their hardy and enterprising boys, who are daily hastening to the 'land of milk and honey.'" A few days later, the *New-York Evening Post* issued its judgment: "It is impossible to prevent the overflow of our population into the unsurveyed lands. You can no more confine the population of the United States within the circle of lands already in market, than you can stop a current of water with a drag net."[34]

Pro-squatter attacks on Clay in the Senate now reflected Panic-intensified class conflict. Indiana Democrat John Tipton thought the Kentuckian merely argued two sides of privilege in American society: "one, the politician in the old States, who is loath to give up the poor but industrious portion of their population; and the other the capitalists, who . . . by attending the public sales and overbidding the poor man, compel him to retire, and content himself with land of an inferior quality." For Lucius Lyon, a Michigan Democrat, only one faction of politicians had good reason to oppose preemption: those advocating Clay's American System. That program, if adopted, would "confine the growing population of the country within the old States," he claimed, "where the poor man will be compelled to become the tenant of some wealthy landlord." Reflecting growing acceptance of pro-settler attitudes in New England, especially among Democrats, Henry Hubbard of New Hampshire, a well-known speculator in western lands and supporter of preemption since 1830, saw the principle as increasing "the moral and physical power of the country"; whether government gained much revenue from land sales was "a secondary consideration."[35]

Daniel Webster's decision to support preemption provided further evidence of speculators joining forces with squatters. Webster, a heavy investor in lands throughout the Northwest, was courting support in the West for another presidential bid in 1840. Public land squatters, he sympathized, "settled and built houses, and made improvements, in the persuasion that Congress would deal with them in the same manner as it has in repeated instances, dealt with others." Adopting the rhetoric of squatters' rights, he found nothing wrong with extending a policy already based in practice, a change far preferable to Calhoun's alternative of ceding federal lands to the states where they lay. Webster cited four general qualities to recommend preemption, each belying the imputation of "frontier radicalism." First, it applied only to those already settled on public lands, and with settlement continuing at such a rapid pace, preemption laws might soon be unnecessary. Second, since the bill made no donation, no actual gratuity, preemption claimants would remain obliged to purchase their claims at the minimum government price. Third, it limited the squatter's right to one quarter section—160 acres—which most westerners considered a reasonable quantity for a farm. Fourth, the policy applied only to "heads of families, or householders, actually settled and residing on the tract."[36]

Things became more tangled on January 27, 1838, when Maryland senator and prominent Whig attorney William D. Merrick proposed an amendment to limit preemption to United States citizens, thus excluding "the hordes of European and other foreign vagrants, knaves, and paupers" who might seek land. This "vicious, corrupt, and debased swarm of outcasts," Merrick called them, would make an "honest and proudhearted" American freeman "rather die in poverty and want, than dwell among such people." Clay agreed, in one of his most "strong and patriotic bursts of eloquence," a Washington correspondent said. "Sir," Clay announced, "I hold that charity begins at home,—that we have no right to make laws for the benefit of the squatters upon our land,—that by giving our domain to these [foreign] interlopers and intruders we rob the old States of what belongs to them as much as to the citizens of the new States." This positive response to Merrick's amendment, which had little chance of passing anyway, further inflamed Democrats, who perceived an attack on the German and Irish immigrants who had flocked to their party. Benton, filled with "a kind of demoniac delight," announced that Clay had at last shown his true colors: "The people of the West will now find

TABLE 5
Sectional Distribution of the Preemption Vote in the House and Senate, 1838

	Senate		House	
	For	Against	For	Against
NEW ENGLAND	6	4	13	9
Maine	1	0	2	0
Vermont	0	2	0	2
New Hampshire	2	0	5	0
Massachusetts	1	1	2	6
Connecticut	2	0	4	0
Rhode Island	0	1	0	1
MID-ATLANTIC	3	7	35	15
New York	2	0	19	4
New Jersey	0	2	0	6
Pennsylvania	1	1	15	5
Delaware	0	2	0	0
Maryland	0	2	1	0
SOUTH ATLANTIC	4	3	13	23
Virginia	1	1	8	6
North Carolina	1	0	1	9
South Carolina	0	2	0	7
Georgia	2	0	4	1
NORTHWEST	8	2	21	2
Ohio	1	1	11	2
Indiana	1	1	5	0
Illinois	2	0	3	0
Missouri	2	0	2	0
Michigan	2	0	0	0
SOUTHWEST	9	2	25	4
Kentucky	0	2	5	4
Tennessee	2	0	10	0
Alabama	2	0	5	0
Louisiana	2	0	2	0
Mississippi	1	0	2	0
Arkansas	2	0	1	0
Total	30	18	107	53

Sources: Congressional Globe, 25th Congress, 2nd session, Appendix, 133; *House Journal*, 25th Congress, 2nd session, 1101.

him out, sir, . . . find out who is who,—sir, who is a friend of the poor, sir, and who is a friend of the rich, sir,—who would aid the foreign money power and who should oppress the foreign poor, sir." Never before, Benton asserted (mistakenly), had federal land policy discriminated against people aspiring to become American citizens. Also mocking Clay, Illinois Democrat Richard M. Young quipped that Merrick was trying to "engraft" a "Native American System" upon the preemption bill. The amendment fell by a vote of 17 to 27.[37]

The question of "squatters' rights" had received more careful examination than ever in this debate of 1838. The Senate passed the preemption bill on January 30, 1838, by a margin of 30 to 18, on a mostly party-line vote, with eastern pro-settlement senators joining westerners in both major parties (see Tables 5 and 6). Clay was one of only four senators from trans-Appalachian states to vote against the bill, and few eastern Democrats sided with him. Webster went with the majority, Calhoun the minority. The measure received assurance of becoming law by Van

TABLE 6

Party Distribution of the Preemption Vote in the Senate, 1838

	Democrats		Whigs	
	For	Against	For	Against
NEW ENGLAND	5	0	1	4
Maine	1	0	0	0
Vermont	0	0	0	2
New Hampshire	2	0	0	0
Massachusetts	0	0	1	1
Connecticut	2	0	0	0
Rhode Island	0	0	0	1
MID-ATLANTIC	3	2	0	5
New York	2	0	0	0
New Jersey	0	1	0	1
Pennsylvania	1	1	0	0
Delaware	0	0	0	2
Maryland	0	0	0	2
SOUTH ATLANTIC	4	2	0	1
Virginia	1	1	0	0
North Carolina	1	0	0	0
South Carolina	0	1	0	1
Georgia	2	0	0	0
NORTHWEST	8	1	0	1
Ohio	1	1	0	0
Indiana	1	0	0	1
Illinois	2	0	0	0
Missouri	2	0	0	0
Michigan	2	0	0	0
SOUTHWEST	8	0	1	2
Kentucky	0	0	0	2
Tennessee	1	0	1	0
Alabama	2	0	0	0
Louisiana	2	0	0	0
Mississippi	1	0	0	0
Arkansas	2	0	0	0
Total	28	5	2	13

Source: *Congressional Globe*, 25th Congress, 2nd session, Appendix, 133.

TABLE 7
Party Distribution of the Preemption Vote in the House, 1838

	Democrats		Whigs	
	For	Against	For	Against
NEW ENGLAND	12	0	1	9
Maine	2	0	0	0
Vermont	0	0	0	2
New Hampshire	5	0	0	0
Massachusetts	1	0	1	6
Connecticut	4	0	0	0
Rhode Island	0	0	0	1
MID-ATLANTIC	30	0	5	15
New York	18	0	1	4
New Jersey	0	0	0	6
Pennsylvania	11	0	4*	5*
Delaware	0	0	0	0
Maryland	1	0	0	0
SOUTH ATLANTIC	13	12	0	11
Virginia	8	2	0	4
North Carolina	1	3	0	6
South Carolina	0	7	0	0
Georgia	4	0	0	1
NORTHWEST	13	0	8	2
Ohio	7	0	4	2
Indiana	1	0	4	0
Illinois	3	0	0	0
Missouri	2	0	0	0
Michigan	0	0	0	0
SOUTHWEST	6	0	19	4
Kentucky	0	0	5	4
Tennessee	2	0	8	0
Alabama	3	0	2	0
Louisiana	0	0	2	0
Mississippi	0	0	2	0
Arkansas	1	0	0	0
Total	74	12	33	41

Source: House Journal, 25th Congress, 2nd session, 1101.
    *Includes two Anti-Masonic Party votes in favor, three Anti-Masons against.

Buren's signature after passing the House by 107 to 53 in June 1838 (see Tables 5 and 7). This decisive victory for preemption seemed to make its permanent installation just a matter of time.

Only a few weeks later, a disgusted Clay again surveyed the impact of Jacksonian rule: "Society has been uprooted, virtue punished, vice rewarded, and talents and intellectual endowments despised; brutality, vulgarism, and loco focoism upheld, cherished, and countenanced. Ages will roll around before the moral and political ravages which have been committed will, I fear, cease to be discernible." With more specific—and positive—regard to preemption, the strongly Jacksonian *United States Magazine and Democratic Review* in September 1838 called it a "morally equitable privilege . . . to the poor man who is willing to reclaim his quarter section from the wilderness, on condition of being suffered to dig from it an honest livelihood by the sweat of his own brow." It represented the "perpetual striving after a better good, a higher perfection of social institutions," and was part of the "restless, progressive, reforming principle" of democracy. The *Arkansas Weekly Gazette*, however, put the political issue more bluntly: "[T]hese SQUATTERS will doubtless bear these [mostly Clay's] epithets in mind when they come to cast their votes for the next President of the United States." The *Milwaukee Sentinel* added: "Most of our 'Squatters' have lately become Freeholders. Will Henry Clay and his supporters longer brand them as 'pirates,' 'vagabonds,' and 'the scape goats of creation,' as they have heretofore done?"[38]

In the several months after the 1838 preemption debate, Clay ironically seemed less preoccupied with the passage of the bill than with the inflammatory language he had employed in characterizing squatters—a discomfort that revealed his own recognition of how much the cultural politics of preemption had changed. "I never used the expressions 'Land robbers or Land pirates,' " he insisted to John B. Dillon, editor of the Logansport, Indiana, *Canal Telegraph*. "I considered the preemptioner a trespasser, and his occupation of the public lands, contrary to law, a trespass; and I contended that the property of the People of the U. S. ought to be protected and guarded as strictly and securely as that of individuals." In retrospect, of course, Clay's choice of words in the Senate mattered far less than his new desire that fellow westerners not think he had insulted squatters (even though he *had* and would again). Even illegal settlers voted, as did others who sympathized with them. It was no longer politically correct, especially in the West, to disparage such people.[39]

To see preemption supported so warmly by Jacksonians he regarded as scoundrels, especially Walker and his old nemesis Benton, outraged Clay and stiffened his resolve. He wanted to believe that such "Goths and Vandals at the Capitol" could not truly reflect the voting public. "Every new infusion of Jacksonianism has been worse than that which preceded it," he complained in June 1839 to his friend Richard H. Wilde, who had been in Europe for several years. "If you were to see some of its late recruits you would wonder how they came here." He told an audience in Baltimore a few months later: "The conclusion was inevitable, that in the matter of plain every day honesty and integrity of character, the official corps [of Jacksonian leaders] were not a fair sample of the people at large." At the same time, of course, the Kentucky senator's own presidential ambitions blazed as ever, and he still saw the American System as his ticket to power. Clay's political aspirations would have been better served by softening his stance on squatters' rights, humiliating as that would have been, but his political economy and his pride both said no. By so doing, he might also have gained greater approval in his own section, as other western Whigs had, at minimal cost to his credibility in the East—especially since Webster, his main eastern rival among the Whigs, now backed preemption.[40]

And so, Clay did not waver. Instead, he adopted an alternative line of attack, depending less on fellow westerners and more focused on possible eastern support. He wrote to his friend Francis T. Brooke on January 7, 1839: "I have been struggling . . . on the Land subject. . . . Whether it will be practicable much longer to save that great interest depends upon the future course of the old States. I can not much longer defeat the combined action of the Administration and the new States." Clay believed that the Whig press in the older states could do more to sway readers on the "threat" to western land, and thus force some seats as well as votes in Congress to change. "It is my opinion" he told New York columnist John O. Sargent on January 14, 1839, "that, if the public could have been awakened to its importance, and to the nefarious projects by which it has been attempted to squander it away and make it subservient to party views, the late Administration would have been overthrown and we should not have been afflicted with the present one."[41]

As the 1840 elections drew near, Clay thought he might turn the worsening Panic to Whig advantage and that of his distribution scheme. Willis Hall reported to him from New York on November 20, 1839, that the "Public Lands are now a prominent familiar & favorite topic with the common people. The depreciation of State bonds, suspension of State internal improvements and the rapidly approaching alternative of State taxation or State bankruptcy will immediately turn the attention of this State to the Public lands with great intensity." Other states faced similar financial crises, making distribution of federal land revenue potentially more attractive than ever. Although once again denied the Whig nomination in favor of William Henry Harrison, Clay did not hesitate to inform political audiences, like one in Hanover County, Virginia, that "the whole public domain is gone if Mr. Van Buren be re-elected." In Nashville, soon after, he asked a largely pro-Jacksonian crowd whether their "new democracy" had realized their hopes and fulfilled the promises made to them four years earlier.[42]

The Democrats, meanwhile, continued to employ the hard times in precisely the opposite way, arguing the necessity—and, they said, the inevitability—of preemption as a promise not only to present settlers but to all future comers as well. Benton, when asked by a group of western Missouri constituents in June 1839 whether they could expect a renewal of the 1838 preemption statute, answered that the updated provision would come in spring 1840. "But whether the act is renewed or not," he contended, "I consider *the spirit of the act as established, and virtually become the law of the land by becoming the law of public opinion.*" If, in practicality, the need no longer existed for elected leaders to legislate on such matters, then it came close to saying that Benton's constituents had a right to do whatever they wanted on the public lands, regardless of government. Few would have been bold enough to make such an assertion twenty years before.[43]

The most interesting change Clay made to his land policy argument from the earlier 1830s was to incorporate the nativist fears of social degeneration communicated to him by friends in the economically distressed Northeast. His support of the Merrick amendment in January 1838 had raised questions not only about the "American" part of the American System, but also about the extent of his sympathy with anti-immigrant northeasterners. Clay may have supported Merrick's idea simply because he believed recent arrivals should stay in the East and find employment as laborers in manufacturing enterprises. Or perhaps he feared that an influx of foreigners, like an uncontrolled multitude of native squatters, might undermine the Americanization of the frontier, bringing westward the kind of immigrant disorder that had threatened eastern cities—and swelled the ranks of the Democrats. In December 1837, he had told an eastern friend: "[I]n the interior where I reside, we experience no inconvenience from the influx of Foreigners. I suppose it is otherwise in the Cities but to what extent I do not know, nor am I able to say what should be the remedy." Then he wrote, "[M]y general preference of every thing native over every similar thing which is foreign, I presume is sufficiently known." In August 1838, Clay had agreed with New York temperance advocate Edward C. Delavan on the need for "guarding the emigrant against vicious practices and habits, upon his landing on our shores." Yet he added, "But may it not be doubted whether emigration to the U States is not already sufficiently great, without the employment of new incitements?"[44]

During the debate on the new preemption bill of early 1841, Clay offered an amendment that would limit the right of preemption to whites only (which passed in the Senate 37 to 1) and further announced that he "opposed on principle . . . the proposition that aliens should be invited from every portion of the habitable globe, to take possession of the public lands." He seemed now to question whether people who had benefited so little from America would reliably support American laws and institutions. Aaron Clark, an exchange broker and former New York City mayor, agreed, informing Clay on January 12, 1841: "The public lands should be the heritage & home of our native citizenry as much as possible & surely in *pref-*

erence to aliens. I am most unhappy when I reflect that our *real* enemies, and the *secret* enemies of our institutions are taking peaceable & unresisted possession of our rich vallies, our cities, ballot boxes & patronage. I hope & trust you will nobly persevere in your advocacy so well proclaimed." Then, on January 20, 1841, Clay declared in the Senate:

> From a view of the whole subject, I am opposed to the [preemption] bill, as impairing the amount of revenue to come into the Treasury during the present year, thereby augmenting a deficit for which provision ought long since to have been made, and as fraught with evils passing all imagination, from the disputes and contests for title among that flood of settlers which is invited from all the quarters of the known world to rush in a mass upon our public domain.[45]

Clay's earlier comments on preemption—and on land policy generally—had not contained strong elements of nativism. But after 1838 they *did*, reflecting not only a Whig anxiety that the societal foundations of republicanism were cracking but also the possibility that opposition to foreigners made the anti-squatter case more persuasive.[46]

Ultimately, of course, the 1841 "prospective" preemption law, Benton's so-called "Log Cabin Bill," passed in a Whig-dominated Congress, with the help of most western Whigs. Although limited to surveyed federal lands, it guaranteed the right of preemption to future settlers, not just those already there. The package included a weakened (and ill-fated) version of Clay's distribution plan to divide land revenues among the states for internal improvements. Although Whigs now held a temporary majority, the Jacksonians had won both the cultural battle for preemption and much of the legendary claim to the frontier—a claim that sympathetic historians have reinforced to the detriment of Clay's reputation. Benton's "log cabin" sobriquet for the legislation reflected the Jacksonian rehabilitation of squatters as hardy, individualistic pioneers, building rough-hewn abodes, symbolic of progress from poverty to fortune. This victory of squatters' rights may have been foreordained when Congress passed the preemption law of 1830; once the door of policy came open to squatters in general, it would have been difficult to close it again. But to see this turn in policy through the eyes of its principal opponent, Clay, is to recognize the full meaning of the change—the extent to which it abandoned earlier, commonly shared assumptions about how Congress should allow the West to be settled. And with the elimination, in just a few years, of the distribution part of the deal, anyone could see which of the two visions for the West had won out.[47]

If an artist can be said to have had the last word on the losing side of a political debate, George Caleb Bingham did. His 1850 painting "The Squatters" immortalized the negative image that had become so politically taboo. An urban Missourian, Whig politician, and long-time Clay supporter (who blamed his own failure to win a seat in the Missouri legislature in 1846 on squatters in his district, who consistently voted Democratic), Bingham knew the subject well. "The Squatters as a class," he wrote in 1850, "are not fond of the toil of agriculture, but erect their rude Cabins upon those remote portions of the National domain, where the abundant game supplies their phisical wants. When this source of subsistence becomes diminished, in consequence of increasing settlements around, they usually sell out their slight improvements, with their *'presentation title'* to the land, and again follow the receding footsteps of the Savage."[48]

—⟡—

Clay steadfastly condemned squatters, not because many of them were poor; indeed they could not have been much poorer than some regular auction-buyers, since auction prices in the 1830s often did not rise far above the $1.25 minimum.[49] And, although he shared the social-fabric concerns of some easterners, he felt no great affinity for the Northeast, where opposition to preemption was strongest, over the West, which had created, nurtured, and elevated him. Nor did his resistance to squatters' rights derive primarily from his hatred of Jacksonian Democratic leaders, who, after 1834, used the issue to attack his economic program and malign him in ways he considered beneath the honor of respectable politicians. Rather, he fought preemption mainly for the reasons he offered both publicly and in private: for him, squatters were men of doubtful character, intruders, trespassers, and bullies, a "lawless rabble," whose apparent lack of moral restraint—and their possible unfamiliarity with native cultural values—threatened to undercut the middle-class concept of republican community embedded in the American System. The rise of such people, and their demagogic, unprincipled spokesmen, is what he thought Jacksonian democracy as a social and cultural movement really represented.

In the end, Clay could neither persuade the westerners of his own party on the issue of preemption nor muster enough support in other sections to offset the increasingly powerful influence of ordinary voters in his own. He would not—and, in his political economy, probably *could* not—address the concerns of squatters in terms that mattered much to them, which included freedom from external forces over their lives, especially that of central government. While he thought traditional concepts of republican virtue and morality had disappeared from political debate, the empathetic words and promises of the Jacksonians did reflect the democratic and libertarian ideals of the day. Even if some western Whigs shared Clay's philosophical opposition to preemption, they faced the overriding danger of voter retaliation back home.[50]

Traditional land policy suited Clay's nationalist vision and his support of a capital-building middle class. Preemption advocates, by contrast, had succeeded by contending that easier access to western land in itself would furnish the way to wealth for those who originally lacked the capital means—and in the process lift the character of the settlers, if it needed lifting. That left no reason for a land system that seemed, in the eyes of its critics, to be based only on distinctions between rich and poor, in that tracts were sold under competitive bidding. While Clay held to his intentions for the West, promoters of squatters' rights stressed an unleashing of individual energies—the opening of lands to all comers, regardless of economic or social status, no matter who benefited most in the end. In this regard, the American System ran against an emerging new set of democratic ideals, what Michigan's Lucius Lyon termed "the moral sense of the people."[51] Challenging Clay's negative portrayal of squatters, such reformers argued that preemption claimants lacked nothing morally. The real social problem, they insisted, was a lingering devotion to an anachronistic land system that fettered the natural rights of western individualists.

Unlike some easterners—Alexander Hamilton and Rufus King of New York, Samuel Foot of Connecticut, Richard Rush of Pennsylvania—who had wanted to restrain the growth of the West, Clay held true to the western "settler ideal." As a defender of the government's traditional policy, however, he differed with fellow westerners who considered any means of settlement good enough as long as it served the goal of populating the frontier as quickly as possible. Clay dared further to ask, as more leaders probably should have, whether it was best to encourage poor families to become frontier farmers, as opposed to other alternatives available to them, such as work in manufacturing and trades. The frontier teemed with aspiring farmers, many of whom would have been better off working at something else. While branded a traitor to his section for saying it, Clay even questioned whether the value of agriculture necessarily outweighed all other economic pursuits.

Clay's campaign against preemption, though a battle he felt obliged to fight, may have been a lost cause from the start. No federal anti-squatter policy could have been enforced by the 1830s. The sheer numbers of illegal settlers on the public domain made that impossible, and political expediency forbade it in any case. John Tipton argued in the 1838 debate that federal law preventing trespass on the public lands had been a "dead letter" for a quarter-century.[52] Had Congress prevented unwanted settlement (and respected Indian rights) by constant military patrolling of the frontier or denying preemption claims from the start, it would have violated beliefs widely shared by white Americans about the dangers of power, the dictates of justice, and the dream of moving west. Central authority could engineer the character of settlement in the West only to the extent that federal administrators could control the westward tide of population. In land policy, as in other parts of his much-heralded, and much reviled, American System, Clay confronted a basic truth of democratic life: in a free society, government cannot accomplish what the governed refuse to accept.

The West Secured?

The framers of the original federal land system thought that to secure the West meant to replicate their most cherished values on the frontier as the waves of migration advanced. They tried to cobble together some basic plans for the gradual westward expansion of republican society, institutions, and beliefs. Those enlightened attempts at republican nation building in the West succeeded sometimes in part, sometimes not at all, and often far from the ways intended. Among the places where the attempts succeeded, at least for a while, was Ohio, the first state to be carved from the old Northwest Territory. And yet even there, earlier hopes had started by the middle of the nineteenth century to give way to mounting disillusionment.

In the small town of Salem, Ohio, on November 29, 1851, George P. Smith, one of its leading citizens, appeared as the evening's main speaker at a town hall meeting. He addressed the "numerous evil tendencies of Land Monopoly" and asserted that "many of our existing laws are detrimental to the progressive spirit of the age." Smith, like many Salem residents, advocated free western homesteads for landless families. Over the previous decade, eastern radicals like George Henry Evans had made the same case for homestead reform on behalf of eastern artisans, especially the exploding numbers of workingmen in cities like Boston and New York. But Smith's concern focused as much on local issues as national ones; he referred to the immediate interests of Salem residents and others in the wider environs of Columbiana County. "True, the Government says the lands are free for any one to purchase, but how are the poor to purchase, when all they can possibly earn must go to pay rents and afford a living?" Smith complained. "The rich can purchase them, and then rent them to the poor, who in consequence, will always remain poor, and their poverty will impoverish others." His presentation included a pair of resolutions, which the meeting quickly endorsed. The first called upon reformers of Columbiana County to "declare their abhorrence to, and detestation of all laws or institutions whereby one man is allowed to hold property in another; or by which any man is allowed to hold or monopolize more land than is actually necessary for the comfortable support of himself and family." The second called for legal changes that would "abolish Tenantry," free the "poor and laboring classes . . . from the oppressive trammels of wealth," and rid the country of "nearly all her paupers and criminals" by making accessible to all the means to earn a livelihood. "Young men, above all others," Smith finished, ought to cast their influence "against land monopoly and for the system of land limitation," instead of turning to "vote for men pledged to support slavery, oppression and wrong!"[1]

At the time of this Salem meeting in 1851, the broad geographical outlines of "Manifest Destiny" seemed nearly complete. The United States by then claimed virtually all of what Americans understood to constitute "the West," and yet, the same expanse that had once helped to bind the nation together now divided it. The Louisiana Purchase, the annexation of Texas and Oregon, and the War with Mexico had stretched the nation's boundaries all the way to the Pacific, while also reinforcing the ambitions of slaveholders and inflaming abolitionist outrage at the further westward spread of slavery. Gold had been discovered in California in 1848, drawing greedy fortune-seekers from every corner of the earth. A trickle of migrants across the continent quickly became a torrent, a mad westward scramble that Congress, by dismantling the nation's original land policy, had already done much to encourage. As for the native peoples still living in the West, no power could remedy their plight, much less save their cultures from near extinction. In 1854, the same year Congress opened the Kansas and Nebraska Territories to slaveholders, lawmakers would also pass—and President Franklin Pierce would sign—the Graduation Act, establishing a scale of minimum-land-price reduction to $1.00 after ten years on the market, 75¢ after fifteen years, 25¢ after twenty years, and 12½¢ after thirty years. The law also allowed preemption claims on graduated acreage, except for lands with valuable mineral deposits or those granted to states for internal improvements. The policy would stimulate the sale of 30 to 40 million acres per year until Congress repealed it in 1862. Ironically, Thomas Hart Benton was not there to reap the glory, nor Henry Clay to register protests. The Missouri legislature in 1851, disenchanted by Benton's newly found free soil scruples, had denied him a sixth term in the United States Senate. Clay, at age 75, had died in Washington of tuberculosis in 1852.

Many Americans, not just in the East but also in the older parts of the West, looked upon the mid-century surge of westward expansion with skepticism, not to say alarm. The new frontier that had unfolded little resembled earlier dreams. But Salem, in east-central Ohio, near the Ohio River, had become a tiny enclave of reformist zeal, a place where early dreams still abided and traditional reform impulses burned white-hot. Publications advancing one or another kind of social

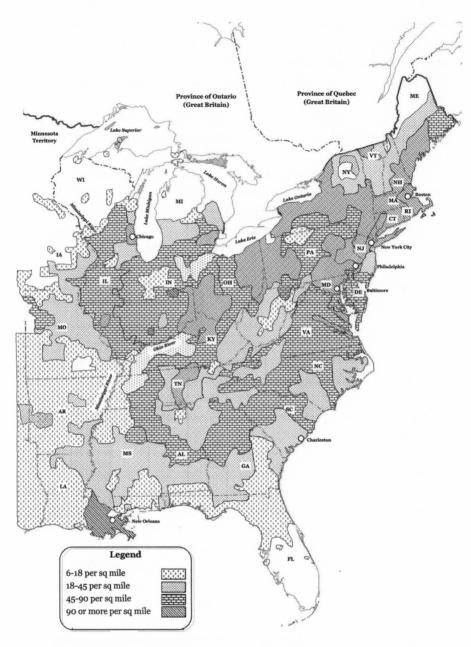

Distribution of U.S. Population East of the Mississippi River, 1850. Map drawn by Margot Gibson-Beattie.

improvement proliferated wildly. Dr. John P. Cope had established the *American Water Cure Advocate* there. The leaders of the Western Anti-Slavery Society, who published the *Anti-Slavery Bugle*, also lived in town. By the 1840s, the surrounding area had become a breeding ground of agitation for homestead reform, largely thanks to another periodical, the *Homestead Journal and Village Register*, published continuously, under varying titles, between 1842 and 1856. Twenty-seven-year-old Quaker Aaron Hinchman, who despised chattel slavery in the South as much as he condemned "land monopoly," took over the editorship in 1847 and held it for several years, tying the paper more closely to the National Land Reform Association of Salem. In fact, newspapers devoted to this land reform initiative mushroomed throughout the state in the late 1840s. An August 1849 issue of the Cleveland *Daily True Democrat* listed fifteen such publications operating in northern and eastern parts of Ohio alone. By 1850, the *Homestead Journal* boasted that it had agents promoting circulation in thirty-eight towns and cities throughout the Northwest, including twenty-seven in Ohio.[2]

While much homestead support came from northwestern parts of the country, the cause was much less popular in the Southwest because of the antislavery undercurrent of the homestead agenda. In a way quite different from earlier radical westerners (like Benton and Edwards), homestead reformers in Salem showed, in microcosm, how republican political and social values of an earlier era could transmute into a reform movement that reflected the stresses and concerns of a relatively new region of the country, where some people saw themselves as distant inheritors of a legacy that mandated a very different kind of social and economic world from the more distressing one developing around them. Established Salem residents, who by 1850 faced a considerable influx of immigrants into their area, a growing population of landless residents, and the lingering effects of the Panic of 1837, had good reason to believe their society was unraveling. Acting more on traditional northwestern than eastern radical impulses, many embraced moralistic causes, like homestead reform, in their effort to preserve treasured cultural values. For them, what historians call the Market Revolution of Jacksonian America made sense only in local terms—in the ways ordinary people of a reform-conscious middle western town experienced change and reacted to it.[3]

Back in 1787, Manasseh Cutler, one of the earliest land speculators in the Old Northwest, had proclaimed that Ohio was destined to be "the garden of the world, the seat of wealth, and the *centre* of a great Empire." Many settlers in the decades to follow arrived in the Ohio country with the same enthusiastic vision. As historian Andrew Cayton has written, Ohio in the early years of the republic constituted "a full-fledged experiment in republican government, in the power of the market, in democratic social organization, and in the necessity of organized competition in politics, religion, labor, and commerce"—a place defined not primarily by urban experience or by its agricultural identity but as a proliferation of villages. Fledgling commercial centers there struggled to develop the institutions and values needed to build from wilderness the new and better society that early-republic visionaries had hoped the West would become. By the 1830s, Ohio *had* become a commercially dynamic place. The third most densely inhabited state by that time, its population increased from 800,000 to 1,500,000 between 1826 and 1840. By 1850, nearly two million people lived there, many of them farmers owning their own property, growing corn or wheat, and herding livestock. Transportation improvement and banking had spurred economic growth, attaching most Ohio producers to an emerging market economy. Canal construction between the 1820s and the 1840s lowered shipping costs and provided further opportunities, as did vigorous railroad building later on. These economic changes led early Ohio settlers from lives of isolation and subsistence agriculture to increasing relationship with, benefit from, and, at times, subjection to, complex and far away economic forces.[4]

The first families to settle in Columbiana County—a large number of them Quakers, like the settlers from Redstone, Pennsylvania, who laid out Salem in 1806—migrated from across the Ohio River, starting in the 1790s. The land, generously watered, proved well-suited for agriculture. In addition, sheep-raising and wool processing would become dominant economic pursuits in the region. Yellow and Beaver Creeks provided ample water power for milling. Extensive deposits of coal and iron held potential for industrialization as well. By 1820, the population of the county had reached 22,033; it increased rapidly to 35,508 in 1830, and by 1840, 40,394.[5]

Between 1830 and 1850, however, the traditional, village-based values that Salem and many other middle western towns once nurtured underwent considerable testing. One reason was obvious: the Panic of 1837. But another, less visible on the surface, was a massive demographic change that took place throughout the region and, indeed, throughout the Northwest. A large part of Ohio's population increase between 1830 and 1850 consisted of immigrants, who came to work on the canals and railroads. The census of 1850 showed 522,734 Ohioans gainfully employed in 237 different occupations, but most of these appeared as "farmers" and "laborers"—269,699 and 86,869, respectively. Ohio remained overwhelmingly rural; in 1850 only four of its cities, Cincinnati, Columbus, Cleveland, and Dayton, had populations over 10,000 (115,535, 17,882, 17,034, and 10,977, respectively). It would seem likely that many of the "laborers" who lived in rural counties worked on farms as well as in small-scale industrial production and the building of transportation improvements. In 1850, non-native inhabitants of Ohio numbered 644,309—32.5 percent of the total population. Of these, 498,317 had migrated from other states (77 percent, mostly from Pennsylvania, Virginia, and New York), and 145,992 came from abroad (23 percent). Of the immigrants, most came from German principalities (70,236—48 percent) or from Ireland (32,779—22 percent). German newcomers sought escape from economic and political crises at home—the estate movement, which claimed the land of many small landowners, and the discontent that led to unsuccessful revolutions of 1848. In Ireland, the potato famine and the growing impoverishment of the landless population would continue to push tens of thousands toward America. Columbiana ranked eleventh among Ohio's eighty-six counties in its number of immigrant inhabitants in 1850, a total of 3,014. The county also had more migrants from the middle-Atlantic states (Pennsylvania, New York, New Jersey, Maryland, and Delaware) than all but six other counties—7,166.[6]

The depression that began in 1837 and lasted until about 1843 pounded the east-central region of Ohio with considerable severity and long-lasting effects. These hard times, even more than those after 1819, exposed the serious problems that market change had generated, along with the ample gains it had brought. If farmers tended to celebrate their vaunted "independence" most in the wake of commercial crises, this was partly because so many others had lost that cherished personal autonomy in those crises. Many Ohioans in places like Salem came to feel cheated by influences in their lives that they regarded as sinister and struggled to understand. The one specter that haunted beyond all others was the fear that economic hardship would force them or their neighbors to sacrifice their most prized possession, the land they owned. Many had already lost their homes. A Salem land dealing agency announced in July 1844 that "descriptions of farms offered for sale, are almost daily coming in." In early-1840s Salem, hard times catalyzed reform agitation. "There are thousands of industrious persons in Ohio, who have *no home*," reported Hinchman in the *Homestead Journal* in July 1847—"no abiding place that they can for a moment call their own—none that they can hope to possess through life." This growing population of Ohioans lived "constantly at the mercy of him who owns the house that shelters them, and the soil that grows their bread. They are not slaves for merchandise—not chattels personal, but hirelings, dependents, *servants* for bread and shelter." The nearby *Portage Sentinel* noted, "The poor landless man is unable to feed, clothe, and educate his family properly, unless he makes a bond slave of himself and them." What census records cannot show, of course, is the emotional and psychological impact of landlessness, the effect on family life, the destruction of one's sense of manhood or personal worth. The *Sentinel* writer implored that such victims would "arise and place themselves upon their inalienable claims to 'Life, Liberty and the pursuit of happiness,' & stand firm as all men should when in an honest position." Milo Townsend, a subscriber in New Brighton, Pennsylvania, wrote to Hinchman: "Your article in the last number of the *Homestead*, headed 'No Home,' appeals to the sad experience of thousands. The soil is as necessary to man's existence as air, sunshine and water, and should no more be monopolized than they."[7]

The humbler classes, contrary to earlier popular understandings, now stood blameless for their misery—at least in the minds of many Salem inhabitants. Poverty resulted from the "innocence" of some falling prey to the "craftiness" of others. The *Homestead Journal* lamented in June 1847 that wealth did not come "at the bidding of the mechanic's tools, or farmer's plough—but he who would get rich, must first turn schemer. . . . Riches are the reward of the speculator's cunning— the broker's craft, and the capitalist's ungodly usury." Another columnist in summer 1847 expressed the anxiety that his offspring might end up no better off than "the terrible fate of the Irish poor," who, escaping desperation in their own country, had arrived to build railroad tracks in Columbiana County: "Did I but know that my children, and my children's children, down through all the long vista of coming time, would never be the victims of a hard cruel poverty— . . . how constant would then be our enjoyment." A speaker before the National Reform Association of Salem in February 1848 also put the matter in terms of a real threat to future generations: his children and those of the audience stood in danger of being "placed in the condition of the Irish peasantry—a condition more to be dreaded than death itself." The war of 1846–1848 further prompted land reformers to blame the system of landholding in America for military aggression against Mexico and the manning of the army sent there to fight. B. B. Davis of Salem believed that such wars could not occur except for the growing number of "vagabonds" throughout the country. "Not one in a hundred of the common soldiers who went to butcher Mexicans," he complained, "were drawn away from comfortable homes."[8]

The *Homestead Journal's* publisher, J. D. Cope, judged in September 1847 that "the spirit of this reform has spread more rapidly in the western States than in the eastern." As one of Cope's contributors, Dr. J. R. Buchanan, saw it, the only remedy for the ills of land speculation, the retardation of internal improvements, the stalling of community growth, the separation of settlers from one another because of "wild tracts," and the inadequacy of schooling in the West lay in the establishment of "a pure republicanism," which at that point seemed possible only beyond the Mississippi, where the chance for economic justice had "never yet been profaned by the complicated systems of social wrong which belong to Europe and her half-regenerate sons in America." Somehow, a cross-national "Party of the Commonwealth" had to come, as the laboring millions of both England and America asserted equal rights to land. "This is the Archimedean fulcrum on which our political lever may move the world," he predicted. Despite reasons to think otherwise, Cope, Buchanan, and many other northern reformers still looked westward for the society of their loftiest dreams.[9]

But so did southern slaveholders, whose aspirations, rooted just as deeply in *their* visions of an ideal republic, would lead fatefully in a different direction. In years to come, the forces that abolitionist critics of the Mexican-American War had dubbed the "slave power" would insist on keeping the West open to slaveholders and pushing a land policy favorable to southern interests. After the war, the Compromise of 1850, part of which would carve out the territories of New Mexico and Utah without proscription of slaveholding, embodied the principle of "popular sovereignty," appeasing southerners and leaving them the frontier access they, too, coveted. The new doctrine, sometimes called "squatter sovereignty," allowed voting residents who lived in the territories, not the federal government, to decide on the legality of slavery—theoretically a democratic solution to the thorny issue. Afterwards, the Democratic Party, eager to unite its northern and southern wings, would take up the banner of "popular sovereignty" in its election campaigns. Following the politically opportunistic leadership of Illinois senator Stephen Douglas, the Democrats would institute the principle again in the Kansas-Nebraska Act of 1854. That law repealed the Missouri Compromise line at 36°30', which had, since 1820, separated slave from free territory west of Missouri, and which organized the territories of Kansas and Nebraska without restriction as to slavery. This new concession to the "slave power" would give rise to a sectional, antislavery, and antisouthern political party, the Republicans, who would carry Abraham Lincoln to power in 1860 and drive most of the slave states to secede from the Union.

By the time it passed in 1854, the Graduation Act, too, reflected more the southern ambition to expand than it did the interests of free-state settlers. The heaviest support for the legislation came from public-land states of the South and Missouri, areas containing the largest proportion of "refuse" land that had remained on the market from 10 to 35 years and where too much federal land had been put for sale in the first place. By this time, the most ardent proponents of graduation—including Robert J. Walker, Daniel Hubbard of Mississippi, and W. R. W. Cobb of Alabama—represented slave states; only one of the ten western House votes opposed to the bill came from a southern public-land state. In the West, especially the Southwest, few land offices would enforce the loosely defined 320-acre maximum on the amount of land a buyer could receive at graduated prices, a provision that had been inserted into the law, graduation advocates *said*, to discourage speculators. But at ground level, perjury, fraud, and undeterred speculation still carried the day. Many a southwestern plantation expanded in the 1850s with the addition of reduced-price marginal lands nearby. Meanwhile, until 1862, southern votes in the Senate (or, in 1860, James Buchanan's presidential veto) blocked passage of homestead bills, with their more definite claim limits of 160 acres per family. Southerners rightly associated homestead reform with the Free Soil and Republican Parties and understood it, again rightly, to be structured against the further expansion of plantation-style agriculture and slavery. The distribution of votes on the several homestead bills that failed in the 1850s shows that the southeastern states most strongly opposed and the middle-Atlantic and northwestern states most heavily favored the bills, a pattern all the more pronounced after the emergence of the Republican Party. To the extent that land policy conflict followed sectional lines, the terms of disagreement separated East and West far less than North and South— but only, of course, until "the great Secession Winter" of 1860–1861.[10]

—◦—

Why did the original nation building intentions that underlay federal land policy run into so much trouble? One answer lies in the early financial instability of the republic, which demanded, among other things, that frontier lands be sold rather than given away. This policy reflected not only the need for revenue but also the belief that landholding in a republic ought to be a privilege that landholders had earned in some way. That understanding dovetailed with republican values of the late eighteenth century and would persist afterwards. As the years passed, however, more and more Americans resented having to bid at auction for a resource they had come to regard as either a simple entitlement or a necessary reward for sacrifices made in settling wilderness.

Another stumbling block for early policy makers, insurmountable until the coming of the railroad, was the enormous size of the western country, stretching at first from the Appalachians to the Mississippi, then doubling with the Louisiana Purchase in 1803. This simple factor of geographical distance hampered the ability of government to control the pace and social character of westward expansion in a time of painfully limited transportation and communication. Some in Congress, and outside, had warned against the acquisition of Louisiana for precisely that reason. By the late 1840s, however, thanks in part to transportation improvements and in part to further acquisitions of territory, fears that the West would split away or become loyal to another power had dissipated. After that, the central question became whether North and South could hold together.

Still another impediment was the expansion and development of market capitalism, with its little-understood business cycle, which manifested itself in two jarring economic depressions, 1819 and 1837. Both of these crises carried unexpected and far-reaching political consequences. Hard times invariably cause people to reassess the world in which they live, along with the beliefs, attitudes, and assumptions that govern it. The economic distress, first in the early and then in the late Jacksonian period, affected public lands issues in this way, creating and later strengthening bottom-up, anti-statist political pressure for changes at the policy-making level.

Most important, fundamental beliefs about society and governance—the influences that guided the decisions of leaders and formed the will of their constituents—changed dramatically between 1785 and 1842. More and more westerners saw central government as an encumbrance rather than a benefit to their individual aspirations, its land policy unduly restrictive where it might have been liberating. After 1830, traditionalists found it increasingly difficult, both culturally and politically, to argue against providing common settlers of little means with easy access to western lands—and on terms much more of the settlers' choosing—than in the earlier days of the republic. The land system had to befit majoritarian democratic forces, as opposed to serving the eighteenth-century republican model that had so strongly motivated the system's designers. Along with this evolution of political philosophy, of course, the emergence of party politics and the spreading of white male suffrage further empowered groups that had never before exercised political clout. Even the lowliest settlers in western regions could sway policy by voting for leaders who promised, however self-servingly, to deliver what their constituents demanded. By the 1850s, the old republic had died. It perished not only from sectionalism and the conflict over slavery but also from the aversion to central authority, the assertive individualism, and the leveling tendencies of nineteenth-century democracy.

For all the political fighting over land policy, the one economic force that would eventually "secure" the West to the Union more than any other would be technology: the telegraph and, most of all, the railroad. In the decade before 1850, the private capital available for internal improvements in the West had shifted in the direction of railroad companies, connecting some of the fastest-growing cities north of the Ohio River: Chicago, Cincinnati, Indianapolis, and St. Louis. State governments, using their legal control over incorporation, eminent domain, and right-of-way, assisted rail projects in the 1840s just as they had earlier road- and canal-building activities. The pivotal departure away from state action came in 1851, with congressional provision for the Illinois Central, the first federal land-grant railway, to receive more than 2,500,000 acres of public land, only a fraction of which it needed for construction. Other grants would soon follow. No less than building roads, banking rivers, and digging canals, the encouragement of railroads helped to consolidate a nation that now stretched to the Pacific. Rail lines built through sparsely settled regions augmented the value of previously unattractive lands, serving the ends of both improvement and settlement. Commercial towns sprouted quickly, farmers enjoyed greater accessibility to eastern markets, and the national government counted on strengthened control over distant extremes of the nation.

Some historians have argued that the disappearance of the old economic issues exacerbated the ongoing sectional crisis over slavery. By mid-century, in any case, most Democrats and Whigs agreed on internal improvement as indispensable to the settlement and development of western lands. In years to come, with southern states absent during the Civil War, the Republican Party of Abraham Lincoln would begin to fulfill some of the long-denied economic promise of strong central governance: a watered-down Homestead Act in 1862, providing 160 acres to household heads who had made a five-year commitment; the Morrill Land Grant College Act, promoting higher education in all states of the Union; and the building of a transcontinental railroad, followed by land grants for other major rail lines in the West (the Atchison, Topeka, and Santa Fe; the Southern Pacific; and the Northern Pacific). In the process, railroad entrepreneurs and others would amass gigantic fortunes, beyond the wildest dreams of schemers back in Benjamin Franklin's day. What of the old republic ideal of keeping too much wealth and economic power from too few hands? This, as well, had been pushed aside, making way for the new. Even so, a Baltimore newspaper in 1871 would boast that 100,000 settlers had become landholders under the Homestead Act, a number more than double the *total* number of people owning land in Great Britain. While rural society in America never had been (and never would be) close to "egalitarian," even for whites, freehold farming and the belief that it carried equalizing power remained the central creed, if not the reality, of westward expansion.[11]

Looking back, the evolution of federal land policy from the 1780s to the 1850s reflected a complex transition in America, from a culture grounded in the values of traditional republicanism to one dominated by a new compound of liberal democracy and *laissez-faire* capitalism. In the West, that meant a general opening of public lands to whoever wanted them, for whatever purpose, no matter the impact on native peoples. The republic's earliest leaders structured the federal land system to provide steady revenue and a slow, systematic settlement of the West by morally virtuous men of stable means, emphasizing careful surveys, organization, and auction sales. After 1789, they looked to an empowered nation-state to govern that process. And yet, the very amorphousness of American society at that time and in years to follow, particularly after 1815, provided room for a multitude of conflicts—a cultural battleground where consensus, order, and government by any sense of original design, especially for the West, proved unsustainable. Far from a republican pursuit of the "common good," "disinterestedness," or even "the national interest," it was political expediency and private greed that became the primary influences on government decision making. In the end, this basic shift in the character of American politics—the influence of sectionalism and the maturing of new social and economic ideas in a rapidly changing society—brought pressures for a dramatic altering of that original land system, relegating key parts of it to the growing collection of long-lost, seldom-lamented relics of the old republic.

Introduction

1. Quotations in this and the next two paragraphs are from Edmund P. Dana, *Geographical Sketches on the Western Country: Designed for Emigrants and Settlers* (Cincinnati, 1819), 9–10, 59, 12.

2. Christopher Clark, "The Agrarian Context of American Capitalist Development," in *Capitalism Takes Command: The Social Transformation of Nineteenth-Century America,* ed. Michael Zakim and Gary J. Kornblith (Chicago, 2012), 13–37, esp. 16. See also Richard White, *The Middle Ground: Indians, Empires and Republics in the Great Lakes Region, 1650–1815* (Cambridge, UK, 1991).

3. On the concept of the "public sphere" as American historians have applied it, see John L. Brooke, "Reason and Passion in the Public Sphere: Habermas and the Cultural Historians," *Journal of Interdisciplinary History* 29 (Summer 1998), 43–67, and "Consent, Civil Society, and the Public Sphere in the Age of Revolution and the Early American Republic," in *Beyond the Founders: New Approaches to the Political History of the Early American Republic,* ed. Jeffrey L. Pasley, Andrew W. Robertson, and David Waldstreicher (Chapel Hill, NC, 2004), 207–50. Also, Brooke, *Columbia Rising: Civil Life on the Upper Hudson from the Revolution to the Age of Jackson* (Chapel Hill, NC, 2010); and David Waldstreicher, *In the Midst of Perpetual Fetes: The Making of American Nationalism, 1776–1820* (Chapel Hill, NC, 1997). On the growing cultural importance of early American newspapers and magazines, see Jeffrey L. Pasley, *"The Tyranny of the Printers": Newspaper Politics in the Early Republic* (Charlottesville, VA, 2001).

4. One of the most persuasive syntheses to argue the entrepreneurial consensus view is Daniel Feller, *The Jacksonian Promise: America, 1815–1840* (Baltimore, 1995). For further commentary, see Feller, "Politics and Society: Toward a Jacksonian Synthesis," *Journal of the Early Republic* 10 (Summer 1990), 135–61; Daniel Walker Howe, "Jacksonianism and the Promise of Improvement," *Reviews in American History* 25 (Mar. 1997), 58–62; and Sean Wilentz, "Land, Labor, and Politics in the Age of Jackson," *Reviews in American History* 14 (June 1986), 200–209.

5. See especially, Paul W. Gates, *History of Public Land Law Development* (Washington, DC, 1968) and *Landlords and Tenants on the Prairie Frontier* (Ithaca, NY, 1973); Malcolm Rohrbough, *The Land Office Business: The Settlement and Administration of American Public Lands, 1789–1837* (New York, 1968); Frederick Jackson Turner, *Rise of the New West* (New York, 1906) and *The United States, 1830–1850: The Nation and Its Sections* (New York, 1935); Raynor Wellington, *The Political and Sectional Influence of the Public Lands, 1828–1842* (Cambridge, MA,

1914); and the finest in recent times, Daniel Feller, *The Public Lands in Jacksonian Politics* (Madison, WI, 1984).

6. Clark, "Agrarian Context," 18–19, and Jonathan Levy, "The Mortgage Worked the Hardest: The Fate of Landed Independence in Nineteenth-Century America," in Zakim and Kornblith, *Capitalism Takes Command* (see n. 2 above), 39–67. For a variety of interpretations of the Market Revolution, see also Charles G. Sellers, *The Market Revolution: Jacksonian America, 1815–1846* (New York, 1991); Daniel W. Howe, *What Hath God Wrought: The Transformation of America, 1815–1848* (New York, 2007); John L. Larson, *The Market Revolution in America: Liberty, Ambition, and the Eclipse of the Common Good* (Cambridge, UK, 2009); and Melvyn Stokes and Stephen Conway, eds., *The Market Revolution in America: Social, Political, and Religious Expressions, 1800–1880* (Charlottesville, VA, 1996).

7. On the need for more social and cultural content in the writing of early-nineteenth-century political history, see Gordon S. Wood, "The Significance of the Early Republic," *Journal of the Early Republic* 8 (Spring 1988), 1–20; and, generally, Pasley, Robertson, and Waldstreicher, eds., *Beyond the Founders* (see n. 3 above). Regarding the impact of republicanism, see primarily Gordon S. Wood, *The Creation of the American Republic, 1776–1787* (Chapel Hill, NC, 1969), *The Radicalism of the American Revolution* (New York, 1992), and *Empire of Liberty: A History of the Early Republic, 1789–1815* (New York, 2010). Also, Daniel T. Rogers, "Republicanism: The Career of a Concept," *Journal of American History* 79 (June 1992), 11–38.

8. William H. Bergmann, *The American National State and the Early West* (Cambridge, UK, 2012), 2; Max M. Edling, *A Revolution in Favor of Government: Origins of the U.S. Constitution and the Making of the American State* (New York, 2003); William J. Novak, "The Myth of the 'Weak' American State," *American Historical Review* 113 (June 2008), 752–72, esp. 758; John L. Larson, *Internal Improvement: National Public Works and the Promise of Popular Government in the Early United States* (Chapel Hill, NC, 2001), 3; and Brian Balogh, *A Government Out of Sight: The Mystery of National Authority in Nineteenth-Century America* (Cambridge, UK, 2009). See also Andrew R. L. Cayton, " 'Separate Interests' and the Nation-State: The Washington Administration and the Origins of Regionalism in the Trans-Appalachian West," *Journal of American History* 79 (June 1992), 347–80. See especially Richard R. John, "Governmental Institutions as Agents of Change: Rethinking American Political Development in the Early Republic, 1787–1835," *Studies in American Political Development* 11 (Sept. 1997), 347–80, *Spreading the News: The Postal System from Franklin to Morse* (Cambridge, MA, 1995), and *Network Nation: Inventing American Telecommunications* (Cambridge, MA, 2010). Also, Richard Novak, *The People's Welfare: Law and Regulation in Nineteenth-Century America* (Chapel Hill, NC, 1996). Eliga H. Gould's *Among the Powers of the Earth: The American Revolution and the Making of a New World Empire* (Cambridge, MA, 2012) examines the subject of nation building in an international context. On the federal government's role in trans-Appalachian development, in addition to Bergmann's *American National State*, see Stephen Rockwell, *Indian Affairs and the Administrative State* (Cambridge, UK, 2010); Patrick Griffin, *American Leviathan: Empire, Nation, and the Revolutionary Frontier* (New York, 2007); Peter J. Kastor, *William Clark's World: Describing America in an Age of Unknowns* (New Haven, CT, 2011); and Adam Rothman, *Slave Country: American Expansion and the Origins of the Deep South* (Cambridge, MA, 2005).

9. For the best broad understanding of the concept of "political economy" in the early republic, see Drew R. McCoy, *The Elusive Republic: Political Economy in Jeffersonian America* (Chapel Hill, NC, 1980). For use of the term "nation," see Gould, *Among the Powers of the Earth*, 10–11. On "frontier" (and various refinements of that word), see Andrew R. L. Cayton, *The Frontier Republic: Ideology and Politics in the Ohio Country, 1780–1825* (Kent, OH, 1986); Gregory H. Nobles, *American Frontiers: Cultural Encounters and Continental Conquest* (New

York, 1997), and "Breaking into the Backcountry: New Approaches to the Early American Frontier, 1750–1800," *William and Mary Quarterly* 46 (Oct. 1989), 641–70; Patricia N. Limerick, *The Legacy of Conquest: The Unbroken Past of the American West* (New York, 1987); and Anne F. Hyde, *Empires, Nations, and Families: A New History of the North American West, 1800–1860* (Lincoln, NE, 2011).

Prologue · "A Great Country, Populous and Mighty"

1. See Drew R. McCoy, "Benjamin Franklin's Vision of a Republican Political Economy for America," *William and Mary Quarterly*, 3rd ser., 35 (Oct. 1978), 605–28. Also McCoy, *The Elusive Republic*. On Franklin generally, see Gordon S. Wood, *The Americanization of Benjamin Franklin* (New York, 2004).

2. On British empire building, see especially Eric Hinderaker, *Elusive Empires: Constructing Colonialism in the Ohio Valley, 1673–1800* (Cambridge, UK, 1997).

3. "Observations Concerning the Increase of Mankind," in *The Papers of Benjamin Franklin*, ed. Leonard W. Labaree et al., 40 vols. (New Haven, CT, 1959–), 4: 225–26. (Hereafter abbreviated *PBF*.)

4. *PBF*, 4: 228–29.

5. *PBF*, 4: 229.

6. Hinderaker, *Elusive Empires*, xii–xiii, 149–50, Franklin quoted on 150.

7. "Observations," *PBF*, 4: 234.

8. Franklin to George Whitefield, July 2, 1756, *PBF*, 6: 468–69.

9. "Reasons and Motives for the Albany Plan of Union," *PBF*, 5: 411–12.

10.-"Pennsylvania Assembly Committee: Report on the State of the Currency," *PBF*, 4: 350.

11. "A Plan for Settling Two Western Colonies," *PBF*, 4: 457.

12. *PBF*, 4: 458.

13. *PBF*, 4: 459–60.

14. Franklin to Peter Collinson, June 26, 1755, *PBF*, 6: 87–88.

15. "The Interest of Great Britain Considered, With Regard to her Colonies, And the Acquisitions of Canada and Guadaloupe, 1760," *PBF*, 9: 73–74; Franklin to Richard Jackson, March 8, 1763, *PBF*, 10: 208.

16. Fred Anderson, *Crucible of War: The Seven Years' War and the Fate of Empire in British North America, 1754–1766* (New York, 2000), 566.

17. On Pontiac's Rebellion and the Proclamation of 1763, ibid., 535–53, 560–71, 633–37.

18. Franklin to Lord Kames, February 25, 1767, *PBF*, 14: 69.

19. Franklin to Cadwalader Evans, February 20, 1768, *PBF*, 15: 52. On the physiocrats, see Elizabeth Fox Genovese, *The Origins of Physiocracy: Economic Revolution and Social Order in Eighteenth-Century France* (Ithaca, NY, 1976).

20. "Comparison of Great Britain and the United States in Regard to the Basis of Credit in the Two Countries, 1777," in *The Writings of Benjamin Franklin*, ed. Albert Henry Smyth, 10 vols. (New York, 1907), 8: 5–6.

21. "Information to Those Who Would Remove to America, September 1782," in ibid., 8: 607. See also "The Internal State of America: Being a True Description of the Interest and Policy of that Vast Continent," in ibid., 10: 120; and Franklin to Benjamin Vaughan, July 26, 1784, in ibid., 9: 245–46.

Chapter 1 · *"Republican Notions—and Utopian Schemes"*

1. Quotations from Madison to Harrison, November 15, 1782, in *Letters of Delegates to Congress, 1774–1789*, ed. Paul H. Smith et al., 26 vols. (Washington, DC, 1976–2000), 19: 391. (Hereafter abbreviated *LDC*.)

2. On the integrating of social and cultural conditions into political history, see Gordon S. Wood, "The Significance of the Early Republic," *Journal of the Early Republic* 8 (Spring 1988), 1–20; Jeffrey L. Pasley, Andrew W. Robertson, and David Waldstreicher, eds., *Beyond the Founders: New Approaches to the Political History of the Early American Republic* (Chapel Hill, NC, 2004); and, generally, Gordon S. Wood, *The Radicalism of the American Revolution* (New York, 1992). On land policy in the post-Revolutionary period, see Peter S. Onuf, "Liberty, Development, and Union: Visions of the West in the 1780s," *William and Mary Quarterly*, 3rd ser., 43 (Apr. 1986), 179–213.

3. On the development of pre-Revolutionary land policies, see generally Paul W. Gates, *History of Public Land Law Development* (Washington, DC, 1968); and Alan Taylor, *American Colonies* (New York, 2001). Also, and more specifically, Stephen Innes, *Creating the Commonwealth: The Economic Culture of Puritan New England* (New York, 1995); and L. Scott Philyaw, *Virginia's Western Visions: Political and Cultural Expansion on an Early American Frontier* (Knoxville, TN, 2004).

4. On the Old World roots of republican political economy, see especially Joyce O. Appleby, *Economic Thought and Ideology in Seventeenth-Century England* (Princeton, NJ, 1978); and William B. Scott, *In Pursuit of Happiness: American Conceptions of Property from the Seventeenth to the Twentieth Century* (Bloomington, IN, 1977), 24–35.

5. On the political philosophy of James Harrington and its influence, see generally J. G. A. Pocock, *The Machiavellian Moment: Florentine Political Thought and the Atlantic Republican Tradition* (Princeton, NJ, 1975). Also Scott, *In Pursuit of Happiness*, chapter 2.

6. Jefferson to James Madison, October 28, 1785, in *The Papers of Thomas Jefferson*, ed. Julian P. Boyd et al., 39 vols. to date (Princeton, NJ, 1950–), 8: 681–83, esp. 682. (Hereafter abbreviated *PTJ*.)

7. See Wood, *Radicalism of the American Revolution*, 11–92.

8. Innes, *Creating the Commonwealth*, 192–236, 91–92, 215.

9. Ibid., 175–77, 214.

10. Wood, *Radicalism of the American Revolution*, 124–29, 308–10; Christopher Clark, *Social Change in America, from the Revolution through the Civil War* (Chicago, 2006), 80; John M. Murrin, "The Great Inversion, or Court versus Country: A Comparison of the Revolution Settlements in England (1688–1721) and America (1776–1816)," in *Three British Revolutions: 1641, 1688, 1776*, ed. J. G. A. Pocock (Princeton, NJ, 1980), 368–453, esp. 387.

11. Clark, *Social Change in America*, 79–88, esp. 80, 82.

12. Data for Caroline and Augusta Counties in Virginia, compiled by the author from Virginia Land Tax Books, 1787 and 1830, Library of Virginia, Richmond.

13. Clark, *Social Change in America*, 84–86.

14. Murrin, "The Great Inversion," 398–401. Also, Woody Holton, *Forced Founders: Indians, Debtors, Slaves, and the Making of the American Revolution in Virginia* (Chapel Hill, NC, 1999), esp. 189–205.

15. Dyer to Judd, July 23, 1775, in *LDC*, 1: 654–56, esp. 654, 2: 249–50n; entry for October 25, 1775, in *Diary and Autobiography of John Adams: Diary, 1771–1781*, ed. Lyman Henry Butterfield, 4 vols. (Cambridge, MA, 1962), 2: 217–18.

16. See Louis W. Potts, "Silas Deane," in *American National Biography*, ed. John A. Garraty and Mark C. Carnes, 24 vols. (New York, 1999), 6: 296–98. On social change in Con-

necticut, see Richard L. Bushman, *From Puritan to Yankee: Character and Social Order in Connecticut, 1690–1765* (Cambridge, MA, 1967).

17. Deane to Samuel Adams, November 13, 1774, in *LDC*, 1: 258–62, esp., 260–61.

18. Deane to Henry, January 2, 1775, *LDC*, 1: 291–92.

19. "Draft of Instructions of the Virginia Delegates," in *PTJ*, 1: 133.

20. *PTJ*, 1: 132–33, and Jefferson to Pendleton, August 13, 1776, 1: 491–94, esp., 492–93.

21. "Third Draft by Jefferson of the Virginia Constitution of 1776," *PTJ*, 1: 362–63.

22. See especially Philyaw, *Virginia's Western Visions*, 1–64.

23. Ibid., 14, 19–20.

24. *Memoir, Correspondence, and Miscellanies, from the Papers of Thomas Jefferson*, ed. Thomas Jefferson Randolph, 4 vols. (Charlottesville, VA, 1829), 1: 29–30, 40; "An Act declaring tenants of lands or slaves in taille to hold the same in fee simple," in *The Statutes at Large: Being a Collection of All the Laws of Virginia . . .* , ed. W. W. Hening, 13 vols. (Richmond, 1808–1823), 9: 226–27; "Bill to Enable Tenants in Fee Tail to Convey Their Lands in Fee Simple," *PTJ*, 1: 560–62. See also Elizabeth Blackmar,"Inheriting Property and Debt: From Family Security to Corporate Accumulation," in *Capitalism Takes Command: The Social Transformation of Nineteenth-Century America*, ed. Michael Zakim and Gary J. Kornblith (Chicago, 2012), 93–117, esp. 94–95.

25. "An act for establishing a Land office and ascertaining the terms and manner of granting waste and unappropriated lands" and "An Act for adjusting and settling the titles of claimers to unpatented lands under the present and former government, previous to the establishment of the commonwealth's land office," in Hening, *Statutes*, 10: 50–65, 35–50; "Bill for Establishing a Land Office and Ascertaining the Terms and Manner of Granting Waste and Unappropriated Lands," *PTJ*, 2: 139–40, and "Editorial Note," 134–35.

26. Gates, *History of Public Land Law*, 49–57, esp. 50.

27. Committee for Foreign Affairs to the Commissioners at Paris, October 6, 1777, *LDC*, 8: 64–65, esp. 64; 13: 454–55n; Gouverneur Morris to the Public, September 4, 1997, *LDC*, 8: 453–55, esp. 454.

28. Gates, *History of Public Land Law*, 51.

29. Arnold to Cahoon, November 4, 1782, *LDC*, 19: 337.

30. Gates, *History of Public Land Law*, 52.

31. "Deed of Cession as Executed," *PTJ*, 6: 577–80, esp. 577, 578.

32. Arthur Lee to John Adams, January 14, 1784, *LDC*, 21: 272–73; Howell to Arnold, February 21, 1784, *LDC*, 21: 380–85, esp. 381.

33. Ellery to Francis Dana, December 3, 1783, *LDC*, 21: 173–81, esp. 177; Howell to Jonathan Arnold, February 21, 1784, *LDC*, 21: 380–85, esp. 383.

34. Howell to Arnold, February 21, 1784, LDC, 21: 383. See also John R. Stilgoe, *Common Landscape of America, 1580–1845* (New Haven, CT, 1982), 99–107.

35. "Report of a Committee to Establish a Land Office," April 30, 1784, *PTJ*, 7: 140–48.

36. "Virginia Delegates in Congress to Benjamin Harrison, with Petition from Inhabitants of Kentucky," February 20, 1784, *PTJ*, 6: 552–55, esp. 553.

37. Grayson to Washington, April 15, 1785, *LDC*, 22: 338–41, esp. 339.

38. Madison to James Monroe, May 29, 1785, in *The Papers of James Madison*, ed. William T. Hutchinson, William M. E. Rachal, et al., Congressional Series, 17 vols. to date (Chicago, IL and Charlottesville, VA, (1962–), 8: 285–87, esp. 286.

39. King to Gerry, May 8, 1785, *LDC*, 22: 384–86, esp. 384.

40. On the Land Ordinance of 1785, see Gates, *History of Public Land Law*, chapter 4. On the changing perceptions of landed property and the "commodifying of land," see Clark, *Social Change in America*, 92–93.

41. Susan Dunn, *Dominion of Memories: Jefferson, Madison, and the Decline of Virginia* (New York, 2007), 40.

42. Gardner to George Bryan, March 19, 1785, *LDC*, 22: 276–78, esp. 277; Grayson to George Washington, April 15, 1785, *LDC*, 22: 339; Howell to William Greene, April 29, 1785, *LDC*, 22: 361.

43. "A Proclamation; by the President and the Supreme Executive Council of the Commonwealth of Pennsylvania," Philadelphia, July 31, 1783, and "A Proclamation by His Excellency Jonathan Trumbull, Governor and Commander in Chief in and over the State of Connecticut," New London, November 15, 1783, broadsides at Library Company of Philadelphia. On squatter policy in the 1780s, see Andrew R. L. Cayton, *Frontier Republic: Ideology and Politics in the Ohio Country, 1780–1825* (Kent, OH, 1986), chapter 1.

44. See Gouverneur Morris to George Clinton, January 26, 1779, *LDC*, 11: 520–21; New York Delegates to George Clinton, February 3, 1779, *LDC*, 12: 17–18, esp. 18. Washington, quoted in Andrew R. L. Cayton, "Radicals in the 'Western World': The Federalist Conquest of Trans-Appalachian North America," in *Federalists Reconsidered*, ed. Doron Ben-Atar and Barbara B. Oberg (Charlottesville, VA, 1998), 77–96, esp. 80. See also, Murrin, "The Great Inversion," 412–13. On land grants to Roman soldiers following their service, see Edward Gibbon, *The Decline and Fall of the Roman Empire*, 6 vols. (1776–1789; repr., London, 1910), 1: 36–37.

45. Ellery to Francis Dana, December 3, 1783, *LDC*, 21: 173–81, esp. 176; Richard Henry Lee to George Washington, April 18, 1785, *LDC*, 22: 345–46; Stuart Banner, *How the Indians Lost Their Land: Law and Power on the Frontier* (Cambridge, MA, 2005), 122–24.

46. David Jackson to George Bryan, July 1, 1785, *LDC*, 22: 490–92, esp. 491; Josiah Harmer, quoted in Patrick Griffin, "Reconsidering the Ideological Origins of Indian Removal: The Case of the Big Bottom 'Massacre,'" in *The Center of a Great Empire: The Ohio Country in the Early American Republic*, ed. Andrew R. L. Cayton and Stuart D. Hobbs (Athens, OH, 2005), 11–35, esp. 18; Samuel Holden Parsons, quoted in R. Douglas Hurt, *The Ohio Frontier: Crucible of the Old Northwest, 1720–1830* (Bloomington, IN, 1996), 145. On violent exchanges between squatters and Indians in the 1780s and before, see Patrick Griffin, *American Leviathan: Empire, Nation, and the Revolutionary Frontier* (New York, 2007), 152–80; and Daniel K. Richter, *Facing East from Indian Country: A Native History of Early America* (Cambridge, MA, 2001), 185, 192, 203, 213. On the Harmer expedition, see William Grayson to James Madison, June 27, 1785, *LDC*, 22: 480–82. On the meaning of "Indianness," see John L. Brooke, "Consent, Civil Society, and the Public Sphere in the Age of Revolution and the Early American Republic," in *Beyond the Founders: New Approaches to the Political History of the Early American Republic*, ed. Jeffrey L. Pasley, Andrew W. Robertson, and David Waldstreicher (Chapel Hill, NC, 2004), 232.

47. Washington to Madison, November 5, 1786, in Hutchinson, Rachal, et al., *Papers of James Madison*, 9: 161–62. Madison replied that Knox's news was "gloomy indeed," but "less so than the colours in which I had it thro' another channel" (166–67).

48. Madison and Rush, quoted in Gordon S. Wood, "Interests and Disinterestedness in the Making of the Constitution," in *Beyond Confederation: Origins of the Constitution and American National Identity*, ed. Richard Beeman, Stephen Botein, and Edward C. Carter II (Chapel Hill, NC, 1987), 73, 71. See also, Woody Holton, *Unruly Americans and the Origins of the Constitution* (New York, 2007).

49. Eliga H. Gould, *Among the Powers of the Earth: The American Revolution and the Making of a New World Empire* (Cambridge, MA, 2012), 12–13. On the Jay-Gardoqui negotiations generally, see Samuel Flagg Bemis, *Pinckney's Treaty: America's Advantage from Europe's Distress, 1783–1800*, rev. ed. (New Haven, CT, 1962); and William Earl Weeks, *Building the Continental Empire: American Expansion from the Revolution to the Civil War* (Chicago, 1997).

50. Williamson to Alexander Martin, September 30, 1784, *LDC*, 21: 796–806, esp. 803.

Chapter 2 · An Embryo of Empire

1. "Memorial to Congress by Inhabitants of Randolph and St. Clair Counties," December 12, 1804, in *The Territorial Papers of the United States*, 26 vols., ed. Clarence E. Carter and John Porter Bloom (Washington, DC, 1934–), 7: 243–47. On squatter appeals and the "shifting language" of settlement, see James Joseph Buss, *Winning the West with Words: Language and Conquest in the Lower Great Lakes* (Norman, OK, 2011), 42–70, esp. 47–49.

2. Richard Henry Lee to George Washington, July 15, 1787, in *Letters of Delegates to Congress, 1774–1789*, ed. Paul H. Smith et al., 26 vols. (Washington, DC, 1976–2000), 24: 356–57, esp. 356. (Hereafter abbreviated *LDC*.)

3. David Hackett Fischer, *The Revolution of American Conservatism: The Federalist Party in the Era of Jeffersonian Democracy* (New York, 1965), 201–26; Gerald Stourzh, *Alexander Hamilton and the Idea of Republican Government* (Stanford, CA, 1970), 129, 139–40; Madison, No. 10 and No. 51, in *The Federalist*, ed., Jacob E. Cooke, (Cleveland, 1961), 56–65, 352–53. See also Gordon S. Wood, "Interests and Disinterestedness in the Making of the Constitution," in *Beyond Confederation: Origins of the Constitution and American National Identity*, ed. Richard Beeman, Stephen Botein, and Edward C. Carter II (Chapel Hill, NC, 1987), 69–109, esp., 91–92.

4. Anne F. Hyde, *Empires, Nations, and Families: A New History of the North American West, 1800–1860* (Lincoln, NE, 2011), 233; Stuart Banner, *How the Indians Lost Their Land: Law and Power on the Frontier* (Cambridge, MA, 2005), 112–49; Gregory Dowd, *A Spirited Resistance: The North American Indian Struggle for Unity, 1745–1815* (Baltimore, 1990), 131–46; Paul W. Gates, *History of Public Land Law Development* (Washington, DC, 1968), 121; and R. Douglas Hurt, *The Ohio Frontier: Crucible of the Old Northwest, 1720–1830* (Bloomington, IN, 1996), 105–19.

5. See Rachel Hope Cleves, *The Reign of Terror in America: Visions of Violence from Anti-Jacobinism to Antislavery* (New York, 2009), esp. chapters 1–3; Albrecht Koschnik, "The Democratic Societies of Philadelphia and the Limits of the American Public Sphere, circa 1793–1795," *William and Mary Quarterly*, 3rd ser., 58 (July 2001), 615–36; and Mathew Schoenbachler, "Republicanism in the Age of Democratic Revolution: The Democratic-Republican Societies of the 1790s," *Journal of the Early Republic* 18 (Summer 1998), 237–61.

6. See Karl-Friedrich Walling, *Republican Empire: Alexander Hamilton on War and Free Government* (Lawrence, KS, 1999); Peter McNamara, *Political Economy and Statesmanship: Smith, Hamilton, and the Foundation of the Commercial Republic* (DeKalb, IL, 1997); Peter S. Onuf, *Jefferson's Empire: The Language of American Nationhood* (Charlottesville, VA, 2000); and Drew R. McCoy, *The Elusive Republic: Political Economy in Jeffersonian America* (Chapel Hill, NC, 1980).

7. Gates, *History of Public Land Law*, 68–71; Andrew R. L. Cayton, *Frontier Republic: Ideology and Politics in the Ohio Country, 1780–1825* (Kent, OH, 1986), chapters 2–3; and Malcolm Rohrbough, *The Land Office Business: The Settlement and Administration of American Public Lands, 1789–1837* (New York, 1968), chapter 1.

8. See Alan Taylor, "From Fathers to Friends of the People: Political Personas in the Early Republic, *Journal of the Early Republic* 11 (Winter 1991), 465–91. Also, Taylor, *William Cooper's Town: Power and Persuasion on the Frontier of the Early American Republic* (New York, 1995), 141–291.

9. Washington, quoted in Andrew R. L. Cayton, "Radicals in the 'Western World,': The Federalist Conquest of Trans-Appalachian North America," in *Federalists Reconsidered*, ed. Doron Ben-Atar and Barbara B. Oberg (Charlottesville, VA, 1998), 81–82; John L. Larson, *Internal Improvement: National Public Works and the Promise of Popular Government in the Early United States* (Chapel Hill, NC, 2001), 17, 12; Eliga H. Gould, *Among the Powers of the Earth: The American Revolution and the Making of a New World Empire* (Cambridge, MA,

2012), 134–36. See also Cayton, "'Separate Interests' and the Nation-State: The Washington Administration and the Origins of Regionalism in the Trans-Appalachian West," *Journal of American History* 79 (June 1992), 39–67.

10. "Extract of a Letter from an Officer in the Western Army, to his Friend in Massachusetts, August 7, 1795," in *Columbian Herald* (Charleston, SC), October 31, 1795; Hyde, *Empires, Nations, and Families,* 233–34; Alan Taylor, *The Divided Ground: Indians, Settlers, and the Northern Borderland of the American Revolution* (New York, 2006), 293–94.

11. *Connecticut Courant* (Hartford), May 5, 1800. The quotation comes from Emer de Vattel's *The Law of Nations* (1758).

12. Hamilton, No. 23, in *The Federalist Papers,* ed. Clinton Rossiter (New York, 1961), 157.

13. "Defense of the Funding System," July 1795, in *The Papers of Alexander Hamilton,* ed. Harold C. Syrett and Jacob E. Cooke, 26 vols. (New York, 1961–1987), 19: 39–40 (hereafter abbreviated *PAH*); [Hamilton], "Purchase of Louisiana," *New-York Evening Post* (New York, NY), July 5, 1803; McNamara, *Political Economy and Statesmanship,* 116–18.

14. "The Continentalist, No. VI," *PAH,* 3: 102.

15. *PAH,* 3: 105.

16. "Remarks on the Ineligibility of Members of the House of Representatives for Other Offices," *PAH,* 4: 216–17; "Constitutional Convention Speech on a Plan of Government," *PAH,* 4: 198; Hamilton, No. 7, in *Federalist Papers* (ed. Rossiter), 61.

17. "Report Relative to a Provision for the Support of Public Credit," *PAH,* 6: 71–72.

18. Gates, *History of Public Land Law,* 122; Madison to Hamilton, November 19, 1789, *PAH,* 5: 526.

19. Hamilton to St. Clair, May 19, 1790, *PAH,* 6: 421; Thomas K. McCraw, *The Founders and Finance: How Hamilton, Gallatin, and Other Immigrants Forged a New Economy* (Cambridge, MA, 2012), 246–68, 360.

20. "Report on Vacant Lands," *PAH,* 6: 502.

21. *PAH,* 6: 502–3.

22. *PAH,* 6: 503–4.

23. *PAH,* 6: 504. See also Hamilton's "Report on the Public Debt and Loans," January 23, 1792, *PAH,* 10: 547.

24. "Report on Vacant Lands," *PAH,* 6: 504.

25. "Second Report on the Further Provision Necessary for Establishing Public Credit (Report on a National Bank)," *PAH,* 7: 320–21.

26. See Coxe's "Draft of the Report on the Subject of Manufactures," *PAH,* 10: 1–23; Adam Smith, *An Inquiry into the Nature and Causes of the Wealth of Nations,* 4th ed., with additions (Dublin, 1785), 1: 413–14, 365.

27. "Alexander Hamilton's Final Version of the Report on the Subject of Manufactures," *PAH,* 10: 258–59.

28. *PAH,* 10: 259; "Address of the board of managers to the Pennsylvania society for the promotion of manufactures and the useful arts," *American Museum* 2 (October 1787), 360–62, esp. 361; "Report on Manufactures," *PAH,* 10: 260. See also "The Politician: Essay on Manufactures," *American Museum* 7 (Jan. 1790), 23–25, esp. 24; and W. Barton, "Remarks on the State of American Manufactures and Commerce," ibid. (June 1790), 285–92, esp. 286.

29. "Report on Manufactures," *PAH,* 10: 265.

30. Rufus King to Elbridge Gerry, June 4, 1786, *LDC,* 23: 331–34, esp. 332.

31. "A Proclamation [Concerning the "Whiskey Rebellion]," September 25, 1794, in *A Compilation of the Messages and Papers of the Presidents, 1789–1897,* 10 vols., comp. James D. Richardson (Washington, DC, 1896), 1: 161–62; Washington to Burges Ball, September 25,

1794, in *George Washington, Writings*, ed. John Rohdehamel (New York, 1997), 884–85. On persistent violence, bloodshed, and disorder in frontier regions, especially between whites and Indians, see Patrick Griffin, *American Leviathan: Empire, Nation, and the Revolutionary Frontier* (New York, 2007). On the Whiskey Rebellion, Thomas P. Slaughter, *The Whiskey Rebellion: Frontier Epilogue to the American Revolution* (New York, 1986).

32. "From the Gazette of the United States," in *Columbian Herald* (Charleston, SC), December 3, 1795; Fisher Ames, quoted in Cayton, "Radicals in the 'Western World,'" 78.

33. "Information to Those Who Are Disposed to Migrate to South-Carolina," *City Gazette* (Charleston, SC), April 22, 1795; "To the Writer of Reply to Remarks, &c," *Columbian Herald* (Charleston, SC), October 21, 1795.

34. On the Tucker family, see Robert J. Brugger, *Beverley Tucker: Heart over Head in the Old South* (Baltimore, 1978). Also see Susan Dunn, *Dominion of Memories: Jefferson, Madison, and the Decline of Virginia* (New York, 2007), 38–41; and E. Lee Shepard, "St. George Tucker," in *American National Biography*, ed. John A. Garraty and Mark C. Carnes, 24 vols. (New York, 1999), 21: 907–8.

35. [St. George Tucker], *Cautionary Hints to Congress Respecting the Sale of the Western Lands Belonging to the United States* (Philadelphia, 1795), 8–9, 11.

36. Ibid., 11, 3, 6, 14.

37. Ibid., 14–15.

38. *The Western Star* (Stockbridge, MA), May 31, 1796; *Annals of Congress*, House, 4th Cong., 1st sess. (1795–1796), 867. On the tumultuous political culture of the nascent republic, see Joanne B. Freeman, *Affairs of Honor: National Politics in the New Republic* (New Haven, CT, 2001).

39. *Annals of Congress*, House, 4th Cong., 1st sess., 860–61, 858–59.

40. Ibid., 859–60, 861–62, 862–63, 865; Cooper, quoted in Taylor, *William Cooper's Town*, 196.

41. Gallatin, quoted in Gates, *History of Public Land Law*, 124; McCraw, *Founders and Finance*, 192–93, 202, 246–49.

42. *Annals of Congress*, Senate, 4th Cong., 1st sess., 83.

43. Gates, *History of Public Land Law*, 125–26; *Annals of Congress*, Senate, 4th Cong., 1st sess., 83.

44. "A Sketch of the Finances of the United States," in *The Writings of Albert Gallatin*, ed. Henry Adams, 3 vols. (Philadelphia, 1879), 3: 155 (hereafter abbreviated *WAG*); Gates, *History of Public Land Law*, 128–30. Unfortunately, the congressional votes on the Harrison bill went unrecorded.

45. Gates, *History of Public Land Law*, 131–32. The House and Senate votes on the 1804 land bill also were not recorded. For the texts of the federal land laws, see *The Public Statutes at Large of the United States of America from the Organization of the Government in 1789 to March 3, 1845*, ed. Richard Peters (Boston, 1848).

46. "First Inaugural Address," March 4, 1801, in *The Portable Thomas Jefferson*, ed. Merrill D. Peterson (New York, 1975), 290–95, esp. 292.

47. Gallatin to Jefferson, October 4, 1803, *WAG*, 1: 157; Jefferson to G. K. Hogendorp, October 13, 1785, in *The Papers of Thomas Jefferson*, ed. Julian P. Boyd et al., 39 vols. to date (Princeton, NJ, 1950–), 8: 633–34.

48. See Richard E. Ellis, "The Persistence of Antifederalism after 1789," in Beeman, Botein, and Carter, *Beyond the Confederation* (see n. 3 above), 295–314; and Ellis, "The Market Revolution and the Transformation of American Politics, 1801–1837," in *The Market Revolution in America: Social, Political, and Religious Expressions, 1800–1880*, ed. Melvyn Stokes

and Stephen Conway (Charlottesville, VA, 1996), 149–76. Also, William H. Bergmann, *The American National State and the Early West* (Cambridge, UK, 2012), chapters 4–5.

49. Gallatin to Jefferson, November 16, 1801, *WAG*, 1: 70; McCraw, *Founders and Finance*, 213, 250–52.

50. Gallatin to William B. Giles, February 13, 1802, *WAG*, 1: 77.

51. On the admission of Ohio, see Gates, *History of Public Land Law*, 288–91; Gallatin to Giles, February 13, 1802, *WAG*, 1: 78, 79.

52. On the Louisiana Purchase, see Peter J. Kastor, *The Nation's Crucible: The Louisiana Purchase and the Creation of America* (New Haven, CT, 2004); and Jon Kukla, *A Wilderness So Immense: The Louisiana Purchase and the Destiny of America* (New York, 2003).

53. "Louisiana," in the *Republican Gazetteer* (Boston, MA), September 8, 1802; King, quoted in Kukla, *A Wilderness So Immense*, 289–90; from the *Columbian Centinel*, reprinted in the *Ulster* (New York) *Gazette*, August 13, 1803.

54. Griffin, *Annals of Congress*, House, 8th Cong., 1st sess. (1803–1804), 443; Elliott, ibid., 451; Thatcher, ibid., 456. For background on House and Senate members, see *Biographical Directory of the United States Congress*, http://bioguide.congress.gov.

55. White, *Annals of Congress*, Senate, 8th Cong., 1st sess., 34.

56. Randolph, *Annals of Congress*, House, 8th Cong, 1st sess., 440; Jackson, ibid., Senate, 41.

57. Jefferson to John Breckinridge, August 12, 1803, in Peterson, *Portable Thomas Jefferson*, 496; Lowell H. Harrison, "John Breckinridge," in *American National Biography*, 3: 457–59; Breckinridge, *Annals of Congress*, Senate, 8th Cong., 1st sess., 60, 61, 65; Cocke, ibid., 72.

58. Jefferson to Breckinridge, August 12, 1803, in Peterson, *Portable Thomas Jefferson*, 496; Gallatin to Jefferson, October 4, 1803, *WAG*, 1: 157.

59. "Second Inaugural Address," in Peterson, *Portable Thomas Jefferson*, 317–18. For the complete address, see Richardson, *Messages and Papers of the Presidents*, 1: 378–82.

60. "Sixth Annual Message to Congress," Peterson, *Portable Thomas Jefferson*, 326. See also Richardson, *Messages and Papers of the Presidents*, 1: 405–10.

61. Gallatin's full "Report on Roads and Canals" is available in *American State Papers: Miscellaneous*, 1: 724–921 (pages 742–921 are appendices). I have relied on the reprinting of it in *The Government and the Economy, 1783–1861*, ed. Carter Goodrich (Indianapolis, 1967), 5–42.

62. Gallatin, "Report on Roads and Canals," 6, 8, 23.

63. Gates, *History of Public Land Law*, 38–39.

64. "Proclamation Requiring Settlers Northwest of the Ohio to Vacate, January 24, 1780," *PTJ*, 3: 266–67; McCraw, *Founders and Finance*, 251–52.

65. Jefferson, quoted in Bernard W. Sheehan, *Seeds of Extinction: Jeffersonian Philanthropy and the American Indian* (New York, 1973), 169; Hyde, *Empires, Nations, and Families*, 235–36. On western coercion, see Robert Owens, *Mr. Jefferson's Hammer: William Henry Harrison and the Origins of Indian Policy* (Norman, OK, 2007). On eastern versus western perceptions of Indian "removal," see Banner, *How the Indians Lost Their Land*, 6, 191–227.

66. Jefferson, quoted in Bergmann, *American National State*, 1. See also Hyde, *Empires, Nations, and Families*, 236; Patrick Bottiger, "Prophetstown for Their Own Purposes: The French, Miamis, and Cultural Identities in the Wabash-Maumee Valley," *Journal of the Early Republic*, 33 (Spring 2013), 29–60.

67. Gallatin to Jefferson, April 16, 1804, *WAG*, 1: 187–88; Jefferson to Gallatin, April 27, 1804, *WAG*, 189. See also Rohrbough, *Land Office Business*, chapter 2.

68. Jefferson to Gallatin, March 31, 1807, *WAG*, 1: 331–32; "Copy of a letter from the Secretary of the Treasury, to Thomas Williams, esq. Register, L. O. East of Pearl River," March 28,

1807, included in *Letter from the Secretary of the Treasury, Transmitting Information in Relation to Settlements Contrary to Law, on the Lands of the United States in the Mississippi Territory, . . .* , January 6, 1811, at Library Company of Philadelphia, 6–7.

69. "Copy of a letter from the Register of the Land Office West of Pearl River, to the Secretary of the Treasury," August 10, 1807, at Library Company of Philadelphia, 8.

70. Ibid.

71. Jefferson to Gallatin, March 31, 1807, *WAG*, 1: 331–32. Badollet and the 1816 petition, quoted in Andrew R. L. Cayton, *Frontier Indiana* (Bloomington, IN, 1996), 266.

72. "Report and bill on the petition of Amos Spafford," February 22, 1816, House Committee on Public Lands, February 22, 1816, printed in Washington, DC, 1816, at Library Company of Philadelphia.

73. Ibid.

74. See Rohrbough, *The Land Office Business*, 89–136.

Chapter 3 · Rise of the Radical West

1. Anonymous letter to the editor, *Weekly Intelligencer* (Richmond, IN), April 17, 1822.

2. *Connecticut Courant* (Hartford, CT), February 27, 1821; *Tennessee Clarion* (Nashville), reprinted in *Brookville Enquirer and Indiana Telegraph* (Brookville, IN), March 2, 1820.

3. "Money," *Indianapolis Gazette* (Indianapolis, IN), July 22, 1823; "Poverty," *Public Ledger* (Wayne County, IN), January 1, 1825.

4. Edmund P. Dana, *Geographical Sketches on the Western Country: Designed for Emigrants and Settlers* (Cincinnati, OH, 1819), 58; Abijah Hammond, *An Address, Delivered before the West Chester Agricultural Society*, October 27, 1819 (New York, 1819), 12.

5. On the causes of the Panic of 1819, see Murray N. Rothbard, *The Panic of 1819: Reactions and Policies* (New York, 1962), and for its impact on land policy, Malcolm Rohrbough, *The Land Office Business: The Settlement and Administration of American Public Lands, 1789–1837* (New York, 1968), chapter 7.

6. "An Act making further provision for the sale of public lands," April 24, 1820, in *The Public Statutes at Large of the United States of America from the Organization of the Government in 1789 to March 3, 1845*, ed. Richard Peters, 18 vols. (Boston, 1848), 3: 566–67. See Benton's remarks introducing the Graduation Bill, *Annals of Congress*, Senate, 18th Cong., 1st sess., 582–83.

7. U.S. Senate, *Memorial of the Legislature of Missouri, for the sale of lands remaining unsold for a certain time after being offered for sale, at the minimum price of fifty cents per acre, and that the residue be given time*, S. Doc. 27, 20th Cong., 1st sess. (serial no. 164), 3. On the variety of backgrounds of preemption petitioners, the deception often practiced, and the expansion of western suffrage to include squatters, see James Joseph Buss, *Winning the West with Words: Language and Conquest in the Lower Great Lakes* (Norman, OK, 2011), 51–56, 48–49.

8. *Richmond Enquirer* (Richmond, VA), October 6, 1818. On the Land Act of 1820, see Paul W. Gates, *History of Public Land Law Development* (Washington, DC, 1968), 141; Daniel Feller, *The Public Lands in Jacksonian Politics* (Madison, WI, 1984), chapter 2.

9. *Niles' Weekly Register* (Baltimore, MD), September 4, 1819, February 5, 1820; Gates, *History of Public Land Law*, 140–41.

10. On Morrow, see Andrew R. L. Cayton, *The Frontier Republic: Ideology and Politics in the Ohio Country, 1780–1825* (Kent, OH, 1986). Also see John R. Van Atta, "Jeremiah Morrow," *American National Biography*, ed. John A. Garraty and Mark C. Carnes, 24 vols. (New York, 1999), 15: 929–30.

11. *Annals of Congress*, Senate, 15th Cong., 2nd sess. (1818–1819), 245.

12. Ibid., 216–17.

13. Ibid., 215–16.

14. Ibid., 217.

15. *Kentucky Reporter* (Lexington), quoted in *Niles' Weekly Register* (Baltimore, MD), September 4, 1819.

16. *Annals of Congress*, Senate, 15th Cong, 2nd sess., 217–18.

17. Ibid., 216.

18. *Annals of Congress*, House, 16th Cong., 1st sess. (1819–1820), 1871; "George Robertson," *Dictionary of American Biography*, ed. Allen Johnson et al., 11 vols. (New York, 1927–1995), 8: 22–23.

19. *Annals of Congress*, House, 16th Cong., 1st sess., 1879, 1886–87.

20. Ibid., 2nd sess. (1820–1821), 162–63. On the voting to abolish the credit system and the subsequent relief acts, see Feller, *Public Lands in Jacksonian Politics*, 26–38, esp. 28. On the significance of the law, see also Brian Balogh, *A Government Out of Sight: The Mystery of National Authority in Nineteenth Century America* (Cambridge, UK, 2009), 180–84.

21. Richard B. Latner, *The Presidency of Andrew Jackson: White House Politics, 1829–1837* (Athens, GA, 1979), 18–21. On the Panic's political consequences in Kentucky, see Rothbard, *Panic of 1819*, 47, 52–55, 154–55; and Lynn L. Marshall, "The Genesis of Grass-Roots Democracy in Kentucky," *Mid-America* 47 (1965), 269–87.

22. *Argus of Western America* (Frankfort, KY), May 11, 1820. For the Senate opposition to the Land Act of 1820, see *Annals of Congress*, 16th Cong., 1st sess., 489, 1901. Speaker of the House Henry Clay did not vote.

23. *Argus of Western America* (Frankfort, KY), December 17, 1823.

24. *Annals of Congress*, Senate, 16th Cong., 2nd sess., 207.

25. Ibid., 209–11. Johnson's speech was reprinted in *Argus of Western America* (Frankfort, KY), March 1, 1821.

26. "Internal Improvement," *The American Farmer* (Baltimore, MD), March 3, 1820.

27. For the Maxcy report, see *Annals of Congress*, Senate, 16th Cong., 2nd sess., App., 1772–84. Also see Virgil Maxcy, "Report with Sundry Resolutions Relative to Appropriations of Public Land for the Purposes of Education, to the Senate of Maryland, January 30, 1821," at Library Company of Philadelphia; Maxcy, "Address to the Worcester County Agricultural Society," *National Aegis*, May 10, 1820; and *Annals of Congress*, Senate 16th Cong., 2nd sess., App., 1775.

28. Letter to the editor, *Baltimore Patriot* (Baltimore, MD), June 6, 1822; Sean Wilentz, *The Rise of American Democracy: Jefferson to Lincoln* (New York, 2005), 207–8; Rothbard, *Panic of 1819*, 94.

29. Virgil Maxcy, *The Maryland Resolutions, and the Objections to them Considered* (Baltimore, 1822), 14; *Annals of Congress*, Senate, 16th Cong., 2nd sess., App., 1780.

30. "Education," *Rhode-Island American* (Providence, RI), May 4, 1821; "The Maryland Resolutions," *Repertory* (Boston, MA), January 17, 1822. Connecticut, New Hampshire, Rhode Island, New Jersey, Kentucky, Delaware, Maine, and Vermont sent their own memorials to Congress supporting the Maxcy idea and asking for a share of the public lands revenue to aid education (see Gates, *History of Public Land Law*, 7).

31. *Annals of Congress*, Senate, 16th Cong., 2nd sess., App., 1782.

32. Ibid., 1783.

33. Ibid., 1773, 1776.

34. The Verplanck report appeared in *Niles' Weekly Register* (Baltimore, MD), August 11, 1821; Steven E. Siry, "Gulian Crommelin Verplanck," *American National Biography*, 22: 331–32.

35. "Report of the committee on colleges, academies, and common schools, upon the message of his excellency the governor, communicating the resolutions of the legislature of Maryland," in *Niles' Weekly Register* (Baltimore, MD), August 11, 1821.

36. *Annals of Congress*, Senate, 16th Cong., 2nd sess., App., 1782–83.

37. *Niles' Weekly Register* (Baltimore, MD), August 11, 1821.

38. "Proposition to Grant Land to the Old States for the Purposes of Education," February 9, 1821, *American State Papers: Public Lands*, 3: 439–40. For a criticism of the Verplanck position, see Jared Sparks, "Appropriation of Public Lands for Schools," *North American Review*, 13 (October 1821), 310–38, esp. 326–31.

39. *Edwardsville Spectator* (Edwardsville, IL), January 22, 1822.

40. Edwards's speech, *Annals of Congress*, Senate, 17th Cong., 1st sess. (1821–1822), 247–68. See John R. Van Atta, "Ninian Edwards," *American National Biography*, 7: 337–38.

41. *Annals of Congress*, Senate, 17th Cong., 1st sess., 250, 261, 263.

42. Governor Edwards's Message to the Illinois Legislature, December 2, 1828, *Illinois House Journal*, 1828–29, 10–39. See also Raynor Wellington, *The Political and Sectional Influence of the Public Lands, 1828–1842* (Cambridge, MA, 1914), 13–20.

43. See Elbert B. Smith, "Thomas Hart Benton," *American National Biography*, 2: 618–20. Also on Benton, see William Nisbet Chambers, *Old Bullion Benton, Senator from the New West* (Boston, 1956); and Elbert B. Smith, *Magnificent Missourian: The Life of Thomas Hart Benton* (Philadelphia, 1958). These touch very sparingly on Benton's involvement in public land policy.

44. Stephen Aron, *American Confluence: The Missouri Frontier from Borderland to Border State* (Bloomington, IN, 2006), 193–94.

45. Thomas Hart Benton, *Thirty Years' View; or, A History of the Working of the American Government for Thirty Years, from 1820 to 1850*, 2 vols. (New York, 1858), 1: 11–12.

46. St. George L. Sioussat, "Some Phases of Tennessee Politics in the Jacksonian Period," *American Historical Review* 14 (1908), 51–69, esp. 52–59. On the Panic and political results in Tennessee, see Rothbard, *Panic of 1819*, 47–52, 153; and Charles G. Sellers, "Banking and Politics in Jackson's Tennessee, 1817–1827," *Mississippi Valley Historical Review* 41 (June 1954), 61–84.

47. Mitchell to Thomas Hart Benton, March 29, 1828, in *American State Papers: Public Lands*, 5: 514.

48. Sioussat, "Phases of Tennessee Politics," 54.

49. Benton, *Thirty Years' View*, 1: 102; Smith to Benton, February 28, 1828, in *American State Papers: Public Lands*, 5: 514; Robert Baird, *View of the Valley of the Mississippi; or, The Emigrant's and Traveler's Guide to the West* (Philadelphia, 1832), 203, 207.

50. Mitchell to Benton, March 29, 1828, *American State Papers: Public Lands*, 5: 515–16; Smith to Benton, February 28, 1828, ibid., 514.

51. Aron, *American Confluence*, 158, 159–60, 195–96.

52. On the Panic of 1819 in Indiana, see Rothbard, *Panic of 1819*, 78–80, 151. See also "William Hendricks' Political Circulars to His Constituents: Congressional Period, 1816–1822," ed. Frederick D. Hill, in *Indiana Magazine of History* 70 (Dec. 1974), 296–344.

53. *Annals of Congress*, Senate, 16th Cong., 1st sess., 360. See Hendricks' speeches regarding state title to public lands in *Messages and Papers of Jonathan Jennings, Ratliff Boon, and William Hendricks*, ed. Logan Esarey, Indiana Historical Collections, vol. 12 (Indianapolis, 1924), 356–84, 386–91. See Jennings's Annual Message, November 28, 1820, ibid., 118, and in the Indiana *House Journal* for 1820, 7–13. The message was covered by the *Vincennes Western Sun* (Vincennes, IN), December 9, 1820; *Vincennes Centinel* (Vincennes, IN), December 16, 1820; and *Corydon Gazette* (Corydon, IN), December 1, 1820.

54. See *Annals of Congress*, Senate, 18th Cong., 1st sess. (1823–1824), 582–83.

55. "Application of Indiana for relief of purchasers and for reduction in the price of public lands," *American State Papers: Public Lands*, 4: 429–30; "Application of Illinois for a Reduction in the Price of Certain Lands," ibid., 148.

56. Finis Ewing to Henry Clay, August 6, 1825, in *The Papers of Henry Clay*, ed. James F. Hopkins et al., 10 vols. (Lexington, KY, 1959–1992), 4: 268 (hereafter abbreviated *PHC*); Message to the General Assembly, December 4, 1827, in *Messages and Papers relating to the Administration of James Brown Ray, Governor of Indiana, 1825–1831*, ed. Dorothy Riker and Gayle Thornbrough, Indiana Historical Collections, vol. 34 (Indianapolis, 1954), 286.

57. Quoted in Benton, *Thirty Years' View*, 1: 103–4.

58. Sloo, quoted in Rohrbough, *Land Office Business*, 92–93; "Squatters," *Illinois Intelligencer* (Vandalia, IL), reprinted in the *Vermont Gazette* (Bennington), March 3, 1830. See also "Florida," *Commercial Advertiser* (New York, NY), May, 13, 1828; "Important Invention," *Daily Commercial Bulletin* (St. Louis, MO), August, 5, 1835.

59. Memorial to Congress by Citizens of the Territory, referred February 17, 1816, in *The Territorial Papers of the United States*, ed. Clarence E. Carter and John Porter Bloom, 27 vols. (Washington, DC, 1934–), 8: 389–90; Tipton to the People of Indiana, June 30, 1834, in *The John Tipton Papers*, ed. Nellie Armstrong Robertson and Dorothy Riker, 3 vols. (Indianapolis, 1942), 3: 62.

60. "Reasons for Graduating the Price of Public Lands in Florida," *American State Papers: Public Lands*, 5: 356; *Florida Herald and Southern Democrat* (St. Augustine, FL), March 7, 1825.

61. House Committee on Public Lands, *Report on a resolution directing an inquiry into the expediency of reducing and graduating the price of public lands, and of making donations to actual settlers*, H.R. Rep. 125, 20th Cong., 1st sess. (serial no. 177), 3–4.

62. "To the Editor," *Arkansas Weekly Gazette* (Little Rock), February 28, 1826; "Squatters on Indian Lands," *Weekly Visitor* (Kennebunk, ME), September 16, 1820; House Committee on Public Lands, *Report upon the subject of granting a right of preemption to settlers on the public lands*, H.R. Rep. 115, 18th Cong., 1st sess. (serial no. 106), 2; and *Report relating to settlers on the public lands*, H.R. Rep. 40, 19th Cong., 1st sess. (serial no. 141), 1–2.

63. "Settlers on the Choctaw Lands in Arkansas," *American State Papers: Public Lands*, 4: 958–59; House Committee on Public Lands, *Report relating to settlers on the public lands*, H.R. Rep. 40, 19th Cong., 1st sess. (serial no. 141), 2; and *Report on the resolution of December 21st, 1825, instructing them "to inquire into the expediency of appropriating a portion of the net annual proceeds of the sales and entries of the public lands exclusively for the support of Common Schools, and of appropriating the same among the several States, in proportion to their representation in the House of Representatives*, H.R. Rep. 88, 19th Cong., 1st sess. (serial no. 141), 7–8.

64. *National Intelligencer* (Washington, DC), reprinted in the *Arkansas Weekly Gazette* (Little Rock), September 20, 1825; U.S. Senate, *Memorial of Sundry Inhabitants of Michigan, Remonstrating against the Passage of the Bill to Graduate the Price of Public Lands, Make Donations thereof to Actual Settlers, and to Cede the Refuse to the States in which they Lie*, S. Doc. 163, 20th Cong., 1st sess. (serial no. 166), 3.

65. "The New Politicians," *Niles' Weekly Register* (Baltimore, MD), January 17, 1829.

Chapter 4 · *"A World within Itself"*

1. Madison to Henry Clay, April [24], 1824, in *The Writings of James Madison*, ed. Gaillard Hunt, 9 vols. (New York, 1900–1910), 9: 183–87, esp. 186.

2. On the American System, see Maurice G. Baxter, *Henry Clay and the American System*

(Lexington, KY, 1995); Merrill D. Peterson, *The Great Triumvirate: Webster, Clay, and Calhoun* (New York, 1987); and, as a part of Whig ideology, Daniel Walker Howe, *The Political Culture of the American Whigs* (Chicago, 1979).

3. Clay to William O. Niles, February 25, 1845, in *The Papers of Henry Clay*, ed. James F. Hopkins et al., 10 vols. (Lexington, KY, 1959–1992), 10: 202–3. (Hereafter abbreviated *PHC*.)

4. Douglas C. North, *The Economic Growth of the United States, 1790–1860* (New York, 1961), 135–55. On the political impact in Ohio, see Andrew R. L. Cayton, *The Frontier Republic: Ideology and Politics in the Ohio Country, 1780–1825* (Kent, OH, 1986), 129–50.

5. Daniel Feller, *The Public Lands in Jacksonian Politics* (Madison, WI, 1984), 78–79, 82–85, 89–90, 96–102, 147–48. On Clay's regional following, Donald J. Ratcliffe, "The Role of Voters and Issues in Party Formation: Ohio, 1824," *Journal of American History* 49 (Mar. 1973), 847–70; and Cayton, *Frontier Republic*, 130–36.

6. "Population--Power--Wealth," *Niles' Weekly Register* (Baltimore, MD), April 14, 1827, 114.

7. Mathew Carey, *Autobiographical sketches: in a series of letters, addressed to a friend . . .* (Philadelphia, 1829), ix; Carey, *The new olive branch; or, An attempt to establish an identity of interest between agriculture, manufactures, and commerce . . .* (Philadelphia, 1820), 183. On manufacturing societies and Carey's role in them, see Lawrence A. Peskin, *Manufacturing Revolution: The Intellectual Origins of Early American Industry* (Baltimore, 2003), 93–118.

8. Mathew Carey, *Addresses of the Philadelphia Society for the Promotion of National Industry* (Philadelphia, 1820), 58–59, 62. Also see, Carey, *Three letters on the present calamitous state of affairs: addressed to J. M. Garnett, Esq., president of the Fredericksburg Agricultural Society* (Philadelphia, 1820), 14–15. On the political economy of the "Old Republicans," see Norman K. Risjord, *The Old Republicans: Southern Conservatism in the Age of Jefferson* (New York, 1965); Charles G. Sellers, *The Market Revolution: Jacksonian America, 1815–1846* (New York, 1991), 113–22; and Feller, *Public Lands in Jacksonian Politics*, 34, 74. For John Taylor's influence, see Paul K. Conkin, *Prophets of Prosperity: America's First Political Economists* (Bloomington, IN, 1980), 43–76; and Robert E. Shalhope, *John Taylor of Caroline, Pastoral Republican* (Columbia, SC, 1980).

9. Carey, *Three letters*, 19–20, 32; Carey, *Addresses*, 195.

10. Mathew Carey, *Essays on political economy; or, The most certain means of promoting the wealth, power, resources, and happiness of nations: applied particularly to the United States* (Philadelphia, 1822), 376, 382. Also see "Reflections on the Subject of Emigration from Europe . . . ," in Mathew Carey, *Miscellaneous essays . . .* (Philadelphia, 1830), 120; and Carey, *Examination of A tract on the alteration of the tariff, written by Thomas Cooper* (Philadelphia, 1824), 62. On the danger of sparse population in frontier areas, see "Reflections on the Subject of Emigration from Europe, with a view to Settlement in the United States: containing Brief Sketches of the Moral and Political Character of this Country," in Carey, *Miscellaneous essays . . .* , 143. Benton argued that graduation would actually *encourage* compact settlement, thus helping the growth of local tax bases, the chance for internal improvements, and the possibility of cooperative agricultural efforts. See Mary E. Young, "Congress Looks West: Liberal Ideology and Public Land Policy in the Nineteenth Century," in *The Frontier in American Development: Essays in Honor of Paul Wallace Gates*, ed. David M. Ellis (Ithaca, NY, 1969), 74–112, esp. 78–79.

11. Carey, *The new olive branch*, 179; Carey, *Addresses*, vii–viii.

12. Carey, *Addresses*, 65; Carey, *Three letters*, 37.

13. Carey, *Addresses*, 65–66. On the mistaken advice to "go back" to the western wilds as a panacea for economic distress, see Mathew Carey, *Address delivered before the Philadelphia*

Society for Promoting Agriculture at its meeting on the twentieth of July, 1824 (Philadelphia, 1827), 29–30.

14. Carey, *Addresses*, 66; Carey, *The new olive branch*, 181.

15. On Carey's admiration of Niles, see Carey, *Autobiographical sketches*, xi. For the Niles-Clay relationship, see in *PHC*: Niles to Clay, July 1, 1822, 3: 246–47; Niles to Clay, March 28, 1827, and Clay to Niles, November 5, 1827, 6: 373–74, 1231–32; Niles to Clay, April 2 (two letters) and 22, and November 22, 1828, and Clay to Niles, November 25, 1828, 7: 210–11, 235–36, 544–45, 548–49; Clay to Niles, October 4, 1829, Niles to Clay, September 17 and October 28, 1830, Clay to Niles, November 8, 1830, and June 3, 1831, Niles to Clay, December 8, 1831, and January 17, February 3 and 28, and July 4, 1832, Clay to Niles, July 8, 1832, Niles to Clay, mid-December, 1832, and December 9, 1833, 8: 108–10, 266–67, 281–82, 292–93, 355–56, 429, 446–47, 456, 469, 549, 551, 604–5, 672; Clay to William O. Niles, February 25, 1845, Clay to Henry Clay Niles, December 13, 1847, 10: 202–3, 389.

16. See "Address of the Committee on behalf of the General Convention of Agriculturists and Manufacturers, and others friendly to the Encouragement of Domestic Industry of the United States, assembled at Harrisburg, 30th July, 1827," *Niles' Weekly Register* (Baltimore, MD), October 13, 1827; Niles to Henry Clay, July 1, 1822, *PHC*, 3: 246; "New Year's desultory Remarks," *Niles' Weekly Register* (Baltimore, MD), January 1, 1820, 290; "Population in the United States," ibid., September 14, 1816, 35.

17. "Political Economies," *Niles' Weekly Register* (Baltimore, MD), November 13, 1819, 162; "Political Economy--No. IV," ibid., July 19, 1817, 321.

18. "Statesmen and Politicians, Political Economy--No. I," ibid., June 7, 1817, 226; "March of the United States," ibid., November 27, 1819, 195.

19. North, *Economic Growth*, 187, 179; Feller, *Public Lands in Jacksonian Politics*, 22; *Niles' Weekly Register* (Baltimore, MD), January 24, 1824, 325; ibid., October 29, 1825, 132.

20. "American Manufactures and the Tariff," *Niles' Weekly Register* (Baltimore, MD), September 24, 1825, 50.

21. "A Compliment of the Season," *Niles' Weekly Register* (Baltimore, MD), January 6, 1827, 289.

22. *Annals of Congress*, House, 17th Cong., 2nd sess. (1822–1823), 750, 940. See also James L. Huston, "Virtue Besieged: Virtue, Equality, and the General Welfare in the Tariff Debates of the 1820s," *Journal of the Early Republic* 14 (Winter 1994), 523–47; and Richard C. Edwards, "Economic Sophistication in Nineteenth-Century Congressional Tariff Debates," *Journal of Economic History* 30 (Dec. 1970), 802–38.

23. "Speech on Tariff," March 30–31, 1824, *PHC*, 3: 716. "Speech on Domestic Manufactures," March 26, 1810, *PHC*, 1: 459–60. On the wide influence of Hamilton's "Report on Manufactures," see Conkin, *Prophets of Prosperity*, 172–77. For the Carey-Clay relationship, see in *PHC*: Clay to Carey, May 2, 1824, Josiah S. Johnston to Clay, August 19 and September 4 and 11, 1824, 3: 745–46, 814–16, 829, 836–37; Clay to Carey, June 6, 1825, 4: 416–17; Carey to Clay, December 1, 1826, 5: 971–72; Carey to Clay, May 15, 1827, and Clay to Carey, May 19, 1827, 6: 563, 568; Carey to Clay, February 10 and 20, 1829, 7: 616, 624; Carey to Clay, October 9, 1830, Clay to Carey, October 25, 1830, and Carey to Clay, March 31, 1832, 8: 279, 280–81, 484; Clay to Carey, December 22, 1838, 9: 259; and Clay to William O. Niles, February 25, 1845, 10: 202–3.

24. On Clay's early career and marriage, see Robert V. Remini, *Henry Clay: Statesman for the Union* (New York, 1992), 15–31; and Thomas Brown, *Politics and Statesmanship: Essays on the American Whig Party* (New York, 1985), 117–53, esp. 120–21.

25. Clay to Cheves, April 19, 1819, *PHC*, 2: 687–88.

26. On Kentucky politics in Clay's era, see Lynn L. Marshall, "The Genesis of Grass-

Roots Democracy in Kentucky," *Mid-America* 47 (1965); and Richard P. McCormick, *The Second American Party System: Party Formation in the Jacksonian Era* (Chapel Hill, NC, 1966), 209–22.

27. Remini, *Henry Clay*, 205–6. On western urban development, see Richard Wade, *The Urban Frontier: Pioneer Life in Early Pittsburgh, Cincinnati, Lexington, Louisville, and St. Louis* (Chicago, 1959), 161–202.

28. "Speech on the Tariff," April 26, 1820, *PHC*, 2: 829–30.

29. *Register of Debates*, House, 20th Cong., 1st sess. (1827–1828), 2831–32. For Adams's message, see *Messages and Papers of the Presidents, 1789–1897*, 10 vols., comp. James D. Richardson (Washington, DC, 1896), 2: 378–92. On Clay's limited role in the debate on the land bill in 1820, see *Annals of Congress*, House, 16th Cong., 1st sess. (1819–1820), 1889, 1901. His vote for the relief bill on February 28, 1821 is recorded in ibid., 16th Cong., House, 2nd sess. (1820–1821), 1249. See also Feller, *Public Lands in Jacksonian Politics*, 27, 87.

30. "Speech on the Tariff," April 26, 1820, *PHC*, 2: 830.

31. Clay to Francis T. Brooke, August 28, 1823, *PHC*, 3: 479.

32. "Speech on the Tariff," March 30–31, 1824, *PHC*, 3: 695.

33. "Speech on the Tariff," April 26, 1820, *PHC*, 2: 833–34; Clay to John B. Dillon, July 28, 1838, *PHC*, 9: 214; *Congressional Globe*, 25th Cong., 2nd sess., App., 129, 132–34, 15–17.

34. "Speech on the Tariff," April 26, 1820, *PHC*, 2: 836; see Clay to Hezekiah Niles, October 4, 1829, *PHC*, 8: 108–10, esp. 109; Ratcliffe, "Role of Voters and Issues in Party Formation," 853, 867.

35. See Peter Passell and Maria Schmundt, "Pre–Civil War Land Policy and the Growth of Manufacturing," *Explorations in Economic History* 9 (Jan. 1971), 35–48.

36. *Annals of Congress*, House, 16th Cong., 1st sess., 1868.

37. *The Selected Writings of John and John Quincy Adams*, ed. Adrienne Koch and William Peden (New York, 1946), 389.

38. Richardson, *Messages and Papers of the Presidents*, 1: 567; *Annals of Congress*, Senate, 14th Cong., 1st sess. (1815–1816), 108.

39. "Speech on Internal Improvements," March 13, 1818, *PHC*, 2: 486–87.

40. Breckinridge to Clay, March 19, 1806, *PHC*, 1: 228. See also *PHC*, 2: 458–9; and *Annals of Congress*, House, 9th Cong., 1st sess. (1805–1806), 191, 206, 228, 234, 236, 241, 248.

41. *Annals of Congress*, House, 14th Cong., 2nd sess. (1816–1817), 852, 853–54, 926. See Madison's veto message in Richardson, *Messages and Papers of the Presidents*, 2: 584–85.

42. "Speech on Cumberland Road," January 17, 1825, *PHC*, 4: 22.

43. *Boston Courier* (Boston, MA), February 9, 1830; John Quincy Adams, *Memoirs of John Quincy Adams, Comprising Portions of his Diary from 1795 to 1848*, ed., Charles Francis Adams, 12 vols. (Philadelphia, 1874–1877), 7: 187. On New England opposition to graduation, see Feller, *Public Lands in Jacksonian Politics*, 96, 133, 182.

44. Rush to Ingersoll, December 3, 1827, in *The Letters and Papers of Richard Rush*, microfilm edition, ed. Anthony M. Brescia (Wilmington, DE, 1980), series 1, reel 15, item 8079; Rush to Mathew Carey, October 7, 1827, ibid., item 7935. See Thaddeus Russell, "Charles Jared Ingersoll," in *American National Biography*, ed. John A. Garraty and Mark C. Carnes, 24 vols. (New York, 1999), 11: 647.

45. See Rush's first annual treasury report in *Register of Debates*, House, 19th Cong., 1st sess. (1825–1826), app., esp. p. 27; also Rush, *Letter from the Secretary of the Treasury, Enclosing His Annual Report on the State of the Finances of the United States*, December 22, 1825 (Washington, DC, 1825), 16–17.

46. Rush to Ingersoll, November 25, 1827, in Brescia, *Letters and Papers of Richard Rush*, series 1, reel 15, item 8053.

47. *Register of Debates*, House, 20th Cong., 1st sess., 2831–32.

48. Rush to Ingersoll, December 3, 1827, in Brescia, *Letters and Papers of Richard Rush*, series I, reel 15, item 8079; Rush to Ingersoll, December 17, 1827, ibid., item 8113; Adams, *Memoirs*, 7: 361.

49. For the Illinois Memorial of February 2, 1829, see *American State Papers: Public Lands*, 5: 624–25.

50. On Ninian Edwards's background, see Ninian Wirt Edwards, *History of Illinois from 1778 to 1833 and Life and Times of Ninian Edwards* (1870; reprinted, New York, 1975).

51. See Governor's message in *Illinois House Journal, 1828–1829*, p. 10 of the message.

52. Ibid., 11–12. See also, Emer de Vattel, *The Law of Nations: or Principles of the Law of Nature: Applied to the Conduct and Affairs of Nations and Sovereigns, translated from the French* (Dublin, 1792).

53. Governor's message, *Illinois House Journal, 1828–1829*, 11–12, 15.

54. Ibid., 16–17, 21–22. On differences between Edwards and Calhoun on this doctrine, see Raynor Wellington, *The Political and Sectional Influence of the Public Lands, 1828–1842* (Cambridge, MA, 1914), 19–20.

55. Archer and Stevenson, quoted in Edward Everett, "The Debate in the Senate of the United States," *North American Review*, 31 (Oct. 1830), 462–546, esp. 467–68; Paul W. Gates, *History of Public Land Law Development* (Washington, DC, 1968), 9; Wellington, *Political and Sectional Influence of the Public Lands*, 17. See also *American State Papers: Public Lands*, 5: 630.

56. Georgia acted on December 30, 1828, Mississippi on February 5, 1829, and Virginia on February 4, 1829.

Chapter 5 · Foot's Resolution and the "Great Debate"

1. *Indiana State Gazette* (Indianapolis), February 11, 1830. For the significance of public lands to the Webster-Hayne Debate, see Raynor Wellington, *The Political and Sectional Influence of the Public Lands, 1828–1842* (Cambridge, MA, 1914), chapter 2; and Daniel Feller, *The Public Lands in Jacksonian Politics* (Madison, WI, 1984), chapter 5. Many modern writers, Feller excepted, have neglected the land policy element. On the debate in general, see Merrill D. Peterson, *The Great Triumvirate: Webster, Clay, and Calhoun* (New York, 1987), 170–83. An interesting account of the debate and its ramifications is Edward Everett, "The Debate in the Senate of the United States," *North American Review* 31 (October 1830), 462–546.

2. See Paul W. Gates, *History of Public Land Law Development* (Washington, DC, 1968), 9–10.

3. For Webster's support for Foot on the graduation issue, see *Register of Debates*, Senate, 21st Cong., 1st sess. (1829–1830), 424. On the perception of Benton's strategy, see Henry Clay to George Watterson, May 8, 1830, in *The Papers of Henry Clay*, ed. James F. Hopkins et al., 10 vols. (Lexington, KY, 1959–1992), 8: 203–4 (hereafter abbreviated as *PHC*). According to Merrill Peterson, Foot's resolution "was not expected to provoke debate," and Webster, though he took no part in framing the resolution, "much preferred Foot's approach to the problem of a surplus of surveyed land" (Peterson, *The Great Triumvirate*, 170, 172). I disagree on both counts.

4. *Boston Courier* (Boston, MA), December 24, 1829. Foot's exact motives have always eluded historians. Many writers have seen him simply as an unwitting pawn of others, as did some at the time (see *Niles' Weekly Register* [Baltimore, MD], February 20, 1830). Paul Gates dismissed Foot as a "confused" Yankee from Connecticut (*History of Public Land Law*, 10). Roy Robbins referred to him only as a senator "who had consistently opposed western influences" (*Our Landed Heritage: The Public Domain, 1776–1970*, 2nd ed. [Lincoln, NE, 1976], 45).

On thin evidence, Raynor Wellington contended that Foot represented eastern manufacturing interests (*Political and Sectional Influence of the Public Lands*, 26–28).

5. On National Republican expectations for the election of 1828, see Daniel Webster to Jeremiah Mason, April 10, 1827, in *The Papers of Daniel Webster, Correspondence, 1782–1852*, ed. Charles M. Wiltse et al., 7 vols. (Hanover, NH, 1974–1986), 2: 184–85 (hereafter abbreviated *PDW,C*); Webster to Samuel Bell, July 29, 1828, *PDW,C*, 2: 356–57; Webster to Nathaniel F. Williams, September 25, 1828, *PDW,C*, 2: 364–65; Henry Clay to Daniel Webster, April 20, and June 7, 1827, *PHC*, 6: 467, 653–54.

6. See Stephanie Kermes, *Creating an American Identity: New England, 1789–1825* (New York, 2008); and Robert Brooke Zevin, *The Growth of Manufacturing in Early Nineteenth Century New England* (New York, 1975).

7. *Niles' Weekly Register* (Baltimore, MD), July 12, 1828.

8. "A Proclamation by Samuel A. Foot, Governor of Connecticut," *Connecticut Courant* (Hartford), October 13, 1834; "Slavery," ibid., March 14, 1820; Herbert Thomas, *Yale Men and Landmarks in Old Connecticut, 1701–1815* (New Haven, 1967), 74. See also, John R. Van Atta, "Samuel Augustus Foot," in *American National Biography*, ed. John A. Garraty and Mark C. Carnes, 24 vols. (New York, 1999), 8: 186–88.

9. *Annals of Congress*, House, 16th Cong., 1st sess. (1819–1820), 1171, 1607; ibid., 2nd sess. (1820–1821), 1211–14. See also, "Motions and Speech on the Admission of Missouri," *PHC*, 3: 18–19; and "Remarks and Motion on Missouri Question," *PHC*, 3: 20.

10. *Annals of Congress*, House, 18th Cong., 1st sess. (1823–1824), 1464–67, 1493–94, 2296–2310 (esp. 2297).

11. Foot to Henry Clay, October 2, 1826, *PHC*, 5: 743–44. For Foot's record in the Senate, see especially the following entries in the *Register of Debates*: Senate, 20th Cong., 1st sess. (1827–1828), 126, 747–48, 785; 2nd sess. (1828–1829), 41; 21st Cong., 1st sess. (1829–1830), 4–5, 7, 16, 30, 31, 438–47 (on restricting public land sales); 342 (internal improvements); 423–24 (opposition to Benton's graduation scheme); 2nd sess. (1830–1831), 334 (internal improvements); 22nd Cong., 1st sess. (1831–1832), 620–21, 668, 1191, 1290–91 (tariff); 979, 1035, 1036 (Bank of the United States); 2nd sess. (1832–1833), 480, 708, 717, 718 (tariff). To further the parallel between Foot's outlook and that of John Quincy Adams, Foot in 1834 would extol the "happy state of society" in Connecticut, where "labor continues to be respected, and secures a just reward; and honest industry rather than wealth, is a passport to public favor, and a qualification for the highest honors" in eyes of the voters. There could be little danger to freedom, he declared, "so long as we continue to encourage the moral culture and improvement of the mind." See Foot's "Governor's Message," *Connecticut Courant* (Hartford), May 12, 1834.

12. For congressional membership and committee assignments during much of the middle period, see Perry M. Goldman and James Sterling Young, *The United States Congressional Directories, 1789–1840* (New York, 1973). Foot said on February 6, 1828, "[N]othing is wanted for the commerce of this country but a free and perfect reciprocity of intercourse and trade." This would not be the language of a man under manipulation by manufacturing interests. See *Register of Debates*, Senate, 20th Cong., 1st sess., 244. For Foot's altercation with Benton on the Tariff of 1828, see *Register of Debates*, Senate, 20th Cong., 1st sess., 747–48.

13. *Register of Debates*, Senate, 21st Cong., 1st sess., 4.

14. Everett, "Debate in the Senate," 465–66; "The Lofty and Surpassing Elevation of Our Commonwealth," *Pittsfield Sun* (Pittsfield, MA), April 1, 1830.

15. *Register of Debates*, Senate, 21st Cong., 1st sess., 5. See J. Chris Arndt, "John Holmes," in *American National Biography*, 11: 81–82.

16. *Register of Debates*, Senate, 21st Cong., 1st sess., 4–6.

17. "Letter from Washington," from the *New York Daily Advertiser* (New York, NY), reprinted in *Connecticut Courant* (Hartford), January 12, 1830. For 1820s New England votes on West-related issues, see Feller, *Public Lands in Jacksonian Politics*, 61, 67, 84–85, 97, 99, 100.

18. Webster, "Second Reply to Hayne" (reported version), in *The Papers of Daniel Webster, Speeches and Formal Writings, 1800–1852*, ed. Charles M. Wiltse, 2 vols., (Hanover, NH, 1986, 1988) , 1: 361–62 (hereafter abbreviated as *PDW,SFW*); *Connecticut Courant* (Hartford), August 10, 1819. On vote to repeal the credit system, see Feller, *Public Lands in Jacksonian Politics*, 28.

19. Governor's Message, *The Watch-Tower* (Cooperstown, NY), January, 8, 1827; "Governor's Message," *Connecticut Courant* (Hartford, CT), May 13, 1828.

20. U.S. Department of Commerce, Bureau of the Census, *Historical Statistics of the United States, Colonial Times to 1970*, 2 vols. (Washington, DC, 1975), 1: 25, 27–31, 33–35.

21. Webster to Letitia Breckenridge Porter, November 19, 1829, *PDW,C* 2: 434–35, esp. 435; "Our Western States," *The Farmer's Cabinet* (Amherst, NH), January 17, 1829.

22. Daniel Walker Howe, "Edward Everett," in *American National Biography*, 7: 629–30.

23. "From the *Dayton Gazette* [Dayton, OH], Dinner to Mr. Everett," *Salem Gazette* (Salem, MA), July 21, 1829.

24. "Dinner to Mr. Everett, Nashville, June 5," *Richmond Enquirer* (Richmond, VA), June 30, 1829.

25. "Advancement of the West," *Connecticut Courant* (Hartford, CT), March 2, 1830.

26. http://www.benningtonmuseum.org/townscape-of-bennington.html; http://www.worcesterart.org/Collection/Early_American/Artists/earl_r/Denny_Hill/discussion.html; http://www.historycooperative.org/journals/cp/vol-01/no-03/lessons/ (accessed, March 19, 2012). On Ralph Earl, see Elizabeth Kornhauser, *Ralph Earl: The Face of the Young Republic* (New Haven, CT, 1991).

27. Songho Ha, *The Rise and Fall of the American System: Nationalism and the Development of the American Economy, 1790–1837* (London, 2009), 92.

28. Donald Cole, *Jacksonian Democracy in New Hampshire* (Cambridge, MA, 1970), chapters 3–4.

29. *New York Commercial [Advertiser]* (New York, NY), quoted in *Boston Courier* (Boston, MA), February 3, 1830; on the appeal of Benton's graduation plan in Indiana, see Daniel Webster to Samuel Bell, July 29, 1828, *PDW,C*, 2: 356–57; Adams, *Memoirs*, 8: 190.

30. Thomas Hart Benton, *Thirty Years' View; or, A History of the Working of the American Government for Thirty Years, from 1820 to 1850*, 2 vols. (New York, 1858), 1: 130–31.

31. Ibid., 131. Paul Gates apparently sided with Benton on all of these points. See Gates, *History of Public Lands Law*, 10.

32. Benton, *Thirty Years' View*, 1: 131.

33. Michael O'Brien, *Conjectures of Order: Intellectual Life and the American South, 1810–1860*, 2 vols. (Chapel Hill, NC, 2004), 1: 46, 531–33; April Folden, "Robert Y. Hayne," in *American National Biography*, 10: 410–11.

34. U.S. Department of Commerce, Bureau of the Census, *Historical Statistics of the United States*, 1: 25–27, 31, 33–35.

35. On South Carolina's exporting economy, see William W. Freehling, *Prelude to Civil War: The Nullification Controversy in South Carolina, 1816–1836* (New York, 1965), chapter 2. On Cooper and Turnbull, see O'Brien, *Conjectures of Order*, 2: 822–26, 896–906. Also, Allen Kaufman, *Capitalism, Slavery, and Republican Values: American Political Economists, 1819–1848* (Austin, TX, 1982), 121–22, 124, 125, 126, 130, 170–71.

36. Kaufman, *Capitalism, Slavery, and Republican Values*, 123–24.

37. *Register of Debates*, Senate, 21st Cong., 1st sess., 33.

38. Ibid., 32.

39. Ibid., 33–34. Hayne later denied that he had meant "to impute to the East hostility towards the West" and claimed that he had "implied none." Further straining credulity, he also denied that he had in mind "the accursed Tariff." "I did not even impute [by name] the policy of Mr. Rush of New England [Pennsylvania]," he wrote. "In alluding to that policy, I noticed its source, and spoke of it as I thought it deserved." See Robert Y. Hayne, *Defense of the South!! General Hayne, in Reply to Mr. Webster, of Massachusetts* (Charleston, 1830), 3.

40. *Register of Debates*, Senate, 21st Cong., 1st sess., 34.

41. [Argument for Acquisition of the Floridas], *PDW,C*, 1: 29–30; Webster to Isaac P. Davis, February 28, 1814, *PDW,C*, 1: 165–67, esp. 166.

42. "Splendid Tribute of Respect," *Connecticut Courant* (Hartford, CT), June 17, 1828.

43. Peter J. Parish, "Daniel Webster, New England, and the West," *Journal of American History* 54 (December 1967), 524–49, esp. 540–43.

44. John Test to Webster, March 29, 1827, *PDW,C*, 2: 181–82, esp. 181; Webster to John C. Wright, April 30, 1827, *PDW,C*, 2: 195–97, esp. 195; Wright to Webster, May 24, 1827, *PDW,C*, 2: 208–10, esp. 210; Samuel Atkinson to Webster, March 5, 1830, *PDW,C*, 3: 24.

45. Webster to Jeremiah Mason, February 27, 1830, *PDW,C*, 3: 18–19. Charles M. Wiltse has argued that Webster began preparing a major statement from the moment he finished reading Calhoun's 1828 pamphlet. See *PDW,C*, 3: 15–16.

46. For discussion of parallels between Webster and Hayne, see William R. Taylor, *Cavalier and Yankee: The Old South and American National Character* (New York, 1957), 110–11.

47. On Webster's role in the "Great Debate," see especially Peterson, *The Great Triumvirate*, 170–83.

48. "First Speech on Foot's Resolution," in *The Works of Daniel Webster: Biographical Memoir of the Life of Daniel Webster*, ed. Edward Everett, 6 vols. (Boston, 1853), 3: 261, 262–63.

49. Ibid., 252–53.

50. "First Speech on Foot's Resolution," ibid., 255.

51. Ibid., 255–56.

52. "Second Reply to Hayne," editorial note, *PDW,SFW*, 1: 286.

53. "First Speech on Foot's Resolution," in Everett, *Works of Daniel Webster*, 3: 257–59.

54. See *Register of Debates*, Senate, 21st Cong. 1st sess., 438–47. Foot's speech was reprinted in installments in the *Columbian Register* (New Haven, CT), June 12 and June 19, 1830. Also on Foot, see the *Norwich Courier* (Norwich, CT), July 14, 1830.

55. "Speech of Mr. Foot, of Connecticut," *Columbian Register* (New Haven, CT), June 19, 1830.

56. Everett, "Debate in the Senate," 465; Jeremiah Mason to Webster, March 8, 1830, *PDW,C*, 3: 27–28, esp. 27; Charles Tait to Webster, March 24, 1830, *PDW,C*, 3: 43; Webster to George Hay, March 12, 1830, *PDW,C*, 3: 30–31, esp. 31.

57. Everett, "Debate in the Senate," 466.

58. Duff Green to Edwards, January 19, 1831, in *The Edwards Papers: Being a Portion of the Collection of the Letters, Papers, and Manuscripts of Ninian Edwards*, ed. E. B. Washburne (Chicago, 1884), 568.

59. Green to Edwards, January 14, 1832, ibid., 578; *Niles' Weekly Register* (Baltimore, MD), November 10, 1832.

60. *Columbian Register* (New Haven, CT), February 27, 1830; Webster to Samuel P. Lyman, August, 10, 1833, *PDW,C*, 3: 265–66, esp. 265; Webster to Albert Haller Tracy, August 10, 1833, *PDW,C*, 3: 266–67, esp. 266. See also, Webster to Ezekiel Forman Chambers, August 6, 1833, *PDW,C*, 3: 260–61.

61. Sevier, quoted in the *Arkansas Weekly Gazette* (Little Rock, AR), March 16, 1830.

62. Feller, *Public Lands in Jacksonian Politics*, 125–36, esp. 130; Gates, *History of Public Land Law*, 225.

Chapter 6 · Whose West?—Alternative Visions

1. Harriet Martineau, *Retrospect of Western Travel*, 2 vols. (London, 1838), 2: 39.

2. Ibid., 35–56, esp. 39–40; David Henshaw, *Letters on the Internal Improvements and Commerce of the West* (Boston 1839), 12; Frederick Hall, *Letters from the East and from the West* (Washington, DC, 1840), 110–11.

3. Joan D. Hedrick, *Harriet Beecher Stowe: A Life* (New York, 1994), 67, 71–72.

4. Martineau, *Retrospect of Western Travel*, 2: 40–44.

5. See Charles C. Bolton, *Poor Whites of the Antebellum South: Tenants and Laborers in Central North Carolina and Northeast Mississippi* (Durham, NC, 1994), 66–83.

6. Ibid., 74–75.

7. *Letters from a Rambler in the West*, No. V: "The East—The West—Enterprise—Agriculture," (Springfield, IL, 1837), Library Company of Philadelphia, 141; *Illinois in 1837; a Sketch Descriptive of the Country, Prominent Districts, Prairies, Rivers, Minerals, Animals, Agricultural Productions, Public Lands, Plans of Internal Improvement, Manufactures, etc. of the State of Illinois* (Philadelphia, 1837), Library Company of Philadelphia, 134–35, 63–64. See also, J. M. Peck, *A New Guide for Emigrants to the West, Containing Sketches of Michigan, Ohio, Indiana, Illinois, Missouri, Arkansas, with the Territory of Wisconsin and the Adjacent Parts* (Boston, 1837).

8. Henry I. Abel, "Traveler's and Emigrant's Guide to Wisconsin and Iowa," broadside, Philadelphia, 1838, at Library Company of Philadelphia; Robert Baird, *View of the Valley of the Mississippi; or, The Emigrant's and Traveler's Guide to the West* (Philadelphia, 1832), 214–15.

9. James Hall, *Statistics of the West, at the Close of the Year 1836* (Cincinnati, 1837), 204, 200.

10. Baird, *View of the Valley of the Mississippi*, 216.

11. James Hall, *Sketches of History, Life, and Manners in the West; Containing Accurate Descriptions of the Country and Modes of Life, in the Western States and Territories of North America* (Cincinnati, 1834), 141; Frederick Hall, *Letters from the East and from the West*, 45.

12. Lyman Beecher, *A Plea for the West* (Cincinnati, 1835), 36–37; Hedrick, *Harriet Beecher Stowe*, 82–83.

13. Lyman Beecher, "A Sermon delivered at Litchfield, on the Day of the Anniversary Thanksgiving, December 2, 1819," included in Mathew Carey, *Addresses of the Philadelphia Society for the Promotion of National Industry* (Philadelphia, 1820), 261–86, esp. 273–74.

14. Ibid., 274.

15. Ibid., 274–75.

16. David T. Kimball, "The Right Hand of Fellowship," in *A Sermon Preached at Ipswich, September 1815. At the Ordination of Rev. Daniel Smith and Cyrus Kingsbury, as Missionaries to the West* (Newburyport, MA, 1815), 23; Philander Chase, *A Plea for the West* (Philadelphia, 1826), 3–4; Daniel Feller, *The Jacksonian Promise: America, 1815–1840* (Baltimore, 1995), 95–117, esp. 100–101.

17. Lyman Beecher to Catherine Beecher, July 8, 1830, in *Autobiography, Correspondence, etc., of Lyman Beecher*, ed. Charles Beecher, 2 vols. (New York, 1865), 2: 224; Paul E. Johnson, *A Shopkeeper's Millennium: Society and Revivals in Rochester, New York, 1815–1837* (New York, 1978), 5; Feller, *The Jacksonian Promise*, 100–103.

18. "An Estimate of the Present and Future Physical, Civil, and Moral Power of the West, Including the Country Watered by the Mississippi and its Tributaries," *Quarterly Register and Journal of the American Education Society*, 1 (April 1828), 61–65.

19. Beecher, *Autobiography, Correspondence*, 224–25; "Republicanism of the Bible," from the *Christian Watchman* (Boston, MA), reprinted in the *Brattleboro Messenger* (Brattleboro, VT), February 19, 1831. On Beecher, see Vincent Harding, *A Certain Magnificence: Lyman Beecher and the Transformation of American Protestantism, 1775–1863* (New York, 1991); and Marie Caskey Morgan, "Lyman Beecher," in *American National Biography*, ed. John A. Garraty and Mark C. Carnes, 24 vols. (New York, 1999), 2: 469–71.

20. "Republicanism of the Bible"; James L. Huston, "Abolitionists, Political Economists, and Capitalism," *Journal of the Early Republic* 20 (Autumn 2000), 487–521, esp. 518–20.

21. Beecher, *Plea for the West*, 35–37, 52, 51.

22. Hedrick, *Harriet Beecher Stowe*, 67–75.

23. Ibid., 69–70; Beecher, *Autobiography*, 2: 239–51, 244; Ronald G. Walters, *American Reformers, 1815–1860* (New York, 1978), 28–29.

24. Beecher, *Plea for the West*, 51–52, 54.

25. Ibid., 28–29, 24, 16.

26. Hedrick, *Harriet Beecher Stowe*, 67, 68, 83.

27. Beecher, *Autobiography*, 2: 420. The records of the Lane Theological Seminary are preserved at the Presbyterian Historical Society, Philadelphia.

28. Baird, *View of the Valley of the Mississippi*, 89. On Walker generally, see James P. Shenton, *Robert John Walker: A Politician from Jackson to Lincoln* (New York, 1961); also James A. Rawley, "Robert John Walker," in *American National Biography*, 22: 511–13.

29. Shenton, *Robert John Walker*, 3–6.

30. Ibid., 2–10, esp. 3.

31. Charles D. Lowery, "The Great Migration to the Mississippi Territory, 1798–1819," *Journal of Mississippi History* 30 (August 1968), 173–92.

32. Christopher Clark, *Social Change in America, from the Revolution through the Civil War* (Chicago, 2006), 102, 126, 136–37.

33. Ibid., 149–51.

34. Letter to editor, *Ariel* (Natchez, MS), August 4, 1826; John J. Audubon, "Hunting the Cougar, or American Lion," *Lowell Mercury* (Lowell, MA), November 4, 1831; John J. Audubon, *Audubon and His Journals*, ed. Maria R. Audubon, 2 vols. (New York, 1897) 2: 443–49.

35. "From Audubon's Ornithological Biography," *Southern Patriot* (Charleston, SC), December 11, 1832; Audubon, *Audubon and His Journals*, 2: 443–49.

36. Audubon, *Audubon and His Journals*, 2: 443–49.

37. On Natchez during Walker's time, see D. Clayton James, *Antebellum Natchez* (Baton Rouge, LA, 1968). Also, Adam Rothman, *Slave Country: American Expansion and the Origins of the Deep South* (Cambridge, MA, 2005), 35, 47, 180, 184.

38. Robert J. Walker, "Public Dinner Given in Honor of the Chickasaw and Choctaw Treaties, at Mr. Parker's Hotel, in the City of Natchez, October 10, 1830," at Library Company of Philadelphia, 3, 5.

39. "Troubles in Alabama," *Journal of Literature and Politics* (Portsmouth, NH), November 2, 1833; "Squatters in Alabama," *American Repertory* (St. Albans, VT), April 22, 1830; *Norwich Courier* (Norwich, CT), April 28, 1830; Daniel K. Richter, *Facing East from Indian Country: A Native History of Early America* (Cambridge, MA, 2001), 241–42. On Governor John Gayle, see "Alabama Governors," Alabama Department of Archives and History, www.archives.state.al.us; and *Alabama Governors: A Political History of the State*, ed. Samuel L. Webb and Margaret Armbrester (Tuscaloosa, AL, 2001).

40. Cass, quoted in "The Alabama Controversy," *Commercial Advertiser* (New York, NY), November 11, 1833. See also, November 11 and 18, and December 17, 1833.

41. Walker's October 10, 1830 remarks, quoted in *American Standard—Extra, Containing the Address of Robert J. Walker, Esq. to the People of the United States on the Subject of the Alleged Frauds of the Public Lands at Chocchuma, Mississippi* (Natchez, 1834), 20–21, 22.

42. Shenton, *Robert John Walker*, 13.

43. *Speech of Robert J. Walker, Delivered at the Union Meeting, held in the City of Natchez, January 1833* (Natchez, 1833), 7, 13, 15.

44. Shenton, *Robert John Walker*, 13–15, 16.

45. Bolton, *Poor Whites of the Antebellum South*, 73–78.

46. Franklin L. Riley, "Extinct Towns and Villages of Mississippi," in *Publications of the Mississippi Historical Society*, ed. Franklin L. Riley, 10 vols. (Oxford, MS, 1902), 5: 335–36; Walker, in *American Standard—Extra*, 21, 24–37.

47. William Haile, to the citizens of the State of Mississippi, March 20, 1828, in *Statesman and Gazette* (Natchez, MS), May 1, 1828; Bolton, *Poor Whites of the Antebellum South*, 67.

48. Shenton, *Robert John Walker*, 17–20.

49. Ibid., 19–21, 1.

50. *The Mississippian—Extra*, "Address of Robert J. Walker, of Madison County, to the People of Mississippi," Jackson, September 26, 1835, at Library Company of Philadelphia.

51. This version of Walker's remarks, made in the Senate on March 31, was reported in the *New York Commercial Advertiser* (New York, NY), April 2, 1836.

52. Espy, quoted in Charles R. Staples, *The History of Pioneer Lexington, 1779–1806* (Lexington, KY, 1939), 215.

53. Frederick Hall, *Letters from the East and from the West*, 132, 134. On land distribution in Lexington, see Stephen Aron, *How the West Was Lost: The Transformation of Kentucky from Daniel Boone to Henry Clay* (Baltimore, 1996), 139–43, esp.140.

54. Hall, *Letters from the East and from the West*, 130. For Clay's landholdings, see *Directory of the City of Lexington and County of Fayette, for 1838 & 1839* (Lexington, 1838), www.rootsweb.com/~kyfayett/fayette.htm (accessed, May 8, 2006). See also Clay to Thomas T. January, October 6, 1838, *The Papers of Henry Clay*, ed. James F. Hopkins et al., 10 vols. (Lexington, KY), 9: 238n (hereafter abbreviated *PHC*),, and for a more extensive statement of his assets, as of 1840, Supplement: 280.

55. Clay to Francis Lieber, September 15, 1834, *PHC*, 8: 747–48, esp. 747.

56. Hector P. Lewis "and Others" to Clay, June 29, 1827, *PHC*, 6: 730–31. For Clay's early belief in building a loyal, public-spirited citizenry, see "Amendment to, and Speech on, the Bill to Raise an Additional Military Force," *Annals of Congress*, House, 12th Cong., 1st sess. (1811–1812), December 31, 1811, 596–602, esp. 598; "Remarks on Payment for Wartime Property Losses." ibid., 14th Cong., 2nd sess.(1816–1817), January 6, 1817, 426–28, esp. 426; and "Motion and Speech on Recognition of the Independent Provinces on the River Plate," ibid., 15th Cong., 1st sess. (1817–1818), March 24–25, 1818, 1468–69, 1474–1500, esp. 1483–84. See also Donald J. Ratcliffe, "The Role of Voters and Issues in Party Formation: Ohio, 1824," *Journal of American History* 49 (Mar. 1973).

57. *Register of Debates*, House, 18th Cong., 2nd sess. (1824–1825), 42–43; "Distribution of the Surplus Revenue Among the Several States for Education, Internal Improvements, &c.," May 11, 1826, *American State Papers: Finance*, 5: 501–5; "Distribution of the Proceeds of the Sales of the Public Lands Among the Several States," February 25, 1829, ibid., 793–97, esp. 797; *Register of Debates*, House, 21st Cong., 1st sess. (1829–1830), 477, 485–86. The Rhode Island petition of 1826 is mentioned in Paul W. Gates, *History of Public Land Law Development* (Washington, DC, 1968), 7.

58. See Daniel Feller, *The Public Lands in Jacksonian Politics* (Madison, WI, 1984), 71–110, 119–42, esp. 133.

59. Friends of Domestic Industry, *Address of the Friends of Domestic Industry, Assembled in Convention at New York* (report), October 26, 1831 (Baltimore, 1831), 21.

60. Ibid., 34–35, 36.

61. Alexander H. Everett, "Memorial of the New York Convention; to the Congress of the United States," March 26, 1832, ibid., 132, 135, 144, 147.

62. Ibid., 150–51.

63. "Speech in the Senate," January 11, 1832, *PHC*, 8: 445. On Benton's influence, the Adams administration's damage to Clay's image, internal improvements votes, and the progress of graduation prior to 1831, see Feller, *Public Lands in Jacksonian Politics*, 71–110, 131–33. Feller proves that the South-and-West alliance was short-lived.

64. Robinson to Edwards, April 1, 1832, in *The Edwards Papers: Being a Portion of the Collection of the Letters, Papers, and Manuscripts of Ninian Edwards*, ed. E. B. Washburne (Chicago, 1884), 583. On the Edwards faction in Illinois politics, see Richard P. McCormick, *The Second American Party System: Party Formation in the Jacksonian Era* (Chapel Hill, NC, 1966), 277–87, esp. 279–81. For the progress of the cession movement, see Feller, *Public Lands in Jacksonian Politics*, 107–9, 134–35.

65. Clay to Francis T. Brooke, March 28, 1832, *PHC*, 8: 481–82.

66. Clay to Brooke, March 28, 1832, and Clay to Ewing, April 14, 1832, *PHC*, 8: 481, 492.

67. Clay benefited from the political economy literature then flooding the Committee on Manufactures, including the published output of Alexander Everett, Daniel W. Coxe, Hezekiah Niles, and others who attended the New York Protectionist Convention of October 26, 1831.

68. Senate Committee on Manufactures, *Report on reducing the price of public lands, on cession of lands to the States; and upon the general policy regarding public lands of the United States*, S. doc. 128, 22nd Cong., 1st sess. (serial no. 214), 3.

69. Ibid., 3–4. On the "forty acre law," see Malcolm Rohrbough, *The Land Office Business: The Settlement and Administration of American Public Lands, 1789–1837* (New York, 1968), 213–14.

70. Senate Committee on Manufactures, *Report on reducing the price of public lands . . . .* , 3–4. See also Clay's "Speech to the Virginia General Assembly," February 7, 1822, *PHC*, 3: 162–67.

71. Senate Committee on Manufactures, *Report on reducing the price of public lands . . .* , 5, 13. See also, Charles G. Sellers, *The Market Revolution: Jacksonian America, 1815–1846* (New York, 1992), 126–27.

72. Senate Committee on Manufactures, *Report on reducing the price of public lands . . .* , 6.

73. Ibid., 6–7.

74. See Feller, *Public Lands in Jacksonian Politics*, 148–49.

75. *Niles' Weekly Register* (Baltimore, MD), April 21, 1832, 122; Rush to Clay, April 23, 1832, mentioned in *PHC*, 8: 494; Dunnica to Clay, June 8 and September 17, 1832, *PHC*, 8: 531, 576.

76. For the political fate of the Land Bill, see Robert V. Remini, *Henry Clay: Statesman for the Union* (New York, 1992), 395, 429, 434, 436. On Jackson's reasons for the veto, see Remini, *Andrew Jackson and the Course of American Democracy, 1833–1845* (New York, 1984), 41–42, 122, 318–21; and Feller, *Public Lands in Jacksonian Politics*, 165–68.

77. Michael F. Holt, *The Rise and Fall of the American Whig Party: Jacksonian Politics and the Onset of the Civil War* (New York, 1999), 136.

78. "Speech on Tariff," March 30–31, 1824, *PHC*, 3: 718–19.

Chapter 7 · *"A Lawless Rabble"*

1. "Invitation to Squatters," *Jamestown Journal* (Jamestown, NY), April 20, 1836; *Portsmouth Journal of Literature and Politics* (Portsmouth, NH), February 11, 1837. See also, *National Gazette* (Philadelphia, PA), February 4, 1837.

2. "TROUBLE BREWING," *New York Commercial Advertiser* (New York, NY), July 7, 1837; *Public Ledger* (Philadelphia, PA), February 5, 1838. See also, *Barre Gazette* (Barre, MA) February 16, 1838; and *Farmer's Cabinet* (Amherst, NH), February 16, 1838.

3. Frederick Jackson Turner saw governmental encouragement of squatters as part of an "emphasis upon equality and democracy" that came to characterize the north central states. To Paul Gates, "preemption was a step toward freeing public land sales from the emphasis on revenue and toward achieving the West's ultimate objective of free lands," which explained why the issue prompted Clay "to a rare expression of hatred of settlers." For Roy Robbins, "it was a victory of pioneer America over the more established eastern order of society" and "the capstone in the democratization of the public land system," whereas Clay "had consistently sided with the Atlantic Coast in its condemnation of the frontier." Though detailing the "administrative nightmare" of preemption legislation, Malcolm Rohrbough paid little attention to Clay or the Whigs. See Turner, *The United States, 1830–1850: The Nation and Its Sections* (New York, 1935), 251–351, esp. 289, 290–92, 351; Gates, *History of Public Land Law Development* (Washington, DC, 1968), 246, 233; Robbins, *Our Landed Heritage: The Public Domain, 1776–1970*, 2nd ed. (Lincoln, NE, 1976), 91, 90; Rohrbough, *The Land Office Business: The Settlement and Administration of American Public Lands, 1789–1837* (New York, 1968), esp. 200–220. More recently, Daniel Walker Howe, *The Political Culture of the American Whigs* (Chicago, 1979); Daniel Feller, *The Public Lands in Jacksonian Politics* (Madison, WI, 1984); Merrill D. Peterson, *The Great Triumvirate: Webster, Clay, and Calhoun* (New York, 1987); Maurice G. Baxter, *Henry Clay and the American System* (Lexington, KY, 1995); and John L. Larson, *Internal Improvement: National Public Works and the Promise of Popular Government in the Early United States* (Chapel Hill, NC, 2001) have provided more balanced consideration of the Clay side, but none explores in detail his position on squatters' rights.

4. *Congressional Globe*, 25th Cong., 2nd sess. (1837–1838), app., 134. Clay's post-1834 speeches on preemption are rich in provocative language used to describe squatters. For other good examples, see ibid., 142–43; app., 15–17; app. 139. For a fascinating debate on what Clay had actually said in his "Lawless Rabble" speech of January 27, 1838, see ibid., 25th Cong., 3rd sess. (1838–1839), app., 55–56, 225–26.

5. See John L. Brooke, "Consent, Civil Society, and the Public Sphere in the Age of Revolution and the Early American Republic," in *Beyond the Founders: New Approaches to the Political History of the Early American Republic*, ed. Jeffrey L. Pasley, Andrew W. Robertson, and David Waldstreicher (Chapel Hill, NC, 2004), 207–50, esp. 229. I differ here from Daniel Feller, who has described preemption as little more than an evolutionary stage of an overall federal land policy that "did not change much" during the Jacksonian years—an "almost trivial" shift when compared to more sweeping revisions advocated, but never adopted, by sectional interests and political parties during the period. See Feller, *Public Lands in Jacksonian Politics*, 194–95.

6. See Adam Smith, *An Inquiry into the Nature and Causes of the Wealth of Nations*, ed. Edwin Cannan, 2 vols. (1776; repr., London, 1904), 1: 128, 357, 356.

7. Clay to William H. Crawford, May 10, 1814, in *The Papers of Henry Clay*, ed. James F. Hopkins et al., 10 vols. (Lexington, KY, 1959–1992), 1: 896–900, esp. 898 (hereafter abbreviated *PHC*); Humphrey Marshall, quoted in Paul W. Gates, *Landlords and Tenants on the Prairie Frontier* (Ithaca, NY, 1973), 14. See also Stephen Aron, "Pioneers and Profiteers: Land

Speculation and the Homestead Ethic in Frontier Kentucky," *Western Historical Quarterly* 23 (May 1992), 179–98, esp. 197; and, generally, Aron, *How the West Was Lost: The Transformation of Kentucky from Daniel Boone to Henry Clay* (Baltimore, 1996). For a later statement of Clay's discomfort with nonresident speculators, see Senate Committee on Manufactures, *Report on reducing the price of public lands, on cession of lands to the States; and upon the general policy regarding public lands of the United States*, Sen. doc. 128, 22nd Cong., 1st sess. (serial no. 214), 3–4. In the same report, Clay recalled the experience of Kentucky landowners living in fear of losing their holdings because of poorly conceived Virginia land laws. Later, in an 1836 speech, he noted the failure of preemption statutes in Kentucky and Tennessee "at an early day" to hold permanent settlers and the fraudulent means speculators had used to take advantage of such laws for their own gain (*Register of Debates*, Senate, 24th Cong., 1st sess., 1248–49). See also, Clay to John B. Dillon, July 28, 1838, *PHC*, 9: 214.

8. Speech to the Virginia General Assembly, February 7, 1822, *PHC*, 3: 161–70, esp. 163–64. On the occupying claimant laws, see Gates, *Landlords and Tenants*, 25–28.

9. Clay to Benjamin Watkins Leigh, February 4, 1823, *PHC*, supplement: 130–32, quote on 131; Gates, *Landlords and Tenants*, 27. On Kentucky's loss of population, see Thomas L. Purvis, "The Ethnic Descent of Kentucky's Early Population, 1790–1820," *Register of the Kentucky Historical Society* 80 (1982), 253–66.

10. For Clay's support of relief for purchasers of public lands, see *Annals of Congress*, House, 16th Cong., 2nd sess. (1820–1821), 1221, 1222. On the belief that Clay had influence with President Adams on land questions, see Finis Ewing to Clay, August 6, 1825, *PHC*, 4: 567–69. For the public lands part of Adams's annual message of December 4, 1827, see *A Compilation of the Messages and Papers of the Presidents, 1789–1897*, comp. James D. Richardson, 10 vols. (Washington, DC, 1896), 2: 390–91. Also see editorial note in *PHC*, 3: 47.

11. On the "forty-acre law," see Rohrbough, *Land Office Business*, 213–14. For Clay's reaction, see Senate Committee on Manufactures, *Report on reducing the price of public lands . . . ,* 3–4. "For fifty dollars," Clay told the Senate on June 20, 1832, "any poor man may purchase forty acres of first rate land; and for less than the wages of one year's labor, he may buy eighty acres" (*Register of Debates*, Senate, 22nd Cong., 1st sess. (1831–1832), 1101–2). He made a similar statement in April 1838: the rate of $1.25 per acre was "so low, so moderate, often so far below the actual value of the land, that every industrious man, however poor, may acquire a permanent home" (*Congressional Globe*, 25th Cong. 2nd sess., Appendix, 563–64).

12. Dwight, quoted in Robert W. McCluggage, "The Pioneer Squatter," *Illinois Historical Journal* 82 (Spring 1989), 47–54, esp., 48–49. See also "Conventions for Adopting the Federal Constitution," *North American Review* 25 (Oct. 1827), 249–78, esp. 273; and "Rain: A Colloquial Lecture," *New-England Magazine* 9 (Oct. 1835), 247–52, esp. 248.

13. "Missouri Hunters," *Brattleboro Messenger* (Brattleboro, NH), July 23, 1831; Chapman to John Tipton, March 4, 1834, in *The John Tipton Papers*, ed. Nellie Armstrong Robertson and Dorothy Riker, 3 vols. (Indianapolis, 1942), 3: 32–33; U.S. Congress, Senate, *Petition of Thomas Osborn, and 270 others, praying Congress not to pass a preemption law, or reduce the price of the public lands*, S. doc. 201, 25th Cong., 2nd sess. (serial no. 316), 1–2.

14. On preemption legislation before 1830, see Feller, *Public Lands in Jacksonian Politics*, 24, 126–29. Clay viewed the direction preemption had taken by 1841 as yet another "wild experiment" of the Jacksonian party—"a thorough, radical, entire change," as described in his Senate speech of January 6, 1841 (see *Cong. Globe*, 26th Cong., 2nd sess. (1840–1841), app., 28–30, 32). See also Clay's Senate speech of February 9, 1837, *Register of Debates*, Senate, 24th Cong., 2nd sess. (1836–1837), 741–42, 759–60, 774–77; Clay to Harrison G. Otis, November 14, 1838, *PHC*, 9: 247–49; and Clay to John P. Kennedy, May 16, 1839, *PHC*, 9: 314–15.

15. For Clay's explanation of his 1834 vote, see "Comment in Senate," January 30, 1838,

PHC, 9: 138. On the Preemption Act of 1830 and the legislative history of preemption in the 1830s, see Feller, *Public Lands in Jacksonian Politics*, 129–31, 175, 185–86; also, Gates, *History of Public Land Law*, 219–48.

16. On the distribution plan, see Clay's speech in the Senate, *Register of Debates*, Senate, 22nd Cong., 1st sess., 1096–1118 (esp. 1108). Early-twentieth-century historians perpetuated an old misrepresentation of Clay's land policy that I wish to correct. Raynor Wellington, in *The Political and Sectional Influence of the Public Lands, 1828–1842* (Cambridge, MA, 1914), advanced the old "revenue" versus "settlement" dichotomy, with Clay strictly on the "revenue" side. Arthur M. Schlesinger, Jr., in *The Age of Jackson* (New York, 1945), credited the Democrats for "the initiative toward actual settlement" (347). Robbins, in *Our Landed Heritage*, associated Clay with "the rising strength of Hamiltonian forces" (36–37).

17. For the political economy of distribution, as understood by both Clay and his supporters, see *Register of Debates*, Senate, 22nd Cong., 1st sess., 1096–1118; Willis Hall to Clay, November 20, 1839, *PHC*, 9: 355–57; Isaac Montgomery to Clay, December 29, 1840, *PHC*, 9: 469–70; "Speech in Senate," January 28 and 29, 1841, *PHC*, 9: 486–94. For Clay's lamentations on what might have been were it not for Jackson's veto of the 1832 land bill, see his Senate speeches of December 29, 1835, *Register of Debates*, Senate, 24th Cong., 1st sess., 48–52, and September 25, 1837, ibid., 25th Cong., 1st sess., 251–69; Clay to William Turner and J. Turner Dodge, February 9, 1839, *PHC*, 9: 284; "Speech in Memphis," February 25, 1843, *PHC*, 9: 801–83.

18. U.S. Congress, Senate, *Memorial of the Legislature of Illinois, to grant pre-emption rights to settlers on public lands*, S. doc. 27, 22nd Cong., 2nd sess. (serial no. 230), 1–2.; U.S. Congress, Senate, *Memorial of the Legislature of Alabama for reduction of the price of public lands*, S. doc. 69, 22nd Cong., 2nd sess. (serial no. 230), 1; U.S. Congress, House, *Missouri legislature on the disposal of proceeds of public lands*, H. doc. 145, 22nd Cong., 2nd sess. (serial no. 235), 2; "Application of Missouri in relation to the adoption of a new system for the permanent disposition of the public lands," February 22, 1833, in *American State Papers: Public Lands*, 6: 612–13.

19. On Evans and other New York radicals, see Sean Wilentz, *Chants Democratic: New York City and the Rise of the American Working Class, 1788–1850* (New York, 1984); and Jamie L. Bronstein, *Land Reform and Working-Class Experience in Britain and the United States, 1800–1862* (Palo Alto, CA, 1999); also, Thomas Skidmore, *The Rights of Man to Property* (New York, 1829), 137–44, 273–83. On the expansion of the public sphere in the early republic, see Brooke, "Consent, Civil Society, and the Public Sphere," 224–30.

20. On the corruption theme, see Michael A. Morrison, "Distribution or Dissolution: Western Land Policy, Economic Development, and the Language of Corruption, 1837–41," *American Nineteenth Century History* 1 (Spring 2000), 1–33.

21. "Speech in Senate," January 28 and 29, 1841, *PHC*, 9: 486–94 (esp. 488); Clay to Thomas Speed, November 1, 1834, *PHC*, 8: 750; Clay to Alexander Coffin, June 11, 1834, *PHC*, 8: 725; Clay to David F. Caldwell, June 25, 1835, *PHC*, 8: 774.

22. For Clay's remarks on the Walker bill and for Walker's response, see *Register of Debates*, Senate, 24th Cong., 1st sess. (1835–1836), 1028–30. For the land policy statement of Walker's Senate committee, see U.S. Congress, Senate, *Report of the Committee of Public Lands on graduating and reducing the price of public lands to actual settlers*, S. doc. 402, 24th Cong., 1st sess. (serial no. 283). In March 1832, Clay's Senate enemies sent to his Committee on Manufactures a resolution for an inquiry into land price reduction and cession, which presumably forced Clay into the awkward position of choosing between his eastern pro-manufacturing supporters and his western pro-settlement constituents. See Clay to Francis T. Brooke, March 28, 1832, *PHC*, 8: 481–82.

23. Clay to Patton et al., April 7, 1836, *PHC*, 8: 840; Clay to Walsh, April 25, 1836, *PHC*, 8: 845–46. See also, Clay to Noah Noble, June 20, 1837, *PHC*, 9: 50–51. On the importance of the 1836 elections and of removing the "Blackguards, Bankrupts and Scoundrels, Profligacy and Corruption" from government, see Clay to John M. Cabanis, June 12, 1835, *PHC*, 8: 773, and Clay to Francis T. Brooke, June 27, 1835, *PHC*, 8: 775–76.

24. "Speech at the Woodford Festival," July 26, 1836, *PHC*, 8: 860–61; *Register of Debates*, Senate, 24th Cong., 2nd sess., 360–76. For Clay's expectations on the impact of the Specie Circular, see also Clay to Matthew L. Davis, July 3, 1837, *PHC*, 9: 54–55. On his view of the political dangers of government by "experiment," see Clay to Gulian C. Verplanck et al., December 8, 1837, *PHC*, 9: 98–100. On the Specie Circular, see Peter L. Rousseau, "Jacksonian Monetary Policy, Specie Flows, and the Panic of 1837," *Journal of Economic History* 62 (June 2002), 457–88.

25. Clay to Letcher, January 17, 1837, *PHC*, 9: 14; *Register of Debates*, Senate, 24th Cong., 2nd sess., 662–63 (esp. 662), 668. If Clay sounded as if he was losing the argument in public, he all but admitted as much in private: "All that I can say is God save the Commonwealth; for I am sure the Devil has now got hold of it." See Clay to Benjamin Watkins Leigh, February 4, 1837, *PHC*, supplement: 267–68. See also *Register of Debates*, Senate, 24th Cong., 2nd sess., 678, 536. For the vote on the Walker bill in 1837, see ibid., 777. On Thomas Ewing, see James Joseph Buss, *Winning the West with Words: Language and Conquest in the Lower Great Lakes* (Norman, OK, 2011), 61–63.

26. "Application of Wisconsin for the extension of the pre-emption laws to the lands recently acquired from the Indians," January 23, 1837, *American State Papers: Public Lands*, 5: 928; U.S. Congress, Senate, *Memorial of a committee of citizens of Illinois, praying the passage of a Preemption Law in favor of Settlers on Unsurveyed Public Lands*, S. doc. 198, 24th Cong., 2nd sess. (serial no. 298), 3. There were also petitions to Congress *against* preemption during the Panic. One of the most interesting came in January 1841 from Daniel W. Coxe, a supporter of transportation improvements in the West. Coxe thought that federal preemption policy threatened his "vested rights" to lands he owned in Louisiana and those of all other landholders in the nation: "[I]f Congress can divest one citizen of his property, and transfer it to another, by legislative enactments," Coxe insisted, then "such power may in time be enlarged and extended from a part to the whole of any estate." See U.S. Congress, Senate, *Memorial of Daniel W. Coxe, praying That his interest in certain lands may not be affected by any legislation of Congress on the subject of pre-emption and settlement rights*, S. doc. 60, 26th Cong., 2nd sess. (serial no. 376). See also U.S. Congress, Senate, *General Assembly of New Jersey on the disposition of public lands*, S. doc. 207, 25th Cong., 3rd sess. (serial no. 340), and U.S. Congress, House, *Resolutions of Massachusetts Legislature on the subject of the Public Lands*, H. doc. 41, 26th Cong., 1st sess. (serial no. 364).

27. U.S. Congress, Senate, *Petition of a number of citizens of Medina County, Ohio, praying a modification of the existing laws regulating the sales of the public lands*, S. doc. 137, 25th Cong., 2nd sess. (serial no. 315), 1. On the Panic of 1837, see Peter Temin, *The Jacksonian Economy* (New York, 1969), 113–37; Edward J. Balleisen, *Navigating Failure: Bankruptcy and Commercial Society in Antebellum America* (Chapel Hill, NC, 2001), 32–41; and Jessica M. Lepler, *The Many Panics of 1837: People, Politics, and the Creation of a Transatlantic Crisis* (Cambridge, UK, 2013).

28. "The Squatters," *New-York Evening Post* (New York, NY), reprinted in *Burlington Gazette* (Burlington, VT), July 10, 1837; Van Buren's First Annual Message, December 5, 1837, in Richardson, *Messages and Papers of the Presidents*, 3: 373–95, esp. 389; "Public Lands," *Richmond Whig* (Richmond, VA), reprinted in *Connecticut Courant* (Hartford, CT), December 23, 1837.

29. *Cong. Globe*, 25th Cong., 2nd sess., app., 15–17 (esp. 16); Joseph Vance to Clay, December 29, 1837, *PHC*, 9: 114–15; Peter B. Porter to Clay, December 15, and Clay to Porter, December 24, 1837, *PHC*, 9: 104–5, 113–14.

30. "Western Land Sales," *Baltimore Gazette and Daily Advertiser* (Baltimore, MD), August 6, 1835; "Western Land Sales," *Commercial Advertiser* (New York), August 17, 1835; "A Government of Squatters," report from the *Milwaukee Advertiser*, reprinted in the *Saratoga Sentinel* (Saratoga, NY), April 18, 1837; "Squatters," report from the *Cleveland Herald*, reprinted in the *Phoenix Civilian* (Cumberland, MD), December 8, 1838; "The Squatters on the Grand River, in Michigan," report from the *Detroit Advertiser*, reprinted in the *Cincinnati Daily Gazette* (Cincinnati, OH), May 31, 1837; "The Public Lands," *Alexandria Gazette* (Alexandria, VA), August 30, 1839. See also *Spectator* (New York), December 3, 1835; *Alexandria Gazette* (Alexandria, VA), December 4, 1835; *Richmond Enquirer* (Richmond, VA), December 8, 1835; *Vermont State Paper* (St. Albans, VT), December 15, 1835; and *New Bedford Gazette* (New Bedford, MA), February 27, 1837.

31. For a further explication of Van Buren's position, see also *Niles' National Register* (Baltimore, MD), September 19, 1840, 40–41.

32. *Globe* (Washington, DC), January 29, 1838; "Speech on the Preemption Bill," January 26, 1838 in The *Works of Henry Clay*, ed. Calvin Colton, 10 vols. (New York, 1904), 8: 87, 90. See also Clay's comments reported in *Cong. Globe*, 25th Cong., 2nd sess. (1837–1838), 142–43; and the note in *PHC*, 9: 134–35.

33. Colton, *Works of Henry Clay*, 8: 92; *Cong. Globe*, 25th Cong., 2nd sess., 136, 137.

34. *Globe* (Washington, DC), January 29, 1838; *New York Evening Post* (New York), January 31, 1838.

35. *Cong. Globe*, 25th Cong., 2nd sess., app., 134, 139, 140–41.

36. Ibid., 135–36. See also Peter J. Parish, "Daniel Webster, New England, and the West," *Journal of American History* 54 (Dec. 1967); and Peterson, *The Great Triumvirate*, 267–68.

37. *Cong. Globe*, 25th Cong., 2nd sess., app., 129–33 (esp. 130); for the vote on Merrick's amendment, see ibid., 133. *Alexandria Gazette* (Alexandria, VA), February 8, 1838.

38. Ibid., app., 614–19 (esp. 615); "How Stands the Case," *United States Magazine and Democratic Review* 3 (Sept. 1838), 10, 4; "Squatters," *Arkansas Weekly Gazette* (Little Rock, AR), May 30, 1838; "Squatters," *Milwaukee Sentinel* (Milwaukee, WI), March 19, 1839. For the Senate and House votes on the 1838 preemption bill, see *Cong. Globe*, 25th Cong., 2nd sess., app., 149; and *Journal of the House of Representatives of the United States*, June 14, 1838, 1101.

39. Clay to John B. Dillon, July 28, 1838, *PHC*, 9: 214. See also Clay to S. Lisle Smith, June 22, 1838, *PHC*, supplement: 272; Clay to Alston B. Estes, June 1, 1839, *PHC*, 9: 321–32, and Clay to J. H. Clay Mudd, September 25, 1843, *PHC*, 9: 860–61. To show readers how little Clay did to tone down his anti-squatter language, even after 1838, the strongly Democratic *Indiana State Sentinel*, on October 18, 1842, ran provocative excerpts of his January 28–29, 1841, Senate speech on preemption. See "Speech in Indianapolis," October 5, 1842, *PHC*, 9: 782–84, esp. 784.

40. "Speech in Washington, DC," December 11, 1839, *PHC*, 9: 363–64; Clay to Richard H. Wilde, June 24, 1839, *PHC*, 9: 328–30, esp. 329; "Speech in Baltimore," August 26, 1839, *PHC*, 9: 338–39.

41. Clay to Francis T. Brooke, January 7, 1839, *PHC*, 9: 266–67; Clay to John O. Sargent, January 14, 1839, *PHC*, 9: 271. Coincidentally, on that same day Sargent, in the *New York Morning Courier & Enquirer*, attacked Clay's opponents in Congress for supporting the land policy of the "present corrupt administration," with the intent to "purchase the votes and favor of the West. He also praised Clay for his "noble disregard of personal consequence" in opposing preemption and urged New Yorkers to stand behind the Kentuckian. See *PHC*,

9: 271n. Similar support came later that month from New York City's Democratic Whig Association. See William Turner and J. Turner Dodge to Clay, January 22, 1839, *PHC*, 9: 274. In May 1839, Clay wrote: "[I]f the Country could be made fully to comprehend the Agrarian aims which are directed against the foundations of all property and all good faith in the Community, I hope it would at last be aroused" (Clay to John P. Kennedy, May 16, 1839, *PHC*, 9: 314–15, quote on 314.) For Clay's public opposition to preemption after January 1838, see *Cong. Globe*, 26th Cong., 1st sess. (1839–1840), 17, 79, 342, and app., 381–84 (Clay's speech was not recorded, but a strong rebuttal by Clement C. Clay of Alabama was); ibid., 26th Cong, 2nd sess. (1840–1841), app., 194, 198, 200–202; "Speech in Senate," January 28 and 29, 1841, *PHC*, 9: 486–94.

42. "Speech on the State of the Country Under Van Buren," June 27, 1840, *PHC*, 9: 426–29, esp. 428; "Speech in Nashville," August 17, 1840, *PHC*, 9: 439–41, esp. 440. Earlier, Clay had received reports that financial distress in North Carolina and Virginia had warmed those states to the land revenue distribution proposal, and similar news from Indiana came shortly after the 1840 election. See Clay to John O. Sargent, January 14, 1839, *PHC*, 9: 271; Isaac Montgomery to Clay, December 29, 1840, *PHC*, 9: 469–70. Also see Clay's lengthy Senate speech to reintroduce the Distribution Bill, January 28 and 29, 1841, *PHC*, 9: 486–94. In an April 1841 letter, he noted how distribution now seemed "indispensable to some of the States" (Clay to Peter B. Porter, April 24, 1841, *PHC*, 9: 522–23).

43. Benton, quoted in the *Connecticut Courant* (Hartford, CT), August 31, 1839.

44. Clay to Alexander Hamilton, December 6, 1837, *PHC*, 9: 97; Clay to Edward C. Delavan, August 20, 1838, *PHC*, 9: 218–19.

45. *Cong. Globe*, 26th Cong., 2nd sess., app., 22–23; Aaron Clark to Clay, January 12, 1841, *PHC*, 9: 477; *Cong. Globe*, 26th Cong., 2nd sess., app., 194, 198, 200–202 (esp. 201).

46. It appears that Clay's appeal to nativism was more for political advantage than from personal conviction; his private correspondence was free of overt bigotry of that kind. In fact, he wrote to Demetrius A. Gallitzin in February 1837: "You do me no more than justice in supposing me incapable of any feelings of prejudice, or entertaining any spirit of intolerance towards the Catholic religion. I have, on the contrary, the highest respect for it, and count among its members some of my best and truest friends." In 1843, he wrote a fellow Kentuckian: "Without regard to Country or their particular Religion, I judge of men by their conduct & character." But he also wrote, "We deprive Native born Citizens, who shew their unworthiness, by perpetrating certain crimes, of the Elective franchise, which ought not to be granted to persons of bad character born in foreign Countries" (Clay to Gallitzin, February 8, 1837, *PHC*, 9: 24; Clay to James Simpson, August 15, 1843, *PHC*, 9: 845–46).

47. The Preemption-Distribution Act of 1841 specified that the distribution of public land proceeds would be suspended whenever the tariff duties exceeded the 20 percent level set by the Compromise Tariff of 1833. When this occurred in mid-1842, President John Tyler (who later that year pocket-vetoed the bill that would have kept Clay's land program intact while tariff duties were raised) ordered an end to the distribution part of the legislation. See Baxter, *Henry Clay and the American System*, 168–71. Also see Clay to Robert P. Letcher, January 6, 1842, and June 24, 1842, *PHC*, 9: 628–29, 719–20.

48. Bingham to the American Art-Union, November 19, 1850, Letters from Artists, vol. 6, American Art-Union Papers, New-York Historical Society, New York City. On Bingham, see Nancy Rash, *The Painting and Politics of George Caleb Bingham* (New Haven, CT, 1991); Paul C. Nagel, *George Caleb Bingham: Missouri's Famed Painter and Forgotten Politician* (Columbia, MO, 2005); Elizabeth Johns, *American Genre Painting: The Politics of Everyday Life* (New Haven, CT, 1991); and David M. Lubin, *Picturing a Nation: Art and Social Change in Nineteenth-Century America* (New Haven, CT, 1994). For similarly negative characterizations

of squatters after 1841, see "The Life and Character of Thomas Paine," *North American Review* 57 (July 1843), 1–58, esp. 4; "Scotch Squatters," *Littell's Living Age* 6 (July 19, 1845), 152; "Everstone," *American Whig Review* 11 (Jan. 1850), 77–98, esp. 95.

49. On land auction prices, see Feller, *Public Lands in Jacksonian Politics*, 194.

50. See Michael F. Holt, *The Rise and Fall of the American Whig Party: Jacksonian Politics and the Onset of the Civil War* (New York, 1999), 136.

51. *Cong. Globe*, 25th Cong., 2nd sess., app., 138.

52. Tipton, "Speech on Pre-emption Bill," January 27, 1838, in Robertson and Riker, *John Tipton Papers*, 3: 519, 51.

Epilogue · The West Secured?

1. *The Homestead Journal and Village Register* (Salem, OH), December 3, 1851, December 17, 1851.

2. Ibid., August 4, 1847, *Daily True Democrat* (Cleveland, OH), August 23, 1849; *Homestead Journal and Village Register*, January 2, 1850; *History of Columbiana County, Ohio, and Representative Citizens*, ed. William B. McCord (Chicago 1905), 223–24.

3. On the homestead reform movement, see especially Mark A. Lause, *Young America: Land, Labor, and the Republican Community* (Champaign-Urbana, IL, 2005), and Jamie L. Bronstein, *Land Reform and the Working-Class Experience in Britain and the United States, 1800–1862* (Palo Alto, CA, 1999).

4. Quoted in Andrew R. L. Cayton, "The Significance of Ohio in the Early American Republic," in *Center of a Great Empire: The Ohio Country in the Early American Republic*, ed. Andrew R. L. Cayton and Stuart D. Hobbs (Athens, OH, 2005), 1, 5; Stephen E. Maizlish, *The Triumph of Sectionalism: The Transformation of Ohio Politics, 1844–1856* (Kent, OH, 1983), 1–2.

5. Henry Howe, *Historical Collections of Ohio*, 2 vols. (Columbus, OH, 1890), 1: 434–66, esp. 434.

6. Hubert G. H. Wilhelm, "The Origin and Distribution of Settlement Groups: Ohio, 1850" (1982), unpublished manuscript, Salem (Ohio) Public Library, 11, 21–24, 25–27, 30–31, 35–36, Appendix A: American Migrants in Ohio, 1850, Appendix B: Immigrants in Ohio, 1850.

7. *Village Register*, January 23, 1844; "Our System of Trade," ibid., June 3, 1845; "Look out for Speculators," ibid.; "Our System of Trade," ibid.; June 24, 1845, "No Home," *Homestead Journal and Village Register*, July 14, 1847; "Reform," reprinted from the *Portage Sentinel* (Ravenna, OH), ibid., June 30, 1847; Milo A. Townsend, "Man's Right to the Soil," ibid., July 28, 1847. See Jonathan Levy, "The Mortage Worked the Hardest: The Fate of Landed Independence in Nineteenth-Century America," in *Capitalism Takes Command: The Social Transformation of Nineteenth-Century America*, ed. Michael Zakim and Gary J. Kornblith (Chicago, 2012), 44–45. On the traumatic loss of faith in self-reliance and individual enterprise as a result of the Panic of 1837, see Scott A. Sandage, *Born Losers: A History of Failure in America* (Cambridge, MA, 2005), esp. 44–69; and Joshua D. Rothman, *Flush Times and Fever Dreams: A Story of Capitalism and Slavery in the Age of Jackson* (Athens, GA, 2012), 292–301.

8. "Labor—Wealth," *Homestead Journal and Village Register*, June 23, 1847; "To all who Labor," ibid., September 9, 1847; "Speech of Mr. Brooke, delivered before the National Reform Association of Salem, February 19, 1848," ibid., March 15, 1848; B. B. Davis, ibid., August 11, 1847.

9. "Extract of a letter to Friend [J. D.] Cope," ibid., September 15, 1847; Dr. J. R. Buchanan, "The Land and the People," ibid., October 27, 1847. For some who disagreed with

the homestead program, see "Letter to the editor," ibid., March 15, 1848; and "Letter to the editor," ibid., September 29, 1847.

10. Paul W. Gates, *History of Public Land Law Development* (Washington, DC, 1968), 184, 190–91. For the vote on homestead bills in the 1850s in the House, see *Congressional Globe*, 31st Cong., 2nd sess, 22, 278; 32nd Cong., 1st sess., 1351; 33rd Cong., 1st sess., 549, 2nd sess., 235–36; and 34th Cong., 1st sess., 1915. For the vote in the Senate, see ibid., 32nd Cong., 2nd sess., 747; 33rd Cong, 1st sess., 1844; 35th Cong., 1st sess., 2426, 2nd sess., 1074–76. On the Republican Party and homestead reform, see Eric Foner, *Free Soil, Free Labor, Free Men: The Ideology of the Republican Party before the Civil War* (New York, 1970), 27–29, 175, 233, 236, 256, 304.

11. *Baltimore Sun*, September 30, 1871, cited in Christopher Clark, "The Agrarian Context of American Capitalist Development," in Zakim and Kornblith, *Capitalism Takes Command* (see n. 7 above), 16, 21–22.

The following discussion just touches on the wealth of sources relevant to subjects addressed in this book. Primary and secondary materials on land-policy development, broadly conceived, are massive in number and span several disciplines. The selected collections and titles listed below represent those I have found especially useful, along with recent works whose full bibliographies may provide a more comprehensive guide to what is sampled here.

Among primary sources, this study depends heavily on the *Annals of Congress* (1789–1824), *Register of Debates* (1824–1837), *Congressional Globe* (1833–1873), and the Senate and House *Journals*, available online at http://memory.loc.gov/ammem/amlaw/lawhome.html. See also *American State Papers, Public Lands* and the U.S. Serial Set for a wide range of government documents, from petitions and memorials to committee reports. Apart from government documents, I have searched a vast array of pre–Civil War newspapers and magazines, rare books, pamphlets, and broadsides, which are more abundant and accessible to scholars than ever before, thanks in part to various online collections that have appeared in recent years. The most notable of these include *America's Historic Newspapers* (Newsbank), *Proquest Historical Newspapers*, Cornell University's *Making of America*, the enormous collection of archives at *GenealogyBank.com*, and the vast digital collections of the Library of Congress. Most of the travel accounts and much of the pamphlet literature used for this study are stored at the Library Company of Philadelphia.

While this book's narrative follows several themes, the problem of governance in the early republic lies at its core. On the role of the federal government in nineteenth-century nation building, see especially Andrew R. L. Cayton's "'Separate Interests' and the Nation-State: The Washington Administration and the Origins of Regionalism in the Trans-Appalachian West," *Journal of American History*, 79 (June 1992), 347–80, and "Radicals in the 'Western World': The Federalist Conquest of Trans-Appalachian North America," in *Federalists Reconsidered*, ed. Doron Ben-Atar and Barbara B. Oberg (Charlottesville, VA, 1998), 77–96. See also Richard R. John, *Spreading the News: The American Postal System from Franklin to Morse* (Cambridge, MA, 1995); William J. Novak, *The People's Welfare: Law and Regulation in Nineteenth-Century America* (Chapel Hill, NC, 1996); John L. Larson, *Internal Improvement: National Public Works and the Promise of Popular Government in the Early United States* (Chapel Hill, NC, 2001); Max M. Edling, *A Revolution in Favor of Government: Origins of the U.S. Constitution and the Making of the American State* (New York, 2003); Daniel Walker Howe, *What Hath God Wrought: The Transformation of America, 1815–1848* (New York, 2007);

William J. Novak, "The Myth of the 'Weak' American State," *American Historical Review*, 113 (June 2008), 752–72; Brian Balogh, *A Government Out of Sight: The Mystery of National Authority in Nineteenth Century America* (Cambridge, UK, 2009); and Eliga Gould, *Among the Powers of the Earth: The American Revolution and the Making of a New World Empire* (Cambridge, MA, 2012).

On the federal government's role in trans-Appalachian development, see Adam Rothman, *Slave Country: American Expansion and the Origins of the Deep South* (Cambridge, MA, 2005); Patrick Griffin, *American Leviathan: Empire, Nation, and the Revolutionary Frontier* (New York, 2007); Stephen Rockwell, *Indian Affairs and the Administrative State* (Cambridge, UK, 2010); Peter J. Kastor, *William Clark's World: Describing America in an Age of Unknowns* (New Haven, CT, 2011); and William H. Bergmann, *The American National State and the Early West* (Cambridge, UK, 2012).

Long ago, Frederick Jackson Turner and his students pioneered the study of the sectional politics of land policy and the West. See Turner's *Rise of the New West* (New York, 1906) and *The United States, 1830–1850: The Nation and Its Sections* (New York, 1935); also see Raynor Wellington, *The Political and Sectional Influence of the Public Lands, 1828–1842* (Cambridge, MA, 1914); and George M. Stephenson, *The Political History of the Public Lands, from 1840 to 1862: From Pre-emption to Homestead* (Boston, 1917). The finest modern study of the politics, sectional and otherwise, of public lands issues is Daniel Feller, *The Public Lands in Jacksonian Politics* (Madison, WI, 1984). Older surveys of the subject include Benjamin H. Hibbard, *A History of the Public Land Policies* (New York, 1939); and Roy M. Robbins, *Our Landed Heritage: The Public Domain, 1776–1970* (Lincoln, NE, 1976).

On the post-Revolutionary period, see Peter S. Onuf, "Liberty, Development, and Union: Visions of the West in the 1780s," *William and Mary Quarterly*, 3rd ser., 43 (April 1986), 179–213. Two brief but exemplary studies that focus on the impact of political belief on pre–Civil War policy are Mary E. Young, "Congress Looks West: Liberal Ideology and Public Land Policy in the Nineteenth Century," in *The Frontier in American Development: Essays in Honor of Paul Wallace Gates*, ed. David M. Ellis (Ithaca, NY, 1969), 74–112; and Michael A. Morrison, "Distribution or Dissolution: Western Land Policy, Economic Development, and the Language of Corruption, 1837–41," *American Nineteenth Century History*, 1 (Spring 2000), 1–33.

On homestead reform and eastern workingmen's movements, more recent works, such as Jamie L. Bronstein's *Land Reform and Working-Class Experience in Britain and the United States, 1800–1862* (Stanford, CA, 1999), Mark A. Lause's *Young America: Land, Labor, and the Republican Community* (Champaign-Urbana, IL, 2005), and Sean Wilentz's *Chants Democratic: New York City and the Rise of the American Working Class, 1788–1850* (New York, 1984), have superseded Helene S. Zahler's classic *Eastern Workingmen and National Land Policy, 1829–62* (New York, 1941).

On governmental administration and the operation of federal land policy, Paul W. Gates and Malcolm Rohrbough wrote the classic works. See particularly Gates's *History of Public Land Law Development* (Washington, DC, 1968) and *Landlords and Tenants on the Prairie Frontier* (Ithaca, NY, 1973), and Rohrbough's *The Land Office Business: The Settlement and Administration of American Public Lands, 1789–1837* (New York, 1968) and *The Trans-Appalachian Frontier: People, Societies, and Institutions, 1775–1850* (New York, 1978).

For the best broad understanding of political economy in the Jeffersonian period, see Drew R. McCoy, *The Elusive Republic: Political Economy in Jeffersonian America* (Chapel Hill,

NC, 1980). McCoy's work built on classics of the "republican synthesis," especially Bernard Bailyn, *The Ideological Origins of the American Revolution* (Cambridge, MA, 1967); Gordon S. Wood, *The Creation of the American Republic, 1776–1787* (Chapel Hill, NC, 1969); and J. G. A. Pocock, *The Machiavellian Moment: Florentine Political Thought and the Atlantic Republican Tradition* (Princeton, NJ, 1975). Among Wood's works, see also *The Radicalism of the American Revolution* (New York, 1992) and *Empire of Liberty: A History of the Early Republic, 1789–1815* (New York, 2010). Also valuable are Peter McNamara, *Political Economy and Statesmanship: Smith, Hamilton, and the Foundation of the Commercial Republic* (DeKalb, IL, 1997); James L. Huston, "Abolitionists, Political Economists, and Capitalism," *Journal of the Early Republic* 20 (Autumn 2000), 487–521; and Thomas K. McCraw, *The Founders and Finance: How Hamilton, Gallatin, and Other Immigrants Forged a New Economy* (Cambridge, MA, 2012). For interpretations that stress "liberalism" over "republicanism," see Louis Hartz, *The Liberal Tradition in America: An Interpretation of American Political Thought since the Revolution* (New York, 1955); Joyce O. Appleby, *Capitalism and a New Social Order: The Republican Vision of the 1790s* (New York, 1984); and John P. Diggins, *The Lost Soul of American Politics: Virtue, Self-Interest, and the Foundations of Liberalism* (New York, 1984). Among surveys of economic thought in the early nineteenth century, see especially Paul K. Conkin, *Prophets of Prosperity: America's First Political Economists* (Bloomington, IN, 1980); Allen Kaufman, *Capitalism, Slavery, and Republican Values: Antebellum Political Economists, 1819–1848* (Austin, TX, 1982); and William B. Scott, *In Pursuit of Happiness: American Conceptions of Property from the Seventeenth to the Twentieth Century* (Bloomington, IN, 1977). On Old World roots of New World political economy, see Joyce O. Appleby, *Economic Thought and Ideology in Seventeenth-Century England* (Princeton, NJ, 1978); and Albert O. Hirschman, *The Passions and the Interests: Political Arguments for Capitalism before Its Triumph* (Princeton, NJ, 1977). On the pre–Civil War South in particular, see Michael O'Brien, *Conjectures of Order: Intellectual Life and the American South, 1810–1860*, 2 vols. (Chapel Hill, NC, 2004).

Differing perspectives on empire building are provided in Eric Hinderaker, *Elusive Empires: Constructing Colonialism in the Ohio Valley, 1673–1800* (Cambridge, MA, 1997); and Bergmann, *American National State*. Also see Karl-Friedrich Walling, *Republican Empire: Alexander Hamilton on War and Free Government* (Lawrence, KS, 1999); and Peter S. Onuf's *Jefferson's Empire: The Language of American Nationhood* (Charlottesville, VA, 2000), *Statehood and Union: A History of the Northwest Ordinance* (Bloomington, IN, 1987), and *The Origins of the Federal Republic: Jurisdictional Controversies in the United States, 1775–1787* (Philadelphia, 1983). See also *Empire and Nation: The American Revolution in the Atlantic World*, ed. Eliga H. Gould and Peter S. Onuf (Baltimore, 2005).

For Indian policy and Native American perspectives on white expansion, good sources include Bernard W. Sheehan, *Seeds of Extinction: Jeffersonian Philanthropy and the American Indian* (New York, 1973); Gregory Dowd, *A Spirited Resistance: The North American Indian Struggle for Unity, 1745–1815* (Baltimore, 1990); Richard White, *The Middle Ground: Indians, Empires, and Republics in the Great Lakes Region, 1650–1815* (Cambridge, UK, 1991); Daniel K. Richter, *Facing East from Indian Country: A Native History of Early America* (Cambridge, MA, 2001); Stuart Banner, *How the Indians Lost Their Land: Law and Power on the Frontier* (Cambridge, MA, 2005); Alan Taylor, *The Divided Ground: Indians, Settlers, and the Northern Borderland of the American Revolution* (New York, 2006); and Robert Owens, *Mr. Jefferson's Hammer: William Henry Harrison and the Origins of Indian Policy* (Norman, OK, 2007).

The literature on the post-1815 phase of the "Market Revolution" is vast and varied. The broader surveys include Charles G. Sellers, *The Market Revolution: Jacksonian America, 1815–1846* (New York, 1992); Daniel W. Howe, *What Hath God Wrought: The Transformation of America, 1815–1848* (New York, 2007); and John L. Larson, *The Market Revolution in America: Liberty, Ambition, and the Eclipse of the Common Good* (Cambridge, UK, 2009). For a shorter, most helpful survey, see Richard E. Ellis, "The Market Revolution and the Transformation of American Politics, 1801–1837," in *The Market Revolution in America: Social, Political, and Religious Expressions, 1800–1880,* ed. Melvyn Stokes and Stephen Conway (Charlottesville, VA, 1996), 149–76. Also useful are the essays in *Wages of Independence,* ed. Paul A. Gilje (New York, 2006) and *Capitalism Takes Command: The Social Transformation of Nineteenth-Century America,* ed. Michael Zakim and Gary J. Kornblith (Chicago, 2012). On the Panic of 1819, Murray N. Rothbard, *The Panic of 1819: Reactions and Policies* (New York, 1962), while dated, remains a standard work, but see also Robert M. Blackson, "Pennsylvania Banks and the Panic of 1819: A Reinterpretation," *Journal of the Early Republic* 9 (1989), 335–58; Stuart Bruchey, *Enterprise: The Dynamic Economy of a Free People* (Cambridge, MA, 1990); and Douglas C. North, *The Economic Growth of the United States, 1790–1860* (New York, 1961). On the building of early western commerce, see Richard C. Wade, *The Urban Frontier: The Rise of Western Cities, 1790–1830* (Cambridge, MA, 1959). Jessica M. Lepler's *The Many Panics of 1837: People, Politics, and the Creation of a Transatlantic Crisis* (Cambridge, UK, 2013) promises to overshadow earlier studies of the Panic of 1837, including Peter Temin, *The Jacksonian Economy* (New York, 1969) and Reginald C. McGrane, *The Panic of 1837: Some Financial Problems of the Jacksonian Era* (Chicago, 1924).

On the social and psychological impact of economic crises in the post-1815 period, see Scott A. Sandage, *Born Losers: A History of Failure in America* (Cambridge, MA, 2005). Among regional, state, and local studies, see Reeve Huston, *Land and Freedom: Rural Society, Popular Protest, and Party Politics in Antebellum New York* (New York, 2000); Craig Thompson Friend, *Along the Maysville Road: The Early American Republic in the Trans-Appalachian West* (Knoxville, TN, 2005); Stephanie Kermes, *Creating an American Identity: New England, 1789–1825* (New York, 2008); Christopher Clark, *The Roots of Rural Capitalism: Western Massachusetts, 1780–1860* (Ithaca, NY, 1990); Winifred Barr Rothenberg, *From Market-Places to a Market Economy: The Transformation of Rural Massachusetts, 1750–1850* (Chicago, 1992); Harry N. Scheiber, *Ohio Canal Era: A Case Study of Government and the Economy, 1820–1861* (Athens, OH, 1968); and Martin Bruegel, *Farm, Shop, Landing: The Rise of a Market Society in the Hudson Valley, 1780–1860* (Durham, NC, 2002).

On the "American System" and the promotion of manufacturing in the early republic, see Maurice G. Baxter, *Henry Clay and the American System* (Lexington, KY, 1995); James L. Huston, "Virtue Besieged: Virtue, Equality, and the General Welfare in the Tariff Debates of the 1820s," *Journal of the Early Republic* 14 (Winter 1994), 523–47; Richard C. Edwards, "Economic Sophistication in Nineteenth Century Congressional Tariff Debates," *Journal of Economic History,* 30 (December 1970), 802–38; Peter Passell and Maria Schmundt, "Pre–Civil War Land Policy and the Growth of Manufacturing," *Explorations in Economic History* 9 (January 1971), 35–48; Robert Brooke Zevin, *The Growth of Manufacturing in Early Nineteenth Century New England* (New York, 1975); and Songho Ha, *The Rise and Fall of the American System: Nationalism and the Development of the American Economy, 1790–1837* (London, 2009). On Clay's regional following, see Donald J. Ratcliffe, "The Role of Voters and Issues in

Party Formation: Ohio, 1824," *Journal of American History* 49 (March 1973), 847–70. Two recent studies that focus on manufacturing development from the Jeffersonian side are Lawrence A. Peskin, *Manufacturing Revolution: The Intellectual Origins of Early American Industry* (Baltimore, 2003); and Andrew Shankman, *Crucible of American Democracy: The Struggle to Fuse Egalitarianism and Capitalism in Jeffersonian Pennsylvania* (Lawrence, KS, 2004). On transportation, Larson, *Internal Improvement* is the new standard, but see also Carter Goodrich, *Governmental Promotion of American Canals and Railroads, 1800–1890* (New York, 1960); and George Rogers Taylor, *The Transportation Revolution, 1815–1860* (New York, 1951). And on communication expansion, it would be hard to surpass Richard R. John, *Network Nation: Inventing American Telecommunications* (Cambridge, MA, 2010).

Studies that explore social transformation in the early republic also are too extensive to be covered here, but highlights include Christopher Clark, *Social Change in America, from the Revolution through the Civil War* (Chicago, 2006); John M. Murrin, "The Great Inversion, or Court Versus Country: A Comparison of the Revolution Settlements in England (1688–1721) and America (1776–1816)," in *Three British Revolutions: 1641, 1688, 1776*, ed. J. G. A. Pocock (Princeton, NJ, 1980), 368–453; Terry Bouton, *Taming Democracy: "The People," the Founders, and the Troubled Ending of the American Revolution* (New York, 2007); Woody Holton, *Forced Founders: Indians, Debtors, Slaves, and the Making of the American Revolution in Virginia* (Chapel Hill, NC, 1999) and *Unruly Americans and the Origins of the Constitution* (New York, 2007); Daniel Feller, *The Jacksonian Promise: America, 1815–1840* (Baltimore, 1995); and Charles C. Bolton, *Poor Whites of the Antebellum South: Tenants and Laborers in Central North Carolina and Northeast Mississippi* (Durham, NC, 1994). On middle-class values in the early republic, see Jennifer L. Goloboy, "The Early American Middle Class," *Journal of the Early Republic* 25 (Winter 2005), 537–45. On the opposing class languages of Jacksonians and Whigs, see Allan Kulikoff, *The Agrarian Origins of American Capitalism* (Charlottesville, VA, 1992).

Among the studies of American western development from the Appalachians to the Mississippi, see particularly John Craig Hammond, *Slavery, Freedom, and Expansion in the Early American West* (Charlottesville, VA, 2007); L. Scott Philyaw, *Virginia's Western Visions: Political and Cultural Expansion on an Early American Frontier* (Knoxville, TN, 2004); Susan Dunn, *Dominion of Memories: Jefferson, Madison, and the Decline of Virginia* (New York, 2007); Andrew R. L. Cayton, *The Frontier Republic: Ideology and Politics in the Ohio Country, 1780–1825* (Kent, OH, 1986); Gregory H. Nobles, *American Frontiers: Cultural Encounters and Continental Conquest* (New York, 1997) and "Breaking into the Backcountry: New Approaches to the Early American Frontier, 1750–1800, *William and Mary Quarterly* 46 (October 1989), 641–70; Alan Taylor, *William Cooper's Town: Power and Persuasion on the Frontier of the Early American Republic* (New York, 1995) and "From Fathers to Friends of the People: Political Personas in the Early Republic, *Journal of the Early Republic* 11 (Winter 1991), 465–91; and Francois Furstenberg, "The Significance of the Trans-Appalachian Frontier in Atlantic History," *American Historical Review* 113 (June 2008), 647–77. Stephen Aron's *How the West Was Lost: The Transformation of Kentucky from Daniel Boone to Henry Clay* (Baltimore, 1996) and *American Confluence: The Missouri Frontier from Borderland to Border State* (Bloomington, IN, 2006) are both valuable, as is his "Pioneers and Profiteers: Land Speculation and the Homestead Ethic in Frontier Kentucky," *Western Historical Quarterly* 23 (May 1992), 179–98. James Joseph Buss, *Winning the West with Words: Language and Conquest in the Lower Great Lakes* (Norman, OK, 2011) is both creative and stimulating. Going beyond the Mississippi, see Patricia N. Limerick, *The Legacy of Conquest: The Unbroken Past of the American West* (New York, 1987); Richard White, *"It's Your Misfortune and None of My Own": A New History of the American West* (Norman, OK, 1991); and Anne F. Hyde, *Empires, Nations, and Families: A New History of the North American West, 1800–1860* (Lincoln, NE, 2011). On the Louisiana Purchase, see especially Jon Kukla, *A Wilderness So Immense: The Louisiana Purchase and the Destiny of America* (New York, 2003); and Peter J. Kastor, *The Nation's Crucible: The Louisiana Purchase and the Creation of America* (New Haven, CT, 2004).

On political development generally, see Gordon S. Wood, "Interests and Disinterestedness in the Making of the Constitution," in *Beyond Confederation: Origins of the Constitution and American National Identity*, ed. Richard Beeman, Stephen Botein, and Edward C. Carter II (Chapel Hill, NC, 1987); Sean Wilentz, *The Rise of American Democracy, Jefferson to Lincoln* (New York, 2005); Jonathan H. Earle, *Jacksonian Antislavery and the Politics of Free Soil, 1824–1854* (Chapel Hill, NC, 2003); Merrill D. Peterson, *The Great Triumvirate: Webster, Clay, and Calhoun* (New York, 1987); Daniel Walker Howe, *The Political Culture of the American Whigs* (Chicago, 1979); Richard P. McCormick, *The Second American Party System: Party Formation in the Jacksonian Era* (Chapel Hill, NC, 1966); Major L. Wilson, *Space, Time, and Freedom: The Quest for Nationality and the Irrepressible Conflict, 1815–1861* (Westport, CT, 1974); Harry L. Watson, *Liberty and Power: The Politics of Jacksonian America* (New York, 1990); Michael A. Morrison, *Slavery and the American West: The Eclipse of Manifest Destiny and the Coming of the Civil War* (Chapel Hill, NC, 1997); Amy S. Greenberg, *Manifest Manhood and the Antebellum American Empire* (Cambridge, UK, 2005); Christopher Childers, *The Failure of Popular Sovereignty: Slavery, Manifest Destiny, and the Radicalization of Southern Politics* (Lawrence, KS, 2012); and Michael F. Holt's *The Rise and Fall of the American Whig Party: Jacksonian Politics and the Onset of the Civil War* (New York, 1999) and *The Political Crisis of the 1850s* (New York, 1978). On the political importance of newspapers and magazines, see Jeffrey L. Pasley, *"The Tyranny of the Printers": Newspaper Politics in the Early Republic* (Charlottesville, VA, 2001). For pre–Civil War voting patterns in Congress, see Joel H. Silbey, *The Shrine of Party: Congressional Voting Behavior, 1841–1852* (Pittsburgh, 1967). Finally, for Republican Party belief and policy, see Eric Foner, *Free Soil, Free Labor, Free Men: The Ideology of the Republican Party before the Civil War* (New York, 1970); Leonard P. Curry, *Blueprint for Modern America: Nonmilitary Legislation of the First Civil War Congress* (Nashville, TN, 1968); and Heather Cox Richardson, *The Greatest Nation of the Earth: Republican Economic Policies during the Civil War* (Cambridge, MA, 1997).

Adams, John, 24, 26–27, 65

Adams, John Quincy, 89, 110, 134, 210; nationalism of, 69, 105; political demise of, 154; pursuing spirit of improvement, 129, 130, 132

Adams (John Quincy) administration, 132–35, 141–42, 144

agriculture: glorification of, in economic programs, 113; manufacturing and, 121–22, 125, 127, 129

agriculturists, 13, 15–16, 58, 68, 120

Albany Plan of Union, 11

American Colonization Society, 179

American empire, 50, 58

American Museum (periodical), 58–59

American Revolution, 20, 22

American System, 7, 89, 113–16, 133, 212, 213, 218, 226, 229, 230; advocates of, 160, 171, 220; home-market approach and, 128; opponents of, 160, 199; political motivation for, 193, 207, 226; revisions to, 194, 196–97, 202, 204

American Water Cure Advocate (periodical), 233, 235

Ames, Fisher, 59, 71

antinationalists, 6, 93, 117

Anti-Slavery Bugle (periodical), 235

anti-statists, 6

anti-westerners, 126

Archer, William S., 137

Arkansas, squatters in, 108

Arkansas Weekly Gazette, 225

Arnold, Benedict, 40

Arnold, Jonathan, 31

Articles of Confederation, 30

Atkinson, Samuel, 162

Audubon, John James, 183–84

Bache, Mary, 181

Bacon's Rebellion, 28

Badollet, John, 83

Baird, Robert, 104, 172–74, 181

Ball, Burges, 60

Bank of the United States, 94, 105, 124, 125, 143

Barton, David, 105, 199

Battle of Fallen Timbers, 51

Bayard, Richard, 220

Beecher, Catherine, 180

Beecher, Edward, 180

Beecher, Lyman, 174–81, 204

Benton, Ann Gooch, 101–2

Benton, Jesse, 101

Benton, Thomas Hart, 95, 136, 162, 197, 233; benefiting from Webster-Hayne debate, 169; celebrating the West, 175; on Clay, 221–22; debate with Foot, 139, 141, 143–47, 154–56; graduation proposal of, 7, 87, 91, 101–8, 111, 122, 195, 259n10; opposition to, 113, 116, 127, 132, 140, 153–54, 166, 199; on preemption, 226–27; supporting free homestead principle, 112; supporting squatters' rights, 181

Berry, William T., 125

Beverly, Robert, 28

Bibb, George M., 209

Bingham, George Caleb, 228–29

Blair, Francis Preston, 94

Blake, George, 195

Boone, Daniel, 152

bounty lands. *See* land bounties

Bowdoin, James, 24

Breckinridge, John, 74, 131

British Empire, 8–9, 10, 11, 19

Brooke, John, 207

Brown, Ethan Allen, 100

Buchanan, J. R., 238–39

Buchanan, James, 239

Byrd, William, II, 28

Calhoun, John C., 140, 165, 220; advocating endowment for permanent improvements, 131; interested in cession, 156, 221; opposition to, 188, 197; on preemption, 223; publishing *South Carolina Exposition and Protest*, 136, 137, 138, 162; supporting Maxcy plan, 98

Canada Pamphlet (Franklin), 13

capitalism, communal, 21

Carey, Mathew, 58–59, 114–15, 117–20, 123, 133, 195

Carroll, Charles, 24

Cass, Lewis, 186–87

Catholicism, 179–80

Cayton, Andrew, 235–36

Cayugas, 49

cession, 31–32, 156, 164, 167, 198–99

Cession of 1784, 96, 136–37, 164

Chapman, John B., 211

character, and westward migration, 174–79

Chase, Philander, 176

checks and balances, 47

Cherokees, 186

Chickasaws, 183

Choctaws, 183

Cincinnati, 164, 170–71; Beecher in, 174–75; immigrants in, 179

citizenship, 19, 39

City Gazette (Charleston, SC), 60

Claibourne, J. F. H., 188

Clark, Aaron, 227–28

class conflict, 3, 62, 84, 93, 121, 154, 220

Clay, Henry, 89, 233; on cession, 198–201; contradicting planter stereotype, 193; on degeneracy in the political community, 213–14; home-market ideas of, 120, 123, 127–28; importance to, of public land policy, 114; on Jacksonianism, 225; land policy of, 194, 198–204, 206, 212; nationalism of, 69, 105; nativist rhetoric of, 227, 228; on nonresident speculators, 208–9; Panic of 1819's effect on, 7, 124; political economy of, 114, 116, 117; political opposition to, 199–200, 220, 221–22; on preemption, 212–16, 219–20, 223–30; presidential aspirations of, 113, 141, 195, 202–3, 207, 212, 226; property of, stolen, 218; protectionist arguments of, 123–24;

responding to strict constructionists, 130–32; on squatters, 128, 129, 206–7, 209–10, 229; on stability of society, 193; sympathizing with anti-relief position, 94, 125; on Walker's land bill, 215–16

Clinton, DeWitt, 147, 150

Clinton, George, 69

Cobb, W. R. W., 239

Cocke, William, 74

colonial America, 8–9, 13, 20–24, 39–40

Columbian Register (New Haven, CT), 168

common fund theory, 32, 99, 111, 164, 165, 200

common good, 21, 39, 98, 142, 164, 202

commonwealth, republican, 19

communal capitalism, 21

Compromise of 1850, 239

Compromise Tariff of 1833, 206

confederacies, political, 86

Connecticut: ceding claims, 32; land grants of, 29; population of, 149; squatters' rights in, 39; Western Reserve of, 37, 50

Connecticut Land Company, 50

consolidation, 165

Consolidation (Cooper), 158

Cooper, Thomas, 157, 158

Cooper, William, 50–51, 56, 63–64

Cope, J. D., 238–39

Cope, John P., 233–35

cotton, short-staple, 182

Coxe, Daniel W., 195, 273n26

Coxe, Tench, 58

Crabb, Jeremiah, 63

Creeks, 186

Crisis, The (Turnbull), 158

Crittenden, John J., 89

cultural tensions, 3

Cumberland Road, 76, 89, 97, 131–32, 161

Cutler, Manasseh, 50, 56, 235

Dallas, Alexander J., 69

Dana, Edmund P., 1–2, 5, 86

Dane, Nathan, 152

Davis, B. B., 238

Davis, Joseph, 189

Deane, Silas, 25–26, 30

Dearborn, Henry, 79

debtor unrest, 90

Delavan, Edward C., 227

Delaware (state), 30, 40

Delawares, 49

De l'Esprit des Lois (Montesquieu), 47

Democratic Party, 188, 203, 239

Democratic Societies, 49–50, 59, 60, 62

denationalization, 101, 130, 159, 167, 200

Desha, Joseph, 125

Dickerson, Mahlon, 194

Douglas, Stephen, 239

Drake, Daniel, 170, 171, 175, 180, 204

Duer, William, 50, 56

Duncan, Joseph, 110, 218

Dunnica, William F., 203

Dwight, Timothy, 210

Dyer, Eliphalet, 24, 25

Earl, Ralph, 153

eastern states: economy of, protecting, 52–55, 57–59, 61; public education in, funding of, 97–98; rising land prices in, 63

education, public, 34, 35–36, 70, 96, 97–100

Edwards, Henry W., 143

Edwards, Ninian, 135–38, 150, 160, 169, 199; advocating cession, 7, 87, 113, 151, 156, 164; condemning traditional land policy, 93, 100–101; opposing the Maxcy plan, 100; opposition to, 127, 144, 165, 167

Ellery, William, 33, 40

Elliott, James, 72

Emerson, Ralph Waldo, 150

empire: 8, 10, 47, 50, 52

"empire of liberty," 58, 68

entail laws, 28, 94

environment, effect of, on behavior, 20

Espy, Josiah, 192

Evans, George Henry, 214, 232

Everett, Alexander Hill, 196–98

Everett, Edward, 150–52, 164, 167

Ewing, Finis, 107

Ewing, Thomas, 216

factions, theory of, 47, 121

factory work, 117–19

Farmers' Bank (Indiana), 105–6

Federalist Papers: No. 10, 47; No. 23, 53; No. 51, 47

Federalists, 47, 51, 62–63, 67; asserting supremacy over the West, 52; elitist policies of, 208; land policy of, 51, 84; opposed to Intrusion Act of 1807, 77

federative principle, 75

fee simple status, 27, 28, 43

Fenno, John, 60

feudalism, 27, 28

Finney, Charles Grandison, 176, 177, 178

floats, 186

Florida, squatters in, 108, 109

Foot, Samuel A., 142–47, 151, 169, 230, 263n11; opposed to graduation, 140; opposition to, 154–56; resolution of, on restricting public land sales, 7, 126, 139, 165–67, 262n3

Foote, Henry S., 189

Force Bill, 191

"forty-acre law" (1832), 207, 210

Frankfort (Kentucky) *Argus*, 94–95

Franklin, Benjamin, 8–16, 22, 24, 58, 67

freeholders, multiplying, 107–8

free homestead principle, 112

free labor, 122

Free Soil Party, 240

free traders, 58, 126–27, 132

Frelinghuysen, Frederick, 65

French empire, 8

Friends of Domestic Industry Convention (1831), 195–96, 269n59

frontier, 6; anarchy in, 31; governance of, 18–19; law enforcement in, 51; military force in, 40–41; political loyalty in, 51; populist forces in, 42–43; transportation improvements in, 51. *See also* West, the American

frontier radicalism, 221

Gales, Joseph, 165

Gallatin, Albert, 50, 64, 66, 69–71, 75–77, 81

Gardener, Joseph, 37

Gardoqui, Don Diego de, 43, 52

Gates, Paul Wallace, 3, 270n3

Gayle, John, 186–87

Gazette of the United States, 60

Genet, Edmond Charles, 60

Georgia: ceding claims, 32; land grants of, 29

Girard, Stephen, 69

government: changes in beliefs about, 241; citizens' indebtedness to, 90; effects of, 1

Graduation Act, 233, 239–40

graduation plan, 87, 91, 101, 102–7, 122, 156, 169; New Englanders divided on, 146; opposition to, 111, 132; preemption tied to, 109, 215; support for, 140, 153–54, 195

Grand Ohio Company, 14

Grayson, William, 35, 39
Great Britain, 12, 13–14, 18, 19, 33, 40, 43, 115
Green, Duff, 167–68
Green v. Biddle, 209
Grenville, George, 14
Gresham's Law, 111
Griffin, Thomas, 72
Gwin, William M., 189

Haile, William, 190
Hall, Frederick, 170–71, 180, 192–93
Hall, James, 173–74
Hall, Willis, 226
Hamilton, Alexander, 64, 116, 123; advocating
    slow westward expansion, 52–57, 59, 230;
    envisioning an American empire, 50; on the
    Louisiana Purchase, 71; political economy of,
    57–58; as treasury secretary, 49, 50, 52–59
Hammond, Abijah, 86
Harmer, Josiah, 41, 49, 208
Harmer expedition, 60, 208
Harmony (PA), 119
Harrington, James, 19
Harrisburg Convention, 157–58
Harrison, William Henry, 67, 79, 226
Harrison Frontier Land Act, 67
Hart, Lucretia, 124
Hart, Thomas, 193
Hartford Convention, 141
Hartley, Thomas, 63
Hay, George, 167
Hayne, Robert Y., 140, 141, 145, 166, 197; debate
    with Webster, 163, 165; responding to Foot's
    resolution, 156–60, 265n39
Hazard, Samuel, 13
Hendricks, William, 106
Henry, John, 65
Henshaw, David, 170
Hinchman, Aaron, 235, 237
History of Kentucky (Marshall), 208
History of the Dividing Line (Byrd), 28
Hogg, James, 24
Holland, James, 63
Holmes, John, 145
Home, Henry (Lord Kames), 15
home-market concept, 116, 117; advantages of,
    119, 121; American system and, 128; damage to,
    133–34; long-range policy for, 123–24; need for,
    120–21, 126–27

Homestead Act, 242
Homestead Journal and Village Register, 235, 238
homestead movement, 235, 239–40
Howell, David, 33–34, 39
Hubbard, Daniel, 239
Hubbard, Henry, 221
Hume, David, 26
Hunt, Jonathan, 139, 159, 194–95

Illinois: cession movement in, 134–35, 151; squat-
    ters in, 108–9
Illinois Central Railway, 241
immigration, European: German, 10, 12, 61, 119,
    171, 179, 221, 237; Irish, 171, 177, 221
improvement projects, 130–32, 242. *See also*
    transportation improvements
Indiana, Panic of 1819's effect on, 105–6
Indiana Territory, petition from, 45
Indians. *See* Native Americans; *individual tribes'*
    names
individualism, 177–78, 241
industrialization, 9, 117–20, 151
Ingersoll, Charles Jared, 133, 195
inheritance, partible, 28
Intrusion Act of 1807, 77, 78, 79, 208
Iron Act, 9
Iroquois, 50
Irvine, William, 17, 31

Jackson, Andrew, 95, 113, 182; election of, 134, 141,
    195; Foot's contempt for, 143; Indian removal
    policy of, 185–87; nationalist policies of, 95;
    and the Nullification Crisis, 168, 191; Specie
    Circular of, 216; vetoing Clay's land bill, 203,
    212–13
Jackson, David, 41
Jackson, James, 73–74
Jackson, Richard, 10–11, 13
Jackson administration, 94, 186, 187
Jacksonians, 94, 102, 106, 125, 143, 150, 163, 178,
    182, 183, 188, 191, 203; Carey's distrust of, 117;
    Clay's resentment of, 207; national policies
    of, 95; on preemption, 214; uniting with the
    Bentonites, 112
Jacobin clubs (France), 49
Jay, John, 43, 52
Jay-Gardoqui negotiations, 52, 59
Jay Treaty of 1795, 52, 63
Jefferson, Thomas, 50, 61, 67–69, 74, 208;

agricultural idealism of, 26–27; on earth as common stock, 19–20; envisioning social reform for the West, 28–29; on improving U.S. transportation system, 75–76; Indian policy of, 78–79; on land distribution, 26–27, 34–35, 37; reshaping Virginia's land policy, 27; squatters' policy of, 77–78; stressing Union, 76; western policies of, 75

Jefferson administration, 74–75

Jeffersonians, 58, 62, 67, 73–75, 117, 124. *See also* Republicans

Jennings, Jonathan, 106

Johnson, Henry, 194

Johnson, Paul, 176

Johnson, Richard M., 94, 95

Judd, William, 24, 25

Kansas-Nebraska Act of 1854, 239

Kendall, Amos, 94, 95, 125

Kentucky, 35; land policy's effect on, 94–95; land speculation in, 208–9; opposition in, to the Federalists, 47; overlapping claims in, 208, 209; Panic of 1819's effect on, 124–25

Kentucky Reporter, 90–91

Kenyon College, 176

Key, Francis Scott, 186–87

Kimball, David T., 176

King, Rufus, 36, 59, 65, 71, 126, 230

King, William R., 199, 202

land: changes in perception of, 36; classes of buyers of, 56; as commodity, 36; crash in, 85–86; distribution of, 20; markets for, 3; ownership of, 19, 21; reform of, after Panic of 1819, 86–87; speculation on, 88, 91

Land Act of 1796, 63–67

Land Act of 1800, 46, 67

Land Act of 1804, 46, 67

Land Act of 1820, 7, 67, 87–88, 93–95, 106, 143, 147, 209–10

land agents, 1

land bounties, 14, 18, 30, 31, 32, 33, 37, 39, 41, 131, 202

land companies, 31–32

land-credit system, 86, 87–93, 111–12, 122

land grants, 14, 21, 97, 242

land offices, 56, 66, 67, 69, 189, 239

Land Ordinance of 1785, 35–39, 46, 51, 57, 62, 66, 96, 207–8

landownership: liberty and, 43, 67–68; principles for, 40

land price graduation. *See* Graduation Act; graduation plan

Lane Seminary, 179, 181

Lawrence, Abbott, 195

Lee, Arthur, 32–33, 34

Lee, Richard Henry, 24, 41, 42, 46–47, 61

Lewis, Hector P., 193–94

Lexington (KY), 192, 193–94

"liberty, empire of," 58, 68

Lincoln, Abraham, 242

List, Friedrich, 115, 132

Livingston, Robert R., 69

Livingstons (New York), 24

Lloyd, Edward, 100

Locke, John, 19–20

Logan, William, 94

Log Cabin Bill, 228

Louisiana Purchase (1803), 53, 70–72, 75, 77, 240

Lyon, Lucius, 220, 230

Macon, Nathaniel, 69, 102, 117, 136

Madison, James, 17, 31, 55, 61, 69, 135; favoring reduced tract sizes, 64; federative principle of, 75; on the Land Ordinance's religion clause, 36; land proposals of, 29, 34; squatters' policy of, 83; on the theory of factions, 47; on transportation improvements, 130; on use of vacant lands, 113; vetoing Bonus Bill, 131

Madison Platform, 69

Malthus, Thomas, 8, 116

Manifest Destiny, 188, 233

manufacturing: agriculture and, 121–22, 125, 127, 129; economic policies and, 113–14; geographical proliferation of, 196–97; morals and, 126; promotion of, 58–59; in the South, 123; threat to, 116–17

market capitalism, 240–41

Market Revolution, 4, 235

Marshall, Humphrey, 208

Marshall, John J., 125

Martineau, Harriet, 170

Mason, Jeremiah, 166

Massachusetts: ceding claims, 32; General Court in, 21; land grants of, 29

Maxcy, Virgil, 95–96, 97, 111

Maxcy plan, 97–101, 144, 159, 194

McCulloch v. Maryland, 96

Merrick, William D., 221, 222

Mexican-American War, 238, 239

Miamis, 49

migration, land policy and, 33

Military District (Virginia), 36–37

Milwaukee Sentinel, 225

Mississippi: constitution of, 186; politics in, 187–92; population of, 182, 183–84

Missouri: graduation scheme in, 105; Panic of 1819's effect on, 102; squatters in, 108

Missouri Compromise, 113, 142, 160, 201, 239

Missouri Crisis, 136, 137, 160

Mitchell, James C., 103, 104–5

Mohawks, 49

money, shortage of, 85

Monroe, James, 34, 126

Montagu-Dunk, George (2nd earl of Halifax), 13–14

Montesquieu (Charles-Louis de Secondat), 47, 74

Montgomery, Thomas, 123

Moore, Thomas P., 125

moral reform, 19, 51, 175–78

Morrill Land Grant College Act, 242

Morris, Gouverneur, 30–31, 39, 42

Morris, Robert, 24, 26

Morrow, Jeremiah, 88–92, 106, 130

Morrow-Robertson bill. *See* Land Act of 1820

Natchez (MS), 185

National Intelligencer, 98, 111, 165

nationalism, 6, 7, 31, 42–43, 117, 120–21, 160

National Land Reform Association, 235

National Republicans, 141, 154, 157, 159–60, 165, 168, 206

Native Americans: provocation of, 18; removal of, 79, 183, 185–87, 189; strength of, 49; survival of, 3. *See also individual tribes' names*

New England: in colonial times, 3, 18, 21, 22, 23, 25; conservatism of, 141; land planning in, 25–26, 34–36; pro-settler attitudes in, 220–21; western policy of, 143–46, 147, 149, 163

New Hampshire, 30

New Hampshire Patriot, 154

New Jersey, 30, 40

New Madrid lowlands, 105

New York: land grants of, 29, 30; land policy in, 40

New York and Mississippi Land Company, 189

New York Evening Post, 217

Nicholas, John, 64

Niles, Hezekiah, 88, 114–15, 117, 120–23, 195

Niles' (Weekly) Register, 88, 98, 112, 116, 120, 168, 202

Noble, James, 106

North America: control of, 9, 12–13, 14–15; settlement of, 9; white occupation of, 3

North American Review, 98, 166, 167, 210

North Carolina, 29, 32

Northwest Ordinance of 1787, 36, 46–47, 51, 55

Norton, John H., 183

nullification, 137–38, 140, 158, 168

Nullification Crisis (1832–1833), 168–69, 191

Observations Concerning the Increase of Mankind (Franklin), 8, 9, 10, 11, 15

Oceana (Harrington), 19

Ohio: and depression of 1837–1843, 237; development of, 115–16, 164; population of, 236–37; settlers of, 91; statehood of, 52; visions for, 235–36. *See also* Ohio country

Ohio Company, 11, 49, 50, 51, 208

Ohio country: Native Americans' victories in, 49; squatters in, 41

Ohio Enabling Act, 70

Old Republicanism, 136

Onondagas, 49

Osborn, Thomas, 211

Ozarks, 105

Paine, Charles, 195

Panic of 1819, 2, 7; class tensions resulting from, 94–95; devastating effect of, on the West, 85–86, 115; effect on Kentucky, 124–25; influence of, on the National Republicans, 114; as key event in Benton's career, 102; land policy issues and, 240–41; land speculation contributing to, 67; Maryland's response to, 96–97

Panic of 1837, 174, 213, 217, 236–37, 240–41

Parsons, Samuel Holden, 41

Peck, John Mason, 172

Pennsylvania, 30, 39

Pettis, Spencer, 195

physiocrats, 58

Pierce, Franklin, 233

Pierce, Joshua, 195

Pinckney's Treaty (1795), 52, 60, 185

Plan for Settling Two Western Colonies (Franklin), 12

plantation agriculture, 18, 33, 59, 122

Plea for the West (Beecher), 174, 179

Plummer, Franklin E., 191

Poindexter, George, 191

Poindexter, John, 189

political conflict, cultural roots of, 4–5

political economy, 2–3, 6, 109, 113, 130, 214, 219; agriculture-based, 118, 136; American, 36, 50, 53; Benton's, 112; British, 16, 19; Clay's, 127, 128, 198, 206, 207, 213, 226, 229; Hamilton's, 57; Jeffersonian, 204; morality and, 175, 178; nationalist, 105, 170; pro-eastern, 134; National Republicans', 157; republican, 68, 76, 114, 136; theory of factions in, 121

Pontiac's Rebellion, 14

Pope, John, 125

popular sovereignty, 239

populism, 42

Potawatomis, 49, 51

Potomac Company, 96

preemption, 7, 39, 45, 67, 83, 87, 102–3, 206, 233; cultural politics of, 225; free-soil implications of, 156; growing support for, 108, 219, 220–21; home-market approach and, 162; limited to whites, 227; opposition to, 110-11, 216, 273; radical approach to, 211; redefined, 213–14; tied to land-price graduation, 109, 110, 215; triumph of, 207. *See also* preemption laws; *individual acts*

Preemption Act (1830), 211–12

Preemption Act (1838), 222–24; debate on, 7, 219–24

Preemption-Distribution Act (1841), 227–28, 275

preemption laws, 169, 186, 216–17, 228

primogeniture, 28

Proclamation of 1763, 14–15, 18, 26, 39, 40

protectionists, 114–15, 116–17, 120–21, 123–24, 132, 188, 195–97

public schools. *See* education, public

Quarterly Journal (American Education Society), 177

quarter-townships, 66, 67

Quebec Act of 1774, 25, 30

Quesnay, François, 15

Quitman, John A., 189

radicalism, 84; frontier, 221; western, 87, 135, 140, 158

railroads, 241–42

Randolph, John, 69, 71, 73, 117, 130, 136

Rapp, George, 119

Rappites, 119

Ray, James B., 107

Raymond, Daniel, 115, 120

rectilinear survey system, 35–36, 56, 66

refuse lands, 33, 36, 105, 107, 145, 212, 239

Relief Act (1821), 143

relief acts, 67, 85, 93, 94–95, 102, 125, 143

Relief (New Court) Party, 94

remainder lands, 37

"Report on a National Bank" (Hamilton), 57–58

"Report on Manufactures" (Hamilton), 58, 116, 123

"Report on Roads and Canals" (Gallatin), 76–77

"Report on Vacant Lands" (Hamilton), 55–57

republic, purpose of, 54

republicanism, 5, 32, 33, 36

Republican Party, 239, 240, 242

Republicans, 62, 64, 67–69, 112; land policies of, 84, 208; Louisiana Purchase and, 71

Revolution of 1800, 50

Reynolds, John, 218

Rhode Island, 30

Ricardo, David, 8, 116

Richmond (Virginia) *Enquirer*, 88, 122

Richmond Whig, 217–18

Ritchie, Thomas, 88, 122

Roane, Spencer, 69

Robbins, Roy, 270n3

Robertson, George, 92–93, 125, 129

Robinson, John M., 198

Rush, Benjamin, 42

Rush, Richard, 126, 132–36, 141–42, 146, 202, 230

Salem (OH), 232–38

Saltonstall family, 25

Scioto Company, 49, 50

Scott, John, 111

Scott, Thomas, 55

Second Bank of the United States, 89, 96, 102, 131, 197

Second Great Awakening, 176–79

sectionalism, 70, 121, 139–40, 151, 241

Senecas, 49

settlement, regulation of, 6

settlers: alternative political universe of, 81; conditions for, 171–74; credit sales for individual, 57; loyalty of, 65–66, 208; new image of, 215; published tracts for, 104, 172–73; southwestern, 190–91. *See also* squatters

Seven Years War, 13

Sevier, A. H., 169

Shawnees, 49, 52

Shays' Rebellion, 42, 51, 60

Shelby, Isaac, 127–28

Skidmore, Thomas, 214

slaveholding, 36

slavery, 160, 241; effect of, on poor whites, 122, 123; opposition to, 112, 142; westward spread of, 233, 239

slave unrest, 24

Sloo, Thomas, 108

Smith, Adam, 8, 15, 58, 117, 122

Smith, George P., 232–33

Smith, Nathaniel, 104

Smith, Oliver H., 162

Smith and Buchanan (financial firm), 96

society, changes in beliefs about, 241

Society of the Cincinnati, 40

South Carolina: antiwestern sentiments in, 60–61; ceding claims, 32; land grants of, 29; nullification movement in, 136, 138, 140, 151, 158, 186, 197; population of, 157; states' rights leadership of, 157

South Carolina College, 157

South Carolina Exposition and Protest (Calhoun), 138, 162

Southern Review, 157

Spafford, Amos, 83–84

Spain, 43

speculators, land, 37–40, 43, 49, 51, 55, 64, 95, 109, 111, 186–91, 208, 209

Spotswood, Alexander, 28

squatters, 77–81; activity of, 87, 108–9; behavior of, 210–11; Clay's impressions of, 128, 129, 206–7, 209–10, 229; clearing, from southern Ohio, 41; commercial benefits of, 190; cultural identity of, 214, 215; Greenville treaty and, 52; hostility toward, 110–11; intimidation of land purchasers by, 218–19; movement into the mainstream, 213–14, 215; murdering Native Americans, 41; petitioning the U.S. Congress, 45–46; political response to, 205–6; portrayal

of, 210–11; protective societies for, 216–17, 218; in the Southwest, 183–84. *See also* squatters' rights

squatter sovereignty, 239

squatters' rights, 7, 39, 181, 186–87, 205, 213, 221, 230

state building, 5, 6

statehood for frontier provinces, 46–47

statists, 6

St. Clair, Arthur, 49, 55

Stevenson, James S., 137

Strong, Caleb, 65

Strong, James, 111

Summary View of the Rights of British America, A (Jefferson), 26, 67–68

Susquehanna Company, 25

Symmes, John Cleves, 50, 56

Tait, Charles, 167

Tallmadge, James, 195

"Tariff of Abominations," 138, 144

tariffs, 4, 70, 75, 99, 114, 128, 133, 138, 143, 144, 147, 198–99, 202

Taylor, John, 61, 69, 117, 136

technology, role of in securing the West to the Union, 241

telegraph, 241

Tennessee: graduation scheme in, 103–5; opposition in, to the Federalists, 47

territories, strict development of, 46

Test, John, 162

Thatcher, Samuel, 72–73

Thomas, Jesse B., 100

Tipton, John, 109, 220, 230

Tomlinson, Gideon, 147–49, 150, 156

Townsend, Milo, 237–38

townships, 35, 39, 56, 57, 62, 66

transportation improvements, 51, 70, 75, 76, 125, 128–30, 162, 196

Transylvania Land Company, 24

Treaty of Cusseta, 186

Treaty of Greenville, 51–52

Treaty of Paris, 13, 33

Treaty of San Lorenzo. *See* Pinckney's Treaty

Trumbull, Jonathan, 39, 65

Tucker, Beverley, 61–62

Tucker, Henry St. George, 61

Tucker, St. George, 61

Turgot, Anne-Robert-Jacques, 15

Turnbull, Robert J., 158
Turner, Frederick Jackson, 3, 270n3

United States: capitalistic transformation in, 36;
centralizing tendencies of, 5; citizens' indebtedness to, 86; coercive power of, 51; cultural
debate in, 141; debt of, 61, 70, 74, 198; financial
credibility of, 49; financial instability of, 240;
General Land Office, 69, 211; Hamilton's view
of, as empire, 52; internal improvements in,
70–71, 75–77; as land creditor, 67; legitimate
opposition in, 62–63; move toward liberal
democracy and *laissez-faire* capitalism, 242–43;
new states in, 31; as plural entity, 6; population
in, 23; property rights held by (1830), 144; purchasing Indian lands, 49; Republicans' control
of land policy in, 67; sectional conflicts in, over
land disposition, 33–34; size of, 52–53, 70–72,
86, 240; states ceding their claims to, 18; surplus produce in, 119–20; surplus revenue for,
194, 198; Treasury Department, 49, 50; treaty-
worthiness of, 43; western radicalism in, 87
United States Magazine and Democratic Review,
225
United States Military Tract, 36–37
U.S. Congress: balance of power in, 140; bringing
states' lands under central control, 29–32;
Committee for Foreign Affairs, 30; debate
over Louisiana Purchase, 72–73; elitism of,
37; House Public Lands Committee, 45; land
sales by, strategies for, 36–38; reinforcing the
armed forces, 51–52; slowness of, in advancing
western development, 49–50; social concerns
of, 4. *See also* U.S. House of Representatives;
U.S. Senate
U.S. Constitution, 47, 51
U.S. House of Representatives: Committee on
Public Lands, 83–84, 111, 213; debate in, over
land sales, 62–64
U.S. Senate: Committee on Manufactures, 199–
200; Committee on Public Lands, 99–100,
199, 202; debate in, over squatters' rights,
219–24; Indian Affairs Committee, 144

value, labor theory of, 112
Van Allen, John, 63
Van Buren, Martin, 95, 197, 206, 215–16, 219,
223–24
Vance, Joseph, 218

Vattel, Emer de, 52, 136
Venable, Abraham, 64
Vermont, 31, 47
Verplanck, Gulian C., 98–99, 100
Vesey, Denmark, 157
Vinton, Samuel F., 110
Virginia: ceding land to the United States, 31–32,
96, 136–37, 164; conflicting land claims in, 34;
land grants of, 29–30; land policy of, 27–31, 40

Walker, Duncan, 181
Walker, Jonathan Hoge, 181
Walker, Robert John, 181–82, 184–92, 197, 204,
215, 219, 239
War of 1812, 83, 84, 114
warrants, settlement, 33–34
Washington, George, 24, 40, 42, 51, 60, 76,
90–91, 193
Washington administration, 51, 53, 63–64
Wayne, Anthony, 51
Wealth of Nations (Smith), 15, 58, 117, 122
Webster, Daniel, 145, 149, 206; anxiety of, about
the West, 152; debate with Hayne (*see* Webster-
Hayne debate); land policy of, 140, 161–65; on
preemption, 223; respect for, 150–51; supporting preemption, 221; touring the West, 168
Webster-Hayne debate, 7, 126, 141, 147, 162–65,
169, 188, 200
Weld, Theodore Dwight, 179
West, the American: auctioning of, 46; capital
in, 125; capitalism and the development of, 4;
as collateral, 52–54, 56; as common property,
30; debtor unrest in, 90–91; development of
delayed by Hamilton, 53–54, 59; diversity of, in
post-1815 period, 115; expansion of during Revolutionary era, 17–18; government's involvement
in settlement of, 18; ideals for, 67–68; investment potential of, 37–38; negative impressions
of, 59, 60; political stability of, 91–92; religious
influx into, 176–80; secured to the Union by
technology, 241; selling of, Jefferson on, 27;
settlement of, 3–6; social development of, 1–2,
9–13, 93, 171. *See also* frontier
Western Anti-Slavery Society, 235
westward expansion: aims of, 32–33; aversion to,
52–57, 59, 73, 230; Confederation Congress's
control of, 46; explanations for, 23; new-state
support of, 74; planning for, 24–26; social
reform and, 28–29; speed of, 74–75

Whigs, 191, 203–4, 206
Whiskey Rebellion (1794), 51, 59–60, 64
White, Hugh Lawson, 216
White, Joseph M., 109–10
White, Samuel, 73
Whitefield, George, 11
whites: inequality among, 182–84, 190, 192–93;
    relations of, with Indians, 166
Whitney, Eli, 182
Wickliffe, Robert, 125
Wilkins, William, 195

Williams, Thomas H., 81
Williamson, Hugh, 31, 43
Wilson, James, 24
Winthrop, John, 21, 37
Woodbury, Levi, 154
Wright, John C., 162

Young, Richard M., 222

zone of cultural competition, 6